The Teaching Archive

The Teaching Archive

A NEW HISTORY FOR LITERARY STUDY

Rachel Sagner Buurma
and Laura Heffernan

The University of Chicago Press   CHICAGO AND LONDON

The University of Chicago Press, Chicago 60637
The University of Chicago Press, Ltd., London
© 2021 by The University of Chicago
Published 2021
Printed in the United States of America

30 29 28 27 26 25 24 23 22 21   1 2 3 4 5

ISBN-13: 978-0-226-73594-8 (cloth)
ISBN-13: 978-0-226-73613-6 (paper)
ISBN-13: 978-0-226-73627-3 (e-book)
DOI: https://doi.org/10.7208/chicago/9780226736273.001.0001

The University of Chicago Press gratefully acknowledges the generous
support of the University of North Florida and Swarthmore College
toward the publication of this book.

Library of Congress Cataloging-in-Publication Data

Names: Buurma, Rachel Sagner, author. | Heffernan, Laura, author.
Title: The teaching archive : a new history for literary study / Rachel
     Sagner Buurma and Laura Heffernan.
Description: Chicago : University of Chicago Press, 2021. | Includes
     bibliographical references and index.
Identifiers: LCCN 2020020789 | ISBN 9780226735948 (cloth) | ISBN
     9780226736136 (paperback) | ISBN 9780226736273 (ebook)
Subjects: LCSH: English literature—Study and teaching. | American
     literature—Study and teaching.
Classification: LCC PR35 .B88 2020 | DDC 428.0071—dc23
LC record available at https://lccn.loc.gov/2020020789

♾ This paper meets the requirements of ANSI/NISO Z39.48-1992
(Permanence of Paper).

Contents

Figures

On Authorship

We have written every line of this book together, and we have elected to list authorship alphabetically. This author order represents neither a hierarchy nor a division of labor.

Introduction

A NEW SYLLABUS

In this book, you will see a series of major literary scholars in a place they are rarely remembered as inhabiting: the classroom. You will watch T. S. Eliot and his working-class students revise their tutorial syllabus in order to reimagine early modern drama as everyday literature written by working poets. You will follow Caroline Spurgeon, one of the first female professors in the UK, as she teaches her first-year women's college students to reconfigure the world of letters by compiling their own reading indexes. You will see I. A. Richards transform large lecture halls into experimental laboratories by enlisting his students as both test subjects and researchers in his poetry experiments. You will encounter Edith Rickert and her graduate students as they invent new methods of formal analysis for poetry and prose. You will watch J. Saunders Redding carefully compose his American literature syllabus so that the class would devote half of its time to Black writers. You will see Cleanth Brooks's students ask him questions about the historical contexts of the poems they read, while Edmund Wilson teaches James Joyce's newly available *Ulysses* alongside Shakespeare and Sterne to women undergraduates and local community members. You will follow poet Josephine Miles as she assigns freshman writing essays designed to get students to think about data rather than merely report it. And you will see how Simon J. Ortiz jettisons the traditional survey course in order to teach Native American literature to community college students.

Along with many others who populate this book, these figures measured out their professional lives by the academic year, the length of the term, and the lecture hour. Like countless other teachers and scholars, they worked—sometimes with students—in special collections archives, in computing laboratories, in private manuscript collections, in major research libraries, and at desks in studies or carrels. But mostly, they worked in classrooms. They worked in classrooms at Bedford College for Women, Southall Grammar School as part of the University of London extension program, the University of Chicago, Elizabeth City Teachers College, Hampton Institute, Smith College, Louisiana State University, George Washington University, Lincoln University, the University of Chicago, Yale University, Harvard University, the University of California, Berkeley, the Institute for American Indian Arts, the College of Marin, and the University of New Mexico. They taught classes of all female undergraduates; they taught working-class adult students; they taught hybrid courses open to undergraduates and the general public; they taught classrooms of high school English teachers; they taught upper-level English majors; they taught dentistry students, freshman composition students, and graduate students. Their classrooms were various: wood-paneled seminar rooms close by dormitories, decaying former gymnasiums a train ride from students' homes, Quonset huts erected hastily during wartime, desk-lined rooms borrowed from elementary schools, communications studios, special collections large and small, and computing laboratories in friendly electrical engineering departments.

The true history of English literary study resides in classrooms like these; most of the study of literature that has happened in the university has happened in classrooms. Counted not just in hours and weeks, but in numbers of people, stacks of paper, and intensity of attention, the teaching of English literature has occupied a grand scale. More poems have been close-read in classrooms than in published articles, more literary texts have been cited on syllabuses than in scholarship, more scholarship has been read in preparation for teaching than in drafting monographs. Within institutions of secondary education large and small, numberless teachers and students have gathered to read both an astonishing number and an astonishing range of texts together. If it were possible to assemble the true, impossible teaching archive—all the syllabuses, handouts, reading lists, lecture notes, student papers, and exams ever made—it would constitute a much larger and more interesting record than the famous monographs and seminal articles that usually represent the history of literary study.

Despite this, the work of classrooms rarely appears in the stories that scholars tell about their past.[1] Histories of the discipline of English almost invariably take the scholarship of professors working at a handful of elite universities as evidence of the main line of the discipline's theories and practices.[2] To do this, they rely on a pervasive assumption: that literary study's core methods have been pioneered by scholars at elite universities, only later to "trickle down" to non-elite institutions, students, and teachers. In this kind of account, historicism comes to the American university via Johns Hopkins, as does structuralism. New Criticism, on the other hand, begins at Yale, and deconstruction makes landfall there. Scholars at major universities innovate; their ideas are disseminated "outward" to less elite universities and "downward"—often, it is imagined, in simplified or distorted form—to the classroom.[3]

Here we will make the case that the opposite is true. As we will show, English classrooms at both elite and non-elite institutions have made major works of scholarship and criticism. T. S. Eliot's important essay collection, *The Sacred Wood* (1920), grew directly out of his three-year course Modern English Literature; the volume centers on works that Eliot read with his students and, more importantly, reflects what he learned from teaching in the format of the Workers' Educational Association tutorial. Edmund Wilson's "The Historical Interpretation of Literature" grew out of the Varieties of Nineteenth-Century Criticism course that he taught at the University of Chicago in 1939. The indexing methods that Caroline Spurgeon practiced with her Art of Reading students at Bedford College for Women inspired her to create the data set of all of the metaphoric vehicles in Shakespeare's plays that she drew on to write her well-known last work, *Shakespeare's Imagery and What It Tells Us* (1935). We can sometimes see these traces of teaching in the many works of scholarship dedicated to classes or students: Wilson's dedication of "Dickens: The Two Scrooges" to English 354, Summer 1939, at the University of Chicago; Cleanth Brooks's dedication of *The Well Wrought Urn* to the students of his English 300-K class from the summer session of 1942, at the University of Michigan, "who discussed the problems with me and helped me work out some of the analyses"; I. A. Richards's dedication to *Practical Criticism* "to my collaborators, whether their work appears in these pages or not"; Edith Rickert's dedication of *New Methods for the Study of Literature* "to all students in English 143, 276, and 376, who by their hard work, lively interest in the subject, and active co-operation in the working out of new methods have made the book possible."[4] *The Teaching Archive* aims not just to show how classrooms have helped create particular books, but to offer readers a new way of seeing the outcomes of teaching, one that will recognize the presence of classrooms within all kinds of published scholarship.

In classrooms, teachers and students have invented and perfected the core methods and modes of literary study.[5] In classrooms, method grows, twining itself around particular texts and particular people. These methods are more various and more mixed than our current accounts allow. In a single semester—or even a single hour—a class might search out the layered registers in which a Keats poem meditates on its own status as literature, admire a particular inflection of the sonnet form, or attempt to synthesize the spirit of an age from a few weeks of readings. They might also conjure the referential significance of details and historical allusions, index a dozen mentions of a literary reference, make fun of a scholarly edition's biased footnote, compare three versions of a novel's first paragraph, and learn to find a failed poem interesting. The downtimes of the class hour also cradle new ways of knowing literature; classes may draw implicit connections to tangentially related current events, dramatize differences between the room's first impressionistic response to the day's chosen poem, refer back to an absent student's claim from last week, offer some chatty preliminary background material, brainstorm deliberately wrong readings of a novel's first sentence, or playfully apply a strong literary theory to a viral meme. When teachers and students turn their collective attention to texts in classrooms, they decide together upon the interest that texts hold; they experiment with creating and conveying value. Perhaps singularly among the disciplines, literary study is enacted rather than rehearsed in classrooms; the answer to the question "Did I miss anything last week?" is truly "Yes—and you missed it forever."

Centering the history of critical method on classrooms also transforms our understanding of the literary canon. Classrooms throughout the twentieth century have sometimes housed the canon that we expect to find—the core works in each period of literary history, the New Critical canon of metaphysical poetry (Donne, Marvell) and modernist experimentation (Joyce, Woolf), the novelistic canon of the Great Tradition (Austen, Eliot, James). But more often, classrooms have been home to a much wider array of texts—texts that teachers and students encounter as both literary and unliterary, or in transition between one and the other. Papal indulgences, paper trails leading to unfinished novels, occasional essays by famous playwrights, poets' notebooks, public frescoes, lives and letters and personal histories, paratextual indexes, and forgotten pornography have all appeared on syllabuses alongside or instead of luminous poems and structurally perfect short stories.

So although we have long seen the classroom as the canon's fortress and main site of reproduction, the archive reveals that this canon has been at best a very incomplete story, and at worst a figment of our imaginations. This is most visible when we turn away from elite research universities and look into the classrooms of a broader array of secondary educational institutions, for several reasons. First, some of these institutions take different approaches to curriculum. In many extension schools, for instance, there was no set hierarchical curriculum for literary study; reading lists were developed contingently in relation to local histories, recent books of interest, and students' demands or experiences. Second, universities often shape curricula around the identities of their student populations; at historically Black Hampton, for example, the English Department described their core American Literature course as "a survey of American prose and poetry beginning with the most important present day Negro writers and going back [to] the most effective writers of the Colonial period."[6] At Hampton, the canon represented the work of Black and white writers in equal measure to accurately reflect their importance to American culture. The class's presentation of great works also demanded attention to the materiality of canon formation and the politics of literacy itself.

This contingent and historicized canon has, we claim, in fact been the dominant model in literary study, though we only see this clearly when we place teaching at the center of literary history. Far from only presenting contextless, aesthetically valuable texts whose selection has come down from on high, most twentieth-century English literature classrooms have in some way discussed the making of literature itself—from how and what famous writers read in childhood to their first failed attempts at literature to their multiple drafts and revisions to their reception by everyday readers and critics and students. Teachers and students often recover the particular political or social circumstances that writers both responded to and shaped. They recover lost connotations within a familiar word's meaning; they draw pictures of old newspapers on the chalkboard; they read the legal decisions that controlled access to controversial texts; they track the publishing networks that determined into what hands certain genres came. This all may sound like fodder for an upper-level or graduate seminar, but our research suggests that students at all levels—perhaps particularly beginning students—have worked to understand the meaning of what is before them through an account of how it was made, and by whom, and under what shaping, but not determinative, conditions.

This new model of the canon is the most surprising discovery of our turn to the teaching archive.[7] And this realization opens up a further insight. Once we see that teachers and students in these classrooms regularly gather around texts that are not traditionally canonical, we can see that literature classrooms are in the business of creating literary value, not merely receiving or reproducing it. Studying the historical or material or biographical life of a literary work isn't ancillary to some more central formal attention to the aesthetic features of a poem or novel, but a core means by which groups of readers have come to take interest in and attach value to texts—to make them, in a sense, literary.[8] And, in fact, the classroom's close attention to the formal features of that poem or novel—the history of classroom-based close reading—turns out to be, from this perspective, yet another way that literary value is made or conveyed. This is to say that literary value *seems* to emanate from texts, but is actually made by people. And classrooms are the core site where this collective making can be practiced and witnessed.

Classrooms offer us both a truer and a more usable account of what literary study is and does, and of what its value is today. This book argues that the value of literary study inheres in the long history of teaching as it was lived and experienced: in constant conversation with research, partly determined by local institutional histories, unevenly connected with students' lives, and as part of a longer and wider story that has never been written down. University teaching can often feel isolated; lacking an account of shared practices, it can seem marooned from the research interests that constitute our main historical narratives and standards of professional value.[9] This long-standing sense of disconnection has grown as institutions prize teaching away from research in tenure files, hiring, and budgetary structures. Restoring a full material history to the ephemeral hours we spend in the classroom will not in itself change institutional structures or revolutionize labor practices. But it will bring a usable history back into view, one that better represents the complex, dynamic work our profession has undertaken in the past, is continuing to perform in the present, and must offer in the future.

Disciplinary History Against the Divide

What we find in the teaching archive overturns nearly every major account of what the history of literary studies has been. Looking at classroom practice—and particularly looking at classroom practice at a wider range of institutions than those usually considered—demolishes the received idea that literature professors once taught a narrow canon that "opened" in the late 1960s and early 1970s. Evidence from the teaching archive also scrambles existing genealogies for twentieth-century methodological change; the teaching archive dispels our long-cherished accounts of the interminable tennis match between eras in which we championed literature for its aesthetic value and eras in which we modeled ourselves after the sciences by producing knowledge about the world in which texts were written. In addition to dissolving the scholars vs. critics divide, the teaching archive likewise dismisses the idea that formalist critics have been the prime architects and champions of undergraduate pedagogy in English. By extension, looking at actual classroom practice suggests that widespread announcements of a contemporary return to the aesthetic are perhaps only the latest return of our perennial method manifestos, recasting the usual figures of method war.

Disciplinary historians of English have, by and large, declined to research in their field. In lieu of creating new knowledge about the history of literary study, chroniclers of English instead recycle and reinterpret a handful of tropes. Figures of opposition and impasse—the bloodless battle, the unbridgeable divide, the mutual exclusion, the cavernous fault line, the central split, the twin poles, the disciplinary pendulum, with its reliably contrapuntal swing—provide the morphology of our tales of literary studies. Marvelously flexible, these tropes determine the plot in which scholars and critics have traded periods of supremacy; these tropes also write the script for contemporary debates. Over time, they have formed a canopy that blocks the sunshine from ever reaching the seedlings of practitioners' own experiences of their teaching and research.

The divide that dogs English studies is imagined by disciplinary historians as a formative one—a late nineteenth-century struggle over whether English professors should evaluate literature or produce knowledge about it.[10] In the nineteenth century, writes Michael Warner in one such account, "a conflict arose between philological scholarship and the literary culture over the study of literature"—at war, we find "genteel urban critics" facing "professional philologists" with "little or no interest in teaching literature." Others include an only slightly different cast of characters: for Wallace Douglas, "college professors of rhetoric" and doctors of divinity, who taught English as the "poor man's classics" to an upwardly mobile middle class, fought against "heady notions about scholarship that were coming out of Hopkins." William Riley Parker sees a battle between "orators" and "philologists"; Franklin E. Court discusses competition between early professors working in a Scottish tradition of oratory and moral philosophy and the late nineteenth century arrival of philologists. Gerald Graff describes a "fundamental disagreement" between "Arnoldian humanism and scientific research."[11] Even those who, like Guillory, admit English's more multifarious nineteenth-century roots in "philology, literary history, belles lettres, [and] composition," still see the late nineteenth century as a moment of conflict, "constitutive of the discipline itself," between literary historians and philologists who treated judgments about literature as matters of fact, and belletristic lecturers who modeled the making of literary judgments.[12] These accounts of conflicted origins cite a handful of late nineteenth-century polemics,[13] usually written by critics, as evidence of an entire period's practices. This handful of essays constitutes what Carol Atherton refers to as the "metadiscourses" of English.[14]

These origin stories about a foundational struggle between philologists (sometimes joined by antiquarians or literary historians) and someone else (oratory professors, humanists, literary men, extension lecturers, doctors of divinity) are staged as a confrontation between scholarly research and undergraduate pedagogy. As Wallace Martin argues, "Pedagogy and criticism stood opposed to scholarship as the basis of a professional formation."[15] Philologists and antiquarian scholars, in this account, have no compelling model of undergraduate teaching. Meanwhile, critic-lecturers are seen as charismatic but amateurish; they are dilettantes or generalists with no compelling model of literary research or scholarship.[16] For Guillory, philologists found it "difficult to devise an engaging undergraduate pedagogy" because they "stopped short of fully interpretive hypotheses, and [their] judgments of quality were usually merely assumed." Meanwhile, "critics presided over interpretations and values, which supposedly had no objective basis and therefore did not qualify for serious academic study," as Graff argues.[17] In other words, philologists or literary historians can't teach, while belletrists can't research. Or sometimes, in a slight twist, critics can teach "the great mass of undergraduates," while scholars thrive in the seminar comprised of a "minority of scholarly or advanced students."[18]

For disciplinary historians, this foundational divide between teacher-critics and scholar-researchers reverberates through the twentieth century. In this account, the twentieth-century history of English literature consists of a contrapuntal movement between historicist scholarship and formalist criticism. Graff's *Professing Literature* is probably the most well-known history that takes the "conflict . . . which has pitted scholars against critics" as a lens through which to understand a century of disciplinary history: "one of the recurrent motifs in the present history," Graff writes, "is the appeal to 'literature itself' against various forms of commentary *about* literature as a cure for institutional dilemmas."[19] Graff is far from alone in seeing twentieth-century literary study as a series of generational-methodological shifts whereby early twentieth-century scholars of philology and literary history are gradually replaced by the New Critics, who emphasize close-reading pedagogy, and who are, in turn, replaced by feminist scholars and Black studies scholars and Marxist historians and cultural studies scholars and new historicists, all of whom restore to view the historical contexts in which poems and canons are made.

This scholars vs. critics or historicists vs. formalists history of literary study has only become more prominent in recent years, which have seen the rise of "new formalism," of "strategic formalism," of "post-critical reading," of "surface reading," and of new defenses of aesthetic experience.[20] These methodological manifestos nearly all begin by recounting our discipline's history as one of contrapuntal method war; they nearly all depict formalist and historicist methods as dramatically opposed.[21] They suggest that a generation of historical or "critical" or "contextualist" scholarship is or should be coming to an end; they suggest that a turn from contexts to texts—to the experience of reading them, to the judgment of their merits, to the apprehension of their forms inside and out in the world—would also constitute a return to what has always been at the core of our profession.[22] This promise of returning to supposedly foundational practices takes on renewed urgency in an era of engineered enrollment decline and other forms of devaluation and defunding, as we discuss in our conclusion. This book declines to take up arms in the method wars. But it does suggest that manifestos like these tend—today and throughout the profession's history—to dominate our metadiscourse while misrepresenting our practice. Even further, the authority of such accounts seems to derive from the glibness with which they characterize the history of practice as starkly divided.

This book rejects the idea that our discipline has been pulled in two directions, that its core has been formed by controversy over method or that its goals of producing knowledge about literature and appreciating literature have been mutually exclusive. Formalism and historicism, we argue, are convenient abstractions from a world of practice in which those methods rarely oppose one another. These abstractions do not describe or refer to actually existing groups of scholars, nor would most practitioners recognize themselves as belonging to such groups. When we look to classroom practices rather than methodological manifestos or critics' high-profile complaints about the professionalization of literary study, we find alternative genealogies for literary study's most familiar practices and longer, continuous histories for literary study's seemingly recent methods. We show, in short, everything you can't see if you believe—following the most-cited documents in disciplinary history—that critics have exercised a monopoly on the governance of literary value and the practice of undergraduate teaching.

Our opening chapters overturn existing accounts of the discipline's origins in a late nineteenth-century battle between teacher-critics and scholar-philologists.[23] We show instead the lost history of research-based undergraduate and extension school teaching. Methods of manuscript research, source studies, and histories of literary periods and figures were often taught in undergraduate classrooms. And not as professional training: these classrooms full of women and working-class adults were not in the business of accrediting students as professional literary scholars.

These students would return to the shop counter or the mine shaft; they would graduate to become stenographers or laboratory assistants. The scholar-teachers who taught them had fully-fledged accounts of the place of literary research in liberal arts and extension education. For these lecturers and tutors—many of whom were themselves unaccredited or playing catch-up in these decades of professionalization—teaching research methods and literary histories to nontraditional students and female undergraduates was a critical practice. Far from the received disciplinary historical scene in which rapt (or bored) students listened to charismatic lectures about great authors, these tutors and students studied how writers worked, how they were paid, and how critics built their reputations. This collective work demystified the ideal of the genius author, allowing students to imagine that they, too, could become writers or critics. Giving students a role in the writing of literature and the production of knowledge was one way the university participated in the nineteenth century's "long revolution," adapting to changes in the idea of what culture was.[24]

The flourishing of literary history and bibliographic research in the undergraduate classroom opened the way to early twentieth-century literary formalisms. Teachers in the 1920s and '30s conducted classroom-based experiments in isolating and enumerating aspects of literary form such as imagery, syntax, sentence length, word count, or rhythm; in doing so, they drew upon their own training in the making of scholarly tools like the concordance and the index. These teachers prompted their students to define and identify and count the elements of literary style by consensus; they believed that this almost mechanical work would serve to cultivate literary sensibilities and tastes. Later, the New Critics would claim to democratize aesthetic sensibility by teaching the poem on the page, but this earlier incarnation of pedagogical formalism differs from New Critical close reading in its transformation of the classroom into a "laboratory" and students into teams of reader-experimenters. Their iterative granular tabulation and interpretation of literature's formal features aimed to reanimate and reveal the poet's own compositional work.[25]

This book also shows the persistence of historical and materialist approaches to literary study through a midcentury long imagined as uniformly New Critical in orientation. In these decades, public-facing literary critics both published in scholarly journals and regularly reviewed books for newspapers and magazines, lectured to general audiences, and served as cultural attachés to the federal government. The classroom practices of these midcentury figures show them turning back to the literary history of the nineteenth and eighteenth centuries in order to revalue authors and texts long regarded as not quite literary. In courses on Civil War–era journalism or nineteenth-century memoirs and letters written by both free and enslaved African Americans, these teachers newly valued as literature documents that had seemed of merely historical interest. Like many of our earlier bibliographers and philologists, these teachers considered the process through which literary reputations and ideas about aesthetic value had been made and unmade.

Our book finds several poet-critics at work through midcentury and the decades after. Yet while this familiar figure has long been associated with the charismatic close reading of the poem on the page, we find them in their classrooms studying poetry rather than poems. These figures—working poets who also taught—practiced a formalism that was tied not to the literary object or the "text" itself but to smaller, more extensive units of poetic production. They tended to focus on continuity rather than rupture, traditions rather than innovations, minor poets rather than major. So, too, were they interested in the relationship between the writing of poetry and the criticism of poetry in the past as well as the present. Their syllabuses' writerly orientation toward literary technique and its literary history constitutes, we find, a robust tradition in its own right but one not currently represented by disciplinary history.

These are some of the ways that a disciplinary historical focus on practice rather than theory reveals interconnections rather than oppositions and continuities rather than ruptures. Together, all of our chapters find longer histories for reading methods that our discipline tends to see as recent developments. The widespread sense that quantitative methods of "distant reading" have been pioneered by male scholars at research universities (with the resources afforded by Silicon Valley and major grant funding) melts away when we look at the earlier twentieth-century women professors, both on and off the tenure track, who used classrooms as the original supercomputers. We show how word counts and tabulations were the basis of collaborative projects undertaken by entire classrooms of students during the first half of the twentieth century. Some of these women also pioneered computational method.[26] Our research reveals, for example, how Josephine Miles led a team to create the first computational literary concordance. Just as quantitative and computational literary method has a long classroom history, so also do identity-based criticism and ideology critique. In every decade of the twentieth century, we find teachers and students choosing to read texts and authors whose interests they shared. Female professors have taught women writers—even women writers contemporary to them—throughout the decades we consider. Ideology critique—imagined, in recent years, as beginning with Fredric Jameson—informs the work of multiple classrooms we study.

The project of counting stock references in literary texts originated with English professors in the 1920s and '30s who did anti-racist work analyzing the circulation of stereotypes.

This classroom-based history of reading methods challenges disciplinary histories that see methods as chess moves in a game of institutional prestige. The most compelling and well-known version of such critical disciplinary history is John Guillory's *Cultural Capital: The Problem of Literary Canon Formation*. *Cultural Capital* appeared in the midst of the culture wars; it offered not a complete history of the discipline but a critical genealogy for its moment. In it, Guillory cautions literature professors against confusing literary representation with political representation. Making the canon more "representative" of minority writers, Guillory argues, was not equivalent to changing political representation; to believe otherwise was to ignore the school itself as a site where social hierarchies are reproduced rather than changed. In Guillory's account, discourses of literary value work above all to secure the high status of literary culture. His history of the core methods of English explains how theorists have worked, over time, to sequester the realm of the "literary" apart from politics and to distinguish literary language from referential speech.[27] Yet for all the power this view assigns to the institution of the school, any sense of its actual existence and workings are curiously absent. Like *Cultural Capital*, many disciplinary histories of the 1980s and '90s considered literature and criticism as institutions. To do so, they relied on a relatively abstract model of the institution—though through its shadowy outlines one could glimpse the solid infrastructure of Yale and Harvard and Oxford.

Our book contributes to the history of the actual institutions that have made the study of English literature. To do so, we draw on the work of scholars such as Gauri Viswanathan, Robert Crawford, Anne Ruggles Gere, and Jonathan Rose, who first included a broader range of schools into "rise of English" accounts.[28] More recently, a great many scholars have expanded the kinds of institutions we typically include in disciplinary histories of English or histories of criticism. Carol Atherton has looked to late nineteenth-century British regional universities; Alexandra Lawrie to 1890s London extension schools; Jennifer McDonell and Leigh Dale to Australian universities; Elizabeth Renker to American land-grant universities and historically Black colleges; Catherine Robson to the American elementary school; Laura R. Fisher to progressive reform institutions like the settlement house, the working girls' club, and the African American college; and Ben Conisbee Baer to public education programs in the 1920s–1940s colonial world; Danica Savonick to CUNY during the era of open admissions. Nancy Glazener and Deidre Lynch have excavated the earlier public (Glazener) and private (Lynch) literary cultures that prepared the professionalization of literary study in the late nineteenth century. And Merve Emre has incorporated mid-twentieth-century institutions of international relations and communications.[29]

Looking at a wider range of institutions restores to view the long history of classroom critique that the last wave of critical disciplinary history obscured. For example, Guillory's claim that a toothless liberal pluralism guided the integration and expansion of syllabuses after the 1970s does not hold weight when we consider the much longer history of fully integrated courses on American literature long taught at historically Black colleges and eventually imported to northern, elite, and predominantly white schools in the United States. Those courses continue to be taught at historically Black colleges and universities today.[30] It is ironic that the wave of critical disciplinary histories—by criticizing and historicizing the institutionalization of aesthetic ideals, canons, and close reading—buried from view the long traditions of classroom-based critique in English. We seek to restore these traditions to view.

Looking at classrooms from a broad range of institutions is crucial in our present moment, when the loss of our sense of higher education as a public good (and accompanying state defunding, private fundraising, and student debt profiteering) has rapidly increased the stratification of higher education. Decades after Graff's *Professing Literature* grappled with the theory wars of the 1980s and Guillory's *Cultural Capital* responded to the culture wars of the 1990s, we find ourselves facing an institutional landscape that the last generation's major disciplinary historians of English hardly anticipated in their most pessimistic passages. In the new millennium, the very value of humanistic knowledge production itself—the unquestioned ground beneath the feet of all participants in the culture and theory wars—seems to be up for debate as economic value replaces all other forms of value in discussions of higher education. The prescient endings of both Graff's and Guillory's books call for us to re-enliven literary study by remaking classrooms. *Professing Literature*'s closing pages recommend that English classrooms become "explicitly historicized" so they may transform the "frozen bod[ies] of knowledge" that students simply receive into "social products with a history that they might have a personal and critical stake in," a change that would counter what Graff sees as the English department's habit of absorbing methodological conflict into institutional structure while systematically excluding conflicts from the classroom.[31] And Guillory's *Cultural Capital* offers a final, counterfactual "thought experiment" in which aesthetic valuation would be untethered from the school and "what we call canon formation would . . . become a much larger part of social life."[32] *The Teaching Archive* begins where *Professing Literature* and *Cultural Capital* end, replacing their wished-for, utopian future classrooms with the many real yet under-studied, under-archived, and undervalued classrooms in which our discipline's history has really been made.

Sources and Methods

Given the long history and vast scope of the teaching of English literature, it is difficult to understand how it has been relegated to footnote status in histories of literary study. Part of the reason is that the history of university teaching is difficult to trace. Teaching's past has escaped from notice because its record is one of ephemeral acts and documents. Text selection, the leading of discussion, the writing and circulation of a seminar paper, reading aloud from a mimeographed sheet of quotations—all these practices, whether rehearsed or improvised, remain largely unrecorded except in occasional retrospective accounts by teachers or (less often) students.[33] We can imaginatively summon the rich ecosystem of manuscript circulation that must have existed in some form around any given classroom from the fifteenth through the twenty-first century: pages of student notes and doodles made during lectures, graded quizzes with scribbled comments, and handouts (some of them with three-hole punches made by more organized students during the era of the three-ringed binder). And most of all, notes: professors detailing—in copious or skeletal fashion, organized by day or by week—the order of the class, the questions to ask, the familiar mundane reminders of due dates and formatting and extra lectures to attend; students' mingled descriptions, interpretations, and dissents from the lecture or conversation around them. If such traces had been preserved, we could imagine a problem of classroom information overload: To which classrooms should we pay most attention? Whose perspective—student, teacher—counts more? How to take genre and convention into account? What of that which we see is disciplinarily significant? What is specific to institution, and what to individual?

But so far, we face the opposite problem. Not having seen teaching as an activity that has a history, we have rarely preserved its traces; scholars often preserve their teaching materials within their lifetimes for reuse, but rarely have they seen them as of interest to other teachers or to future scholars. It should not therefore surprise us that the material traces of teaching have rarely found their way into well-cataloged university archives. The relative infrequency with which teaching papers have been preserved attests to the fact that at every step of their potential preservation, they have tended to be devalued—by teachers who don't think of them as worth preserving, by booksellers and libraries who purge them when a scholar's papers are bought or accessioned (over and over—"they threw the teaching papers away"; "she threw the teaching papers away before she gave us her files"), and by catalogers who are given limited time and resources for cataloging them or describing them in finding aids. Unlike drafts of published papers, which have the alibi of existing as evidence of an ultimately peer-reviewed, polished, published scholarly artifact, teaching papers are the often-embarrassing remnants of a process undertaken almost always under less-than-ideal conditions. (Upon learning about our project, many scholars we know have threatened to go straight home and bury the evidence accumulated in their old hard drives and paper files in order to keep them from someday falling into the hands of people like us. Few, it seems, would want their teaching papers to be taken—or mistaken—as examples of anything.)

Striking exceptions to this rule exist. Occasionally a beautifully preserved teaching archive surfaces: Caroline Spurgeon's papers include both her own student notes and her teaching notes, apparently nearly complete. Beautifully bound in red and black leather with embossed gold titles and neatly indexed, they are interleaved with materials like the letterpress-printed examples of her own research notes that she handed out as guides in her Art of Reading class for first-year students of English. Archivists at Royal Holloway, University of London, have cataloged Spurgeon's archive in exquisite detail, their care for her notes matching or even exceeding her own. Spurgeon also preserved her research notes; the thousands of cards containing her quantitative research into the metaphors of Shakespeare and his contemporaries reside in the Folger Shakespeare Library. She intended that her heroic, informational scholarship would be open to the use of future scholars, not just the basis of her own publications.

Spurgeon's archive is one real example of a kind of fantasy: a single gemlike instance of what all scholars' archives might have looked like if individuals and institutions had valued teaching much more than we do. Her notebooks offer a view of what teaching materials could look like if we imagined them being reused by others in new classrooms and preserved as a record of an important activity with traceable as well as trackless results. But the teaching materials left behind by most scholars of literature look nothing like this. When they are preserved at all, syllabuses, lecture notes, and handouts tend to be accidentally archived along with more valued materials—drafts of scholarly essays, review clippings,

FIGURE 0.1. Caroline Spurgeon kept her student notes and her teaching notes in leather-bound volumes (1880s–1910s) with the names of the courses embossed in gilt on the spines. Here we see the notes she took in W. P. Ker's Form and Style course and his English Prose of the 19th Century at the University of London, as well as notes for her courses the Art of Reading and Style, which she taught at Bedford College for Women. RHC PP 7 Archives, Royal Holloway, University of London.

or correspondence. While piecing together the teaching materials of midcentury man of letters Edmund Wilson, we discovered a page from a typescript draft of his article "The Historical Interpretation of Literature" on the verso of Wilson's draft syllabus and first-day lecture for his Varieties of Nineteenth-Century Criticism class.[34] Other teaching materials survive because they are intended for publication. For example, famous New Critic Cleanth Brooks's lectures for English 71 appear in his archive in Yale's Beinecke Rare Book and Manuscript Library in multiple neatly organized typescript drafts, audio-recorded and then transcribed by a typist at Bantam Books in anticipation of their (never-realized) publication as a book. T. S. Eliot's class notes have not survived, nor have his students' papers, but his letters, the official lecturers' reports he filed each year, and most of all the published syllabuses for his three-year Modern English Literature tutorial class help us understand how his teaching changed over time in response to his developing sense of who his students were and how they learned. Other figures' archives yield thousands of pages of class notes filed by text (in the case of Josephine Miles) or class (in the case of J. Saunders Redding); for some professors, the only extant traces of their teaching are in their publications.

These material-textual traces of teaching help us rediscover some of the rhythms of the lecture hour, the temporality of the course's week, and the semester-long social life of the class. To move from material texts to reading practices, we draw on the methods of book history and cultural sociology. These methods help us avoid the common temptation of mistaking a book's contents for its use—of interpreting, for example, the pedagogical framing in popular classroom anthologies as evidence of actual classroom practice. We have also benefited from the subset of material text scholarship concerning the history of scholarly practices by Ann Blair and William Clark. As Clark notes, "One can learn much from the material practices of academics—about the nature of academic work from the transformation of the lecture catalogue, about the constitution of the research library from the battle over its catalogues, about the commodification of academics from tables evaluating them."[35] Likewise, we have benefited from those critics who have looked beyond the metadiscourses of English to generate accounts of critical and reading practices that constitute what Stefan Collini, playing on "normal science," calls our discipline's "normal criticism."[36]

Are the figures and institutions in this book representative? Yes and no. The relative difficulty of tracking down teaching papers means that chance and serendipity as well as informed selection guided our choice of figures and institutions. However, though the book looks in detail at only a handful of figures and classrooms, wherever possible we include contextualizing detail about contiguous teachers and similar institutions by including the papers of colleagues who taught down the hall, across the street, or across the country. In this book, T. S. Eliot's syllabuses sit alongside the hundreds of other University of London extension syllabuses and lecturers' reports we studied. Josephine Miles's exams and class notes and noun counts take context from Berkeley's course catalogs as well as from her colleagues' and successors' teaching in the Berkeley English Department. Simon J. Ortiz's syllabuses come into focus in relation to other courses taught in the College of Marin's Ethnic Studies Department as well as Native American studies courses at San Diego State University and the University of New Mexico. Regardless of whether these figures are representative or unusual, they are clearly not exemplary in the sense of being models we hold up for possible emulation, though some of the past teaching we describe seems new and exciting now.

Ten Courses in Seven Chapters

The Teaching Archive's seven chapters retrace the steps of traditional histories of literary study while considering a greater range of institutions than such histories typically examine. Geographically, the book begins in the UK in the 1910s and '20s and then shifts, as disciplinary histories often do, to the United States for the decades from midcentury through the 1970s. Along the way, we see how teaching materials radically transform our understanding of some of the key texts, figures, and moments that feature centrally in existing histories. At the same time, we also profile a series of figures who are well-known in their subfields but rarely incorporated into broader histories of the discipline.

Chapters 1 and 2 take up the interconnected worlds of women's colleges and extension schools to reveal the deeply collaborative and research-based nature of these classes held for women and working-class students around the time of World War I. Chapter 1 considers the Art of Reading, taught at Bedford College for Women in 1913 by eminent early modernist Caroline Spurgeon. Spurgeon's Art of Reading course was devised to guide beginning students through the process of academic research. She started by teaching them how to pull a volume off a library shelf and quickly skim its pages, and ended by modeling the creation of polished personal indexes with her own letterpress-printed notes on John Ruskin's *Unto This Last.* For Spurgeon, this seemingly informational work of indexing actually enacted John Henry Newman's ideal of liberal education as the "extension" of knowledge. Indexes demystified literature, showing students not only how a work was made, but also suggesting how they might make it differently. Spurgeon and her research team spent most of the 1920s and early 1930s doing this same kind of indexing work with Shakespeare's corpus in preparation for what became her magisterial work of distant reading, *Shakespeare's Imagery and What It Tells Us* (1935). Her extensive indexing of the vehicles of the plays' metaphors—the stars, jewels, and seas that seem to exist only to lend their properties to lovers' eyes or enemies' ambitions—finds the plays' most literary parts in the material existence of Shakespeare's everyday life. Some literary critics disparaged Spurgeon's masterwork as merely informational, but when we restore the context of her teaching, the critical force and conceptual claims behind her work's referentiality snap into focus.

Chapter 2 takes up the three-year Modern English Literature tutorial that T. S. Eliot taught between 1916 and 1919 under the auspices of the University of London Joint Committee for the Promotion of the Higher Education of Working People. Like Spurgeon, Eliot taught several extension courses for working adults during the war years. Drawing on a wide array of extension syllabuses and lecturer's reports from this decade, we describe how early twentieth-century tutorials like Eliot's were quite radical in design: students and tutors wrote their syllabuses together, and tutors encouraged their students to perform original research and to draw on the unrecorded histories of their work and their families to revise existing disciplinary knowledge. Eliot's course gradually adopted the ethos of this institution. His Modern English Literature syllabuses and lecturer's reports show that as the three-year class proceeded, Eliot acceded to his students' interests and requests, rewrote essay prompts to accommodate their work schedules, and reorganized his syllabus away from individual authors and toward more interconnected themes and questions. In their third year together, Eliot refused to teach the contemporary literature syllabus his students desired because he did not "favor the study of living authors."[37] But he accepted their second choice of early modern literature and composed a syllabus for his working-class students that presented Elizabethan poets and playwrights as working writers. When the tutorial ended in 1919, Eliot transformed the syllabus into the essays of *The Sacred Wood* (1920). Identifying that work's origins in Eliot's classroom allows us to reinterpret it entirely, understanding Eliot's famous canon reformation not as an astringent and elite valuation of minor poets, but as a reading of literary history guided by the extension school's favoring of collective work over individual genius.

Whereas our first two chapters show teachers and students learning to value literature by researching it, chapter 3 turns to two figures—I. A. Richards and Edith Rickert—who used their classrooms to stage dramatic experiments in literary reading. We look at several iterations of the Practical Criticism course that I. A. Richards taught at Cambridge University before and after the publication of *Practical Criticism: A Study of Literary Judgment* (1929). Scholars have long seen *Practical Criticism* as a dour text promising to import rigor and standards into undergraduate English studies. Yet whereas the book *Practical Criticism* exhaustively cataloged and corrected students' reading errors, in the Practical Criticism class, Richards addressed his students as fellow researchers rather than study subjects. Edith Rickert, another 1920s pedagogical experimenter, enlisted the students in her University of Chicago course Scientific Analysis of Style to help her invent the "new methods for the study of literature" that would appear in her 1927 book of that title. Both Rickert and Richards demanded from students not polished readings of literary works, but their cooperation in the process of gathering and organizing bits of data about the formal properties of texts and the interpretive decisions of readers. Like other classroom experimenters and organizers of literary laboratories in the 1920s, Richards and Rickert believed that their new methods would elevate the discernment of individual students, but only in the context of what Richards called "co-operative inquiry."[38] They believed that collective literary study be considered as a valuable social activity both itself and as a tool for elevating individual judgment.

The next chapters of *The Teaching Archive* turn to the decades around midcentury to offer a new, more accurate story of one of the most familiar and important stages of our discipline's development. Chapter 4, like chapters 1 and 2, offers a strong case for how teaching papers from institutions rarely centered by histories of literary study upend accepted disciplinary narratives. In it we turn to the racially integrated English literature courses taught by J. Saunders Redding from the 1930s through the 1970s. Redding is remembered today as one of the makers of the African American literary canon, his fifty-year career bookended by two major publications: *To Make a Poet Black* (1939) and the seminal anthology (with Arthur P. Davis) *Cavalcade: Negro American Writing from 1760 to the Present* (1971). Publication of the latter coincided with Redding's appointment as the first African American professor of literary criticism in the Ivy League and cemented his reputation as the "dean of African-American studies" even as his own institutional vision for American literature's integration was eclipsed by the rise of Black studies programs.[39] In this chapter, we return to the materials that remain from Redding's years teaching in southern historically Black colleges in the 1930s, '40s, and '50s, where he and others first developed survey courses that presented American literature as the collective history of white and Black authors writing with urgency and immediacy about their material and social circumstances. "Until relatively recent times, writing by both black and white Americans had little to do with aesthetics either as philosophy or in practice," read the opening premise of the Negro in American Literature syllabus that Redding taught regularly at the Hampton Institute and later carried to Cornell and other northern universities in the 1970s.[40] Redding's courses abandoned formally conscious texts in order to explore genres that documented the vast and strange collection of American lives ignored by official histories. Disciplinary histories, focused on elite, predominantly white universities, have seen curricular integration as a matter of adding Black writers to preexisting syllabuses or offering specialized classes in African American literature; we restore to view an earlier classroom-based model that offers us a new vision of the relation between critical race studies and the teaching of literature.

In chapter 5, we follow Redding's historicist critical values into the classrooms of Edmund Wilson and Cleanth Brooks. These two teachers at first seem quite opposed: Brooks, a formalist; Wilson, a historicist; Brooks, a critic with a close relationship to disciplinarity; Wilson, a critic with a close relationship to journalism and reviewing. We might imagine what we will find in Brooks's classroom, for even to mention the New Critical classroom evokes familiar images: rows of desks filled with GI Bill students, mimeographed poems on a single page, a charismatic, democratic teacher intent upon clearing away all of the "specialized rubbish . . . standing between the reader of a poem and the poem."[41] Above all, the New Critical classroom is remembered, with loathing or longing, as the place where close reading provided literary critics with a powerful account of both their specialization and their wider appeal. Yet in the actual classroom of Brooks's Contemporary Poetic Theory and Practice at Yale University in 1963, we find discussions of historical references, off-the-cuff paraphrasing, and the sketching of author biography as often as (and as preparation for) the masterful formalist reading familiar to us from books like *The Well Wrought Urn*.

In the second half of chapter 5, Edmund Wilson's teaching materials further challenge our received sense that a literature free from politics and history dominated midcentury classrooms. We follow Wilson's career as he travels through several universities from the 1930s through the 1960s. We begin with the Introduction to James Joyce course that Wilson offered for Smith College undergraduates and the general public in 1942. Wilson's account of how a text like Joyce's *Ulysses* changes through a reader's multiple returns helped him explain to the students and townspeople who attended his lectures how literary value changes over historical time. Wilson's critics complained that his historical relativism left him without a true account of literary value, his work plagued by a "tendency to think, and in fact to hope, that literature was about to become something else," as Robert Martin Adams wrote in a 1948 review of Wilson's *The Triple Thinkers*.[42] Adams was correct that Wilson failed in his attempts to fix his critical values in print, yet in his temporal, worldly classrooms, Wilson's account of literary value's historicity attained its full expression. From Wilson's 1942 Joyce course, we turn to his 1958 Use of Language in Literature course, which explored literature's changing capacity to reference the world. Along the way, we consider as well how his courses on Charles Dickens and Civil War journalism taught students how to transform literature into "something else." In Wilson's classrooms, we see how historical inquiry creates its own aesthetic and mode of value—one that links texts to life experience rather than sanctifying them within a timeless canon, one that sees literary value accrue to texts as they are read and reinterpreted over time by varying readerships.

Chapter 6 turns to the archives that remain from Josephine Miles's five decades of teaching at the University of California, Berkeley. Miles was an early practitioner of quantitative and proto-computational approaches to literary study, beginning with her 1938 doctoral thesis, for which she "counted" Wordsworth's "feelings."[43] By the 1950s, Miles was collaborating with the electrical engineering lab at Berkeley to make the very first computational concordance in the humanities. Alongside this lost history of early distant reading, we consider Miles's decades of notes for teaching English 1A, Berkeley's freshman composition course. Miles taught this class as a workshop; to her mind, even the supposedly practical pedagogy of the New Critics trained at "Harvard or Yale" expressed a will to mastery she abhorred, a style in which "you ask a bunch of students to read the work and then you tell them all where they're wrong and you tell them how to really read the work."[44] We describe how Miles's focus on the sentence as foundational to composition shaped her research—research in which she pursued a method for quantifying the sentence structures of five hundred years of poetry. In turn, Miles's quantitative scholarship gave her a unique account of the value of freshman composition to society. Whereas the New Critics set literary and poetic form in opposition to scientific modes of writing and knowing, Miles believed that poems, English 1A papers, and handmade data sets all required decisions about representativeness and selection, qualification and connection. In her writing workshops, Miles taught students to write meaningfully about the world and its data from their own distinct perspective.

Chapter 7 takes our book into the 1970s, following Simon J. Ortiz, an Acoma Pueblo poet, critic, and professor, as he developed his introductory survey of Native American literature between 1977 and 1979 for the Ethnic Studies program at the College of Marin in the California community college system. A visiting instructor who had already studied and taught both literature and creative writing at several different kinds of higher-education institutions, Ortiz needed to accomplish a challenging task: constructing a syllabus that would allow him to teach an oral tradition mistakenly described as past or vanished alongside a contemporary literature that Ortiz did view as a real resurgence after a relatively silent time. As he moved from institutions serving Native American students to an institution serving a diverse group, Ortiz reckoned with how to form a literature whose meaning was tied to the everyday lives of people from a wide variety of cultures and geographies into a single-semester survey. After teaching a first version of the course—a traditional survey that moved from pre-contact oral literature through anthropologist-mediated life writing to the present "renaissance of Native American literature"—Ortiz radically rewrote his syllabus. In his revised syllabus, each week triangulated traditional oral story, historical narrative, and contemporary fiction. This new format, inspired in part by N. Scott Momaday's acclaimed *The Way to Rainy Mountain* (1969), replaced the traditional survey's search for an authentic, pre-contact version of an oral tradition with a vision of the last five hundred post-contact years as the center of Native American national literary tradition. Ortiz theorized this literature of survivance and continuance in his famous 1981 essay "Towards a National Indian Literature."

Our book thus draws to a close in the 1970s, famously tumultuous years for higher education in America. These years saw student-led efforts to form new programs of study, to diversify faculty and student bodies, and to expand curricular offerings. Some of the figures we profile in this book either saw, firsthand, the changes afoot or helped to enact them. Josephine Miles's students at Berkeley were heavily involved in the free speech movement; Miles redesigned class assignments around it and encouraged students to write poetry about it. By 1971 she was chairing the Ad Hoc Committee on Women in the Department at Berkeley that added a "course on women and literature" to the curriculum and took "affirmative action" to recruit women for faculty and teaching assistantships.[45] In the spring of 1969, J. Saunders Redding began teaching at George Washington University just as SDS students were occupying Maury Hall and Monroe Hall. Redding was hired to teach as part of the American Studies program, which had just separated from the English Department and commenced debating whether their junior proseminar on American intellectual history should teach students all about "Emerson and transcendentalism" or "class structure."[46] Redding and Clarence Mondale co-taught the general education course for the department that spring and organized it around the concept of "polarities": "America vs. Europe, city vs. country, black vs. white."[47] The following year, Redding became the Ernest I. White Professor of American Studies and Humane Letters at Cornell University. Cornell's Africana Studies and Research Center was founded in 1969; the number of other new Africana Studies centers and Black studies programs founded at universities across America in the following years could very nearly be tallied by the number of visiting lecturer invitations that Redding received: Rhode Island College, the University of Illinois at Urbana-Champaign, Howard University, the University of Pennsylvania, Swarthmore College, UC Berkeley, UC Irvine, and UMass Boston are a few of the schools whose offers he accepted, but he rejected many, many more.

Ortiz, in turn, spent the summers of 1974–76 teaching at Navajo Community College (now Diné College), the first tribal college in the United States. Later that decade he would move from the College of Marin to the University of New Mexico to become a part of the newly forming Native American Studies Center and to take over Leslie Marmon Silko's courses in the English Department after the publication and critical success of her book *Ceremony*.

It may seem, then, that our history of classroom-based literary study stops short of the era that changed everything—the era in which worldly politics finally burst in upon the hermetic classroom, the era in which disciplinary knowledges were transformed by critique. In literary study, in particular, "post-1968" serves as shorthand for a twinned opening of canon and method that we associate with the demands of identity politics, the arrival of cultural studies and continental theory, and eventually the rise of new historicism and postcolonial studies. Yet, as we show, a fuller history of how teachers and students have practiced English at all kinds of twentieth-century universities overturns our collective sense that something closed was opened in 1968 and after. The seven chapters of this book show how classrooms throughout the twentieth century have been hospitable to some of the key aspects of method and ethos that we associate with "post-1968" English. A history like this one allows us to give up— finally and forever—the idea that "traditional" English was confronted, in these decades, with what Gerald Graff called the "disruptive novelties" of "black studies, feminism, Marxism."[48] To recover the ways that our discipline has been hospitable to these texts and modes of thought is not to claim that universities throughout the twentieth century welcomed the students and teachers who incubated them, nor is it to suggest that universities today have overcome the problems of access and equity that student movements shed light on in the 1960s and '70s. Yet making our histories more reflective of the discipline's actual composition is one pathway forward. The question of how to read this history in a present moment in which legislatures, parliaments, and universities have casualized academic labor—and the labor of teaching specifically—is one we address in our conclusion.

CHAPTER 1

Caroline Spurgeon, *The Art of Reading (1913)*

Beginnings and Beginners

Caroline Spurgeon meticulously preserved her teaching notes. Collecting them in indexed, leather-bound volumes, one per class, she identified them by embossing the course titles in gold on their spines.[1] The inky blue-black leather volumes, often with copies of the printed syllabuses pasted into the front, offer a detailed record of the classes she taught during the first decades of the twentieth century: The Age of Johnson; English Prose, 1798–1832; Shakespeare as Historian; The English Novel; English Literature, 1700–1760; Style; The Art of Reading; Poetry of World War I; Mysticism; Poetry of the Romantic Revival. Spurgeon also preserved her student notes. These notes, bound in red leather volumes of the same size and style, provide a record of courses taught by her University College London professor W. P. Ker, including Form and Style I and English Prose of the Nineteenth Century. We can track Spurgeon reusing certain passages from Ker's lectures—sometimes verbatim, sometimes transformed. In glimpsing the transmission of knowledge from Ker to Spurgeon and from Spurgeon to her own students, we also begin to understand how Spurgeon imagined future teachers might make similar use of her lectures.

Spurgeon's teaching notes endure because she viewed them as worthy of preservation, organization, and even decoration quite apart from their possible afterlives as publications. Spurgeon's lecture notes contain none of the grand pronouncements or magisterial interpretations that one might expect from such expensive-looking volumes. And while Spurgeon did occasionally deliver a fully drafted lecture on a topic like Tennyson's early work or Johnson and his era, her notes do not contain the polished prose speeches of a charismatic lecturer. More typical are the materials from her Art of Reading class, in which she spent most of the class time giving her students minute instructions on how to take effective reading notes. Her notes for this class contain lectures written in shorthand, marginal citations of the sources she read to develop her class plans, lists of topics for student papers, and printed reproductions of her own research notes that she distributed to her students as examples. Trained as an early modernist, Spurgeon was familiar with the conventions and practices of manuscript preservation used by generations of collectors, librarians, and scholars. Like the humanists she studied, Spurgeon ensured that her own manuscript notes would be preserved intact and available to others for reference. The material form of her notes thus makes an argument about the classroom's place in the world of scholarship and its role in the transmission of knowledge.

Spurgeon's classrooms form a part of a long genealogy of literary study—one that stretches back to the colonial schools, Scottish universities, working men's colleges, women's colleges, and urban universities in which the modern discipline of English had its beginnings.[2] Spurgeon's own life and career brought her into contact with nearly all of these institutions. Born in India in 1869 to an army family, Spurgeon was orphaned by the time she was ten. After several years in Germany and France, she was sent to school in England.[3] She began her university-level study at King's College and the nonsectarian University College London, where sixty years earlier Thomas Dale had become the first professor of English language and literature in 1828.[4] At King's College, Spurgeon studied with Ernest de Sélincourt and Lilian Faithfull. At UCL she studied with Ker, who had himself been trained at the University of Glasgow and later helped shape the new English degree at Oxford.[5] Spurgeon went on to pass university examinations in English literature and language at Oxford in 1899 but did not receive a degree because of her gender.[6] In 1901 she began teaching at Bedford College for Women as an assistant lecturer in English. Around the same time, she met Frederick James Furnivall, who had helped found the London Working Men's College, as well as multiple literary societies, including the Early English Text Society and the Chaucer Society. Spurgeon had originally planned to write a doctoral thesis on George Eliot's historical context and philosophical influences, but with Furnivall's encouragement, she instead took up research on the history of Chaucer criticism.[7]

In 1911 Spurgeon received her doctorate from the Sorbonne based on her work *Chaucer devant la critique en Angleterre et en France depuis son temps jusqu'à nos jours*, later published in English as *Five Hundred Years of Chaucer Criticism and Allusion, 1357–1900* (1918–28).[8] In 1913 she was named Professor of English Literature at the University of London, becoming the first woman professor of English literature in England, and became chair of the newly formed Department of English Literature at Bedford.[9] With her longtime companion Virginia Gildersleeve (for many years the dean of Barnard College) and other collaborators, she founded the International Federation of University Women in 1919. In 1921 she served on the Newbolt Committee, contributing to their 1921 report, *The Teaching of English in England*. In 1928 she published *Keats's Shakespeare: A Descriptive Study Based on New Material*, followed by *Shakespeare's Imagery and What It Tells Us* (1935). Later in her life, she spent time in both England and America, visiting Gildersleeve in New York frequently. She died in Arizona in 1942.

The "rise of English" story that Spurgeon's career and teaching materials tell is one that has been obscured by too-pat tales of clashes and compromises between humanist pedagogues and philologist scholars.[10] Nineteenth- and early twentieth-century English studies, we are told, consisted of two separate strains: the belletristic tradition of cultivating appreciation for English literature in the lecture halls of provincial universities, women's colleges, and extension schools, and the scholarly tradition of antiquarianism and philology practiced in elite universities like Oxford and Cambridge. In this story—told by scholars including D. J. Palmer, Terry Eagleton, Franklin E. Court, and John Guillory—extension school and women's college lecturers were "concerned merely to encourage the reading of great authors of the past,"[11] while the philologists and literary historians at well-established universities had "difficulty . . . devis[ing] an engaging undergraduate pedagogy" because they stopped short of interpretation and evaluation, tending instead to "overemphasize memorization of historical facts."[12] Spurgeon's own rigorous teaching of literary historical research methods to students at Bedford and the University of London extension school reveals these accounts of an English pedagogy caught between humanist appreciation and antiquarian memorization to be mere caricature.

Witness, for example, the lecturer's report that Spurgeon submitted to the University of London Board to Promote the Extension of University Teaching for her 1915–16 Age of Johnson course. These bureaucratic summaries of class attendance and student performance in extension courses, typically brief, tended to become even shorter after the start of the war in 1914. Reporting on his Shakespeare and England course, held in Walworth Road in the same term as Spurgeon's Age of Johnson course, Mordaunt Shairp tersely noted that the "attendance at this course has been small, and for this, the zeppelin raid of October 13th, was largely responsible," but that the classes were nevertheless "a success," with discussions admittedly sometimes straying "rather far afield, due to a desire to bring Shakespeare to bear on everyday problems and interests."[13] Spurgeon's report, by contrast, filled the whole of the allotted blank form, her signature squished in at the very bottom.[14] She began by describing the unusually intense, project-driven organization of her course. "The system," she wrote, "is not that of lectures + paperwork, but the more advanced one of close individual research on the parts of each student in a comparatively limited field."[15] During class gatherings, her working-class students presented "specially prepared papers" describing their original research on manuscripts from the British Museum.[16] The only nod to the war comes when Spurgeon notes that while students have "much appreciated" the experience of working firsthand with manuscripts at the British Museum, this archival "side of the work has not been developed as much as desk work, as owing to the war, many MSs have been inaccessible."[17] Spurgeon's teaching of advanced literary historical methods to her students stands out even within what was in general a very ambitious and rigorous set of extension school courses. She did note that "at first the seminar was very uphill work" because when asked to undertake original research using primary sources, her students "were somewhat puzzled at first and perhaps in some cases discouraged." And yet, she recounts, "by the second term they began to get a grip on the method."[18] Spurgeon's Age of Johnson, like T. S. Eliot's extension school course Modern English Literature, which is described in the next chapter, shows how teachers refused to offer working-class adult students generalist overviews or introductory work aimed at redressing missed opportunities. Instead, Spurgeon and others like her invited their students to plunge into the center of scholarly research by reading and interpreting the sources for themselves.

As in her Age of Johnson course, Spurgeon's Art of Reading course notes show her teaching centuries-old methods of literary historical scholarship and reference tool making to beginning students so that they could participate in the creation of knowledge about literature.[19] Her teaching papers show, as well, that Spurgeon had a fully-fledged theory of the humanistic value of these research methods. She saw them as a core part of a liberal arts education, rather than as training for a profession.[20] In her Art of Reading course, Spurgeon taught her students that proper practices of note taking and literary research would help them read in order "to come into contact with another mind" as well as to experience the movement of "a living knowledge" as it passed from person to person and institution to institution.[21] The kind of reading Spurgeon taught was detailed, granular, and even grinding; it required the repetitive opening of myriad tiny referential connections from the book to the reader's previous knowledge and experience. Unhooking finished texts from their fixed places in constellations of valued literary works, Spurgeon taught her students to excerpt and reorganize them, to treat their citations as dangling loose ends to be followed out, and to see the hidden as well as the overt connections between the single text and its multiple points of origin, circulation, and reception. The goal, she told her students, was not "the mere heaping together or memorization of facts." Liberal education, which she described as "a discipline and an enlargement of the mind," required not rote fact gathering, but "acting on these facts and ideas—digesting, coordinating, and assimilating them." Paraphrasing John Henry Newman, Spurgeon explained that education happens when "we feel our minds to be growing and expanding . . . when we not only learn, but refer what we learn to what we know already"[22]—what Newman calls the "extension" of knowledge.[23]

Spurgeon's published research, like her teaching, sought to reimagine literary works as formations that both gathered references and inspired further writing. Spurgeon regarded the history of literary criticism and literary opinion—including the budding opinions of her own students—as a central part of the history of literature. Spurgeon's multivolume *Five Hundred Years of Chaucer Criticism and Allusion* shows how the canonical Chaucer was created over time via a long, uneven tradition of transmission, commentary, and criticism. She therefore included commentary on both authentic and spurious works, since Spurgeon was less interested in recovering a "true Chaucer" than in tracking the creation of an author figure. In *Keats's Shakespeare: A Descriptive Study*, Spurgeon transcribed all of the marginalia in John Keats's copy of the complete works of Shakespeare. She summarized and analyzed Keats's markings, compared "various kinds of reminiscence of thought or verbal likeness between *The Tempest* and *A Midsummer Night's Dream* on the one hand, and *Endymion* on the other," and included a complete "accurate reprint of all the marks, annotations, and under-linings in the text of four plays in Keats's small seven-volume edition of Shakespeare."[24] Like *500 Years of Chaucer Criticism and Allusion*, *Keats's Shakespeare* revealed how the institution of literature was made through practices of citation and reference.[25] Spurgeon's most famous work, *Shakespeare's Imagery*, was based on her own and her research assistants' careful cataloging of each metaphor in Shakespeare's works; they used indexical methods very like those she taught in the Art of Reading.[26] At the time of its publication, many reviewers complained that *Shakespeare's Imagery* was a mere reference tool. But understanding Spurgeon's teaching methods reveals the literary theory implicit in *Shakespeare's Imagery*. Spurgeon's method, born in her classrooms, set aside Romantic ideas of inspiration and genius in order reveal the min-ute, quotidian practices of note taking, citation, and reference that, over time, became literature.

The Art of Reading (1913)

In her 1913 Art of Reading course, Spurgeon taught her students how to practice the kind of reading that regarded books as both gathered refer-ences and incitements to further writing. The course taught students how to see and make the extensible connections between books, the world, and themselves that Spurgeon borrowed from Newman's writing. Day by day and week by week, Spurgeon walked her students through the steps of scholarly reading. She explained how to take a book off the shelf and get to know it, how to take notes and how to use them, and how to recon-struct and read the network of citations on a topic. The course ended, as Spurgeon intended, just at the point where students would begin to write a research paper. By showing them how to prepare to write their own research papers, Spurgeon taught them to see published texts as the finished products of a similar process. Her research methods course, that is, contained an embedded theory of literature.

What kind of students were learning to read from Spurgeon? The Art of Reading met at a time of rapid change and growth for Bedford. Founded as the Ladies' College in Bedford Square in 1849 to provide nonsectarian education to women, Bedford became a pathway to a formal degree in 1878, when women became eligible to sit for examinations for University of London degrees. And in 1900, when the University of London trans-formed from a degree-granting body to a teaching university, Bedford, along with many other colleges in London, became one of its schools. In *A History of Bedford College for Women*, Margaret Tuke notes that in 1909 there were fewer than three hundred students at the college; by 1920 the student body had more than doubled.[27] The year 1913 saw Spurgeon teaching at a Bedford College that had just relocated from a few over-crowded houses at 8-9-10 York Place, off Baker Street, to a new campus in Regent's Park. With the move to Regent's Park, Bedford became increas-ingly residential, with the college constructing new dormitories to meet demand.[28] At the same time, because of an increasing number of public scholarships and other forms of financial aid, students from a wider vari-ety of socioeconomic backgrounds began to enroll. In the early decades of the century, and especially after the war, Bedford students also were becoming more career-minded. By the 1930s, a majority of Bedford grad-uates were choosing careers in secondary schools; others went on to train for secretarial work, went into business, or engaged in scientific research.[29] A few Bedford students enrolled to study for advanced degrees, but as Tuke explains, new opportunities for women that were then opening up at Oxford and Cambridge made Bedford less appealing for those seeking advanced degrees.[30]

As the first head of the English Literature Department (newly separated from the English Language Department) at Bedford, Spurgeon was responsible for shaping a new curriculum.[31] Part of her vision involved the rigorous teaching of reading and research methods. This curriculum included introductory classes like the Art of Reading (methods from which she also integrated into her summer teacher education course),[32] as well as a new seminar for the department's Honors students, "by means of which they received excellent training in methods of research."[33] As she did with her extension school students, Spurgeon taught her Bedford students to coordinate information into knowledge; by rising above a mass of seemingly unrelated details, they could gain a clear and unifying perspective. For Spurgeon, this was the main goal of undergraduate literary research, one that put it at the center of the English literature curriculum.

On the first day of the Art of Reading course, Spurgeon explained to her students that she knew that a class on reading might seem "v. elementary as a subject for a course of lectures." "We have not come to College to learn how to read, we know that already," she imagines students new to Bedford might say in response to her announcement of the course subject. She also ventriloquizes the slightly different complaints of the upperclasswomen: "There may be many things we do not know, but as most of our work consists in reading + the use of books, surely we know somethg. abt. that"! Years ago she herself, Spurgeon admits, "wld not have dreamt of speaking on this subject. I wld have assumed that by the time she came up to College that a student did know to some extent 1) What reading is 2) How to organize it 3) How best to make use of books." Yet recently, Spurgeon continues, she had come to realize that this is not the case. Reading is in fact difficult because "it is at the same time a science + an art; + we are too apt to assume—particularly those of us who have a natural capacity for handling + using books—that every student knows by nature how to read."[34] By "reading," she clarifies, she means not literal literacy—"the act of knowing your letters + being able to make out words + their sense in combination—as we may read a notice or a newspaper." Rather, "reading" in this context "really means study, the art of using + getting the best out of books, + probl out of a good many books. So that genl speaking fr my pt of view, the going thru once of a book or a play or a poem, is not in this sense of the word 'reading' it."[35] And the main mistake people—"in general" but "especially women"—make is to confuse the first meaning with the second, and therefore read too passively, devouring books "in quantities in a purely receptive spirit." This kind of reading, for Spurgeon, is useless. Real reading, by contrast, is vigorous and active (and perhaps not incidentally, best described with metaphors more associated with masculinity); it is "a conflict of 2 minds," "a continual struggle," "a voyage of discovery," "an adventure"; it is a "meeting with a new mind + new ideas."[36]

In these lectures, Spurgeon taxonomizes two kinds of literature and four types of reading. Our reading methods, she tells her students, will depend heavily upon the kind of literature we are reading: informational or inspirational. As she explains, "Lit has been divided into 2 kinds, and broadly speaking it may be so divided, tho' in nearly all great literature the two kinds co-exist, altho' one usually predominates. (1) The inspiring kind (2) The informing kind." In the category of "inspiring," she puts Keats's and Shakespeare's sonnets and John Milton's *Samson Agonistes*, "but also a great deal of prose, Carlyle's *French Revolution*, Charles Lamb's *Dream Children*." The "informational" category includes "good critical essays— Dryden, Hazlitt," along with histories by Edward Gibbon and Thomas Babington Macaulay, biographies like James Boswell's *Life of Johnson*, and the philosophies of Francis Bacon and David Hume. And yet, as she repeats several times over the course of her lectures, "the greatest lit. will both inform + inspire us."[37]

Turning to the four kinds of reading, Spurgeon next explains the first type: informational reading. When we read for information, we might study the literature of Queen Anne's age in order to "realise the difft forces at play, social + political" or read "Defoe's pamphlets + reviews in order—primarily—to gain inform abt these forces." Or—to take a more complex example—in studying Milton "in order to understand his life + work we must have a clear view of the civil + religious strife in England in 17thC; what were difft. points of view, what was the precise history of the struggle?" And "up to a point" but "with great care," we read more important works "of philosophy or reflection" that reveal "the theories and the mind of a writer" in this same informational way—works like "Bacon's Art of Learning, Hobbes's Leviathan, Burke's Speeches, and Carlyle's Sartor Resartus."[38]

The second kind of reading is also informational, but it is different because it grapples with concerns of aesthetics and intentions. In this second kind of reading, we read "for criticism—in order to judge of a work + express our opinion about it." In this second kind of reading, we become responsible to the entire work, for we are no longer just skimming or searching for information. When we read in order to criticize, Spurgeon explains, we must be systematic. We must build our own working model of the text upon which we will base our judgments. Both the first and second forms of informational reading require students to learn to use scholarly tools. Spurgeon notes, "It is in this class of work that we make best use of the system of slips wh. I shall go into more fully later. To read, pencil in hand, + making use of slips is indispensable for these 1st + 2nd types of reading; for it is the only sound + scholarly method of collecting, sorting + arranging your facts + your points."[39]

More briefly, Spurgeon mentions the other reason we read: to be inspired. Like informational reading, inspirational reading has two different motivations. One is to "read for the pleasure of coming into contact with great minds. This is one of the most fruitful + educative kinds of reading, + our attitude here is somewhat dift [from that of informational reading]—will return to this later." When we read for information or to criticize, "we must take careful notes, we must verify and co-ordinate our knowledge," while when we read "to come into contact with great minds," we must "gather up all our forces of mind, to be ready to criticize, to refute, to disagree." Accurate note taking is essential to each of the first three types. The fourth type is different. When we "read in order to feel," we need not take notes, verify, and coordinate; instead, we must cultivate ourselves and "attune ourselves to see + to feel."[40] Spurgeon is less specific in her lectures about how we might undertake this kind of cultivation and achieve this sort of seeing and feeling. She reminds her students that though it is important, reading for feeling will not be central to the class: "In what I am going to say now, I am thinking of the first 3 kinds of reading."[41]

In the next meeting, Spurgeon discusses the conditions necessary for the reading and handling of books, suggesting that there are physical prerequisites for effective reading. In this kind of study, your focus will be "concentrated, your attention absolutely absorbed."[42] It is important, she notes, not to study for more than four or six hours a day to avoid fatigue. One must also "get into the way of handling books—so as to get at the centre of a book at once, the book lover + student will always read the title page + publisher" because "old publishers convey a whole history" and even "modern publishers have certain traditions."[43] The student encountering the book should read the table of contents and note its arrangement; sample some bit of the book to begin to judge it, noticing "the style, length of words + paras, presentation, all v indicative." From doing this, "the practiced reader in 3 minutes investigation can get a pretty good idea of whether he wants to read a book or not, + what sort of service it will be to him." This is important in order to make sure you "use books as tools" rather than being "overwhelmed" by them. Master your books, or be mastered by them, Spurgeon sternly warns: "If all the time you are reading, you keep co-ordinating yr. knowledge, grouping it—relating it—keeping a clear thread of the main principles—you will be able to mount above it, and not allow it to mount above you and oppress you."[44]

To model the techniques for achieving mastery of books, Spurgeon offers examples drawn from her own research on Ruskin in the later weeks of the course.[45] How, she asks, should one set out to navigate the "very vast" worlds of information that exist in relation to Ruskin's life and thought? The possibilities are myriad: "Endless problems are raised in connection with him, endless lines of thought may be looked at. For instance various aspects of his work: art critic, artist, interpreter of nature, geologist, social reformer, education, ethics, literary + critical work, as a prose artist, etc."[46] Even to "take one branch—social reform" is to alight upon an "enormous subject, + one which throws light on the [major] forces of the whole 19thc in England, + goes far to explain the condition of things today."[47] Spurgeon assumes at the outset that "you have read R's life (Cook + Collingwood) + know some of his work" as background. The next step is to exploit the resources of the Library Edition of the Works of John Ruskin. To do this, she recommends that you begin with the index and look up "Social Reform." There you will find yourself "referred to Political Economy—nearly 2½ pages given to it. See + read." Having consulted the index, "You will next turn to vol 17 of Lib edn where you will find R's 3 chief writings on Pol. Econ"—*Unto This Last*, *Munera Pulveris*, and *Time and Tide*. The Library Edition also includes, she notes, "an admirable introd. on the whole subject, + a valuable app. of Letters + Speeches + Notes." Spurgeon provides a quick summary of that introduction's useful points: its tracing of the main currents of Ruskin's writings on political science; its account of British political science at the time of Ruskin, in addition to "v. full refs to the newspapers of 1860, wh: shows you the attitude R. had to fight against"; and "a full list of books on this specl side of R's work." You should of course "make a note of these and look them up."[48]

After using the Library Edition itself as an index to your core set of materials, your next task is to read intensively using the note-taking system. Earlier in the semester, Spurgeon had instructed her students how to use slips or "fiches" in order to support systematic note taking. "Suppose you are studying some author—steeping yourself in his work + thought—if that is going to be of any permanent + practical use to you afterwards, you need to make some record of your study." Slips are important "in order to secure order + convenience of ref. You can arrange them + shuffle them + sort them as you never can entries on a notebook or on a sheet of paper. Have them all the same size. Card or paper."[49] Now, in order to capture your thoughts about Ruskin, Spurgeon urges, the real work begins. You will "set to work to read carefully R's primary books on this point, + here your series of slips begins in earnest. Here is where your own resources are called into play, your natural power of seizing important points." You will have two main types of slips, "those giving refs to the actual facts of R's theories" and "those tabulating your own views, + working towards various lines of investigation."[50] Her example of the type of slips giving references lists a set of Ruskin's definitions of wealth, value, labor, and riches along with a quick list of his objections to the old "Political Economy." She offers two examples, the first a set of judgments of Ruskin's ideas, the second a set of "peculiarly fine or notable passages" in categories such as "the power of rousing emotion," examples of "striking comparisons," of "good concrete illustrations of an abstract point," and of

UNTO THIS LAST.

Good concrete illustrations of an abstract point.

§5.	p. 6.	Does not always follow that persons are antagonistic because their interests are (mother and children).
§32.	p. 49.	Analogy between circulation of wealth and blood.
§36.	pp.55-6.	Working of modern Political Economy.
§59.	p. 112.	The economical usefulness of a thing.
§73.	p. 145.	The comparison of Capital to a root or bulb.

FIGURE 1.1. Caroline Spurgeon's printed example of her own notes detailing "Good concrete illustrations of an abstract point" in John Ruskin's *Unto This Last.* Spurgeon distributed these printed examples in her Art of Reading class at Bedford College in 1913, to show students how to move from taking "rough notes" on a text to a final index of a text, tailored to the notetaker's particular project. RHC PP 7/3/1/20 Archives, Royal Holloway, University of London.

the connection of his work on political economy with other areas of his thought, like his "views on art."[51]

Spurgeon claims that research and note taking require not rote copying and sorting, but value judgments—recording this and not that, subordinating one point to another. For example, ideas that were important to Ruskin might be of little importance to your understanding of him, while ideas of minor importance to Ruskin might transform your understanding of his life. The researcher, Spurgeon emphasizes, encodes her own ideas in the very structure and organization of her note taking. Like Josephine Miles, who is discussed in chapter 6, Spurgeon insists that students understand how seemingly technical choices and apparently banal scholarly practices require thoughtful consideration because they encode perspectives.

Spurgeon's course culminated in an exercise that required students to move from page-by-page note taking to an index of a work whose hierarchy would reflect their individual perspective on it. To show them how to do this, Spurgeon passed out printed examples of her rough notes toward an index to Ruskin's *Unto This Last* along with copies of her rough index and her final index in order to demonstrate in detail. She points out that "in Rough Notes there is no arrangement" and "certain points are repeated." In the rough index, the repetition goes away and the order follows Ruskin's book, proceeding chapter by chapter and page by page. The final index then imposes the reader's own order. In the final version, "what has happened in making the Index is that the ideas have been grouped, concentrated, the movement made clear by accentuating certain points."[52] For example, in Spurgeon's rough notes the definition of "value" is tied to page 118, where it appears in *Unto This Last*; in the final index, it appears alongside other definitions at the top. Likewise, Spurgeon gathers the multiple definitions of wealth that appear throughout the rough notes into a single entry, also at the top. Other rough notes never appear in the final index at all. For Spurgeon, making your own index to a work like *Unto This Last* unravels it into a set of strands that you can reorder and reconnect.[53]

After unfolding the process of scholarly research over the weeks of the Art of Reading class, Spurgeon finishes by suggesting, almost as an afterthought, some of the essays about Ruskin one might write after creating "some body of knowledge upon which to work." She suggests, for example, that an essay on Ruskin's influence on present-day social reform and thought would build from this knowledge base by tracking his influence on William Morris. It could use print sources, "making investigation of all kinds by studying a good deal of the newspapers and periodicals of

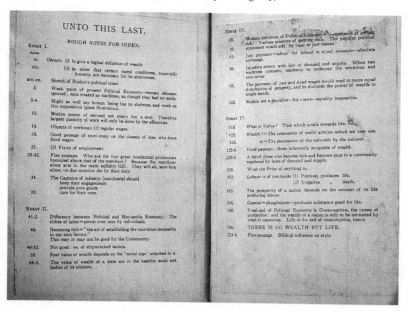

FIGURE 1.2. Caroline Spurgeon's "Rough Notes for Index" (1913) of Ruskin's *Unto This Last*. She pasted these class handouts into her Art of Reading notebook containing her course lectures. RHC PP 7/3/1/20 Archives, Royal Holloway, University of London.

the last 20 years," as well as interviews with "some of the old members of [the] Working Men's College" to see what effects Ruskin's teachings had on the present Labour Party. One could also "study the reforms of the last 20 years in education, elementary and technical, in social matters such as wages, houses for the poor, old age pensions, in questions of land and property" in order to "trace how much of it is directly owing to this one man." Having done all this, one will then have "some insight, some working knowledge, some body of material bearing on one fraction of the life work of Ruskin."[54] But despite her brief suggestions of other ideas for paper topics, Spurgeon makes it clear that actual essay writing is a different study, outside of the scope of her class.[55] The art of literary research that Spurgeon models in such detail can be an occupation and an end—at least temporarily—in itself.

By showing her students how to move from the Library Edition of Ruskin to a personal index of *Unto This Last,* by teaching them step-by-step how to decompose Ruskin's writing so that they could then recompose it into the shapes of their own interpretations and arguments, Spurgeon not only demystified the production of scholarship, but also

UNTO THIS LAST.

INDEX.

PAGES.

Two main objects of the book:

xi. §2. (1) to give a logical definition of wealth.
xiii. §4. (2) to show that certain moral conditions, especially honesty, are necessary for its attainment.

xvi-xx. §6. }
102. §54. } *Ruskin's political creed.*

Definitions.

118. §61. Value.
58, 64-5. 123, 125, 156. §§37, 40, 62, 64, 77. } Wealth.
136. §69. Price.
142. §72. Labour.
146. §73. Capital.

Objects for the workman to attain.

18. §13. (1) Regular wages.
21-3. §§15, 16. (2) Fixity of employment.

Defects of present Political Science.

2. §§1-3. (1) Human element ignored—men treated as machines, pp. 3-4. Good illustration.
150. §75. (2) Object 'money gain' not 'mouth gain.'
151. §76. (3) Belief that a demand for commodities is not a demand for labour. Mill's colossal error.

41-2. §28. *Difference between Political and Mercantile Economy.*
150. §76. The final end of Political Economy is consumption, the crown of production. The wealth of a nation is only to be estimated by what it consumes. Life is
§77. the end of consumption, hence

156. THERE IS NO WEALTH BUT LIFE.

Notable passages.

10. §8. Motive power of human being not steam but a soul.
18. §13. Good passage of semi-irony—bishops, physicians, etc., have fixed payments.
25-32. §§17-25. Very good passage—why the soldier, etc., is honoured above the merchant.
128-9. §65. Those who become rich and poor in a community regulated by demand and supply.
125-6. §64. Those inherently incapable of wealth.
173-4. §85. Ending—Biblical influence on style.

The most original and important part of the book.

(1) The definition of wealth as worked out in Essay IV.
18-21. §§13-14. (2) The insistence on the need for fixity of wages
90-96. §§50-53. *irrespective of the demand for labour.*

FIGURE 1.3. Caroline Spurgeon's final "Index" (1913) to Ruskin's *Unto This Last*. Whereas the rough index orders the entries chronologically, following the order of the book, the final index reflects the reader's orders of importance. RHC PP 7/3/1/20 Archives, Royal Holloway, University of London.

the production of great works like *Unto This Last*. When she escorted her extension school students to the British Museum to perform original research during World War I, Spurgeon taught them to see for themselves the materials that went into the creation of the bound works of literature they held in their hands back in the classroom. And in her Art of Reading class, Spurgeon taught students to index Ruskin for themselves, using scholarly tools to break down an intimidating work of a towering figure into its component parts preparatory to making their own claims about some aspect of the work. In all of these courses, Spurgeon taught her students to see themselves as agents in the creation and circulation of scholarly knowledge, a project that was ongoing and infinitely extensible. And she showed them how, in drawing on and contributing to scholarly knowledge, they were themselves contributing to the value of literary works and the shaping of literary reputations. In the decades that followed, Spurgeon amplified this method and turned it to the most canonical writer in the English language in order to make him, temporarily, into an everyday man walking around in the world. Counting and charting Shakespeare's metaphors, Spurgeon sought to show that his writing process relied upon the quotidian details of the everyday life around him. Indexical work, she hoped, could render these details visible to twentieth-century readers so that they could see the very ordinary origins of the works they often encountered as sacrosanct and mystified.

Unraveling the Canon: Shakespeare's Imagery and What It Tells Us *(1935)*

Shakespeare's Imagery and What It Tells Us, Spurgeon's best-known and last-published major scholarly work, undoes the fixed and finished form of the canonical work even more methodically than her classroom work does.[56] She published *Shakespeare's Imagery* after a decade of "gradually selecting, sorting, and classifying" "the whole of Shakespeare's images"— all of his figures of speech—contained in his complete works, as well as images drawn from the plays of many of his contemporaries. Spurgeon intended the volume to be the first of several book publications resulting from this decade of research.[57] She also hoped "eventually to publish the material itself, so that other students can check and perhaps extend it, in order that it may serve as data and a starting-point for further research of various kinds."[58] By slowly separating out, categorizing, and visualizing Shakespeare's metaphors, Spurgeon sought to return Shakespeare's work to everyday life. She did this not by historicizing and contextualizing

Shakespeare's plays, but by treating the plays as "documents" or "data" that would help her reconstruct the material world that had surrounded Shakespeare as he wrote.[59]

Turning her attention to the most literary part of the works of the most canonical English writer in history, Spurgeon undoes their literariness by returning these figures to what she speculated were their origins in the everyday world surrounding Shakespeare at the time of his writing. As she explained, her primary interest in Shakespeare's images was "in their stuff, and what this stuff or content tells us."[60] Using what she saw as a decidedly new method, Spurgeon first mined Shakespeare's works to extract the similes and metaphors from the text in which they were embedded. Having removed them from their context in Shakespeare's plays, Spurgeon then snipped the link between tenor and vehicle, setting the former aside to carefully catalog the latter. So in "they'll take suggestion as a cat laps milk," she discards "they" and "suggestion"—the fiction's referents— and preserves "cat" and "milk," cataloging them under taxonomies that include categories and subcategories like "nature" within which "growing things," "weather," and "sea" appear; "animals," including "four-footed," "birds," and "fish"; and "body," under which we find "body action," "food," and "sickness."[61] Spurgeon thus creates the raw material for a totally different mapping of Shakespeare's works out of the nonreferential aspects of his fictional worlds—the metaphors—and reimagines them as the referential content she claims they once were.[62] Rereading the vehicles of Shakespeare's metaphors as real worldly things that he encountered in his daily life, she unravels the tightly knit formal unit of the metaphor (or "image" in her language) to return its component parts to the world of the not-yet-literary. As *Shakespeare's Imagery* unfolds, the central point becomes this slow decomposition of finished and canonical works into an index of things that interested Shakespeare and the writers of his time, things they noticed and eventually made into literature—from Shakespeare's detailed observations of birds and his love of green vegetables to Bacon's attraction to the world of books and learning to Christopher Marlowe's preference for the city over the country.

This new method offered a more objective view of Shakespeare's plays, Spurgeon suggested, because it bypassed the evaluative and canonizing moves of criticism through indiscriminately collecting together *all* of Shakespeare's uses of figural language.[63] While many critics had already examined selected Shakespearean images from across his corpus, in her preface Spurgeon explains that "the novelty of the procedure I am describing is that *all* his images are assembled, sorted, and examined on a systematic basis, the good with the bad, the disagreeable with the unpleasant, the coarse with the refined, the attractive with the unattractive, and the poetical with the unpoetical."[64] Not selected to illustrate a "preconceived idea or thesis," "they are studied, either as a whole, or in groups, with a perfectly open mind, to see what information they yield, and the result comes often as a complete surprise to the investigator."[65] In a section of a chapter on "Shakespeare's Tastes and Interests," for example, Spurgeon argues that Shakespeare's "interest in needlework" can be concluded from the very specific knowledge displayed in figural references to "a bodkin, a silken thread, a twist of rotten silk, or an 'immaterial' skein of sleave or floss silk and needles, threaded and unthreaded" in plays including *Love's Labour's Lost, Much Ado about Nothing, Coriolanus,* and *King Lear.*[66] She notes that the range of Shakespeare's references to daily life indicate his familiarity with very modest domestic settings, especially in comparison with the more opulent references to domestic settings she finds in some other playwrights, and tracks the way Shakespeare's references to food become more precise while exponentially expanding in number in works he wrote after 1594.[67]

But more is at stake in this conceptual flattening of tenor and vehicle than a claim to objective literary analysis—a goal that actually recedes as the book unfolds across fifteen chapters, eight appendices, an extensive index, and seven charts accompanied by interpretive text. Throughout *Shakespeare's Imagery,* Spurgeon pulls away from the sense of any play as an organic whole or a finished work, instead using Shakespeare's writing to generate an imaginative map of the earliest moments of its composition— the instances that Roland Barthes theorizes as the jotting down of brief "notula" as they occur to the author in real time.[68] Spurgeon's criticism seeks to reveal literature as living rather than canonical by thinking about how literature might be composed from a variety of the author's referential, iterative, everyday experiences. What emerges is Spurgeon's desire to decompose Shakespeare's complete works into a data set that lets us study everyday life in Elizabethan England, and Shakespeare's everyday life in particular.[69] We can of course learn about Shakespeare indirectly from his finished plays, she notes, but we can also "add a little to our detailed knowledge of Shakespeare as a person by studying the data he has left us, incidentally and by the way as it were, embedded in his images."[70] Setting aside the conventional sources and methods of historicist work long familiar to her, Spurgeon turned to the plays' metaphors as a new angle on her old interest in the details of literary composition and the process of canon formation.

Critics noted the apparent tension between her interest in recovering the texture of everyday experience and her discarding of the usual apparatus of historicist literary study that seemed to many a more reliable method for carrying out her goal. As one annoyed reviewer complained, *Shakespeare's Imagery* avoids "any of the more concrete facts of the poet's life," virtually ignoring Shakespeare's biography.[71] And Spurgeon distances herself not just from biographical detail, but also from studies of Shakespeare's reading. Emphasizing "the difference between references and images," she dismisses the "lists of Shakespeare's references to various things, the law, school-books, learning, the Bible, religion, and so on" that had "been made out by enthusiasts who desire to prove from them that he at one time had been a lawyer's clerk or a schoolmaster, or that he was a Protestant or a Roman Catholic."[72] Accusing "reference-hunters" of ideological bias, she suggests that the unselfconscious way an author reaches for a metaphor differs completely from the more self-conscious referencing of a published work.[73] Yet if Spurgeon rejects traditional contextualisms, she also suspends any interest in a taxonomy or "formal classification" of the forms of metaphors she examined, since "for my purposes at the moment I do not need therefore to distinguish and analyze the various kinds of image: the sunken, the decorative, the expansive and so on; or to dwell on the differences between metaphor, simile, personification, metonymy, synecdoche and the like."[74] Her assertion of the importance of metaphor in her introduction along with this rejection of the classification of types of metaphor reminds us of her commitment to the unliterariness of this kind of literary study.[75]

Spurgeon's apparent disinterest in literary greatness or critical evaluation rubbed some critics the wrong way. Many of her reviewers suggested that *Shakespeare's Imagery* was more a concordance than a work of criticism; review after review framed Spurgeon as an information worker whose writing could nevertheless profitably be used as raw material by more brilliant (usually male) critics.[76] To take just one example of this kind of complaint, Stanley Hyman, in his 1948 retrospective assessment of her work and career, accuses Spurgeon of an almost comical short-circuiting of the connections between the language of Shakespeare's plays and the facts of Shakespeare's life.[77] Hyman suggests that Spurgeon's contributions to scholarship are achieved not through "superior insight but merely through her opening up a new area of information, the image-tabulations, as though she had discovered another lost book like Keats's Shakespeare."[78] Although he admits, grudgingly, that Spurgeon was a rare unifier of scholarly and critical methods, his final assessment is that her book is a reference tool superficially disguised as a scholarly monograph. Spurgeon's work on Shakespeare, in Hyman's final analysis, "did not venture very far, or cover even that distance very well." Yet "some of the subtlest and most important criticism of our day has been, and will increasingly be, enabled to venture far indeed because of her work," including "cluster criticism" by Edward A. Armstrong and Kenneth Burke.[79]

But some saw a different kind of value in the very qualities of Spurgeon's method that Hyman derided. As Rachel Hannon wrote in 1944, Spurgeon's work held out the alluring promise that "by an almost mechanical means we baser mortals can come upon a grasp of poetic values instantly apparent to Sidney, Shakespeare, Shelley, or Coleridge."[80] For Hannon, the "almost mechanical" nature of Spurgeon's *Shakespeare's Imagery* research demystifies the creation of "poetic values" in a way that lets everyday people connect to and understand it. Hannon's reading was rare among early reactions to Spurgeon's work, but if we reimagine *Shakespeare's Imagery* as graduating from the Art of Reading classroom, suddenly it snaps into focus, becoming the dominant—even obvious— reading of the book. In *Shakespeare's Imagery* as in the Art of Reading, Spurgeon uses mechanical methods to create literary sensibilities. In both her classroom and her research, she seeks to reveal the quotidian materials and methods that writers use to make literary works, and the slow, collective, accretive process through which critics, scholars, and readers all contribute to forming literary figures with particular reputations. As we will see in the next chapter, in doing this Spurgeon shared more than a little with Eliot, whose own methods were different but who also sought to reveal to his students the working methods and everyday practices of canonical writers.

The Art of Reading and the Idea of the University

Reviewers of *Shakespeare's Imagery* encountered the book in the context of the late 1930s and early 1940s debates between literary critics and literary scholars over the proper modes and methods of English.[81] Since Spurgeon mostly refrained from positioning her work within contemporary debates on method, others were free to elaborate the polemical statements about method they believed her work implied, or to cast her as the plodding scholar whose books, weighted down by numbers and graphs, belonged on the reference shelf. In her teaching, by contrast, Spurgeon spoke quite fully about the relation between her methods and her theories, drawing strong connections between how she taught students to read and the place of literary scholarship in the liberal education of the whole student.

It was in her classroom, that is, rather than in the introductory pages of her monographs, that Spurgeon most fully theorized method. In the first lecture for the Art of Reading, for example, Spurgeon turned to John Henry Newman's *Discourses on the Scope and Nature of University Education* to explain how a research methods class on indexing and note taking might grant them a new appreciation of literature and help them discover their own ideas and values. Acquiring knowledge, as she was teaching them to do, was merely one of the preconditions of being "educated," Spurgeon explained. "When I say 'educated' I mean that liberal educn which I think it is the function of the Univy to give us, + which consists at one + same time in a discipline + an enlargement of the mind," she continued. This enlargement requires that the "mind must act upon facts + ideas, not just passively absorbing . . . [but] digesting, co-ordinating, and assimilating them." This work of coordination and assimilation "is done by fitting in what we learn to what we already know, by comparing ideas, by connecting the past with the present—in short by possessing a knowledge not only of things but also of their relations." Characteristically, after summarizing and explaining Newman's ideas to her students, she also gives them the full citation and suggests that they read the source for themselves: "I am touching here on a difficult subject, + I do want you to understand what I mean, and I would refer you therefore to the best exposition I know of what a liberal education means + in what it consists. Chapter V of Card Newman's The Scope and Nature of University Education—the ch called 'Liberal knowledge viewed in relation to learning.'" As they advance in the course, Spurgeon told them, "It will become ever more clear to us that it is not what we read or how much we read, but that it is the way our minds re-act upon what we have read that matters—+ that is the only thing that matters."[82]

For Spurgeon, as for Newman, cataloging and indexing information offered a material way of teaching students to build connections between their objects of research and their own lives. Spurgeon was particularly interested in Newman's vision of the university as a place for liberal education. In this view, the university was not the domain of the solitary researcher but a place where students—learning from teachers and from each other—began the lifelong work of assimilating newly acquired knowledge to their existing understanding of the world. University teaching for Spurgeon was not the rote dissemination of a fixed body of knowledge created elsewhere and by others. Rather, it involved the refinement, assimilation, and what Newman called the "extension" of knowledge. In the "University Teaching" section of his book, Newman refers to "a living teaching" that "is a something, and does a something."[83] This idea of a teaching that is not merely a scene of rehearsal or transmission, but that has tangible transformative and creative effects on its participants and on the world, was one in which Spurgeon believed. Like Newman, Spurgeon saw the research classroom as a place where students and teachers collectively created value by connecting their work to what they already knew, to each other, and to possible but not yet existing future audiences.

Spurgeon's careful curation of her own teaching papers testifies to this vision of university teaching as the extension of knowledge. Her preservation and organization of her own teaching notebooks—with tables of contents and indexes, with standardized marginal notes and title pages— has the intended effect of making them available not just to her future self, but to other scholars and students. Like her plan to open the extensive data set she compiled in order to write *Shakespeare's Imagery* to other scholars, her organization of her teaching notebooks also points outward. Using the familiar apparatus of scholarly research, she makes her lecture notes and their many references to other works and lectures as legible as possible so they may be repurposed by later generations seeking to extend their own knowledge.

Spurgeon's is one of the few archives we found in which teaching materials are carefully organized and preserved by their creator with an eye to their future survival and potential use by others. Our collective devaluation of our own teaching materials has made repositories' preservation of them difficult to justify and therefore unlikely. This combination of forces is in part responsible for the mass amnesia about the history of teaching in English literary studies—and, we suspect, in many other disciplines. But even more than this, mass amnesia about the history of teaching has dramatically affected the current shape and status of teaching in the university, as we discuss further in this book's conclusion. Spurgeon's teaching archive thus forms a figure for a kind of fantasy that we seek, in this book as a whole, to edge toward reality. The teaching archive we need today might look like a collective version of Spurgeon's individual one: an archive produced by a history in which we collectively valued teaching enough to treat teaching materials—notes, syllabuses, exams—as worth preserving, circulating, sharing, and citing. Spurgeon's notebooks— bound by Spurgeon, expertly cataloged and curated by Royal Holloway archivists and librarians—are the model for a counterfactual but imaginable archive of teaching's past.

CHAPTER 2

T. S. Eliot, Modern English Literature (1916–19)

T. S. Eliot, we are often told, almost single-handedly shaped the twentieth-century literary canon. His dramatic reformation of critical taste, literary historians hold, began with *The Sacred Wood*. In that 1920 volume of essays, Eliot quietly replaced the major figures of English literature—William Shakespeare, John Milton, John Keats, Alfred Tennyson—with an array of minor Elizabethan and Jacobean playwrights and metaphysical poets. He also introduced concepts, such as the dissociation of sensibility, that would shape anthologies and literary histories for years to come. E. M. W. Tillyard, for instance, recalls how *The Sacred Wood* inspired an entire generation of Cambridge students to turn from Romantic, expressive poetry to the metaphysical "poetry of ideas." Stefan Collini credits Eliot with establishing the midcentury's "'Holy Trinity' of poetry, drama, and the novel" and with effectively decanonizing the Victorian essayists and moralists. And critics such as Nicholas McDowell describe how *The Sacred Wood*'s once iconoclastic judgments and assertions came to determine how scholars narrate seventeenth-century literary history.[1]

But even more than Eliot's new canon, his reformation of critical method is the force that scholars feel has most powerfully determined the course of literary study in the twentieth century. As John Crowe Ransom wrote in *The New Criticism* in 1941, "One of the best things in [Eliot's] influence has been his habit of considering aesthetic effect as independent of religious effect, or moral, or political and social."[2] Indeed, many argue that *The Sacred Wood*'s anti-Romantic canon paved the way for the New Critics' redefinition of literature as impersonal and detached from the immediate circumstances of its composition.[3] John Guillory, for instance, argues that Eliot's canon reformation—Eliot's preference for minor poets (John Donne, John Dryden) over major authors (Shakespeare, Tennyson)—encoded an entirely new set of literary values. *The*

Sacred Wood, Guillory says, recentered literature's authority on its ambiguity and nonreferentiality. For Guillory, English professors reaffirm these values in the "pedagogical device of close reading" when they attend to how texts mean—to their forms and figures—rather than to what they say.[4] In this sense, Shakespeare, Keats, and Tennyson may remain central to the university literature curriculum, but the way they are taught since Eliot makes them fall in line with the new canon's silent redefinition of literariness.[5]

Yet while imagining that *The Sacred Wood* determined the texts and practices of countless twentieth-century literature classrooms, scholars have overlooked the actual classroom that made *The Sacred Wood.* As Ronald Schuchard recounts, Eliot taught Modern English Literature, a three-year tutorial course, to working-class adults from 1916 to 1919.[6] The course, offered under the auspices of the University of London Joint Committee for the Promotion of the Higher Education of Working People, met on Monday evenings in Southall at the local grammar school.[7] The students included a "very intelligent grocer who reads Ruskin behind his counter" and several "(female) elementary schoolteachers, who work very hard with large classes of refractory children all day but come with unabated eagerness to get culture in the evening."[8] During their first two years together, the class worked through a collectively determined syllabus of nineteenth-century novelists, poets, historians, and social critics. For the third year of the course, Eliot's students requested Elizabethan literature. Eliot obliged, and together they came up with a syllabus that included works by Thomas Kyd, John Lyly, Christopher Marlowe, George Peele, Robert Greene, Shakespeare, John Webster, Ben Jonson, and Francis Beaumont and John Fletcher. In the spring of 1919, Eliot turned his work from the tutorial's third year into a series of book reviews on early modern literature. Six of these reviews would become essays or part of essays in *The Sacred Wood.*

In order to reveal how Eliot's Modern English Literature tutorial shaped *The Sacred Wood,* we reconstruct the class's social life and institutional contexts. Unlike the two large lecture-based extension courses Eliot also taught in these years—an eleven-week course, Tendencies in Contemporary French Thought, in Yorkshire through the Oxford Extension Delegacy in 1916 and a twenty-five-week course on Victorian literature at Sydenham for the London City Council in 1917—Modern English Literature convened a small group of students for three years of intensive, discussion-based study. The course's tutorial format derived from the demands of the Workers' Educational Association (WEA) for forms of extension education that would give working-class students a central role in knowledge production and a forum in which to share their experiences and knowledge. As Albert Mansbridge, president of the WEA, put it, "The relation of tutor and student in a University Tutorial Class . . . is entirely different from the ordinary relationship of teacher and pupil. The teacher is in real fact a fellow-student, and the fellow-students are teachers."[9] Following the tutorial format, the students of Modern English Literature took a lead role in selecting their tutor, choosing course topics, setting reading lists, determining the amount of time the class spent on each author, and conducting individual research. In his first end-of-year report, Eliot described the class as "experimental and tentative."[10] Whereas the audiences for his lecture courses were "extremely intelligent but somewhat passive," he found his tutorial students more engaging. As he wrote to his father, "Monday evening is one of the moments of the week that I look forward to. The class is very keen and very appreciative, and very anxious to learn and to think."[11]

The materials that remain from Modern English Literature show that Eliot was anxious to learn as well. Eliot's syllabuses, lecturer's reports, letters, and notes provide a record of how he adapted his teaching to the tutorial form and to the WEA's ethos of equal exchange. Over the course of the tutorial's three years, Eliot revised his syllabuses in response to his students' interests and requests, and adjusted assignments to the pace of their work schedules. This required structural changes. Specifically, Eliot jettisoned the format of his first-year syllabus, which had moved chronologically through disconnected studies of representative authors, to offer instead a densely interconnected syllabus that foregrounded the material working conditions of past writers. As he explained in his reports, this new organization served the practical purpose of encouraging his busy students to pursue sustained research with the confidence that their work would remain relevant to class discussion over the course of several weeks. Like other WEA tutors, Eliot learned how to shift the gravity of his course so that Modern English Literature approximated a dialogical exchange rather than a hierarchical dissemination of culture or knowledge.

As Modern English Literature became more and more communal, the class developed a vision of literary history that placed workers at its center. The class's movement away from a syllabus of solitary geniuses to a syllabus peopled by men and women who used source texts, wrote for audiences, adopted influences, manipulated conventions, and collaborated with peers reflects not only Eliot's pedagogical strategizing but also the class's burgeoning literary values—specifically, their valuation of authorship as work. Returning to the material practices of writing—newly revealed as imitative, repetitive, sometimes paid or patronized—allowed

Eliot and his working-class students to draw connections between the tutorial course's own sociality and the social lives and working practices of the writers they studied. Together, the class came to prize workaday writers like John Ruskin and John Dryden—writers whose uneven work became valuable not for its formal perfection but for the way it enabled the future work of other writers. This model of literary value as continued, collective work—made in Eliot's classroom and enshrined in *The Sacred Wood*—derives, we argue, from the WEA. When we set the three years' worth of materials from Modern English Literature in the context of other WEA extension tutorials offered in these same years, the influence of that tutorial on both the thematic concerns and the literary values of *The Sacred Wood* snaps into focus.

Our ability to reconstruct the effects that Eliot's extension tutorial had on *The Sacred Wood*—and thus on some of the discipline's core theoretical conceptions—depends on the University of London's preservation of the syllabuses, course descriptions, lecturer's reports, and graded assignments of courses taught under the auspices of the Joint Committee for the Promotion of the Higher Education of Working People. The survival of so many of these documents is unusual, yet even when these materials exist, they are often ignored by disciplinary historians. As Jonathan Rose and Alexandra Lawrie have argued, historians of education as well as major disciplinary historians of English like Terry Eagleton and Chris Baldick have caricatured extension schools as simple ideological state apparatuses[12] without examining archival evidence for what happened in their classrooms—evidence that shows, in some cases, how extension classes created many of the central practices and methods of our discipline.[13] Lawrie, for example, credits literature extension lecturers such as R. G. Moulton with devising the method of "inductive criticism"— a formalist approach "that dispensed with issues of canonicity or literary reputation"—decades prior to the invention of New Critical close reading.[14] Rose likewise hints at how the working-class students in these courses affected the development of disciplinary methods and knowledge, particularly in the discipline of history.[15] Turning to extension tutors and their students, in other words, does more than supplement or diversify existing histories of literary study; it requires that we radically rewrite them.

Extension Education and the Tutorial Course

Before we can reconstruct how Eliot and his students read Elizabethan literature in the year before *The Sacred Wood* appeared, we must first

describe how the ethos and practices of working-class extension education shaped Eliot's teaching. By the time Eliot began teaching extension
education courses in 1916, the university extension movement in England
was more than fifty years old, with an established if flexible set of conventions for convening and running courses in local centers around the country.[16] From its beginnings, university extension developed through partnerships among local centers, workers' groups, religious organizations,
charismatic individuals, city boards, and university bodies. As Lawrence
Goldman writes, the movement "has no easy and obvious delineations,
no clear and unambiguous margins; it spills across educational and institutional boundaries."[17]

Though extension schools worked in concert with universities, in the
early twentieth century the extension movement positioned itself as fundamentally at odds with the university as an institution. Parent universities may have considered their extension programs peripheral, but the
WEA countered that extension school students made major contributions
to the production of knowledge. They further argued that Oxford and the
University of London needed working-class students much more than
working-class students needed them. John Burrows, in his history of adult
education at the University of London, offers an anecdote that captures
the disagreement: when the WEA president, Mansbridge, challenged the
assumption that extension students enrolled to receive knowledge, R. B.
Haldane, chairman of the Royal Commission on University Education in
London, asked pedagogically, "Well, of course, a university is a body that
imparts knowledge?" Mansbridge replied, "And may I venture to say that
it receives it—students [from tutorial classes] may go right beyond the
university degree, dealing with first class research."[18] Indeed, the WEA
maintained that only through an "education devised by working men in
company with scholars" would the disciplines produce a usable account
of England's national past and future. "The movement," Mansbridge
wrote, "has linked up the experience of Universities with the experience
of life outside."[19]

The WEA thus rejected the idea that extension courses merely disseminated existing knowledge downward. It also suggested that the collective social relations of knowledge production in the extension school
were as important as the knowledge produced. "Tutorial classes," Mansbridge wrote, "are less than nothing if they concern themselves merely
with the acquisition or dissemination of knowledge. They are in reality
concerned with the complete development of those who compose them,
and indeed of the common life."[20] Such collective ideals were shared by
the first wave of tutorial students,[21] who explicitly rejected the proposed

model whereby the most talented among them would receive prizes and admission to parent universities.[22] Whereas parent universities saw university extension as a "ladder" that individual students might climb, rung by rung, into the upper regions of the university proper, the WEA argued that universities and their extension programs together already formed a "highway of education"—a broad path linking several locations by which one could reach a variety of destinations.[23]

The classroom archive verifies these two hallmarks of the extension tutorials: a deeply collaborative ethos and a curriculum that positioned working adults as coparticipants in the discovery of unrecorded knowledge. Records show that before the tutor even set foot in the classroom, tutorials were convened through a process of negotiation: tutors offered a list of proposed courses, and the students at a local center would choose a topic.[24] The extension delegacy would compare the tutors' offerings with the interests submitted by students and offer a tutor to a group of students for approval. Tutor and students then spent their weeks and months together reading a subject that they had collaboratively chosen. The contingent arrangement of tutorial topics was not merely a convenient mechanism; it was an expression of core extension school values mandating that social relations and students' interests, not a fixed topic imposed by a tutor or institution, should lead the formation of a tutorial.

Extension organizations published syllabuses for the chosen classes through their associated university's press.[25] More public than teaching documents are usually imagined to be, these printed syllabuses acted as advertisements to potential students and guides to enrolled ones, as well as records designed to inform the wider public about the extension school's work. They were also part of an important archive, annually bound into volumes that helped record the extension school's history. But despite their printed form, extension school syllabuses were flexible documents, responsive to the changing needs of the class and to the necessary indeterminacy of the twenty-four-week lecture series or the three-year tutorial. For extension students not only collaborated with teachers to determine curricula and course offerings; they also helped create reading lists and weekly topics.

Extension school syllabuses draw attention to their own contingency. The headnote to Alice Davies's 1913–14 syllabus for Some Writers of the XIXth Century and After explains that the lectures make "no attempt to deal fully with any of the three periods treated. The subjects have been chosen by the students and tutors jointly, purely on the basis of their inclinations." The syllabus for B. L. K. Henderson's tutorial Aspects of Victorian Literature (1919–21) remarks that after the first year, "the class will be in a position to discuss whether it wishes to go further into the treasury of the same period, to ascertain the relationship of Victorian writers to those of an earlier period, or to those who have followed in their footsteps." Mabel Atkinson's syllabus for Social History of England from 1860 (1911–12) notes that her course's method of combining industrial history with economic theory was developed in response to her students, who "desired to study the economic development of England from 1760 and at the same time wished to acquire the elements of economic history."[26]

Flexibility around course topics was possible because, unlike traditional university courses, extension classes were not offered as part of a sequenced curriculum. Course topics often reflected, instead, contemporary relevance or student interest. R. St. John Parry explained in 1920 that "it is natural that a class of mothers should begin with 'The History of the Home'; that a class of young conscripts from the woolen trade of Yorkshire should be found interested in the study of wool, its history and its treatment; that economics and the history of industry should be the favourite subjects of Tutorial Classes for working men."[27] Industrial and economic history courses were common,[28] as were courses exploring the present state of the working class, such as Gilbert Slater's The Worker and the State or J. Lionel Tayler's The Condition of the People.[29] Courses featured contemporary social issues; reading lists often included recent publications such as Maria Montessori's The Montessori Method (1912), W. E. B. Du Bois's The Souls of Black Folk (1903), Emilia Kanthack's The Preservation of Infant Life (1907), Beckles Willson's The Story of Rapid Transit (1903), and C. S. Myers's A Text-Book of Experimental Psychology (1909). Syllabuses reveal how tutors incorporated new knowledge into their course plans; M. Epstein, who taught his Descriptive Economics tutorial several times in the 1910s, added new lectures such as "The Cash Nexus" in response to theoretical developments or student demands.[30] During World War I, many courses sprang up to cover aspects of the conflict, including R. H. U. Bloor's Ideals and Issues of the Present Struggle (1917), Mabel Palmer's Problems of Social Economics Arising from the War (1916), Mordaunt Shairp's The Literary Inspiration of the Great War (1919), and Arnold Freeman's The Economic Problems of Demobilisation (1916), which Freeman taught at Southall, down the hall from Eliot's Modern English Literature.[31]

Extension courses also invited students to create knowledge by incorporating various kinds of research-based classwork.[32] Historians of extension education tend to focus on data about the small proportion of tutorial students who completed the fortnightly papers required to receive course credit.[33] Such data was submitted in lecturer's reports and preserved in the board records of extension schools, but syllabuses tell a different story about what constituted coursework. From fieldwork to oral presentations to at-home experiments to archival research, extension students completed a wide range of activities never documented by institutional record keeping. S. S. Brierley's 1917–18 psychology course asked students "to keep note-books for practical work, in which will be recorded both the experiments performed in class and those carried out at home."[34] Caroline Spurgeon took her Age of Johnson students to the British Museum to conduct original manuscript research, as described in the previous chapter. Tayler's course Life in the Home taught students "how to keep a life-album" on the model of Francis Galton. R. P. Farley's three-year tutorial in sociology began in 1911 with the yearlong course Poverty: Suggested Causes and Remedies, in which students made "visits of observation" designed "to bring the members of the class into actual touch with the problems discussed and with various methods of dealing with them." E. H. Pringle's Modern Economic Problems course, offered in 1912–13, included student presentations on farming, "investment of trade union funds," and the minimum wage, which drew on personal experience as the beginning of research.[35]

In many cases, extension courses advanced directly to firsthand research and independent study in acknowledgment—rather than willful ignorance—of students' busy work lives. In his lecturer's report for The Life of the Nineteenth Century as Represented in Literature (1914), A. A. Jack describes the "attemptive atmosphere" of his class, in which "everyone was trying to get something out of it and to make use of what was being put before them." His "chiefly poor" students, Jack wrote, "take much interest, work with energy in their spare time, and made very marked progress," quickly coming to "strongly express their desire to have more detailed study of particular authors."[36] Like Jack, Eliot encouraged his students to proceed directly to deep reading precisely because their work lives often prevented them from keeping up with the syllabus. In his lecturer's report for the first year of Modern English Literature, Eliot wrote, "I ask the students all to read some particular work on the current author, in order that there may always be a common basis for discussion; but when (as is usually the case), a student has very little time, I recommend further reading of one author in whom the student is interested, rather than a smattering of all." He also requested that the library obtain copies of books, such as "Mill's *Utilitarianism,* or Renan's *Life of Jesus* . . . and also a few historical works covering the period" that were not on the course reading list but would be of interest to his students.[37] Eliot's dismissal of the kind of class that would offer students a uniform "smattering" of culture echoes extension education's promise to critique and expand disciplinary knowledge rather than simply transmit it.

These untallied instances of research-based classwork point toward the WEA's internal standards for judging the effectiveness of its courses. Distinct from parent universities' bureaucratic attention to the quantity and quality of papers submitted by credit-earning students, the WEA measured the success or failure of a university extension course by the collective life that the course engendered. Mansbridge described the range of social formations that emerged in parallel to the tutorials: gatherings of students' families and friends, preparatory seminars to get potential future students up to speed while they waited for a course opening, essay circles, and weekend study groups. And there were many senses in which tutorials might "carry on their work beyond the three years" formally allotted to them.[38] Extension boards and delegacies tracked how many students went on to write for local newspapers or take further courses; they recorded how many tutorials kept their original composition and moved on as a group to a new subject.[39] In some cases, students extended the life of the tutorial by becoming (unpaid) tutors themselves. The members of a tutorial at Longton, Industrial History of England, traveled to surrounding villages to teach the material to new groups of working people; a group of Yorkshire manual workers finished their tutorial and commenced teaching short courses; and tutorial students in North Staffordshire began their own local education program. Though the term "extension education" came from the idea of extending the central research university's mission outward to reach "the people," in practice the idea of the "extension" of knowledge through collective social life came to characterize the work and study of the students themselves.

Turning to Eliot's Modern English Literature syllabuses, we will show how the values of the WEA tutorial transformed his teaching over the course of the class's three years. Eliot's pedagogy—his shift to an emphasis on self-guided research, his willingness to revise readings and assignments to follow his students' interests, and his focus on creating conditions that enabled his students to have a sustained investment in course topics in the second and third years of the course—testify to his absorption of the WEA's tested practices and general ethos. These practices also increasingly informed the vision of literary culture that Eliot developed in his tutorial and in his writing. Drawing on historicist approaches to literature that emphasized the interconnections between writers, Eliot taught his students to recognize the everyday working conditions under which authors wrote; together, the class developed an idea of literature as a collective cultural enterprise rather than a series of great works by great figures. By importing the WEA's values into the scene of literary study, Eliot created the conditions in which his students could recognize themselves in the working writers of the literary past.

Eliot in the Classroom

Like the leaders of the extension movement, Eliot had a vexed relationship to the modern research university. In August 1916, just a month before he began teaching his first two extension courses, Eliot elected not to return to Harvard to take up an assistant professorship. Gail McDonald imagines how difficult this decision must have been for Eliot, given his family's multigenerational devotion to education.[40] But entering the world of British extension education let him reject the American system of formal education and the life scripted for him within it while joining an educational institution of a very different kind. The first in a series of dissenting institutions that Eliot affiliated with over the course of his career, the extension school allowed Eliot to act as a source of culture for schoolteachers, copy clerks, and the occasional grocer while occupying a position at once marginal and central—marginal to the world of the Oxford or Cambridge common room but central to the extension school movement's reimagination of the national system of higher education.

Eliot's syllabuses for his three-year Modern English Literature tutorial let us tell the story of his growing affiliation with the dissenting institution of the WEA. Receptive to the WEA's animating belief that working-class students could make culture rather than merely receive it, Eliot learned to adapt the pace and topics of his tutorials to give his students a guiding role. The syllabuses themselves evidence these ongoing adjustments. While the first year focused on a series of Victorian authors in the style of the accustomed university literature survey class, the headnote to the syllabus explains that the course is "organized by topic rather than by lecture," giving the class flexibility to linger on some authors and skim over others, rather than binding a given author to a particular week.[41] After covering Tennyson, Robert Browning, Thomas Carlyle, John Henry Newman, Charles Dickens, William Makepeace Thackeray, George Eliot, Matthew Arnold, minor novelists (Benjamin Disraeli, Thomas Love Peacock, Charles Reade, and Anthony Trollope), the Brontës, and George Borrow, the tutorial moved on to Ruskin and there remained, giving up the syllabus's final weeks on Edward Fitzgerald and George Meredith to linger with Ruskin, taking time to consider him both as a "stylist" and a "social and moral reformer."[42] It seems likely that the "four evenings" the class spent on Ruskin would have drawn on Eliot's students' work experiences and worldviews; their decision to forgo the planned final weeks on Fitz-gerald and Meredith shows how the students decided together as a class what they valued and thus how they would spend their time.[43]

The second year's syllabus even more clearly reflects the needs and interests of Eliot's students, who asked Eliot if they could "start with Emerson," which they did, in a course that otherwise exclusively covered British literature of the late nineteenth century.[44] After Ralph Waldo Emerson, the class moved to William Morris, Dante Gabriel Rossetti, Algernon Charles Swinburne, Walter Pater, Samuel Butler, and Robert Louis Stevenson and then closed with "The 'Nineties,'" Thomas Hardy, and a con-cluding week comparing "the later part of the nineteenth century with the earlier."[45] As this list suggests, the scope of the second-year syllabus had been reduced: it contains only nine authors or topics, as compared with the fifteen that Eliot proposed for the first year. This syllabus is also more interconnected: Morris, Pater, and Rossetti are all considered in relation to Ruskin, and Swinburne in relation to the preceding figures. Eliot's lec-turer's reports indicate that he was emphasizing connections among these authors to enable students to write more papers. After a first year in which only three students had completed papers, Eliot thought that he might reorganize the course around "subjects" rather than individual authors:

> I do not wish to slight the personal element, but if the course can be arranged on the basis of subjects—instead of passing from one man to another, I think more papers would be written; as the members are deterred by thinking that before they can read a book and write about it, the author will have been dropped.[46]

Eliot also included a list of potential paper topics at the end of the second-year syllabus, including "Emerson and His Circle," "Socialism in Litera-ture," "Art for Art's Sake," "Medieval Influence in Poetry and Prose," "Nat-uralism," "The Celtic Revival," and "The Drama." At the head of this list of paper topics, Eliot promises that these "subjects will be proposed in connection with each lecture" so that students can "plan three or more papers on related subjects."[47]

Over the course of the first two years of Modern English Literature, then, Eliot began to imagine a tutorial in which interconnected subjects replaced authors. His third-year syllabus on Elizabethan literature turned this corner. Structured around the cultural histories, collaborations, and literary forms that reveal the connections among authors, the third-year Modern English Literature syllabus entirely dispenses with the move-ment from "one man to another" in favor of reanimating a literary culture in which Elizabethan dramatists emerge as working writers for the audience of Eliot's working-class students.

This reimagining of the canon of early modern literature as a kind of writers' workshop seems like an inspired bit of teaching, but it was also the practical response to the impasse at which Eliot and his students arrived at the end of their second year together. The first two years' syllabuses had proceeded chronologically through nineteenth-century British literature, and the students seem to have expected that the third year's syllabus would cover contemporary literature. Eliot, however, did "not favour" the study of "living authors."[48] When his students requested a year on Elizabethan literature as their second choice, Eliot happily acceded. What excited him most about the prospect, he explained to his mother, was the opportunity to revalue a literature that had been continuously respected but never effectively judged: "My Southall people want to do Elizabethan Literature next year which would interest me more than what we have done before, and would be of some use to me too, as I want to write some essays on the dramatists, who have never been properly criticised."[49] These essays eventually became part of *The Sacred Wood*.

The Sacred Wood's central exhortation is to rescue works that have been more esteemed than read; instead of approaching them in a "canonical spirit," Eliot urges readers to recover their "living force."[50] Behind *The Sacred Wood*'s revaluation of Elizabethan literature (especially the dramatists) is the work of the third year of Modern English Literature, in which Eliot taught Elizabethan literature not just in place of the requested contemporary literature syllabus, but as a contemporary literature. The picture of the Elizabethans as "living authors" that Eliot invented in response to the desires of his extension school students became the foundation of *The Sacred Wood*'s imagination of Elizabethan literature.

For Eliot, historical facts could reanimate dead literature. When he later looked back on his years of extension teaching in "The Function of Criticism," Eliot remembered the methods he used to help his students criticize early modern drama. In particular, he emphasized how historical information could lead students to the "right liking" of bygone literature. If he presented students "with a selection of the simpler kind of facts about a work—its conditions, its setting, its genesis," Eliot noted, Elizabethan drama could come to seem as immediate as a recently published poem.[51] *The Sacred Wood* likewise emphasizes the role of historical knowledge in evaluation. In his essay "Euripides and Professor Murray," for instance, Eliot describes how recent anthropological scholarship, by making the past "as present to us as the present," allows readers to form fresh critical opinions about long-dead authors: "If Pindar bores us, we admit it; we are not certain that Sappho was *very* much greater than Catullus; we hold various opinions about Vergil; and we think more highly of Petronius than our grandfathers did."[52]

Eliot may have recalled his role in the extension classroom as that of a guide presenting facts to his students, but his letters from the extension years suggest that the biographical and historical information with which he peppered his lectures sometimes put him on unnervingly equal footing with his students. In 1917, while he was teaching Modern English Literature at Southall and lecturing on Victorian literature at Sydenham through the London City Council, Eliot wrote a self-deprecating letter home about his newfound talent for assembling the sorts of "superficial information" about authors that his students already had:

> Lately I have been at a point in my lectures where the material was unfamiliar to me: I have had to get up the Brontës for one course and Stevenson for the other. Of course I have developed a knack of acquiring superficial information at short notice, and they think me a prodigy of information. But some of the old ladies are extraordinarily learned, and know all sorts of things about the private life of worthies, where they went to school, and why their elder brother failed in business, which I have never bothered my head about.[53]

Here, Eliot's students augment his hastily gathered facts with the kind of tidbits one might cull from late Victorian–style literary gossip columns and journalistic lives of authors. Tutor and students volley bits of information—rapidly collected from several sources, cut adrift from a body of ordered knowledge—that are typically circulated among those who have difficulty judging what is worth putting and keeping in one's head. Yet in the tutorial, these "simpler kinds of facts" do not mark the absence of critical judgment. Instead, they become a preparation for it, helping convert authors from revered figures of the English literary tradition into knowable, everyday writers whose lives and times can be discovered in local libraries, or even in the kinds of superannuated periodicals one might find in a coffeehouse or railway waiting room.

Eliot's liberal use in lectures of authorial biography, scenes of writing, composition techniques, and the critical chatter that amounts to literary reputation not only drew on the kinds of knowledge his students already possessed but also reached out to students by moving the focus from the forbiddingly aura-laden work to the more familiar worker. In the third-year syllabus for Modern English Literature, Eliot reconstructed the world in which poets and playwrights wrote, surrounded by their varied source

3

ELIZABETHAN LITERATURE.

[This syllabus is divided by subjects and not by lectures. It is suggested that students should prepare themselves by reading some of the texts indicated. For reference and supplementary reading a bibliography is printed at the end of this syllabus.]

I.—THE EARLIEST FORMS OF DRAMA.

Popular festival and religious rite. The "liturgical" drama. The Guild plays. Difference between "miracle" plays, "moralities," and "interludes." Examination of several examples. Their peculiar charm and their essential dramatic qualities.

READ: *Everyman, Abraham and Isaac*, and the *Second Shepherds Play*.

II.—THE REVIVAL OF LEARNING.

The Renaissance in England, and its effect upon the Drama. John Bale and Heywood. Influence of humanism not always beneficial. Study of Latin literature: Seneca and Plautus. Beginnings of blank verse. Development of set tragedy and comedy. Italian influence.

READ: *Gorboduc* or *Ralph Roister Doister*.

III.—THE ELIZABETHAN STAGE.

Popularity of the Theatre. The theatres of Shakespeare's time: their construction, the audience, its character and its demands, the players and their life. The playwright: his task and his life. The continuous adaptation of old plays to current needs. Why Elizabethan life and thought found its most adequate expression in the theatre.

READ: The first chapters of *G. P. Baker: Development of Shakespeare as a Dramatist*.

TC-145 (2) DI 60 C & S
3/90 10/10/18 (14952)

FIGURE 2.1. The first page of T. S. Eliot's third-year syllabus (1918) for his Modern English Literature course, taught under the auspices of the Joint Committee for the Promotion of the Higher Education of Working People, University of London. Eliot revised his syllabuses in the second and third years of the three-year course in response to his students' interests and requests. Senate House Library, EM 6/6/5, University of London.

materials, collaborators, influences, and daily pressures. Eliot designed the first weeks of the syllabus to conjure up the Elizabethan playwrights' world, starting with popular festivals and religious rites as the earliest forms of drama, followed by a section on the classical tradition and other influences on drama. Another early unit took up the material world of the

Elizabethan stage. In it, Eliot and his students covered stage construction, audience demands, and the playwright's "continuous adaptation of old plays to current needs."[54] Reading George Pierce Baker's *The Development of Shakespeare as a Dramatist* (1907) set the scene for understanding the collaborative working life of Elizabethan dramatists and enabled Eliot's students to see Shakespeare as being of his time.

After these opening weeks on the source material and social life of Elizabethan drama, the class moved on to a set of interconnected weeks on Elizabethan playwrights, taking up several playwrights each week to trace influences, compare different examples of a single genre, and view collaborations. The class read Kyd's *Spanish Tragedy* alongside *Titus Andronicus* and *Hamlet* to compare different examples of the tragedy of blood and to contrast treatments of stock situations. They studied Greene and Peele alongside Marlowe, as playwrights influenced by Marlowe's style. In a week on "The Chronicle Play," the class read *The True Tragedy of Richard, Duke of York* with *Richard III* and *Henry VI* to glimpse the "traces of Marlowe, Peele, Greene, and Shakespeare" in that unattributed play.[55] From a first year dominated by single-author figures to a final year that sought connections among authors in the material contexts of their world, Eliot's syllabuses demonstrate his iterative development of an approach to teaching literary history that demystified great authors to reveal them as working writers.

The critical judgments that anchor *The Sacred Wood* fully emerge in the final weeks of the third-year syllabus. Eliot's descriptions under each heading become lengthier and the language becomes noticeably evaluative: "greatest," "highest point," "beauty," "greatness." These markers of highest praise are awarded not to Shakespeare but to Ben Jonson, George Chapman, Thomas Dekker, Thomas Heywood, Thomas Middleton, Francis Beaumont and John Fletcher, and John Webster. Yet even in this turn from historical contextualism to evaluation, Eliot deemphasizes the final, polished literary work and the singular author. The greatness of these lesser-known writers can be found, for Eliot, in the scene rather than in the complete play; it is fully realized only in the collective literary culture, not in any individual. Despite the fact that "the greatest of Shakespeare's followers is undoubtedly John Webster," Eliot describes Webster's greatness as specific to subgenre: "his skill in dealing with horror; the beauty of his verse." Instead of offering exemplary individuals who are complete models of greatness, these post-Shakespearean playwrights are great as a collective effort toward the perfection of a particular form: "Each of the later dramatists has some unique quality, and in them English blank verse reaches its highest point."[56]

Coming in the final weeks of the three years that Eliot and his tutorial students spent together, this culminating vision of a set of unheralded playwrights whose value becomes apparent only when viewed as a collective takes on shades of the WEA's conviction that the value of tutorials becomes most apparent not in local records of individual papers submitted but in the context of the "common life."[57] This ethos of extension education emerges as an explicitly literary value in *The Sacred Wood*, in which Eliot famously turns from great works to minor authors, whose uneven and collaborative work on existing literary forms enabled subsequent writers to continue the work of making literature.

Southall *in* The Sacred Wood

When Modern English Literature ended in the spring of 1919, Eliot's students gave him a copy of *The Oxford Book of English Verse* inscribed "with the gratitude and appreciation of the students of the Southall Tutorial Literature Class May 1919."[58] Eliot spent the next several months transforming his lecture materials into book reviews, publishing thirteen reviews of criticism and scholarship on early modern literature by the spring of 1920. Six of these reviews would become essays in *The Sacred Wood*, including "A Romantic Aristocrat," "'Rhetoric' and Poetic Drama," "Hamlet and His Problems," "Notes on the Blank Verse of Christopher Marlowe," "Ben Jonson," and "Philip Massinger." In other essays of *The Sacred Wood*, figures from the early modern syllabus—Marlowe, Sir Thomas Elyot, Lyly, Webster, and Middleton—reappear.

Initial reviewers of *The Sacred Wood* were unaware of the extension classroom in which Eliot had most recently read this minor canon of poets and dramatists. To them, the essays' turn from major and beloved authors to more minor ones seemed elitist. They saw in Eliot's manner "the traces of a superior attitude,"[59] "the coolness of the dandy and the air of a man of science,"[60] the censoriousness of "the traditional Plymouth Brother,"[61] and "the detachment of the great surgeon."[62] Eliot, they imagined, was setting an impossibly high critical standard. As one critic put it, "He assumes that art, in the sense of work of 'eternal intensity,' is something rare, exquisite, requiring intelligence for its apprehension, and indeed never understood save by a select minority."[63] And where early reviewers saw Eliot sequestering literature away in a laboratory, an exclusive heaven, or a surgical theater, modern-day critics have figured Eliot's beautiful prison as the classroom. Disciplinary historians like Guillory have suggested that Eliot's new canon gave birth to a specifically academic style of literary reading particularly associated with the classroom—a style of reading that attends exclusively to literary technique and form and forgets that literary texts were written in and about an everyday world.[64]

But understanding Eliot's extension school teaching opens an entirely different reading of *The Sacred Wood*. That volume's characteristic gesture—its rejection of the major authors to which literary culture pays lip service and its appreciation of the subtler virtues of more workaday writers—draws on the WEA's attempts to revise authoritative, disciplinary knowledge by incorporating working-class history and experiences. When Eliot asserts, in those essays, that not all old literature is good literature—when in "The Perfect Critic" he faults Arnold for treating the masters of the past as "canonical literature" or in "Ben Jonson" describes Jonson as more admired than read—he refers almost directly to his own refusal to offer his busy students a mere "smattering" of culture with a reading list composed of long-admired major authors.[65] Likewise, *The Sacred Wood*'s appreciation of how historicism prepares past works for fresh judgment expresses lessons Eliot learned during the three-year transformation of his syllabuses from an inert set of representative writers to an Elizabethan world of "living authors." "We need an eye," Eliot writes in *The Sacred Wood*, "which can see the past in its place with its definite differences from the present, and yet so lively that it shall be as present to us as the present."[66]

The minor canon of *The Sacred Wood*, like the literary world Eliot conjured in his classroom, relies on a communal vision of a literary past and future. This world is peopled not by great authors, but by scholars, editors, readers, critics, and translators of variable abilities. The works that Eliot commends in *The Sacred Wood* are those written with no eye to posterity but rather for the immediate use of other writers in the tradition. The greatness of these works derives not from their enduring, transhistorical formal properties but from their connectivity. They represent an incremental improvement of literary forms borrowed from previous authors; the uneven quality of their work invites future writers to take up the pen to improve on them. In this way, Philip Massinger "prepared the way for Dryden," while in Dryden resides the last "living criticism" of Jonson.[67] This principle of valuing works that allow for literary culture's continuation—a principle that informs, for example, Eliot's favoring of Dryden, through whom many lines flow, over "the Chinese Wall of Milton," after which blank verse suffers "retrogression"[68]—mirrors the WEA's rejection of individualized accreditation and its valuation of tutorials for the cultural formations they engendered.

The WEA's "highway" of education thus guided Eliot's creation of a genealogy of minor poets who constitute the literary tradition. Eliot also borrowed from his tutorial a way of valuing the works of these minor figures. The seminar's circulation of the "simpler kind of facts about a work" from teacher to student as well as from student to teacher resurfaces in *The Sacred Wood*'s treatment of information as necessary to literature's flourishing.[69] Indeed, Eliot's rejection of the Romantics in *The Sacred Wood* stems from this principle. According to him, the Romantics "did not know enough"; their literary production "proceeded without having its proper data, without sufficient material to work with."[70] Depending on the supremacy of individual genius, they worked without the aid of "second-order minds"—that is, without the help of those critics who were numerous and unburdened enough to "digest the heavy food of historical and scientific knowledge" through which the literary past becomes present and usable.[71] *The Sacred Wood* is full of admiration for the paratextual apparatus of mediocre critics: the appendixes to George Cruikshank's essay on Massinger "are as valuable as the essay itself," Charles Whibley's introduction to Thomas Urquhart's *Rabelais* "contains all the irrelevant information about that writer which is what is wanted to stimulate a taste for him," and Professor Murray may be an awful translator of classical poetry but is thanked for bringing us "closer" to the classics through the medium of historical scholarship.[72] Just as the Modern English Literature tutorial saw Eliot drawing on the kinds of information circulated by editors, scholars, and biographers and welcoming his students' fluency in bits of fact as preparatory to taste formation, so does *The Sacred Wood* recognize the value of the preparatory, informational work of criticism.

And just as Eliot's tutorial used bits of information to open up a vision of past authors as working writers, *The Sacred Wood* draws on historical and biographical information to call up the sociality of writing practices. Eliot describes Marlowe "with the Aeneid in front of him" writing *Dido* "to order" and imagines Jonson composing *The Masques of Blackness* in tandem with Inigo Jones designing its scenery.[73] In his essay on Massinger, Eliot argues, "To understand Elizabethan drama it is necessary to study a dozen playwrights at once, to dissect with all care the complex growth, to ponder collaboration to the utmost line."[74] Using textual collation techniques to track revision practices, Eliot debunks myths of literary genius and the spontaneous creation of formally perfect works by revealing the incremental labor that goes into the creation of a poem or play. Examining examples of Marlowe's self-revision and his borrowing from Edmund Spenser, Eliot explains that, "somewhat contrary to usual opinion," Marlowe was not a genius but "a deliberate and conscious workman."[75] Indeed, when Eliot does esteem a Romantic—as in the case of William Blake—it is because textual scholars had dispelled Blake's self-mythologizing to reveal the conscious work of revision evident in his drafts: though "Blake believed much of his writing to be automatic," his manuscripts express that a "meticulous care in composition is everywhere apparent in the poems preserved in rough draft . . . alteration on alteration, rearrangement after rearrangement, deletions, additions, and inversions."[76] This insistent emphasis threaded throughout *The Sacred Wood*, not just on writers as careful and meticulous craftspeople but on the everyday, laborious work of writing "to order" as "workmen" in groups, has its origins in Eliot's ad hoc attempt to enable the incremental work of his own students through reanimating the working practices and conditions of Elizabethan writers for them. Tracing this pedagogy into *The Sacred Wood* reveals how the momentary work of the classroom grows into a theory of literature.

In *The Sacred Wood*, of course, as in the Modern English Literature classroom, the gathering of information that reanimates the working lives of writers is not its own end; it is the preparation for critical judgment. Yet in neither book nor tutorial is critical judgment atemporal, objective, or fixed. The social life of the WEA seminar served for Eliot as an education in taste and the materiality and temporality of aesthetic judgment. In *The Sacred Wood*, these lessons reappear in Eliot's sense that certain books, such as Arthur Symons's *The Symbolist Movement in Literature*, are valuable in different ways at different moments of a life span, and how additional life experience can reorient one's relationship to a major text. In the introduction to *The Sacred Wood*, Eliot explains that though "the faults and foibles of Matthew Arnold are no less evident to me now than twelve years ago, after my first admiration for him; but I hope that now, on rereading some of his prose with more care, I can better appreciate his position."[77] Throughout *The Sacred Wood* remain traces of his early classroom's sense that the arc of one's life and one's momentary and changing circumstances necessarily and meaningfully shape valid critical judgments.

But above all, the Modern English Literature tutorial is present in *The Sacred Wood*'s conviction that people make literary value. Eliot's call to transform canonical texts into the "living force" of literature is for him a necessarily social endeavor. Like the classroom in which this transformation began, Eliot's essays do not transmit a singular set of literary values. Instead, they maintain a varied world in which thousands of small exchanges between writers and readers, editors and teachers and students, climb inside poems and plays; only later do these social exchanges come to seem to emanate from literary works themselves. In Eliot's extension school classroom, we find the lived origins of what calcified into our received idea of the Eliotic canon. But by expanding our understanding of where literary study has actually happened to include classrooms like

Eliot's, we can see how canons are made rather than merely received. Now, in a moment in which literary study threatens to become the exclusive property of elite and private universities alone, we must build and preserve accounts of how classrooms at institutions of all kinds have discovered our core methods and made our critical classics. This is true not only of *The Sacred Wood*, but also of I. A. Richards's *Practical Criticism*—one of the subjects of our next chapter.

I. A. Richards, Practical Criticism (1925), and Edith Rickert, Scientific Analysis of Style (1926)

To my collaborators, whether their work appears in these pages or not.
—dedication to *Practical Criticism*

This book has not been written; it has grown.
—*New Methods for Literary Study*

The Experimental 1920s

In 1925 I. A. Richards began running a Cambridge English course in which he conducted a collective experiment in the reading of poetry. Week by week, Richards would distribute sheets of three or four poems without authorial attribution to his students. He asked the students to spend a week evaluating each poem in about one hundred words, and then collected these "protocols." Richards discovered that not only did his students differ widely in their evaluations of each poem—quite often ranking sentimental howlers more highly than sonnets by Donne—they, in nearly all cases, misunderstood the "plain sense" of each poem.[1] In 1929 he published the results of this experiment as *Practical Criticism: A Study in Literary Judgment*. The volume documented his students' protocols, classified their most common reading errors, and set forth a method for teaching English students how to identify the "Four Types of Meaning" to be found in a poem. Richards intended for this "new kind of documentation" to improve "educational methods . . . for developing discrimination" among students of literature.[2]

Historians of the discipline remember the methodical and exacting *Practical Criticism* as a bomb thrown into a settled and genteel literary academy that admired, rather than analyzed, literature. There was an "element of brutality" to Richards's experiment, Raymond Williams argues:

he drew back the curtain of literary instruction to reveal that for all their "assured taste and competence," his students had not learned the very simple skill of how to read a poem.[3] Richards's documentation of what Paul Fry calls his Cambridge students' "appallingly incompetent" protocols pointed to a likely epidemic: "If gold could rust to this degree, then what could be expected of more abundant baser metals?" Cleanth Brooks wondered after reading Richards's 1929 volume.[4] Almost universally, historians of the discipline argue that Richards's Practical Criticism experiments brought rigor to the literary lecture: where other lecturers invoked authorial reputations and static hierarchies of literary greatness, Richards studied and taught the foundations of literary judgment—how to read a poem and judge its merits. Richardsian "close reading was rigorous reading, the opposite of loose or distant or offhand appreciation or criticism," writes Michael Wood.[5] Again and again, Richards is invoked as the figure who transformed English from a dilettantish profession into a discipline, lighting the way to a more modern, focused, and democratic future for literary pedagogy.[6] His project seemed imbued with the authority of the scientific disciplines from which he borrowed the format of his monograph, which included sections on "The Condition of the Experiment," "Documentation," "Analysis," and "Summary and Recommendations." As Joseph North argues, Richards placed English "on something like the scientific footing required in order to qualify it as a discipline within the modern research university."[7]

Yet though literary historians credit Richards with the nearly single-handed reform of English literary study, *Practical Criticism* recorded the results of just one of the many pedagogical experiments being run and described in print during these decades.[8] Even a cursory glance at the thicket of education journals, university reports, new curricular plans, and K–12 manuals of the 1920s shows that humanistic educators, in the United States especially, were turning their classrooms into experimental laboratories and their discipline-based curricula into integrated projects. Titles like *An Experiment in Project Curricula; An Experiment in Teaching; An Evaluation on Extensive and Intensive Teaching of Literature: A Year's Experiment in the Eleventh Grade*; and *An Experiment in History Teaching with Colored Charts* abound in these years. It has become traditional in literary studies to think of Richards as borrowing from other disciplines— behaviorism, neuroscience, linguistics, semantics[9]—yet his rhetoric and methods of experiment would fit easily in the table of contents for nearly any 1920s-era issue of the *English Journal* for grammar, high school, and college English teachers. Allen Tate, in his 1929 review of *Practical Criticism*, recognized Richards as part of this new breed of "laboratory" reformers: "Mr. Richards has succumbed to the prevailing belief that you get education when you get ingenious education methods."[10]

This burst of articles written by and for English teachers often promised, like *Practical Criticism*, to overturn staid methods of literary pedagogy. These innovators wished to replace lectures with seminars, the "recitation method" with the "laboratory method," broad surveys with intensive reading, and narrowly disciplinary aims with a wider interdisciplinary scope. They shared these plans in articles with titles like "Teaching Books Instead of Authors."[11] Frank Aydelotte's 1912 *English as Training in Thought*, for instance, records a multiyear Indiana University experiment in replacing the popular introductory "rapid survey of English literary history from Alfred or Chaucer to Tennyson" with a "literary study of literature" that would give students "some notion of literature as a record of thought" in order to avoid "standardization."[12] O. J. Campbell describes reforms to the Introductory Course in Literature at Michigan to replace an historical survey with a study of fewer texts: "We do not cultivate glibness about authors of whom they know nothing but words of critical praise or blame"; instead, the course helps students "learn to exercise their judgement."[13] Like Richards, these other reform-minded scholars of the 1920s believed that their classroom-based experiments with newly intensive forms of reading could open the gates of literary appreciation to students without prior training or literary backgrounds.

Richards's Practical Criticism courses at Cambridge take on an entirely new cast when we see them as one of many such educational experiments and English curriculum reforms in that decade. Richards's work comes to seem like a copy rather than the original, a part of the mainstream of experimentation rather than a bold strike against a hidebound literary establishment. He becomes part of the larger movement within English departments to convert the traditional introductory historical survey into a reading-focused seminar. Once we look at other experimental English classrooms from this time, Richards seems far from the most innovative experimenter; he is neither the most dedicated collector of systematic data about student reading and interpretation, nor the most visionary theoretician of literary pedagogy.

That title might go instead to someone like Edith Rickert, professor in the English Department at the University of Chicago. Rickert's *New Methods for the Study of Literature*, published two years before *Practical Criticism* appeared, records the reading experiments conducted with her graduate students in English 376: Scientific Analysis of Style during the mid-1920s.[14] In English 376, Rickert invited her students to devise a series of methods for comparing and visualizing literary texts by focusing on very particular aspects of their form—imagery, sentence lengths, word choices, rhythms, connective phrases, and so on. As she explained in *New Methods*, these experiments drew upon "the methods of code analysis used in the Code and Cipher Section of the Military Intelligence in Washington" she had learned while working there during World War I before John Manly invited her to teach courses at the University of Chicago in 1923.[15] Rickert recognized the project as pedagogically experimental; she thought that "the educational value of the work lies largely in the fact that students become keenly interested in it and are constantly devising and suggesting new and better methods." The footnotes in *New Methods* memorialize this classroom collaboration by diligently recording the names and "suggestions of the students."[16]

Students from Rickert's graduate classes went on to devise their own experiment in collective reading, published as *A New Approach to Poetry* in 1929 with final author credits given to Elsa Chapin and Russell Thomas. *A New Approach*, the students write, "has grown from a careful application in classroom practice lasting through two years, of the principles of Professor Edith Rickert's book, *New Methods for the Study of Literature*." For the project, the students ran their own undergraduate class at the University of Chicago with "thirty young men and women" in the "Autumn Quarter of 1928." This class collaborated with schoolteachers from Minneapolis, Chicago, San Antonio, Provo City, Seattle, and elsewhere to test the reading methods upon grammar school students. As the authors write in the book's introduction, "Anyone who has tried out adaptations of Professor Rickert's methods for the analysis of style knows the amusing avidity with which boys and girls set to work with colored crayons and schemes of charts, definitely to prove the existence in a poem of the patterns of the rhyme, use of color imagery, proportion of characteristic sound-qualities, or some other exquisite device which has caught their attention and which they wish to explore more intimately."[17]

The similarities between the Rickertian and the Richardsian experiments in reading are quite striking. *New Approach*, for example, experimented with giving students poems without any indication of authorship. The students were asked to discuss them in the light of their knowledge of poetical elements—that is, of the imagery, rhythm, and sound patterns— with no comment from the instructor."[18] Like *Practical Criticism*, *New Approach* reproduces students' comments, identifying them by protocol number within the text and by name in footnotes. Just as Richards had discovered with dismay that his Cambridge students almost universally preferred bad poems to "Landor, Hopkins, Belloc, De Quincey, and Jeremy Taylor at their very best!," Chapin and Thomas describe the results of a classroom experiment that found students preferred a bad poem ("The Optimist" by Grenville Kleiser) to a good one (W. E. Henley's "Invictus").[19] And the poems in Chapin and Thomas's *New Approach* as well as in Rickert's *New Methods* included many that Richards himself taught in these same years. For all of these teachers, contemporary poetry—by writers H.D., John Gould Fletcher, Walter de la Mare, Robert Graves, and Thomas Hardy—was especially well-suited to pedagogical experimentation because its detachment from longer literary histories and traditions rendered its formal aspects more immediately perceptible.

The first moment that we see Richards alongside Rickert and her students thus gives us an uncanny shock: Rickert seems like a lost (and female) version of Richards. But within the broader context of the pedagogically innovative 1920s, we can see their classrooms as part of the ferment of experimentation and change that was bubbling up in elementary schools, high schools, and college. Like their peers, Richards and Rickert were seeking not just to mold their students into a certain kind of reader or subject, but to transform their classrooms into research laboratories. We have lost sight of this in the case of Richards especially. *Practical Criticism* has long been misread as a book that seeks to objectively reveal student weakness, offering instructors "a foolproof test of the student's unaided perception."[20] But as a return to Richards's classrooms will reveal, Richards intended *Practical Criticism* as a documentation of an iterative experiment in collective reading, one that he continued to restage and write about in the decades that followed its publication.

By returning to the classrooms that invented these new methods of literary reading, this chapter uncovers the history of how formalist reading practices began as attempts to harness and theorize the power of groups—seminars, lecture halls, reading clubs—to elevate the discernment of individuals. Though we can and should think of them as literary formalists, both Richards and Rickert turned away from the literary text conceived as an organic whole or an aesthetic experience: Richards, by focusing his lectures upon the degrees and varieties of misreading, and Rickert, by breaking texts down into quantifiable qualities and classifiable characteristics. They demanded from students not carefully crafted interpretations of literary texts, but their cooperation in the process of gathering and organizing bits of data about readers and texts. They both envisioned a future in which their experiments multiplied across classrooms of all grades, involving more and more readers in the production of data about the interpretation of literature. Both teachers believed that these experimental methods would, in Rickert's words, "awaken the senses and sharpen the perceptions of the mere reader," not through the teaching of individualized discernment, but through the engagement of students in what Richards called "co-operative inquiry."[21]

Practical Criticism *vs. Practical Criticism*

Of all the canonical works of literary criticism and scholarship we discuss in this book, Richards's *Practical Criticism: A Study in Literary Judgment* enjoys the closest connection to classroom teaching. The book offered itself as "documentation" of the "experiment" that Richards conducted in the two Practical Criticism courses that Richards taught at Cambridge in 1925 and in 1927. Richards's students' protocols from each course are reproduced as part of the book, and though Richards does not name his students, his commentary on their protocols reflects his familiarity with them—their generational tastes, the other courses they take, their leisure reading. *Practical Criticism* is also imagined to shape the practices of countless future classrooms. Richards is credited with planting the idea that the most important and effective skill that literature professors can teach is how to read a poem, and *Practical Criticism* is almost universally cited as the foundational text for the major twentieth-century pedagogical tradition of "close reading."[22]

Perhaps because Richards's published volume is so explicit about its connection to the classroom, few scholars have consulted the bound and unlined notebooks in which Richards recorded his notes and lectures for his many iterations of the Practical Criticism courses. Instead, they take the book as a stand-in for the courses.[23] Yet the notes and sketches and lecture drafts that Richards left behind afford an entirely different understanding of his classroom. Most crucially, as we will describe, the notebooks show how Richards enlisted his students as collaborators rather than research subjects. Readers of *Practical Criticism* have seen Richards's experiment as objective and controlled, but the notebooks show that the Practical Criticism courses were deliberately uncontrolled experiments: Richards described his hypotheses to his students in advance, including his expectations that their individual readings of each poem would differ. He enlisted their help and relied upon their good-faith willingness to compose and submit their protocols as anonymous and aggregated data rather than polished, individually authored work. Week by week of each course, he solicited the help of the class in developing an analysis of where the protocols had gone wrong. And he began each new iteration of the experiment by summarizing the results of the last. In the lecture hall, it was clear that Richards reran the experiments not to verify initial findings but to build upon them with the help of each new group of students and voluntary participants.

Richards's sprawling experimental pedagogy project, Practical Criticism, lasted from 1924 until at least 1957. Richards first began setting the reading experiments he used in these courses for the Davison Prize competition in the Cambridge English Department in 1924. He offered his first Practical Criticism class as an eight-week course that began on October 20, 1925. He ran the course again in the Michaelmas term of 1927, reusing and revising some of his lecture notes from the 1925 course while adding new poems. In December 1927, when the second course had finished, Richards drafted the introduction to *Practical Criticism* and spent the following spring and summer of 1928 writing the remainder of the book. When Richards published *Practical Criticism* in the beginning of 1929, he intended it to stand as an interim report upon those first two experimental courses. Indeed, he was already teaching a third iteration of the course, this time a sixteen-week version, in 1928–29 as the book went to press. And Richards continued to run his Practical Criticism experiments for years after the publication of *Practical Criticism*. In addition to the 1928–29 iteration, he ran the course at Harvard and Radcliffe in 1931, and again at Bryn Mawr the following year. His 1933 article "15 Lines from Landor" reports on these later experiments. Returning to Cambridge, he ran a prose version of the course in 1935, Practical Criticism, Prose. The results of this experiment he analyzed in *Interpretation in Teaching* (1938). As late as 1957, Richards was reporting on the results of classroom-based experiments in reading for a public television program titled *The Sense of Poetry*. Richards's teaching notebooks, then, help us to uncover the ongoing pedagogical experiment of which the book *Practical Criticism* recorded one part.

Richards has become known as the earliest champion of close reading, yet he rarely practiced it in the classroom. His main pedagogical commitment was not to textual exegesis, but to the idea that classrooms were sites of ever-changing, ever-refining experimentation: "The field for . . . experimentation is, of course, the classroom, which has not yet, in spite of Plato, received due recognition as the philosophic laboratory," he wrote in *Speculative Instruments*.[24] For him, it was these classroom experiments in reading—rather than any exegetical program or routine—that would remediate students' errors of interpretation and judgment. Though readers of *Practical Criticism* have tended to focus on Richards's theory of poetic meaning (the "Four Kinds of Meaning"), the book ends with an often-overlooked section titled "Summary and Recommendations," in which Richards calls for classroom teachers everywhere, including in grammar schools, to host their own experiments in collective reading. Recovering Richards's actual teaching practices confirms that, for him, only the collective attention to and analysis of readerly error could help individual readers improve.

Yet while the Practical Criticism notebooks help establish the difference between Richards's pedagogic experiments and the close-reading pedagogies inspired by *Practical Criticism*, the notebooks also show how Richards's lectures in the first two courses provided the basis for the book itself. In the first Practical Criticism course, given in the fall and winter of 1925, Richards distributed two sets of unattributed poems. The first contained Philip James Bailey's "Festus," Christina Rossetti's "Spring Quiet," Donne's "Holy Sonnet VII," "Easter" by Reverend Geoffrey Studdert Kennedy ("Woodbine Willie"), and a passage from Byron's *The Island*. The second set, distributed two weeks later, contained an Edna St. Vincent Millay sonnet, Gerard Manley Hopkins's "Spring and Fall, to a Young Child," J. D. C. Pellew's "The Temple," and D. H. Lawrence's "Piano." Richards's lecture drafts show that he spoke in the first week on "The Conditions of the Experiment" and in the second week on his account of the psychology of reading from *Principles of Literary Criticism*. In the third week, he discussed his students' responses to Bailey's "Festus" and Rossetti's "Spring Quiet"; in the fourth week, he covered their responses to Donne's "Holy Sonnet VII." In the fifth week, he discussed their responses to Kennedy's "Easter"; their responses to the Millay sonnet and Pellew's "The Temple" in week 6; the Hopkins protocols in week 7, and the Lawrence protocols in week 8. Richards skips Byron entirely ("No Byron" began the notes for lecture 6) and leaves that poem out of *Practical Criticism*, but the others all appear, comprising eight of the volume's thirteen poems and protocols. Richards ran the Practical Criticism course again in the Michaelmas term of 1927. He reused and revised his lecture notes from the 1925 course, particularly his notes on the first two lectures. But this time, he handed out new sets of poems, including Alfred Noyes's "For the 80th Birthday of George Meredith," a poem by G. H. Luce, Thomas Hardy's "George Meredith," a selection from Wilfred Rowland Childe's *Ivory Palaces*, and Henry Wadsworth Longfellow's "In the Churchyard at Cambridge." These Michaelmas-term poems become the final five of *Practical Criticism*'s thirteen-poem series.

Though Richards's lectures were the basis of *Practical Criticism*'s chapters, his lecture notes also show a clear difference between how he conducted his pedagogic experiments in practice and how he later represented them in print. At the podium, Richards was clear that the experiment would fail without student cooperation. Richards opened his first

Practical Criticism course on October 20, 1925, by introducing the class as a collective experiment vulnerable to failure: "This course is an experiment. An attempt to do something which so far as I know has not been tried before. That being so it's very likely to go wrong. Both you + I shall try to do [something] new."[25] Further into the hour, Richards said, jokingly, "If the experiment doesn't come off as it is quite likely it won't, I shall just cancel the course, so you must not be surprised if this happens." When he gave the course again in 1927, Richards began, "This course is an experiment—An experiment that requires a peculiar kind of cooperation from you. On a former occasion the results were very remarkably interesting. But it is by no means certain that it will always come off. Whether it comes off or falls flat depends as much upon you as upon me."[26]

In order to make sure that the experiment would not fail, Richards carefully instructed his students how to approach their reading. In *Practical Criticism*, Richards glibly explains that he instructed his students merely to "comment freely" upon the authorless poems he distributed; he emphasizes that he took care "to refrain from influencing" the students' responses in any way.[27] In the lecture notebooks, Richards gave much clearer instructions. Richards explicitly encouraged his students to view their responses to these poems as bits of anonymous and aggregated data, quite different from the typical submission of student work in English courses. Thus, in the first lecture, Richards implored the class not to overthink matters, not to take too much time, and not to write too much: "What I'm going to do is to hand out a sheet of poems. The authors are not indicated. And you will not know most of them. But it doesn't seriously matter if you do know them. I want you to take the sheets away and spend a certain amount of time—it needn't be very long— . . . reading them and writing short comments upon them." Richards emphasized that he was not seeking a fully formed reading of each poem; instead, he invited students to "serve up your view in the form of notes, as rough as you like. . . . Refrain as hard as you can from writing more literature about the literature which I put before you." He requested that they try only to say "definite things . . . try mainly to put down the kernel, the core, the essential motive of your opinion, if you can get at it."[28] Richards's instructions encourage his students to try to locate their most baseline, unreflective responses to poetry and then to tie those responses to evidence if possible. Several years later, in *Interpretation in Teaching*, Richards was even clearer about the provisional nature of the protocols: "These scraps of scribble are not more than faint and imperfect indications—distant and distorted rumors—of the fleeting processes of interpretation we are trying to study. They are never to be read by the letter (another of the

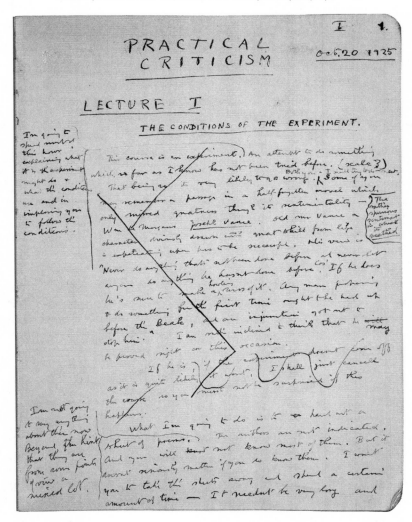

FIGURE 3.1. I. A. Richards's lecture notes for the first day of his first Practical Criticism course at Cambridge University, October 20, 1925. Notebook 21, I. A. Richards Collection, Pepys Library. By permission of the Master and Fellows of Magdalene College, University of Cambridge.

tired pedagogue's besetting sins); they do not tell their own story; they are mere clues for us to place and interpret in our turn."[29]

Richards's opening instructions also framed the student protocols as demographic data. In order to ensure that each protocol represented a single reader's response, Richards asked his students to avoid discussing their protocols with each other. In the 1927 course, he warned: "The temptation to collect a few opinions from other people before making up one's own mind is what this experiment is most likely to be wrecked upon." "It would spoil the whole thing," he explained, "if instead of a number of independent personal opinions we got only the findings of a number of overlapping committees. I beseech and adjure you: do not form little committees."[30] In order to alleviate student anxiety about sharing their untested opinions, Richards explained that he would assign each student a number and use these to identify the protocols in lecture. He also encouraged them to enlist other participants from outside the course if possible: "If you find any other people interested enough to write out their views by all means enlist them . . . let me have them numbering them 17A for example"[31]—to indicate their position as student 17's recruit. Finally, in 1925 Richards also asked his students to record a number of other demographic variables: whether they'd had a classics education; how many times they'd read through each poem; and whether, under normal circumstances, they would have given each poem more than a single reading. A few years later, he added a question about gender. Survey questions like these further encouraged students to consider their written protocols as submissions of data to be aggregated and valued as much for its failures as its successes.

In the lecture hall, Richards indicated that he expected—and even hoped for less-than-perfect readings from his students. In the third iteration of the course in 1928–29, Richards joked, "Don't take too much trouble over them—if you do we may miss some possibilities of amusement. And may I ask anyone who is tempted to pull my leg to refrain?"[32] Richards reassured his students not to worry if they had not much to say about a poem on first perusal. "Personally I will freely confess that whenever anyone puts a poem in my hands and expects me to say what I think of it what I say has nothing to do with the poem." "Very few people," he continued, "even with the best will in the world can judge poetry in one attack. For both the reproduction of the poem and the judging of it are complicated delicate and difficult matters which no one can do freely at all hours of the day and night. And there is a great deal of Humbug in pretending as we all do to be able to do so."[33] Reassuring his students that their responses would not be judged lacking in relation to some preexisting critical ideal, Richards suggested that their protocols might help him to unearth what he hypothesized was an enormous variation in readers' responses: "As the experiment will make very plain, probably no two people in this room will get the same experience while reading."[34]

By confessing his own difficulties in mustering an immediate response to poems—"Very few people can form an honest judgment on anything without hard work and in less than a week," he assured them—Richards framed his students' protocols as exercises in frankness: a collective liberation from the oppressive social performances of literary judgment. Richards suggested that it is "rather a relief to say all this especially in a place like Cambridge, which is crowded out with highwaymen of all grades always ready to put a pistol to one's head and say 'Now! tell me at once what you think about that Pirandello or your critical reputation isn't worth 5 minutes purchase.'"[35] In opposition to this sort of shibboleth taste testing, Richards presented his classroom as an island of sanity and sincerity, in which he and his students alike could give up this "sham" performance of literary judgment and begin to dispel the false illusion, created by "social chatter about literature and the arts," that "we do agree about them more than we do."[36] The experiment, it seems, was never about revealing that students should be able to read but can't; rather it was presented as a collective venture in liberatory disillusionment—a group refusal to engage in the meaningless talk that typically papers over individual uncertainty and personal response.

Richards's students, then, understood that their protocols were preliminary rather than culminating; they understood, that is, that they were responsible for providing fodder for the course itself. As in seminar discussion, in which everyone must agree to contribute their only partially formed commentary so that discussion may proceed and become more refined over the class period, Richards presented the work of the protocols as precursory. Explaining the give-and-take schedule for the course—in which Richards and his students would trade sets of poems for protocols—he explained that "next week you will bring them back and give them to me so that I can (1) analyze the views you express (2) classify them and then (3) lecture upon them. Lecturing partly [on the poems] but chiefly on your views so you may see the whole thing does demand a peculiar collaboration."[37]

In actual format, the Practical Criticism lectures resembled not a sanitized laboratory but a scaled-up and formalized version of the smaller, discussion-based seminar. Richards was not a masterful interpreter of poems, dazzling scores of students with his fascinating readings of Donne's "Holy Sonnet VII" or Byron's *The Island*. Rather, he primarily lectured on the protocols his students submitted, often beginning the hour by tallying the "results" of the submissions and then continuing on to read the protocols aloud and comment upon them. Opening the sixth lecture on responses to the sonnet by Millay, for example, Richards read the tally of responses:

Out of 62

17 declared themselves baffled as to its sense

14 appear to have fathomed it

7 are doubtful cases

and 26, no less, appear to me to have <u>not</u> understood it <u>without them-</u>
<u>selves knowing that this was the case.</u>

Now [clearly?] this is a very lamentable state of affairs![38]

In lecture, Richards's epithets for readers were affectionate rather than scolding. And these opening tallies seemed designed, at least in part, to show the students that they were all in good company. Before discussing any individual protocol that someone would know was theirs, he always pointed out that his examples were all representative of a larger group of similar responses.

In his lectures on readerly error, Richards emphasized that he made the same kinds of mistakes as his students. He often used the second-person plural to capture a broad community of erring readers. In 1925, lecturing on the protocol responses to the Woodbine Willie poem, Richards introduced the widespread problem of "sentimentality." There are "few words we use more often than sentimentality," Richards began. "I've counted up that in our protocols, [sentimentality] is used no less than 28 times as a term of abuse about W.W. and 5 times in senses which don't imply condemnation."[39] Because "we constantly use words like Sentiment[alit]y without any definite meaning," Richards prepared the class to move further; to try to gather, from the evidence, what exactly is meant by this quasi-aesthetic epithet.[40] Richards often used the second-person plural to present critical difficulties as widely shared; he also, in lecture, drew upon protocols to stage a kind of discussion, to conjure up an interlocutor, or to give voice to valid critical opinions. In the Woodbine Willie lecture, for example, Richards read one student's indignant response to the poem's first-person female speaker who "vow[s] that my life lies dead": "If the girl's life were lying dead she wouldn't write like this. Why she's thoroughly enjoying it!" Presumably pausing for a big laugh, Richards continued in measured tones, "We mustn't push this too far. Shakespeare heroes don't talk like any actual men. But the point is a good one. The peculiar kind of gusto in the words is fatal to the pathetic effect."[41]

Many recall the enormous popularity of Richards's Practical Criticism lectures. In his biography of Richards, John Paul Russo gathers accounts describing how the lectures were "so popular that at times they had to be held in the streets. It was said that this had not happened since the Middle

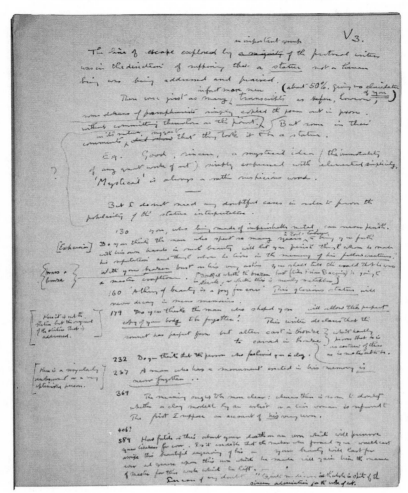

FIGURE 3.2. Notes for Lecture V of I. A. Richards's 1928–29 Practical Criticism course. Richards numbered the student protocols and then lectured upon them, simulating the regular rhythm of seminar discussion, in which student commentary takes center stage. Notebook 7, I. A. Richards Collection, Pepys Library. By permission of the Master and Fellows of Magdalene College, University of Cambridge.

Ages."[42] Others remembered finding seats on windowsills, or seeing Richards climb upon a table to address the overfull hall.[43] Such reports may seem to verify our received sense that Richards was an innovator—Russo suggests that the lectures were popular because he was "analyzing poems in a close, systematic way."[44] But Richards spent more time on the protocols than the poems. The popularity of the course was due to Richards's incorporation of the voices of his students into the lectures themselves. Like a tutor in a small seminar, Richards stepped aside in order to make his students' commentary the center of attention. Presumably more than some other styles of lecturing, the Practical Criticism lectures mimicked the rhythm and content of the small group discussion in which students reflect upon their classmates' interpretations of a primary text in the spirit of collective venture.

In *Practical Criticism*, Richards's interim report on these first two Practical Criticism courses, Richards offers instructions for other educators wishing to repeat his experiments. Richards's final "Summary and Recommendations" section includes two subsections—titled "The Teaching of English" and "Practical Suggestions"—in which Richards imagines the future that his book opens up. In this future, reading experiments may be conducted in all kinds of classrooms—beginning perhaps with "advanced classes in the Universities but it would be rash to say how far from the Elementary School we need in the end stop."[45] Richards implies the possibility that all sorts of different experiments might produce all kinds of results. His goal was not, in other words, the controlled experiment culminating in a verification of his findings, but rather the dissemination of the conditions of the experiment itself, in which more and more students and teachers gather to reckon collectively with the gothic cathedral of misinterpretation.

Laying out his "suggestions towards a remedy" for the problems of misinterpretation that the book illustrates, Richards begins by noting that he "is not aware of any work that has been done" on the model of *Practical Criticism*. "I have not yet heard of any schoolmaster who may have attempted to make a *systematic* discussion of the forms of meaning and the psychology of understanding part of his teaching." Indeed, Richards goes further and states that he has met quite a few schoolmasters who "treat the suggestion with an amused or indignant contempt." He ventriloquizes a harried teacher already overwhelmed by the challenge of instilling a single orthodox meaning into the minds of his students: "'What! Fill the children's heads with a lot of abstractions! It is quite hard enough already to get them to grasp *one* meaning—THE MEANING— let alone four or sixteen, or whatever it is! They couldn't understand a word you were talking about.'"[46]

"But even if any teacher should have wished to experiment in this way," Richards continues, "it is difficult to see where he would have obtained his intellectual instruments from." He points out, "Even the theory of football has been more thoroughly inquired into" than the "theory of interpretation." "One would expect," Richards continues, "that our libraries would be full of works on the theory of interpretation, the diagnosis of linguistic situations, systematic ambiguity and the functions of complex symbols; and that there would be Chairs of Significance or of General Linguistic at all our Universities." But far from libraries filled with works on significance and endowed chairs on linguistic meaning, Richards finds not a single "respectable treatise on the theory of linguistic interpretation in existence," and "no person whose professional occupation it is to inquire into these questions and direct study in the matter."[47]

In the absence of a theoretical school of interpretation, Richards imagines that the path forward lays in the reduplication of reading experiments like his, in classrooms across the country. "Progress in this direction can be made," Richards writes, "through such experiments as the one upon which this book is based." "However incomplete, tentative, or, indeed, speculative we may consider our present views on this subject, they are far enough advanced to justify some experimental applications, if not in the school period than certainly at the Universities."[48] Because there are no theoreticians to guide practice, Richards suggests that teachers might, like him, run their own classroom experiments: gathering evidence, classifying and analyzing, interpreting, and beginning to draw conclusions.

Richards imagines that such widespread classroom experiments in reading would serve another important purpose: by revealing misprisions and misinterpretations to be the norm rather than the exception, individual readers would be forced to give up the illusion that language is easily understood. "We are with difficulty persuaded that we have much to learn about language, or that our understanding of it is defective," Richards writes, and so the "first condition for improvement in the adult's use of language must be to disturb this ludicrous piece of self-deception." It is only in the collective space of the classroom, in which a "systematic publicity is given to these ordinary phenomena of misinterpretation," that individuals can finally be persuaded to identify their own faulty readings. "We are quicker to detect our own errors when they are duplicated by our fellows," Richards writes, "and readier to challenge a pretension when it is worn by another."[49] In other words, for Richards, the key to the success of these classroom-based experiments is that the myriad misinterpretations, false ideas, and basic errors of comprehension are collected and reviewed by the class together. As Richards notes, "Language is primarily a social product, and it is not surprising that the best way to display its action is through the agency of a group."[50]

These final sections suggest that, for Richards, the Practical Criticism classroom experiments served not only to diagnose misinterpretation but to alleviate it. Richards's experiments had thrown light upon individualized problems of aesthetic apprehension and reading comprehension. But fixing these problems would be a matter for the group, not the quiet reader; accordingly, *Practical Criticism* disseminated a pedagogical program rather than a reading method. The final sections of the book offer up a plan for turning collective attention to the obstacle-ridden pathways of interpretation, a classroom-based method for undertaking the necessarily collective process of disillusionment.

Each of the post-1928 iterations of Richards's Practical Criticism course extended and explored Richards's claim that his method of classroom-based experimentation could serve not only to diagnose individual misinterpretations but to correct them. Whereas the first two Practical Criticism courses had focused upon the matter of "literary judgment"—as the book's subtitle reminds us—Richards came to realize that his students' errors of comprehension were amplifying their disagreements over literary value. As he explained to his students in his third course in 1928–29, "if one reader thinks a poem is about a Monarch and another thinks it is about a mountain there is no need to feel astonished if they disagree about its merits." A complete understanding of the poem, Richards had come to see, must precede the evaluation of its worth: "Unless we have really read the poem correctly we are in no position to judge it."[51] In the coming years, Richards began to regard comprehension as the proper focus of his classroom experimentation, and to nudge the matter of literary judgment to the wings; for him, a "correct" interpretation could be achieved as classroom consensus, while he began to regard evaluation—the practice of "criticism" per se—as an increasingly private matter.

In the 1928–29 course that Richards taught as *Practical Criticism* was coming to press, he attempted to separate out this question of comprehension—making out the "plain sense"—from the apprehension of poetic form and the establishment of literary judgment. As he explained to the 1928–29 class:

> Something . . . disconcerting appeared from the comments that were written [in last year's course]. It was this. The reading, the interpretations that were given to the poems (in nearly all cases) were as varied as the opinions. Readers didn't at all agree as to what the poems were about, as to their meaning. . . . What came out, almost overpoweringly, was that readers differ immensely in their power to construe sense—to make out its meaning.[52]

Accordingly, Richards planned to organize the sixteen-week course into three phases. Whereas his instructions for the protocols in previous years had simply asked students for "short comments" about the essence or core of their "opinion" on each poem in all sets, this year he designed different prompts for each set. For the first set—an excerpt from Walter Savage Landor's *Gebir*, the same Millay sonnet he'd used in the past, and Hopkins's "Binsey Poplars"—Richards asked the students to provide a "paraphrase" of each. "Going to ask you to do something that may seem a little tedious this week," Richards explained, "to make paraphrases of the [three] passages of verse I have had printed."[53] Richards explained that the instructions would be different for the next set of poems: "After this paraphrasing experiment, I am going on to various other experiments roughly in the same lines. Issuing sheets of poems with some particular request each time. Each experiment is designed to throw light, if possible, upon some one outstanding difficulty in criticism." In the third week, Richards planned to distribute the second set of poems—Percy Bysshe Shelley's "When the Lamp is Shattered" and Alexander Pope's "Elegy to the Memory of an Unfortunate Lady"—and ask students to address, in their protocols, matters "dealing with the apprehension of Form in Poetry."[54] A third set of poems—Ella Wheeler Wilcox's "Let Them Go" and Walter de la Mare's "The Flower"—would focus on literary judgment by asking students to "say briefly whether you like or dislike these poems and why."[55]

The new, more directive protocol prompts that Richards distributed in the 1928–29 course noticeably changed his students' orientation toward the poems. In previous years, as we've seen, students were encouraged in a vaguer way to submit their responses as subjective data for aggregation. Now, however, in the case of the paraphrase protocols, it began to seem like there would be right and wrong answers. Explaining the protocol prompts on the first day, Richards warned his students that writing the paraphrases might take some time but would be satisfying in the end: "I know they took me very much longer in the experimental paraphrases I made before selecting them. But the trouble is well spent and even has some of the attraction of a game. I have found it more interesting than doing cross-word puzzles or acrostics." As in previous years, Richards warned his students to "avoid consulting friends until you have satisfied yourselves as to the meaning of the passages. It's much more likely that two or three people should between them arrive at an exact interpretation. They cancel out one another's aberrations." "Possibly in this experiment," Richards half-joked, "everybody will return perfectly correct interpretations. If this happens the future of English Studies will indeed be rosy. Though the experiment will be a failure from the point of view of this course. But it will, in any case, be interesting to

Say briefly whether you like or dislike these poems and why:

I

Let the dream go: Are there not other dreams
In vastness of clouds hid from thy sight
That still do crown the heights with golden beams
    And yet shall pierce the mist with arrowy light?
    What matters one lost vision of the night?

Though the hope set, are there not other hopes
    That yet shall rise like new stars in thy sky?
Never any soul in sightless darkness gropes
    Except by some sad failure of the eye.
    Blindness alone sees every hope gone by.

Let the love die. Are there not other loves
    As radiant and as full of sweet unrest
Flying through time like snowy-pinioned doves?
    They yet shall come and nestle in thy breast,
    And thou shalt say of each, " Lo, this is best!"

II

Horizon to horizon, lies outspread
The tenting firmament of day and night;
Wherein are winds at play; and planets shed
Amid the stars their gentle gliding light.

The huge world's sun flames on the snow-capped hills;
Cindrous his heat burns in the sandy plain;
With myriad spume-bows roaring ocean swills
The cold profuse abundance of the rain.

And man—a transient object in this vast,
Sighs o'er a universe transcending thought,
Afflicted by vague bodings of the past,
Driven toward a future, unforeseen, unsought.

Yet, see him, stooping low to naked weed
That meeks its blossom in his anxious eye,
Mark how he grieves, as if his heart did bleed,
And wheels his wondrous features to the sky;
As if, transfigured by so small a grace,
He sought Companion in earth's dwelling-place.

Please retain the same identification numbers as before.
I should be grateful if you would record :
    1. Whether you are in your 1st, 2nd, 3rd, Nth Year.
    2. Whether masculine or feminine.

FIGURE 3.3. One of the poem sheets that I. A. Richards distributed in his 1928–29 Practical Criticism course at Cambridge University. Richards added a new demographic question this year, on gender, for he had found in the first two courses that "the women-writers were of average higher discernment than the men," as he wrote in *Practical Criticism: A Study of Literary Judgment*. Notebook 7, I. A. Richards Collection, Pepys Library. By permission of the Master and Fellows of Magdalene College, University of Cambridge.

see what differences this direct attention to the meaning prior to judgment makes."[56]

Though Richards had planned to move on from the paraphrase exercise to higher-order questions of poetic form and literary judgment, in practice the 1928–29 course spent almost the entirety of its sixteen weeks dealing with this foundational matter of "making out the meaning." Questions of poetic form and literary judgment receded perpetually into the distance. At the end of the first eight weeks, Richards marveled that he had spent the entire Michaelmas term on the act of paraphrase.[57] Listing the ten critical difficulties from *Practical Criticism*, Richards explained that "what I have been trying to do this term has been to deal as fully as time has allowed with <u>Difficulty No. 1 Making out the Meaning</u>." After his standard opening two lectures, covering conditions of the experiment and his theory of the psychology of reading, Richards had devoted the next five to the first set of poems and his students' faulty paraphrases of them, leaving the Pope and Shelley protocols to the wayside: "I've given five lectures out of a total of sixteen to this (instead of one and a half) in part because this proportion 5/16 represents I think the comparative importance of this initial difficulty of criticism."[58] As Richards had explained at the start of the course, "This business of reading [^interpreting][59] poetry is much more difficult than we ordinarily believe. It's really the central, the root difficulty, of criticism. It is very nearly the whole difficulty," and "nobody," not even established critics, "is safe" from the dangers of misinterpretation.[60]

What seemed to be happening, for Richards and his students, was that "Difficulty No. 1," "Making out the Meaning," began to involve other aspects of interpretation that were numbered further down the list. It became harder and harder, as the class continued, for Richards to view higher-order questions of sensuous imagery or rhythm and meter or even historical context as external to the primary problem of making out the "sense" of a poem. This slippage began with the course's third poem, Hopkins's "Binsey Poplars." In the case of Hopkins, Richards explained in lecture 7, readers often experience the poem's "subject" and its "form and vocabulary" as two distinct aspects difficult to "join" together. This seeming split between the poem's content and its form caused readers to dislike the poem: "out of 100 paraphrases" there were "70 against, 30 for" the poem. Richards argues that "more familiarity with Hopkins's peculiar technique might overcome this difficulty. I remember feeling precisely the same obstacle myself when I first attempted to read him. The difficulty has worn off. But this special torturing and twisting of language has another reason and justification."[61] In "Binsey Poplars," for example,

"Hopkins is trying to reflect the movement of the aspens etc (ie part of the sense) in the movement of his verse. The effect is to make those who expect verses to be primarily governed by their sense find an extreme obscurity in Hopkins."[62] As Richards proceeded, it seemed more and more that aspects of poetic form such as Hopkins's rhythmic mimicry of trees in the wind became, for Richards, inseparable parts of a poem's sense. The course both deferred the question of poetic form, but also began to assimilate it, in the case of individual poems, under the heading of "Making out the Meaning." As Richards explained, he was attempting to focus on "the interpretation of the sense of poetry and how through the sense we can aim at the feeling and tone and how feeling and tone confirm and adjust our interpretation of the sense. And so forth" in a Möbius-strip undoing of his own numerical classifications.[63]

At the beginning of the Lent term for the 1928–29 Practical Criticism course, Richards introduced an even more complex example of the kinds of operations necessary to determine a poem's plain sense. He began:

> Last term you will recall considerable attention [to] problems of the inter-
> pretation of poetry. The moral—to summarize the results so far as there
> were any—being: The poem (the whole compound of feeling and thought
> and attitude etc in which as readers of poetry we are interested) is not a
> thing which at all inevitably or necessarily arises in the reader's mind. It
> has to be recreated by the reader. And this recreation is an intricate process
> which easily goes wrong. On the whole it is much more likely that we shall
> misinterpret a poem—or interpret it imperfectly—than that we shall get
> the poem at a first reading.

This applies, Richards explained, "not only to difficult, abstruse, intricate, and highly condensed poetry—it applies equally to simple poetry— unless it happens to be simple poetry written by people very like our- selves, written in our own age, and built out of feelings thoughts and atti- tudes which can be presupposed to be ready prepared in us by the cultural conditions in which we have grown up."[64]

To illustrate his point that simple poetry from other eras can be dif- ficult to construe, Richards turns to the ballad: "Consider, for example, the imaginative transition required if we are really to read, to enter into the body of thought and feeling that should be conveyed by a Ballad. Say, Sir Patrick Spens."[65] The biggest barrier to understanding ballads, Rich- ards explains, is our contemporary expectations about what poetry is and does: "Recall the difficulty so many adults feel in taking such a bal- lad as anything more than a quaint relic of bygone times in these days of cross channel steamers. Or still more in reconstituting that state of group solidarity—the social attitude of poetry—which makes ballads of any sort possible. Nowadays if we listen to poetry in a group we do so in an artificial, not a natural, mood."[66]

Continuing on, Richards argues that the proper reading of ballads can be even further complicated by the fact that many have "been rewritten in part in the 18th Century." In these cases, Richards explains, a reader must reconcile: "(1) The original; (2) The 18th Century overlay (in some ways as difficult if not more difficult to get at than the original); and (3) Our contemporary modern consciousness." Copying the verses of "Sweet William's Ghost," Richards underlines the recognizably eighteenth-century diction and word order in lines like, "No more the ghost to Margret said" and "Evanish'd in a cloud of mist."[67] "Now," Richards explains, "the plain sense" of this ballad about a retreating ghost "offers no difficulties." What's more difficult to recover, however, is the sense in which the ballad, which was never "quite serious ever for the original ballad singer and his audience" gained a new "quality of . . . amusingness" for the eighteenth-century "man who added in" the new lines. "The result is that though the ballad may still be poetry, for the changed readers it has become a different kind of poetry"—violently so, in a case like this, for "jokes more than any other literary products grow stale and flat in the course of time because they depend so much on social conditions, what the audience is used to, and so forth." "The moral of this," Richards wraps up, "is that the reading of poetry—if by that we mean not a mere diversion, a way of passing time in a harmless and dignified fashion—but a serious attempt to produce the outlook and attitudes of other people—is extremely difficult."[68]

To read through Richards's actual lectures for the 1928–29 course is to feel as though one is watching Winnie-the-Pooh and Piglet track the Woozle. As the weeks passed, Richards and his students found themselves always circling back to the question of "making out the plain sense." Setting out each week once more in pursuit of plain sense, they found themselves discussing an astonishing number of complex questions of poetic form and historical context. Moving from meter to imagery to onomatopoeia to semantic change to generic distinctions to the past social contexts for poetry to the whims and tastes of past compilers and editors, the class abandoned the planned progressive march through increasingly higher-order critical difficulties. They pursued instead a perpetual set of matters almost preliminary to basic comprehension. *Practical Criticism* attempted to taxonomize reading operations, to define them and separate them and order them; Practical Criticism was devoted instead to folding these "extremely difficult" operations under the basic and foundational question of figuring out what a poem means. Like the classroom-based experiments that Richards ran year after year, the lectures themselves speak of a commitment to starting, over and over again, at the beginning.

Finally, the fact that Richards lingered so long in 1928–29 with the protocol responses that attempted to paraphrase his first three poems demonstrates how and why Richards's democratic pedagogical vision differed from that of the New Critics who followed him. Where Cleanth Brooks, for example, defined poetry as that which can't be paraphrased, Richards devoted an entire course to the practice (and even planned a never-written book on the topic with C. K. Ogden as a follow-up to *Practical Criticism*).[69] To Brooks's mind, it was "heresy" to paraphrase poetry, for prose summaries would always fail to capture the most important element. Yet though Richards cared as much as Brooks about the singularity of poetic language, he did not teach with poems at the center of his classroom. Instead, he centered students' interpretations of poems. Like Edith Rickert, who, as we will see, spent class after class having her students invent elaborate systems of notation with which to identify and quantify aspects of poetry, Richards also asked students to make, collectively, an equivalent for the poem: a translation of it, a consensus-based interpretation. Both Rickert and Richards held as their goal the creation of an intelligent and discerning individual reader. And both knew that such readers were made not by silent study, but in the laboratory of the classroom, where students' collective attention could create the sharpest possible sense of the text's meaning.

New Methods for the Study of Literature

Before *Practical Criticism*, there was Edith Rickert's *New Methods for the Study of Literature*. Also a record of classroom-based experiments in reading, Rickert's book did not find the same popularity. Published in 1927, the book had a second impression in 1928, but by July 1934 it was declared out of print. Yet the influence of Rickert's class the Scientific Analysis of Style had a longer reach. Her many students went on to write theses based upon the quantitative methods that they learned in her classroom; they experimented with their new methods in high school and college classrooms of their own; and they published books developing related strategies for wider reading audiences. This second generation of experiments and experimenters that Rickert's work created was the same effect that Richards envisioned when he closed *Practical Criticism* with a "Summary and Recommendations" aimed at other teachers.

Though *New Methods* has been all but forgotten, Rickert is still remembered today as a medievalist scholar and as coeditor, with John Manly, of the massive variorum manuscript project *The Text of the Canterbury Tales: Studied on the Basis of All Known Manuscripts* (1940). Like her contemporary Caroline Spurgeon, Rickert trained as an early modernist scholar. After graduating from Vassar in 1891, she taught high school around Chicago for several years before enrolling in graduate school at the University of Chicago.[70] At Chicago, Rickert studied early modern literature and culture, learning the skills of bibliography and paleography in her graduate classes. Her dissertation project was a new edition of the fourteenth-century *Romance of Emaré*. When Rickert's dissertation adviser was out of town during her scheduled defense, John Manly, who had just joined the department in 1898, stepped in to conduct her examination. This was the first meeting of what would become a lifelong collaborative relationship.[71]

After graduating from Chicago, Rickert moved to England, where she made a living writing novels, short stories, and journalism. During those years, she also remained part of the medievalist community. In London she befriended Frederick James Furnivall, philologist and founder of the Chaucer Society.[72] She prepared several translations of medieval texts, including *The Babees' Book*, a book of "medieval manners for the young" based on Furnivall's collection of treatises depicting the domestic life of "Englishmen in former days."[73] Rickert conducted research at the British Library on behalf of American scholars such as Eleanor Prescott Hammond and Manly, and kept up her own scholarship as well, publishing "The Old English Offa Saga" in *Modern Philology* in 1904 and an edition of *The Romance of Emaré* based on her dissertation in 1907.

After Rickert returned to the United States in 1909, she worked in the magazine industry in Boston, New York, and Philadelphia for the next five years. In addition to short stories, Rickert wrote features on college and work life for women's magazines. For *Ladies' Home Journal*, for example, Rickert edited and wrote a four-part series titled "What Can I Do?" on how women could make money while staying home. Another, "What Has the College Done for Girls?," featured the results of Rickert's "Personal Canvass of Hundreds of Graduates of Sixty Colleges" to consider whether and how colleges were failing their female students.[74] One series somewhat prefigured Richards's *Practical Criticism* experiments. Titled "As 100 College Girls Write Letters," the column describes how Rickert wrote to the 1912 graduating class of "our six leading women's colleges, with a view of finding out the kind of letters that our college graduates, after sixteen years of schooling, would write." Rickert graded each of the replies and verified her judgment by having "an English teacher of long experience in a city High School" to mark them "as if they had been sent in as exercises by her own pupils." The majority of the letters, Rickert reports, received grades of C or D, with only three A's in the whole bunch. As in Richards's *Practical Criticism*, Rickert's column includes commentary on excerpts from the letters themselves, and attempts to review "the various flaws in these letters," concluding that "*the girls do not know how to say what they mean.*"[75]

Around 1914, Rickert returned to the University of Chicago and began teaching summer courses as an "assistant" in the English Department, resuming her place among the medieval and Renaissance scholars. In 1918 the Department of State recruited John Manly, who had been a hobbyist cryptographer since childhood, to join the codebreaking effort in Washington, DC. Manly assembled a team to bring with him to Washington, including Charles Beeson, associate professor of Latin; David H. Stevens, a young English instructor; Thomas A. Knott, associate professor of English; Edgar H. Sturtevant, assistant professor of linguistics; and Rickert.[76] Together, this group worked directly under Herbert O. Yardley, commander of the US Army's cryptographic section during World War I. David Kahn recounts how Rickert and Manly together broke the "Waberski" code. The official twelve-step transposition cipher, named for the German double agent found with a 424-letter cryptogram sewn into his sleeve, featured "multiple horizontal shiftings of three- and four-letter plaintext groups ripped apart by a final vertical transcription."[77] Rickert and Manly solved it in a "three-day marathon of cryptanalysis" and immediately boarded a train to San Antonio to testify in the trail against Waberski, the agent who had blown up the "Black Tom" munitions depot in New York Harbor in 1916. On the strength of Manly's testimony, Waberski was sentenced to death. Yardley would later recall this episode as the cryptographic section's greatest wartime achievement.

After the war, Rickert and Manly returned to Chicago, inspired to remake humanities scholarship on the model of their urgent, collaborative wartime codebreaking. Elected president of the Modern Language Association in 1920, Manly gave an inaugural presidential address that called upon English professors to undertake more ambitious collaborative projects. "The general impression produced by a survey of our work is that it has been individual, casual, scrappy, scattering," Manly wrote. This piecemeal approach to scholarship has left humanists unable to "point to large, unified achievements" when requesting funding, instead finding their work "unified only under the subject headings in the valuable Index to the Publications recently issued."[78] Manly also argued that individualist scholarship benefited faculty working at well-endowed institutions but left others out in the cold. His address called for greater coordination to support shared access to library materials and manuscripts, for new language and dialect preservation projects, for the preparation of annotated scholarly editions, and for the creation of field- and topic-specific MLA interest groups. Manly also introduced the idea of more public-oriented programs: "I think provision should be made both in these special groups and in our public meetings for those members of the Association and of the public who are not interested in research but none the less care for literature in a large and intelligent way."[79] Several years later, in 1924, Stanley Greenlaw echoed Manly in his presentation to the Association of American Universities, "Recent Movements for Co-operative Research in the Humanities." Greenlaw argued that humanities researchers needed organizations and funding to coordinate research projects and share materials just as much as scientists did; while the handful of large research universities conducting graduate education already had these facilities, the research capabilities of PhDs taking jobs at other kinds of institutions was hampered by a lack of coordination.[80]

In 1924 Manly and Rickert began their own major collaborative humanities effort, known as the Chaucer project. Their goal was to establish an authoritative text of *The Canterbury Tales* by assembling all known manuscripts and tracking down, through public records, details about Chaucer and his time that would contextualize and order the extant versions. That same year Rickert was named associate professor in the English Department and began teaching courses on Chaucer in the summers and the fall to students who would participate in the research for the project.[81] In the spring terms, Rickert and Manly would travel to England to gather and inspect manuscript copies of the *Canterbury Tales* and look for details about Chaucer's life in public records. The rest of the year they spent in their Chaucer "laboratory" in Wieboldt Hall, where they and their graduate student assistants would analyze manuscripts and gather information about the medieval world, eventually recording "some three million pieces of information on sixty thousand collation cards."[82] The project lasted for the remainder of Rickert's academic career; she was named full professor in 1930 and died in 1938, just two years before the publication of the variorum edition. *The Text of the Canterbury Tales: Studied on the Basis of All Known Manuscripts* lists Manly and Rickert as coeditors, credits Margaret Rickert—Edith's sister and an art historian—for a chapter on illuminations, and names "Mabel Dean, Helen McIntosh, and others" on the title page for their "aid."[83] Rickert's own *Chaucer's World*, a compendium of materials "discovered by her and her assistants in their exhaustive search of the public records in London" for details about Chaucer's life and time, was published posthumously in 1948.[84]

Rickert's *New Methods* pedagogical project shared some of the Chaucer project's incremental and collaborative modes of manuscript description, textual interpretation, and historical and biographical research—not to mention the methods she and Manly had used to break codes during the war. Yet the book also developed out of Rickert's experiences reading, writing, and teaching contemporary literature. Like most of the poems Richards included in *Practical Criticism*, the texts included in *New Methods* were culled from recent publications; their detachment from historical context rendered them ripe for the kind of formal analysis that Rickert believed had been lagging in literary study. In the introduction to *New Methods*, Rickert points to recent advances in the "scientific" study of the "environment" of literature—the investigation of sources and influences, of history and biography, and even of geographical setting. She notes that it has become normal to see college-level students producing original research like "History of the Curtain Raiser" and "The Contemporary Reception of Gray's *Elegy*." And while this work is important, despite its sometimes seemingly minute scale—"every thesis of this type is a block in the foundations of truth"—the study of "literature itself, as distinct from its environment," was not similarly developed. The solution, writes Rickert, "so far as I can see, is to try to find new and practicable methods of analysis by which the qualities of literature can be perceived as well as felt."[85]

Before Rickert began teaching the courses in which she developed the formalist reading practices of *New Methods*, she coauthored several textbooks with Manly that focused on technique in contemporary writing. The first of these, *The Writing of English* (1919), prefigures the experimental pedagogy boom of the coming decade. It begins, "Do you like to write? Probably not." In it, Rickert and Manly encourage instructors to replace that old-fashioned practice of the "daily theme"—that "laborious putting together of ideas, without audience and without purpose, hated alike by student and by instructor"—with their new "methods" for "stimulating the student to take a more active part in the cooperative work of education."[86] In their introduction, Rickert and Manly explain that the book had "grown out of experiment at the University of Chicago with sections of freshmen who, being below the standard for entrance, were required to take additional training before they could be admitted to the regular freshman course in English."[87] They report that over two-thirds of their sample set of one hundred remedial students—"Russians, Poles, Lithuanians, Chinese, Japanese, and young people of many other nationalities"—were writing at or above freshman standards at the end of the course. The book included a section on "technique" with sections on the sentence, the paragraph, narration, description, exposition, argument, and another section with "practice" prompts related to "newspaper work," "the short story," "the one-act play," "letter-writing," "criticism," and "verse." ("Convert the prose below into a sonnet," reads one prompt from the verse section.)[88]

After *The Writing of English*, Rickert and Manly published two modern literature textbooks, *Contemporary British Literature: Bibliographies and Study Outlines* (1921) and *Contemporary American Literature: Bibliographies and Study Outlines* (1922), designed to aid "students and studious readers" in "working out and applying their own standards of criticism." Just as the composition textbook emerged from Rickert's freshman writing courses, these contemporary literature workbooks were likely inspired by Rickert's contemporary literature courses. Noting the lack of student guides to contemporary literature, Rickert and Manly compiled the books "to suggest materials, outlines, and methods of work, which will enable students to form intelligent judgments of individual authors and to discover and appraise for themselves the outstanding literary tendencies."[89] The textbooks listed contemporary authors alphabetically, with biographical headnotes and bibliographies of major works. Certain entries also included "Suggestions for Reading," a "distinctive feature" of the book in which Rickert and Manly make critical observations about the author's style and then prompt readers to attend to certain features or test observations.[90] The entry for Arnold Bennett, for example, includes a prompt that encourages readers to "Note his photographs of people and backgrounds in the *Five Towns*. Observe his use of plan, his method of shutting the point of view, his choice of details. List details which could have been noted only by one long familiar with what he describes." A suggestion for Dorothy Richardson prompts readers to "compare her as to method" with James Joyce, Wyndham Lewis, and May Sinclair.[91]

Rickert and Manly's contemporary literature textbooks offered a method to focus the individual reader and direct their attention to particular formal aspects of an author's style. By 1922 Rickert had become interested in developing more collective methods by which to sharpen readers' discernment. That summer, Rickert's graduate-level English 143a: Contemporary Literature course began to develop the systems of counting and graphing that would become part of *New Methods*. The following summer of 1923, she taught Contemporary Literature again, now as English 219. By 1924 Rickert felt that she had enough material for a book. She sent a proposal to Gordon J. Laing, director at the University of Chicago Press, emphasizing the importance of the book's collaborative quality. As she explained, "Throughout the book I shall make use of the work of students, giving due credit, of course. The book will thus become the result of the cooperative effort of some twenty or thirty people." Rickert said that while she planned to continue the work through her "graduate research course," that she and Manly had discussed the possibility of developing "an undergraduate course having for its definite aim the cultivation of taste," perhaps a "course for sophomores, to follow up what is done for freshman in English 40," which would "at once create a foundation sale for the book here at the University."[92]

Rickert predicted that she would have a complete manuscript by the end of 1924, but as she continued to teach the course, the content of the book continued to develop: "From the beginning, the ideas suggested were caught up by the students and developed; crude methods were improved; new methods were proposed. Very early it appeared that the work would not progress rapidly without a textbook; but the material assembled for such a book would not remain stationary long enough to be printed. Even in the galleys, some chapters were largely rewritten."[93] As Manly notes in his introduction, Rickert's students "have remade the methods not once, but many times."[94] In the summer of 1925, Rickert taught English 276: Contemporary British Literature and English 376: Studies in Contemporary British Literature. The course description for the latter now advertised that the class would pursue "investigations in style and technique." By the summer of 1926, Rickert had her own course name for the New Methods project—English 376: Scientific Analysis of Style. In 1927 *New Methods for the Study of Literature* was finally published.

Rickert's teaching papers have been lost, but by piecing together her comments in *New Methods* on particular students and classes, publication records, and course catalogs, we can reconstruct how that volume was made in her classrooms. For example, Rickert mentions that in the summer 1922 Contemporary Literature course, she and her students first attempted "to work out scientifically some of the phenomena of tone color and rhythm"—techniques that would make their way into chapters 5, "Rhythm," and 6, "Tone Patterns," in *New Methods*. During the following summer of 1923, a new set of Contemporary Literature students devised methods "for the study of imagery, of words, of sentences, and of visual devices." Their readings and visualizations became the basis for chapters 2, "Imagery," 3, "Words," 4, "Thought Patterns," and 7, "Visual Devices," in *New Methods*. The book credits particular students with the discovery, creating, and working out of the new methods. Rickert specifies what phases of an experiment a student might have worked on; for example, in a method requiring the visualization of sound, she gives credit to "Harriet Barker, who thought of the use of the musical scale; Lalla J. Davis, who first worked with classified sounds and the clef; and Helena Callis, who devised a mechanical method of recording. These students, however, are not responsible for the method as developed further." Rickert also credits students with useful suggestions for tools: Vernon Horn, for example, suggests keeping track of images using color-coded index cards. Rickert also includes footnoted "suggestions . . . made after the book went to press" on how to achieve greater accuracy when tallying word length, or how to achieve better graphical representations of word counts.[95]

The methods that Rickert and her students developed worked by zeroing in on very carefully defined textual characteristics and using both "statistical" and "graphical" means to study them.[96] Each chapter of the book considered an aspect of poetic form—imagery, words, sentences, rhythm, tone patterns, visual devices. Suggestive rather than prescriptive, each chapter introduced several possible ways a group of readers might classify and analyze an aspect of form. For example, chapter 2 offers seven different ways one could classify the imagery in a literary work. Readers could tag images based on "sense appeal" to one of the five senses; they could consider whether an image is part of a catalog or series; they could determine which images drew on "ready-made" language and which were fresh inventions. Readers could define images based on their "sources of . . . experience" or study their literalness or figurativeness. Considering the work as a whole, readers could measure the "proportion of imagery to non-imagery" or consider how "choice of imagery" was determined by "author's temperament and experience, theme, or purpose." Each chapter also included exercises for conducting these analyses. To study the proportion of imagery to non-imagery in a text, for example, Rickert recommends the following method:

> To get the proportion of imagery to the entire content, the most economical way is to buy a cheap edition of the work to be studied, so that the pages can be marked. . . . Underline with a continuous line all the words that are combined by a single act of attention to form one image. . . . When the images have been marked for a page, the simplest way to take the proportion is to count the images (disregarding the number of words in each) and the lines on the page or in the poem, and to express the result as a ratio.[97]

Alongside this statistical approach, one might visualize the proportion of images graphically by drawing thick black or dotted lines to represent imagery or non-imagery in each line of a poem. The book gives examples of this graphical approach using Sara Teasdale's "I Shall Not Care" (28 percent imagery) and H.D.'s "Oread" (100 percent imagery). A footnote adds that one might include more information by coding the solid lines by color, "to indicate different sense appeals."[98]

Likewise, the chapter on "tone color" offers methods for noticing repetition, rhyme, alliteration, assonance, and consonance. Examples of repetition draw on James Joyce's *Portrait of the Artist as a Young Man* and Matthew Arnold's "machinery" passage from *Culture and Anarchy*; readers are directed to examine repetition in Victorian prose by choosing passages of "one thousand words each" from works by Arnold, Newman, and Carlyle. Rickert compares intentional alliteration in Meredith's "Love in the Valley" and Ruskin's description of St. Mark's from *The Stones of Venice* with unintentionally occurring alliteration in "a sentence chosen absolutely at random" from "the book that happened to be nearest at hand" (*St Botolph Aldgate: The Story of a City Parish, Compiled from the Record Books and Other Ancient Documents*). She follows with an exercise directing the reader to "in any newspaper mark the alliteration. Decide how much of it is of the obvious type, which is so easily overdone, and how much of it is due to accident. Make experiments in reduction of the obvious and in omission of the accidental cases."[99] The chapter culminates with a set of graphs and charts that compare the tone color of Tennyson's "And murmuring of innumerable bees" with Poe's "The tintinnabulation of the bells." Pointing to the graphical representation of stressed and unstressed syllables, consonant matters, and high vs. low tones, Rickert summarizes the differences this way: "Both use the middle register of sounds almost exclusively. But in T, there is an uninterrupted drone of nasals and liquids, with a 'buzz' at the end, highly suggestive of humming bees; in P, a 'ringing' sound, sharply introduced, is repeated several times, and, after an interval, is repeated again with an echoic effect at the end. The whole is surely as suggestive of bells as Tennyson's line was of bees."[100] Here and throughout the text, Rickert emphasizes that charts and graphs can reveal "differences which do not appear in reading."[101]

Some of the statistical and graphical practices in *New Methods* draw upon older forms of notation in literary studies. For example, the "Imagery" chapter recommends a method whereby students keep a notecard per image to record each of the images' characteristics and classifications.[102] The final product resembles both descriptive bibliography cards and reference cards. Likewise, the chapter "Thought Patterns," on sentence structure, includes exercises that build upon traditional modes of sentence diagramming.[103] The "Words" chapter features several charts inspired by the field of stylometry; for example, a chart made by Rickert's student Ruth M. Norris compares the use of monosyllables in the writing of William Sharp "and his other self," Fiona MacLeod, proving

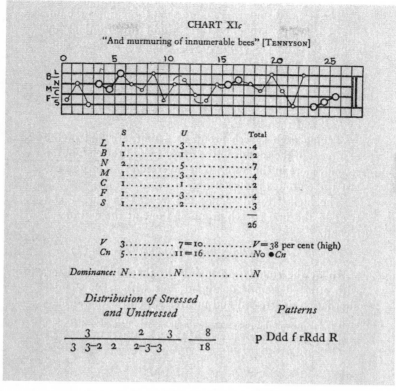

FIGURE 3.4. Chart XIc from Edith Rickert's *New Methods for the Study of Literature*. This chart depicts the sounds (on a clef), proportion of vowels to consonants, proportion of stressed to unstressed syllables, and the consonant patterns of a line from Alfred Lord Tennyson's "The Princess." Copyright © 1927 by The University of Chicago. All rights reserved.

that "notwithstanding Sharp's effort to disguise his style, the resemblance is striking." A chart on the next page, drawn up by Rickert's student Inez Perley, compares the first 1,000 lines of Shakespeare's *Richard II* to the first 1,000 lines of Marlowe's *Edward II*.[104] (At least one reviewer noted that Rickert's methods could be used not only to stimulate "actual enjoyment of [literature] thru the senses" but for "literary detective work." Because, the reviewer goes on, the methods "bring out with extraordinary accuracy those personal qualities of style by which we recognize this or that author . . . any lover of literature may start experimenting for himself and may make actual discoveries of authorship.")[105]

Other methods offered in the book seem drawn, at least in part, from the fields of rhetoric and composition, with their familiar exercises of imi-

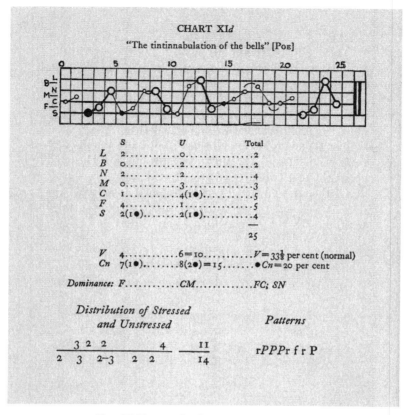

FIGURE 3.5. Chart XId from Rickert's *New Methods for the Study of Literature* depicts the sounds (on a clef), proportion of vowels to consonants, proportion of stressed to unstressed syllables, and the consonant patterns of a line from Edgar Allan Poe's "The Bells." Copyright © 1927 by The University of Chicago. All right reserved.

tation, translation, or substitution. For example, in the "Imagery" chapter, students are invited to consider how imagery is affected by an author's temperament and experience by reading John Masefield's "Cargoes"—a poem about "the contrast between the splendors of ancient civilization and the cheapness of our own." The student should "make a list of the images used in each stanza. Then write after each image others that might have been used and combine them in different ways to see the effect. Change the words describing the ships themselves, as well as those that tell of their cargoes; change the periods of civilization and the countries. Combine your results in different ways (with mental apologies to Mr. Masefield) in either prose or verse. At the end of this experiment you will realize how greatly the author's intention affects the choice of imagery."[106] Likewise, the "Visual Devices" chapter teaches readers to attend to the ways that line breaks, punctuation, spelling, capital letters, and italics "have a marked stylistic effect" by altering these "to get as many different effects as possible from the same words" in Alfred Kreymborg's "Ritardando," E. E. Cummings's "Four Poems," and Carl Sandburg's "Smoke and Steel."[107]

Yet most of the methods Rickert and her students introduced seemed entirely new—a graph paper method for using squares to represent modifiers within a sentence, a pie chart for color imagery in the work of a single poet. Accordingly, their invented terminology was a bit idiosyncratic. "Poise," for example, they adopted as a term for function and position of a sentence within a paragraph; the accompanying diagram of poise in the opening passage of Joyce's *Portrait of the Artist* seems quite inscrutable and unreproducible. But Rickert was untroubled by the provisional nature of her terms. They were "so new," she writes in *New Methods*, that they were "valuable mainly for opening up the way to further study of this kind." Particular classifications may be "proved or disproved by further experiment." The charts and summaries given, Rickert emphasizes, are not entirely idiosyncratic. Rather, they have been made "over and over again" and may form the basis for an interpretation of literary language based on a consensus rendering. (Some chapters even note the number of total students in agreement or disagreement about a classification.)[108] Such consensus could eventually "substitute for the impressionistic, hit-or-miss, every-man-for-himself method of approaching literature."[109] It is the confidence of the groups of people who have made these experiments upon which Rickert relies when she states her confidence in them: "That the method, however altered and improved, will eventually bring results of a new kind in the study of literature is, I believe, the opinion of the group who have been working with it."[110]

Reviews of *New Methods* were so split that the University of Chicago Press used the controversy for a second round of marketing; one press release describes how "the apparent strangeness of Miss Rickert's methods caused a furor in the pedagogic world."[111] Many reviewers worried that Rickert's methods would be taken up by dour and dull schoolteachers with disastrous results. One review by Homer Woodbridge, titled "Literary Suicide," warned that Rickert's methods "will make a strong appeal to that numerous class of teachers of literature who have never had a glimmer as to what it is all about." Woodbridge foresaw the "rebellion of healthy youth against such pedantic foolery" as counting "the PVF sequences in a passage of Ruskin."[112] William Wilbur Hatfield, editor of the

NCTE's *English Journal*, wrote to the Press late in 1926, refusing to print an excerpt from the book in the journal: "As a method of literary study in high schools Miss Rickert's plan would do untold harm and high school teachers are all too ready to accept it." Recalling his own youthful dabbling in analytic methods after reading L. A. Sherman's *Analytics of Literature* (1893), Hatfield conceded that "the harm lies not so much in the study itself as in the fact that teachers will substitute this sort of work for actual dealing with the content of literature, which is far more important."[113] The *English Journal* review of *New Methods* echoed Hatfield's characterization of Rickert's book as the old pedantry dressed up as new methods: "The analytic method in literature once enjoyed a large popularity as many of us who were practiced upon in our school days know to our cost."[114] In the *London Mercury*, J. C. Squire depicted the feminized and mechanized future portended by Rickert's "handling of all these 'items' of literature" via "lines, squares, charts, leads of eight colours, index cards, and the adding machines of Professor Rickert's pupil, Miss von Christ." (Rickert had credited von Christ, in a footnote, for tallying a phonetic chart on an adding machine.) "Professor Rickert's ingenuities might be developed in deadliness," Squire warned, "machines which punch little holes in little cards, signifying by each little hole a special feature, as age, nationality, colour, and a dozen items besides" could come to "eliminate all but one or two girls from [Rickert's] classes, and in a year's time report to the world the precise constituents of the work of all good poets and prose writers."[115]

Other reviewers, however, recognized how Rickert's methods could serve to focus students' attention on the formal aspects of literature. In the *New Republic*, Allen Tate welcomed Rickert's *New Methods*, predicting that "it will tend to lift the teaching of a fine art out of the current muddle of moral exhortation and propaganda" for "it concentrates on literature as art" through an act of translation—"a dislocation of the total aesthetic experience."[116] The *London Times* commended Rickert's "extremely ingenious attempts to find statistical and graphical methods by which the varied manifestations of the different elements of style in literature may be properly understood."[117] Llewellyn Jones, literary editor of the *Chicago Post*, wrote that what "Miss Rickert has given us is a series of Vernier scales for the closer reading of narrative, essay, and poem. They call our attention sharply to subtleties that in ordinary reading we only feel vaguely: thereby increasing the sharpness of our ordinary reading."[118] Only one skeptical reviewer questioned whether Rickert's students were led closer to literature or simply to each other: "Professor Manly praises his colleague's method for the 'delight' it offers its users 'of sharing in the very processes of creative thought.' But from Professor Rickert's text it appears that this is a pleasure they share chiefly with one another."[119]

Such was the furor surrounding the book that Rickert's own students spoke up in defense of the methods. In response to Francis P. Donnelly's review of *New Methods* in the *Saturday Review of Literature*, Rickert's student Martha F. F. von Christ (she of the adding-machine fame), wrote to the paper: "I am one of those unfortunate creatures, one of those personages so utterly lost to any appreciation of the 'ancient rhetoric,' so completely secure from the impact of any emotional delight in literature, as to sign away my soul to the demon of science and take a course or two under Dr. Rickert. Indeed, I may as well confess the full extent of my depravity and say that I heartily enjoyed the courses." Christ described how she applied Rickert's methods to a study of Walter de la Mare's "The Listeners." Conceding that Rickert's methods take a great deal of time— "my study . . . occupied the greater part of one summer and even then, I did not feel that it had exhausted the subject"—she describes how even as "little as I did (I made statistical studies of De la Mare's use of rhyme and accent, his line-length, his stanza, and his use of tone-color), after it was all over, I felt myself able to approach the questions, 'What place has *form* in the production of this artist's effect? How is *form* responsible for such effects?' with some hope of an intelligent answer."[120] Donnelly, noting that Rickert's book had already stimulated a number of "Chicago theses," had argued that "what is wanted in education" is not more scholarship but rather "a Ph.D. degree for creative work"; he cited G. P. Baker's playwriting workshops at Yale and William Hughes Mearn's 1925 book on his Dewey-inspired progressive pedagogy, *Creative Youth*, as models for future programs.[121] In her response, Christ agrees that the "creative art must ever lead; the studious art, follow," but argues that this is the "whole point of Dr. Rickert's work": "she is trying to find a method of study which will give to him who can never write and who has no desire to write, a power of keen delight in the finer shades of literary art."[122]

As *New Methods* came to press in 1927, Rickert's students planned to further develop her methods. In the summer of 1927, Dr. Mildred Lambert taught English 376: Scientific Analysis of Style in Rickert's stead. Lambert was a Chicago graduate, one of Manly's students, who had taught at Grinnell College and the University of Minnesota. During that course, Lambert and her students began work on a poetry textbook inspired by *New Methods*. Rickert's text worked well for graduate courses in English, but her students wanted to create a simplified version for secondary classrooms. Many of them were high school or junior college teachers—Elsa Chapin had taught at Miss Gamble's School for Girls in Santa Barbara and the Summit School for Girls in St. Paul; Russell Thomas had taught high school in Gibson City, Illinois, and was concurrently teaching at the University of Chicago High School; Martha von Christ was teaching at Crane Junior College in Chicago.[123] That summer of 1927, they began devising their methods, which included crayon underlining poetic images by color, classifying poetic images by the senses in five-column charts, and using ¼-inch ruled graph paper to chart poetic rhythm line by line.

In the fall of 1927, these students returned to their own classrooms and began to experiment with their students and even supervise more widespread experimentation in the schools of their region. Ed M. Rowe, for example, returned to Provo City, Utah, in the fall of 1927 and sent out poems, questions, and technical exercises to local high schools. "English Teachers Are Testing Poems" read a headline in the *Y News*, the BYU student newspaper. The article describes how area teachers have been "testing a series of poems sent out by the University of Chicago." The poems are accompanied by "questions and suggestions for a scientific analysis of style" inspired by Rickert's "very interesting book on new methods for the study of literature," the article explains. The "criticisms and suggestions" of local teachers "will be of assistance to the writers and publishers of a book that will be of service to high schools and junior colleges throughout the United States." Rowe, who had taken courses with Rickert and then Lambert in the summers of 1925–27, taught his own Contemporary British Literature course at BYU that spring, and it's likely that his undergraduates helped facilitate this "investigation of Miss Richart's [*sic*] new methods."[124]

The University of Chicago Press put the resulting book under contract in early 1928, describing it to educators as "the product of Miss Rickert's students who formed a large committee to work out a textbook for high schools as a cooperative project."[125] The Press prepared to market the book alongside *New Methods*; the latter forming the "theory" and the former the "practice"—both designed "to sharpen literary perception."[126] In their responses to the Press's marketing questionnaire, Rickert's students emphasized that their "scientific types of analysis hopes to cut through" the tendency of schoolteachers to insist on "making masterpieces teach 'lessons' or demonstrate 'truths' approved by the transitory fashions of the era in which they happened to be teaching." In place of this "sentimental distortion of values," their book would put the student in touch with "the essential primary meaning of the artist." The coauthors explain that they're planning to use mostly "contemporary verse" "so that the language will present no difficulties in shades of meaning or strangeness of form to young students."[127]

The book was eventually published in August 1929 as *A New Approach to Poetry*, just a few months after *Practical Criticism*. The large committee that had undertaken the project from the beginning was, by that time, whittled down to two coeditors, Elsa Chapin and Russell Thomas. The three-part book opened with extensive quotation from Alfred North Whitehead's *Science and the Modern World*, in which Whitehead asserts that "general training should aim at eliciting our concrete apprehensions, and should satisfy the itch of youth to be doing something."[128] Part 1 of the book introduced "tools" for "doing something" with poetry. In four chapters on imagery, rhythm, sound patterns, and the typographical shapes of poems, Chapin and Thomas reproduced examples of charts and exercise work for classroom use. Chapter 1, for example, reproduces Wilfred Gibson's "Before Action," Elinor Wylie's "August," John Masefield's "Cargoes," and other poems in which students had, using crayons, underlined each image in the poem by color. Chapter 2 explains how to make a rhythm graph of Kipling's "The Gypsy Trail" using "graph paper ruled in quarter inch squares: across the top of the sheet number the squares, first counting the syllables of the longest line in the poem. . . . Let the lower edge of our quarter-inch squares represent unstressed syllables; the upper will represent stressed syllables."[129] Further chapters describe experiments with end rhyme and consonant/vowel patterns, as well as line breaks and typographical shaping.

Like *New Methods* before it, *A New Approach* valued these exercises of classification and visualization as process rather than product. The point of quantifying and categorizing poetic elements was to stimulate close discussion and consensus-building around the concrete particulars of actual poems. "We may not agree" on what constitutes a visual or aural image or whether a syllable is stressed, they write, but "our disagreements are as instructive as our agreements."[130] They note that existing terms for poetic form can often serve to paper over generalizations or misapprehensions. For example, in their chapter "The Sound of Words," they encourage teachers to avoid terms like "alliteration, assonance, and consonance" as "the use of these words has been based far too much on traditional conceptions of their character, and far too little on close study of vowel and consonant repetition as they actually occur."[131] Likewise, basic categorizing can be useful for identifying false presupposition. In the chapter on imagery, they describe how a set of University of Chicago undergraduates, "girls and boys from Middle West farming country, with no experience of New England flowers," coded Amy Lowell's "night-scented stock" from "The Garden by Moonlight" as black-and-white or Jersey brown. "The instructor became curious" about this collective error and realized that nearly half the class "were framing romantic pictures of the 'night-scented stock' familiar to them in the capacious barns of their Home Counties" rather than the cone-clustered, fragrant flower by the same name. "From the teacher's point of view, then, the chart was invaluable."[132] Because these methods are designed to be refined through use, they treat their own categories and objects of study as evolving; a footnote, for example, mentions that they've dropped one of Rickert's six categories of alliteration, "eye alliteration," "because Professor Rickert is not sure of its validity."[133]

While part 1 of *New Approach* adapted Rickert's *New Methods*, parts 2 and 3 struck out into new textbook territory. Part 2, titled "Adventures in Discovery," reproduced over eighty mostly contemporary poems, organized thematically according to topics such as "The World of Waters, Winds, and Weathers" or "Feather, Fin, and Fur," to be used as "an interesting field for explorations" of the type modeled in part 1.[134] Many of these poems and their poets—including Eliot's "The Love Song of J. Alfred Prufrock," H.D.'s "Oread," poems by de la Mare and Millay—appear also in both *New Methods* and in *Practical Criticism*, or in Richards's earlier *Principles of Literary Criticism*. Part 3, titled "Puzzles," addresses critical questions such as "How are we to judge a poem as 'good' or 'bad'?" and "What *is* poetry?" by drawing upon "actual class discussions" and student work.[135] For example, chapter 1, "Poetry and Prose," describes an experiment in which students were given three pieces of writing, "without any indication of authorship": an excerpt from the *New International Encyclopedia* entry for "poplar," an excerpt on the poplar from Logan Pearsall Smith's *Trivia* (1926 edition), and a section of John Masefield's "Sonnet XLVI" on a tree. The "students were asked to discuss them in the light of their knowledge of poetical elements—that is, of the imagery, rhythm, and sound patterns—with no comment from the instructor."[136] Quoting extensively from five student responses (identified in a footnote as the work of "Vivian Wasser, Margaret Dean, Mrs. Leah Clawson, Lester Freudenthal, Harvey Greenleaf"), they analyze and discuss how the students drew distinctions between "'pure' prose, poetic prose, and 'pure' poetry," explaining that the excerpts were chosen to show that "there can be no hard and fast line drawn between prose on the one hand, and poetry on the other."[137]

New Approach also detailed an experiment uncannily similar to Richards's *Practical Criticism*, as at least one reviewer noted.[138] In Chapter 2 of part 3, "'Good' Poetry—The Problem of Taste," the authors describe an experiment in which they distributed two poems, one "good" and one "bad," to two classes of thirty students. The students were asked, "with no preliminary remarks from the instructor," to "write as fully as possible on each." Like Richards, Chapin and Thomas reproduce the poems (Grenville Kleiser's "The Optimist" and W. E. Henley's "Invictus") without identifying the authors, and, like Richards, they discuss and quote extensively from the anonymized student writing they collected. Yet the *New Approach* experiment differed from *Practical Criticism* in a crucial way: they distributed the poems to two different classes: one "which had been discussing the nature of poetry for a month" and one that had not.[139] They found that "in each group" about "half the class" preferred the "bad" poem ("The Optimist") to the "good" ("Invictus"). But "there was an encouraging feature, nevertheless": "Those who objected to 'The Optimist' among the students of poetry had very definite reasons for condemning it."[140] Turning to the students who preferred "The Optimist," Chapin and Thomas take up the questions of sentimentality and stock response upon which Richards also dwells. Like Richards, they argue that "people who expect only rest and relaxation from art are rejecting one of the most powerful aids to a fuller and freer life which life itself has to offer." Yet they are not as dire about students' preference for sentimental or moralizing poetry. For they note that most students who prefer "The Optimist" self-correct once introduced to a theory of poetry: "Of our class of thirty, only three or four are confirmed, determined wearers of rose-colored glasses. The others are persons who have never thought about art at all."[141] When students come to understand, through class discussion, that "poetry—any art, for that matter—grows out of a keen understanding of universal human difficulties, and deals with these difficulties in the highest spirit of which the human being is capable," they can recognize poetry that falls short of this standard, and "they find themselves on the road to a sound basis for making art an element in their lives." "All of us who have watched this discovery grow in the eyes of students know from what singularly unpromising beginnings it may spring," they add.[142]

In the end, the key difference between *New Approach* and *Practical Criticism* is simply that *New Approach* pays open and direct testimony to the experimental class work that served as the impetus for both projects. In both books, collective experiments in the reading of poetry serve as not only the diagnostic but, crucially, as the corrective tool for student misapprehension. *New Approach* more explicitly identifies how its exercises do more than simply "satisfy the itch of youth to be doing something," but serve as occasions for shifting readerly attention to the concrete particulars of individual poems and starting the work of consensus-building around definitions of poetic form.[143] Just as Richards ceded his own lecture platform to his students' written protocols, Chapin and Thomas recommend that "the teacher, as an individual, must remain part of the background."

Instructors should "refrain from statements of personal preference and opinion which will hamper and sometimes destroy that purely independent growth of individual response to certain poems which the student must recognize freshly and independently as valuable for him." The teacher's only role is "to give the student tools" and "necessary facts about the nature of poetry" and "to insist with austerity that the student know what the poet has said, that is, that a thorough and intimate understanding of the text is the only adequate basis for opinions about the poem."[144]

Like Richards, Rickert and her students believed that to read poetry well was to receive an act of communication—to make, as Richards said, "a serious attempt to produce the outlook and attitudes of other people."[145] Over the decades that followed, this communication model of poetry came to seem positivistic—a naive account of both poetic creation and of the practice and value of reading poetry. Yet for these 1920s teachers, this model of poetry's value was never located in the poems themselves. It lay instead in their experimental and democratic classrooms, which centered the work of consensus-building through the step-by-step establishment of descriptive norms, through the shared commitment to exposing individual idiosyncrasies to the bracing light of collective scrutiny. Like their countless peers from the same decade—some who did and some who didn't publish their own experiences of experimental classroom practices—Richards, Rickert, and her students were determined to demystify literary taste, which had seemed in general culture to be a matter of individual development and discernment or innate capacity, by returning to its building blocks. They imagined that collective attention to matters that seemed hardly literary at all would end by bringing these students closer to literature. However, the question—indeed, the test—of whether this might be true was itself perpetually deferred in favor of further experimental work on method. After the publication of *New Methods*, English 376 returned to the catalogs for 1929, 1930, and 1931, renamed, by then, English 376: New Methods for the Study of English. Rickert's students Chapin and Thomas and many others returned to their classrooms across the United States to continue their own experiments with the new methods. Richards continued to run his Practical Criticism courses through the 1930s, '40s, and '50s, and those courses, in turn, influenced other future critics and professors: versions of the Practical Criticism experiments were run throughout the twentieth century.[146] In the end, it is these countless experimental laboratories—this long tradition of students researching themselves reading poetry—that should command our attention when we think about the history of literary study, and particularly the history of literary study in the classroom.

J. Saunders Redding, The Negro in American Literature (1944) and American Biographical Literature (1976)

The teachers we have studied so far were skeptical of the concepts of the major author and the great work. Spurgeon, Eliot, Richards, and Rickert knew very well how editors, scholars, and bibliographers had worked incrementally over the course of centuries to assemble authoritative texts. They saw how the critical tradition made and remade author figures like "Shakespeare" and "Chaucer" over time. Their classroom teaching demystified these ideals in order to induct their students into the scholarly, critical, and authorial work that constituted the literary tradition. In this chapter, we turn to another teacher whose pedagogy worked to dismantle the concept of "pure literature" and the mystique of romantic authorship. For J. Saunders Redding, these particular concepts were born of racism. Like the related concept of "objective" history, these ideals functioned to segregate disciplinary knowledge, rendering African American writing unliterary and African American lives and letters unhistorical. The materials that remain from Redding's five decades' worth of teaching show how Redding practiced critique in order to reconstitute American literature as written by white and Black authors alike. His pedagogy was invented in historically Black colleges and universities in the Jim Crow South and, much later, carried north to newly integrated colleges and universities. Redding's teaching aimed, he wrote, to "rid the minds of whites and blacks alike of false learning, and . . . promote for blacks and whites alike a completely rewarding participation in American life."[1]

Redding studied and taught in universities almost continuously from 1924 through 1981. He and his peers entered the academy on the heels of the Harlem Renaissance. They formed what Lawrence P. Jackson calls "the Indignant Generation"—the first "bona fide generation of African Americans with access to colleges, graduate schools" and funding from "liberal, integrated institutions" such as Yaddo and the Julius Rosenwald

Foundation.[2] Obituaries and biographies tend to gloss over the complicated details of Redding's many-layered career, but his archival papers, held at Brown's John Hay Library and the Hampton University Archives, give a clearer picture.[3] Born in 1906 in Wilmington, Delaware, Redding left home at seventeen to begin his college education at Lincoln University, before moving to Brown University, from which he graduated in 1928. He spent the late 1920s teaching at Morehouse College; when he was let go for his radical viewpoints, he returned north to complete his MA at Brown in 1931 and his doctorate at Columbia University in 1934.[4] Redding spent the remainder of the '30s chairing English departments and teaching literature courses (as well as the occasional economics class) at several southern Black colleges: Louisville Municipal College, Southern University in Baton Rouge, Elizabeth City College in North Carolina. During this time, he published his critical monograph on "the literature of the Negro," *To Make a Poet Black* (1939), a book that Henry Louis Gates has called "the first serious attempt at canon formation in our tradition."[5] From 1938 onward, he served as a consultant, along with Margaret Mead and Henry Nash Smith, on "American Cultural History" to the Library of Congress.[6] In 1940 Redding accepted a Rockefeller grant from the University of North Carolina to write a documentary account of southern Black life. *No Day of Triumph* appeared in 1942, and the following year Redding was hired by Hampton Institute, where he would remain through 1965, becoming the James Weldon Johnson Professor of Creative Writing in 1956. In the 1950s, Redding published in a range of genres including his biographical history *They Came in Chains: Americans from Africa* (1950), a book of autobiographical reflections titled *On Being Negro in America* (1951), and a campus novel, *Stranger and Alone* (1950). Through the 1950s and '60s, he reviewed books for a wide range of newspapers and periodicals. In the 1960s, he served as director of Research and Publication at the newly formed National Endowment for the Humanities.[7] He also helped academic presses conform to new multi-ethnic publishing guidelines by reviewing their manuscripts for elisions or misrepresentations of the contributions of Black Americans and Americans of other races to American history.

In 1969 Redding was hired as a founding faculty member in George Washington University's newly independent American Studies program. He taught and co-taught courses for several years, including the Mind of the Negro in 1969. In 1971 Redding was hired by Cornell University as the Ernest I. White Professor of American Studies and Humane Letters, becoming the first African American scholar to hold an endowed professorship in literary criticism in the Ivy League. Redding's return to the northern Ivies that would not hire their own African American graduates in the 1930s coincided with the publication of his major anthology, co-edited with Arthur P. Davis, *Cavalcade: Negro American Writing from 1760 to the Present* (1971). These years saw the founding of hundreds of Black studies programs in universities across the United States, and Redding accepted more than a dozen requests to teach as a visiting scholar at colleges and universities including Rhode Island College; Swarthmore College; University of Illinois at Urbana-Champaign; Howard University; the University of Pennsylvania; University of California, Berkeley; University of California, Irvine; and University of Massachusetts Boston.[8] Redding officially retired from teaching in 1978; he passed away in 1988. The opening line of Cornell's memorial notice quotes Gates describing Redding as the "veritable dean of Afro-American literary critics."[9]

Yet Redding's reputation as the "dean of Afro-American literary critics" has outlived his generation's institutional vision for an integrated American literature—a vision that Redding himself first introduced in *To Make a Poet Black* (1939). In that monograph, Redding reordered a canon of African American writing around his appreciation of its historical embeddedness. Unlike earlier anthologies of "Negro literature" and their companion volumes of criticism from the 1920s and early '30s, which tended to focus on the interplay of invention and tradition in New Negro poetry, Redding's book offered a "history of Negro thought in America." Crucially, Redding declared that "the literature of the Negro has been a literature of purpose or even necessity."[10] His critical analyses of speeches, early novels, and memoirs focused on the circumstances of their composition and framed Black American literature as particularly fertile ground from which to grapple with problems of realist representation.

Critics today rightly see *To Make a Poet Black* as a foundational text for African American literary studies. Yet if we look solely to Redding's published work, largely focused on the literature and culture of Black Americans, we get only half the picture of his integrationist approach to literary study. In Redding's teaching materials, we can see that Redding integrated "Negro writing" into American literature by emphasizing the extent to which *most* American writing was unaesthetic and tied to its historical circumstances. "Until relatively recent times, writing by both black and white Americans had little to do with 'pure literature' and aesthetics either as philosophy or in practice," reads the course rationale and a final exam question for the Negro in American Literature course that Redding repurposed for decades.[11] "Writing by black Americans is American writing," the rationale continues, "and it cannot be lopped off from the corpus of American literary expression without doing grave harm to the corpus as an instrument of cultural and social diagnosis."[12] In Redding's class lectures and course reading lists, we find his vision of an integrated American literature. It was a vision centered around realist texts and documentary form. As we will describe, Redding's courses from the 1930s through the 1970s turned away from consciously literary texts in order to explore the memoirs, letters, pamphlets, and autobiographies that documented a vast and strange collection of American lives. While Redding's published work fits squarely into Kenneth Warren's narrowed definition of African American literature as Jim Crow–era literature with a "necessarily instrumental view of the political urgency and utility of black writing" in its project to protest segregation, Redding's classroom teaching shows how this political urgency gave rise to an entirely new and fully-fledged approach to literary history that became foundational to later disciplinary developments not only in English, but in American studies and history.[13]

Though Redding had a pedagogical vision for an integrated America, the colleges and universities in which he taught were themselves instruments of segregation. And though, as Jackson describes, Redding's generation was the first to be taught in white universities and funded by integrated foundations, Redding's writing from the 1940s and '50s is critical of northern white universities and southern Black colleges alike. Indeed, Redding's criticism of higher education institutions is the thread that connects nearly all of his publications, from his damning account of the high suicide rate among lonely Black students at New England colleges in the 1920s in *No Day of Triumph* to his critique of the "Negro schoolmen" of the South as "terrific snobs, the true bourgeoisie" in that same volume, to his embittered campus novel, *Stranger and Alone*, to his account of the "dulling effect" that race consciousness had had on his teaching and his scholarship in *On Being Negro in America*.[14] Archival materials, as well, tell the story of Redding's restlessness at different points in his career: here a letter from a department chair at Hampton complaining that Redding "diverted himself with magazines" at faculty meetings, there a few letters from Redding seeking alternate appointments to relieve him of teaching at Hampton.[15] And newly opened FBI files show that Redding's colleagues at several of his first teaching appointments were informing the FBI of Redding's activities.[16] Such materials index the alienation that Redding himself documented across years' worth of texts that build upon and quote each other. We are thus reminded that Redding's pedagogical project of integrationism remained tenuous, critical, and unfinished by the 1960s and '70s.

It was as an integrationist scholar with an unfinished project that Redding protested the formation of Black studies programs in the late 1960s.

"There are American studies into which Negro materials should be structured," Redding wrote in an internal response to a document outlining "An Approach to Black Studies" at George Washington University in 1969, but "there are no black studies." For Redding, validations of Black experience and Black aesthetics rested upon racial essentialism and political separatism; he warned against offering "black courses" for "black students," and he personally rejected many invitations to visit universities as a race representative or an expert in "black experience."[17] Established and respected by that time, Redding published his critiques of Black studies and the Black Arts movement in both mainstream venues such as the *New York Times* and scholarly journals as well. The critics, authors, and scholars at the forefront of those movements in return painted him as a timid assimilationist and a comfortable establishment figure. This characterization of Redding has endured, so that he is often today misidentified as an apolitical aesthete—a "color-blind" poetry critic, in the words of one scholar[18]—remembered, as Michael Lackey argues, for his critique of Black essentialism rather than his earlier critiques of white essentialism.[19] Stephanie Brown writes that Redding was "excoriated for holding positions deemed too radical in the 1930s and insufficiently radical in the 1960s."[20]

While histories of Black studies have discarded Redding as a literary scholar uninterested in politics, histories of literary study have also failed to preserve his legacy or the classroom model and methods of his generation's integrationism. Indeed, disciplinary histories of English in America, focused as they are on northern elite universities, tend to see integrationism as a late 1960s phenomenon, in which student movements demanded the belated integration of curricula and faculty, and English departments accommodated them by adding contemporary fiction by Black writers to preexisting courses. The years just before Redding joined the faculty at Cornell in 1971, for instance, saw the foundation of the Africana Studies and Research Center in 1969 after student protests and the takeover of Willard Straight Hall that same year. And in the English Department, curricular integration began in 1967 with the addition of Richard Wright, Ralph Ellison, and James Baldwin to course reading lists for American Literature, Twentieth-Century American Literature, and an honors course on "the political novel."[21] The incorporation of these few select African American writers to preexisting courses at Cornell is an example of Lawrence P. Jackson's argument that elite universities—beguiled by the difficult modernist novel and its power to transform the individual reader—welcomed writers like Wright, Ellison, and Baldwin but had a harder time incorporating the Indignant Generation's works of social realism.[22]

Looking away from elite universities such as Cornell, however, we find in the English classes taught at southern Black colleges an entirely different approach to an integrated literary study, with a robust history dating back to the 1930s and even earlier.[23] When Redding arrived at Hampton in 1943, for instance, the English Department had been for several years teaching its English 411–412: American Literature course (later English 311–312) as a backward-looping survey that began with "the most important present day Negro writers" before "going back to the most effective writers of the Colonial period." The description of American Literature in the Hampton course catalog notes that "considerable time and emphasis are given to the contributions of Negro writers," which "are treated as an integral part of American literature." The class was conducted by "lectures, socialized recitations, individual and group reports, and panel discussions"; it promised to approach literature "in such a way as to give the student an appreciation of the fullness of life in the United States" along with "sufficient historical and biographical material to meet the needs of prospective teachers and to place writers in proper perspective."[24] At the same time, the department offered English 314: Negro Literature (renamed the Negro in American Literature in 1947), which covered

> the works of Negro writers of prose, poetry and drama from their first efforts in the United States to the present day, with emphasis on their interpretation of Negro people, the constantly changing situations they have encountered, and their reaction to these situations. Emphasis on major writers. Attention to minor writers, as well as to white writers whose interpretations of the Negro have influenced American opinion and literature.[25]

These two integrated historical survey courses, always adjacent in the course catalog, were taught at Hampton for decades.

When Redding came to Cornell in 1971, he brought with him this approach to integrationist literary history that had been standard for decades in English departments of southern Black colleges. But this practice, which has been invisible to previous disciplinary histories, is precisely the alternative history that warrants resurrection today. Redding introduced, for example, English 365: The Negro in American Literature into the department's curriculum, using and updating notecards he kept from his days teaching English 312: The Negro in American Literature at Hampton. In it, he taught Wright (*Native Son*), Ellison (*Shadow and Act*), Gwendolyn Brooks (*Annie Allen*), and Baldwin (*Notes of a Native Son*), and even Black Arts writers like LeRoi Jones and Addison Gayle, but within a long, multi-generic tradition that also included Gustavus Vassa, Phillis Wheatley, George Moses Horton, Charles Chesnutt, Harlem Renaissance writers, and fellow scholar-critics Robert Bone and Hugh Gloster.[26] Redding also taught the department's upper-level seminars on Shakespeare and Studies in American Literature in 1971.[27] He revamped the latter to serve as "[a] comparative study of selected black and white American writings preliminary to an assessment of their contribution to the corpus of American literature."[28]

It is worth pausing to consider the difference between the integrated American literature syllabus that Redding carried from southern Black colleges to Cornell, and the supplemental model that added a few contemporary Black novelists to existing courses, invoking a majority/minority model of representation. Without scrutiny, both models may seem informed by what John Guillory has described as the "liberal pluralist" logic whereby authors on a syllabus are imagined to "represent . . . different social groups," with Redding's syllabuses simply according greater representation to Black Americans.[29] But Redding's syllabuses offer a difference not of amount but of kind. For they open, we argue, an alternative to the "let your voice be heard" liberal pluralism that Guillory describes.[30] Redding presented American literature as a body of writing fundamentally shaped by politics and history: abolitionist speeches by Black writers and anti-historical descriptions of happy enslaved people in the work of white writers alike answered the demands of political and historical exigency. What we stand to gain by recovering the syllabuses that Redding carried north, then, is a model for integrating reading lists that rejects the analogy between inclusion on a syllabus and inclusion in American political life.

Redding's integrationism, like the literary theory that underpinned it—his reading of all American literature as "literature of necessity"—comes most fully into view when we consider its roots in his classroom practices. In his published scholarship, Redding kept a tight focus on Black literature, culture, and society. In his classroom materials, however, we can see how his critical assessment of African American literature formed the basis of a new account—one that would much later become dominant within American studies—of both American literature and history. To understand how Redding revalued realist genres and developed a critical account of the politics of representation, we must begin with his two earliest works, *To Make a Poet Black* (1939) and *No Day of Triumph* (1943). We then turn to Redding's 1954 course called the Novel to see how his documentary aesthetic informed his teaching of literary fiction. Among other things, his lectures on Dickens's *David Copperfield* prepared students to read novels as transmuted records of real historical lives. Moving from Redding's midcentury course focused on the novel to his 1976 American Biographical Literature course, we can see the culmination of Redding's decades-long project of gathering, from mostly "non-literary" materials, the true record of America's past as at once a basis for solidarity and a bulwark against false promises of national belonging.

The Novel (1954)

The defining project of Redding's generation was that of representing America to itself for the first time—and this was for Redding a particularly *literary* project. This documentary ambition—which was shared, as Jackson points out, by many writers, photographers, and filmmakers and funded by agencies like the Works Progress Administration in the 1930s—was never for Redding simply about discovering what was already there. Historically speaking, most Black lives from the past lay off the written record; thus, Redding's *They Came in Chains: Americans from Africa* (1950) imaginatively re-created sketches of the lives of figures like Sojourner Truth.[31] Redding was keenly aware, especially after his own 1940 plunge into social realism with the Rockefeller-funded *No Day of Triumph*, that realism often reflected not the world but the social values of a specific class of readers and granting institutions. "Facing reality," he wrote, "was a job for the novelist."[32]

Redding had these questions of realist representation already in mind in 1939's *To Make a Poet Black*, where he began to reread African American writing for glimpses of a past populated by Americans unfamiliar and strange. In that volume's historical overview of African American literature, he had treated but ultimately set aside major "literary" figures like Phillis Wheatley, Jupiter Hammon, and Frederick Douglass to turn instead to figures like William Wells Brown, a writer of "slightly more than ordinary talents."[33] The William Wells Brown section of *To Make a Poet Black* shows Redding working through the problems and promises of the documentary aesthetic. Brown's sprawling oeuvre—which included abolitionist polemics; plays that drew on Shakespeare as well as burlesque, parody, and minstrelsy; histories; and novels—offered a glimpse of many more lives than his own. For Redding, Brown was of interest precisely because he lacked discrimination: "An impressionable man all his life," Redding wrote, Brown was "touched by nearly everything he heard and saw, absorbing much that was odd and valueless along with that that was solid and worthwhile."[34] In an under-archived and inadequately chronicled world, Brown's attraction to very important social and historical materials as well as apparently ephemeral happenings became a crucial source for Redding. As Redding wrote, "Historically more important in the development of Negro literature than any of his contemporaries, he was also the most representative Negro man of the age, for he was simply a man of slightly more than ordinary talents doing his best in a cause [abolitionism] that was his religion." By contrast with the "too exceptional" Frederick Douglass, for example, Brown was a nearly unconscious conduit for "the thoughts and yearnings of thousands of what he was pleased to call his 'countrymen.'"[35]

It was Brown that Redding seemed to take as a model when, one year after *To Make a Poet Black* was published, he somewhat reluctantly accepted a commission from the Rockefeller Foundation through the University of North Carolina to, as he recalled it, "go out into Negro life in the South." By 1940, of course, this kind of documentary project had an expected literary form inhabited by expected types, if not stereotypes, and producing particular effects on the reader or viewer. Redding worried, "I knew what they wanted and I thought I knew vaguely what I wanted, and the two things were not the same. Their wants were simple and direct. Mine seemed neither." The University of North Carolina and the Rockefeller Foundation viewed the problem as one of ethnographic observation or data collection. For Redding, by contrast, the expectations of granting organizations and academic institutions were already narrowly bound by the strictures of a delimited aesthetic form. Hedging his bets, Redding recalls accepting the commission: "'All right,' I said. 'But I can't promise you what I'll find.' I was still questing, still lost."[36] As he elaborates in the opening autobiographical chapters of *No Day of Triumph*, his quest was to belong "to something bigger than myself." In language reminiscent of Brown's unconscious contact with the "thoughts and yearnings of thousands," Redding described his search for "not a family merely, or institution, or race; but a people and all their topless strivings; a nation and its million destinies" (a line that Redding self-quoted eight years later in *On Being Negro in America*).[37]

Redding's sense that his own documentary aesthetic was at odds with the expectations of the institutions that commissioned him was correct. Reviewers complained that *No Day of Triumph* was in no sense a representative text, beginning with the meandering route Redding took through Virginia across Tennessee, into Arkansas, and down through Mississippi into Cajun Louisiana: "Really, though, Professor Redding's book is not a story of American Negroes, nor of Negroes at all; rather it is a highly personalized account of the experiences of a man on the road, picking likely spots for adventure."[38] Neither did Redding's sketches of Black southerners meet the expectations held by readers. Many objected to what they saw as a disproportionate focus on comic or depraved figures, accusing Redding of "choosing exotic rather than significantly typical incidents."[39] One reviewer actually counted the pages allotted to such figures: "Mike Chowan, a Communist-American, gets 10 pages; a small-town-big-doctor gets 10; . . . Attorney Coe Harvis of the West Virginia mines gets 20; . . . Rosalie Hatton, a high society pervert, gets 25."[40] Redding's narrative habit of tarrying with such seemingly extraordinary characters left readers feeling that no comprehensible story of racial degradation or racial uplift had been told: Redding "fail[s] to indicate sufficiently the inner meaning of what he deals with."[41]

Reviewers' complaints that *No Day of Triumph* had randomly recorded southern Black life without any organizing principles of discrimination and valuation recalls how Redding revalued the oeuvre of Brown for precisely these qualities of indiscrimination. Redding had offered a picture of southern Black life unorganized by the middle-class values aligned with the conventions of documentary realism. "He is the first Negro," Richard Wright wrote in his introduction to the volume, "to break with the ideology of the talented tenth."[42] Giving up those bourgeois conventions for the representation of society, Redding hoped to open instead a new vision of American life unbounded by the narrative conventions that valorize racial or familial belonging.

Redding's revaluation, in *To Make a Poet Black*, of writing like Brown's that did not transcend its immediate historical circumstances to access a higher meaning thus built a literary history for his own writing in works such as *No Day of Triumph*. There, too, we see Redding developing a new conception of authorship in which authors such as Brown do not so much speak for their race or age as unconsciously capture it by preserving for the future those odd details and meaningless sketches that seem not yet valuable or important. Turning now to the notes that Redding kept for the yearlong class the Novel that he taught at Hampton in 1954, we can see how the critical values and practices of realist representation that formed the core of Redding's project produced a new reading of the novel and its history. The full syllabus and reading list for this course have not survived, but Redding's second semester notes for the classes he spent on Charles Dickens's *David Copperfield* have. In them, we see Redding redescribing the genre of Dickens's novel along the lines of *No Day of Triumph*: as a hybrid of reworked personal history, social observation, and literary convention. In his lecture on *David Copperfield*, he considered specifically the ways that apparently valueless and random scenes from life get reworked as literature.

Redding's notes for the Novel course were entirely organized in outline form with occasional passages transcribed or taped in. His lectures on Dickens begin with a timeline of Dickens's life and an overview of "influences upon him." Influences include "A. General conditions of the world" ("a. Industrial development"; "b. Growth of Cities"; "c. Own city living") and "B. Family + Friends" ("a. Particularly his father—shoe-blacking factory"; "b. mother" "c. Maria Beadnell"). Under the name of Dickens's unrequited young love, Maria Beadnell, Redding starts a subcategory: Dickens's "growth of self pity—poverty" and transcribes the following passage from Forster's *Life of Dickens*:

> He was a very little and a very sickly boy. He was subject to attacks of violent spasm which disabled him for any active exertion. He was never a good little cricket-player; he was never a first-rate hand at marbles, or peg-top, or prisoner's base; but he had great pleasure in watching the other boys, officers' sons for the most part, at these games, reading while they played; and he had always the belief that this early sickness had brought to himself one inestimable advantage, in the circumstance of his weak health having strongly inclined him to reading.[43]

Redding underlined the final words of this passage, "health having strongly inclined him to reading," in order to contest them. Redding's next outline section on Dickens's influences in fact focuses on the *lack* of literary influences on Dickens: "C. But a strong inclination to reading is questionable." Under this heading, Redding concedes the importance of Fielding ("whose influence upon him is neglected") and Smollett ("from whom he learned to write picaresque and picaresque characters") but notes that beyond these two forebears, there are "few allusions in Dickens that can be tabbed as having come either from wide or important reading."[44]

Redding thus reframes Dickens as an author who, like Redding's preferred writers and orators in *To Make a Poet Black*, was not particularly literate in the tradition of "wide or important reading." Yet Dickens was, in Redding's view, influenced by other, less illustrious print sources. Here begins the densest, most revised and highlighted section of Redding's outline, which has, until this point, proceeded quite neatly. Here, Redding listed some of these less illustrious sources, including "contemporary journals," "Penny Dreadfuls that were popular in his day," and writers of popular sketches of urban and rural life from the 1820s, '30s, and '40s, including "Pierce Egan—Life in London, Theo. Hook, Robt. Surtee's Sporting Sketches (Jorrocks)," and "Charles Whitehead—Sunny Side of London Life." Around this list Redding inserted a number of sidebar boxes and drew pink highlighter lines to connect these magazines and urban sketches to three separate categories: not just category "C." dealing with the question of what Dickens read and did not read, but also "D. His own journalism," and "E. His attachment to his social class." By focusing on the print world of London that surrounded Dickens in his early years and to which his own journalism contributed, Redding avoids the question of direct influences and actual reading. In place of such literary genealogy, he shows his students both the workaday literary productions that represented London to a nineteenth-century, middle-class readership. The cross-linked outline captures, too, Dickens's own contributions to this genre. Under "His own Journalism," Redding planned to discuss a few qualities of Dickens's parliamentary reporting, including its "sense of immediacy" and "sense of urgency." Redding notes as well that Dickens's journalism demonstrates Dickens's "knowledge of contemporary problems + personality types" and showcases his "habit of observation."[45]

Redding's background lecture on Dickens moves from the broad historical shifts of the era to matters of biography, including intimate family relations, books that Dickens did and did not read, and places he lived. Indeed, the logic of the outline suggests that Redding considered his final cross-linked section, devoted to the murky soup of early Victorian popular print culture, to be part of a narrowing focus on Dickens, the man and the author. In other words, these print journals, sketches, and novels-turned-stage plays—all of which are contrasted by Redding to "wide and important reading" and comprise what we might think of as "historical" materials—here become biographical, a part of Dickens himself. In these notes we can see the pedagogical method behind Redding's claim, in his American literature syllabuses, that there is no "pure literature." Even a major author like Dickens, Redding shows his students, is shaped not by singular literary influences, but rather by an entire print world and the ideology implicit within it.

Redding's expanded sense of what is contained within an author like Dickens leads him, in this lecture, to an equally expansive sense of what is contained within a novel. Redding begins his lectures on *David Copperfield* by contradicting those critics, including Percy Fitzgerald, Alice Meynell, and F. G. Kitson, who have treated the novel as "strictly autobiographical."[46] Redding contends instead that only a "small part" of that book, "probably no larger than the autobiographical sections of Great Expectations," can be said to directly represent Dickens's life. This may seem like a quibble, given that the entirety of his remaining lecture—pages of notes—are devoted to tracing the connections between Dickens's life,

Forster's biography, and that novel. In other words, Redding objects to "strictly" autobiographical readings of the novel not in the name of the novel's pure invention, but in order to develop a thicker account of how details from life make their way into novels.

For instance, just after Redding asserts that only a "small part" of the book can be said to be strictly autobiographical, Redding's notes read, "Curious circumstances in this connection: He sweated over the title." Redding lists the prospective titles:

> The Copperfield Disclosures—Being the personal history, experiences,
>   + observation of Mr. David Copperfield—etc.
> The Copperfield Records—Being, etc.
> The Last Living Speech + Composition of David Copperfield
> The Copperfield Survey of the World as it Rolled[47]

He comments, "Curious, because all of these titles suggest that he was involved in the conscious idea of doing an autobiographical work, and was simply seeking the proper disguise for it."[48] For Redding, the prospective titles for *David Copperfield*—which suggest both confession and documentation—prove that Dickens planned the work to be autobiographical. Further, "it is significant," Redding writes, that "David's initials are Dickens's own backwards." Yet neither this tiny code, nor the "curious circumstances" of the titles Dickens sweated over are, for Redding, clues that point to the book's disguised, personal content. Instead, Redding treats the title variations and title initials as figures for how Dickens takes portions of his life and repurposes them for the novel.

Restating again that the novel is "not autobiographical in any strict sense," Redding qualifies that "it is, however, A. a Reflection of his Youth . . . [the] essential features of his boy[hood] are there." (Here Redding inserts but then crosses out the qualifier "but not always facts.") For Redding, the outlines of David's experiences were roughly Dickens's own: "David's toil in Murdstone + Grinby's warehouse stacks up rather nearly with Dickens's experiences in the blacking factory," for instance. So, too, Redding points out, "there are passages in the novel that passed into it directly from the notes he kept for his autobiography (or vice versa)." Redding pastes in a memory of Dickens's that Forster transcribes:

> I remember one evening—that I went into a public house on Parliament Street, which is still there though altered, at the corner of the short street leading into Cannon Row, and said to the landlord behind the bar, "What is your very best—the VERY *best*—ale a glass?" For, the occasion was a

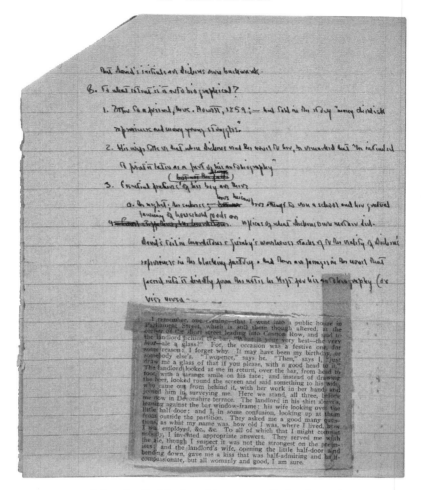

FIGURE 4.1. J. Saunders Redding's teaching notes on Dickens's *David Copperfield* for his 1954 course The Novel at Hampton Institute. Jay Saunders Redding Papers, John Hay Library, Brown University.

festive one, for some reason: I forget why. It may have been my birthday, or somebody else's. "Twopence," says he. "Then," says I, "just draw me a glass of that if you please, with a good head to it." The landlord looked at me in return, over the bar, from head to foot, with a strange smile on his face; and instead of drawing the beer, looked round the screen and said something to his wife, who came out from behind it, with her work in her hand, and joined him in surveying me. Here we stand, all three, before me now in Devonshire terrace. The landlord in his shirtsleeves, leaning against the bar window-frame; his wife looking over the little half-door; and I, in some confusion, looking up at them from outside the partition. They asked me a good many questions, as what my name was, how old I was, where I lived, how I was employed, &c., To all of which that I might commit nobody, I invented appropriate answers. They served me with the ale, though I suspect it was not the strongest on the premises; and the landlord's wife, opening the little half-door and bending down, gave me a kiss that was half-admiring and half-compassionate, but all womanly and good, I am sure.[49]

The passage reappears almost verbatim in David Copperfield, where it is joined by other random scenes that Dickens recalls from his youth, as chronicled by Forster, such as sitting on a bench in London and watching street dancers perform.

Yet Redding's crossed-out insertion, "but not always the facts," indicates that Redding is thinking and teaching about how such moments from life become incorporated into fiction but are also subject to what he describes, to his students, as the "tendency to idealization." Redding explains that Dickens's women and his fathers are often "true to types"— are indeed the "apotheosis of types." The marvel here, Redding argues, is that "as types they are remarkably credible and alive, in spite of the tags with which he labels them and it is not the spurious, one dimensional type of the newspaper or caricature (though Dickens sometimes uses his cartoon draughtsman's technique)." Redding suggests, in other words, that Dickens is using his life, but transmuting it too, according not only to his personal idealizations but also to accepted social conventions and ideological constructions. "Literature must be based upon more or less well-established conventions, upon ideas that have some roots in the general consciousness, upon ideas that are at least somewhat familiar to the public mind," Redding had argued a decade prior.[50] If one thinks of David Copperfield as strictly autobiographical, as many critics have done, Redding argues, then you cannot trace how the book emerges, transmuted, from its historical moment.

In his midcentury course the Novel, then, we see Redding using print culture and biography and historical events not as backdrops through which to interpret or make sense of novels, but as source materials for the making of them. In doing so, he draws attention to the particular ways in which realist genres like the novel select from and refigure the real worlds they purport to represent. He draws students' attention to the particular ways that class-based ideology gives figural shape to the novel's realisms. And, finally, he shows students how novelists like Dickens draw not from

the high literary tradition but from the low and ephemeral world of journalism and mass culture. In the second half of this chapter, we will see
how Redding remained concerned, through midcentury and after, with
these questions of representation and representativeness; he lingered for
years in the literary intersection where the paths of autobiography, social
realism, and history met.

American Biographical Literature (1976)

In the same decade in which Redding taught Dickens's *David Copperfield*
as a novel, an autobiography, a work of social observation, and a chronicle
of history, Redding was himself writing in those multiple genres. In 1950
Redding published a semi-autobiographical campus novel, *Stranger and
Alone*, as well as a four-century history of African Americans, *They Came
in Chains: Americans from Africa*. "It is refreshing when a student of literature turns to the writing of history," one reviewer noted.[51] The following
year saw the publication of *On Being Negro in America*, Redding's autobiographical account of the psychological impacts of racism. *An American
in India: A Personal Report of the Indian Dilemma and the Nature of Her
Conflicts* appeared in 1954. An account of Redding's State Department
trip to India, it reads as part travel narrative and part reflection on American values. *The Lonesome Road: The Story of the Negro's Part in America*
(1958) compiled short biographies of notable figures; on the book jacket,
Redding's publisher described him as a "well known social historian."[52]
In 1956 Redding was named the James Weldon Johnson Professor of Creative Writing at Hampton, and he began work in the final years of the
1950s on a sequel to *Stranger and Alone*.[53]

Redding's book reviews from this decade show how he valued writing
that stood at the crossroads of history and literature, autobiography and
chronicle—books whose testimony challenged official, racist histories.
Herbert Aptheker's *A Documentary History of the Negro People*, published
in 1951 with a preface by W. E. B. Du Bois, put into print a variety of African American manuscript materials, as well as selections from William
Lloyd Garrison's *Liberator*, Black newspapers, pamphlets, and government records. The *New York Times* declined to review it, but Redding did,
positively, and taught and cited it for decades.[54] Reviewing Manie Morgan's *The New Stars: Life and Labor in Old Missouri* (1949)—a collection of
letters, diaries, and dictated memories of Morgan's life on a Missouri slave
plantation—Redding wrote about the superiority of first-person stories
to scholarly history:

Let scholar-historians say what they will, there is no such thing as objective history. Probably the closest thing to it is the newspaper story written by an honest journalist. But even such history as the journalist writes we read with our emotions. If it were not for the play of emotion upon fact, history would be dull stuff indeed, and it would never be productive of its only worthwhile result—truth. And truth is emotional. And historical truth (not fact) is personal.

Thus historical truth is more likely to be found in memoirs, memorabilia, ana and autobiographies than in the works of those historians who pride themselves on objectivity. A chapter from a slave's autobiography is worth as much as three chapters of Buckingham's Slave States of America. And the more naive the writer of autobiography is, the more likely is his work to be revealing of the truth.[55]

Redding also valued what he called "the use of imagination in historical research."[56] Reviewing Truman Nelson's *The Sin of the Prophet,* a fictionalized history of the courthouse riots at the Massachusetts trial of escaped slave Anthony Burns, Redding wrote that Nelson's was a "narrative which reveals—with truth and humor and compassion—those subtle relationships in life, those causes and effects which are likely to escape us when we read either history or romance."[57] Of George Lamming's *In the Castle of My Skin*, Redding marveled, "There is no way to classify this beautifully written, heart-stopping book. To call it autobiography would be as untrue as to call it a work of fiction; yet it has the quality of both, and something more." Like *John Brown's Body,* Redding said, Lamming's book showed "how a magical poetry can recreate a wholly unpoetic and disenchanting world."[58]

By the end of the 1960s, Redding had left his position at Hampton. After a serving as the director of Research and Publication for several years at the newly formed National Endowment for the Humanities, Redding was hired by George Washington University to teach in their American Studies program.[59] At GWU, Redding taught History 173–174: The Negro in American History, Am Civ 175: The Mind of the Negro, and Am Civ 273: Materials in American Negro Culture, a graduate seminar. He also co-taught, with Clarence Mondale, the program's new yearlong American Thought and Civilization course, Am Civ 71–72.[60]

The same year that Redding was hired, George Washington University's new Black Student Union convinced the university to make scholarships to recruit five African American students from Washington, DC, and to require all student organizations to have a nondiscrimination policy.[61] The following April, SDS students occupied Maury Hall, then Monroe Hall a few weeks later. In between the two occupations, Mondale circulated a draft proposal for a Black Studies program at GWU.[62] Redding sent it back with heavy revisions and critique; among other things, Redding objected to the formation of remedial courses specifically for Black students and to the name of the program ("'black studies' . . . is the most disingenuous put-on"). He advocated instead for all lower-level courses in "American history, sociology, literature, education, etc." to "give full recognition to the contributions of black people to our culture" and "address the problems of racism."[63]

The following year, Redding published an opinion editorial in the *New York Times* that drew a distinction between Afro-American Studies and Black Studies. In it, Redding identified with students "at predominantly white" universities who feel their courses "lack relevance" and view their textbooks as "primers of white supremacy." For evidence, Redding points to Henry Allen Bullock's *A History of Negro Education in the South*, which won the Bancroft Prize in 1968 while presenting America's racist past and present as "historical accident." Carefully separating essentializing concepts of Black identity and Black studies from Afro-American Studies, Redding argues that the latter "are basically American studies" since "a line of historical continuity and cultural and social development peculiar to America has generated a new breed of black man with a new and different orientation to life, with a demonstrably different psychological and emotional structure from that of his 'brothers' in Africa." Redding continues, "A scholarly, painstaking pursuit of this line of continuity, with all of its myriad branches, is a proper and legitimate academic pursuit. White scholars would not and should not be barred from the pursuit. Such a pursuit would necessarily be interdisciplinary."[64]

In high demand by the fall of 1969, Redding accepted visiting positions at Rhode Island College and Swarthmore College, and a faculty position in the English Department at Cornell University. Returning to English departments from his brief stint in an interdisciplinary American studies program, Redding carried with him that vision of a fully integrated American literature, more historical than aesthetic, that he had taught for decades at Hampton and outlined in the *New York Times* as a pathway forward. He also worked on two publications that anthologized literary and historical materials. The first was a 1969 anthology for high school students, *The Negro in American History*, that aimed, in the words of its editors (Mortimer Adler and Charles Van Doren), "to turn teachers into scholars and pupils into students."[65] The three-volume anthology was organized, like the American Literature survey at Hampton, in reverse chronological order. Redding wrote the introduction to volume 1, *Black Americans, 1928–1968*. And in 1971 Redding and Arthur P. Davis published their landmark anthology, *Cavalcade: Negro American Writing from 1760 to the Present*.[66] Identified as a gathering of "writing" rather than literature, *Cavalcade* anthologized the work of nineteenth-century and twentieth-century African American historians alongside poets and novelists.

Around 1975, just as he was retiring from Cornell but still teaching as a visitor at the University of Pennsylvania and Howard University, Redding designed a new syllabus, perhaps his last. Titled American Biographical Literature, it constituted, in many ways, his vision for an integrated American studies. The course's subtitle, Aspects of American Cultural and Intellectual History,[67] and its rationale used interdisciplinary language and highlighted the tension between actuality and ideality, between America in reality and American in imagination:

> An examination of the biographies and/or autobiographies of selected writers, thinkers and participant-observers, with a view to defining their responses—both anecdotal and philosophic—to fundamental aspects of American thought, culture, and social behavior in the late 19th and first half of the 20th century. What is the American? Crevecoeur asked the question more than two centuries ago. Because it is important to know who we are, who we think we are, and how we conceive ourselves, this seminar is another attempt to find answers.[68]

Redding's course rationale contains an implicit historical argument. The invocation of Crevecoeur's colonial *Letters from an American Farmer* alongside the post–Civil War historical framework of the course itself—which began with *The Education of Henry Adams* and ended with *The Autobiography of Malcolm X*—contraposes reality and ideality. The question of "what is the American?," Redding implies, can be answered only in the aftermath of Emancipation. And though the course begins in the late nineteenth century, it built upon the challenge to official histories of America posed by the newly published and anthologized testimonies of enslaved people and slavers.[69]

The texts for the course included a mixture of biography, autobiography, and ghostwritten autobiography, featuring figures drawn the literary and journalistic worlds that Redding knew well. Redding arranged the "order of reading and discussion" chronologically by the subject's life span rather than by publication date, underscoring that the course's focus was the study of America rather than of individual authors.[70] Beginning with Henry Adams's retrospective look at the nineteenth century, the class then read Justin Kaplan's *Mr. Clemens and Mark Twain*, a biography that explored the tensions between "the Hartford literary gentleman and the sagebrush bohemian."[71] Next they studied Jane Addams's *Twenty Years at Hull-House* and W. E. B. Du Bois's *Dusk of Dawn*, both social studies as much as autobiographies. From Du Bois they turned to Yale American studies professor R. W. B. Lewis's *Edith Wharton: A Biography*, which won the Pulitzer and the Bancroft awards the year that Redding taught the course. Next they read Lincoln Steffens's *Autobiography* about growing up in California and muckraking for *McClure's*, followed by Theodore Rosengarten's *All God's Dangers: The Life of Nate Shaw*, a biography of Alabama sharecropper Ned Cobb based on transcripts of interviews that had been published just the year before. After that, the class considered the life and aftermath of literary modernism with Arthur Mizener's *The Far Side of Paradise: A Biography of F. Scott Fitzgerald*; Malcolm Cowley's story of ex-patriot life among the modernists in Paris, *Exile's Return*; and Wallace Stegner's biography of Utah-born *Saturday Review* editor Bernard DeVoto, *The Uneasy Chair*. The final four texts were all African American autobiographies: Richard Wright's *Black Boy*, Redding's *On Being Negro in America*, James Baldwin's *Notes of a Native Son*, and Alex Haley's *The Autobiography of Malcolm X*. Alongside *Dusk of Dawn* and *All God's Dangers*, they made a syllabus composed half of Black and half of white writers—the same model that Redding had used for American literature courses since the 1940s.

Redding's secondary readings for the course justify the course's treatment of biography and autobiography as valuable contributions to the study of American history and culture. In particular, the collateral readings looked to African American historians' extensive work with testimonials, first-person narratives, and documentary materials as a path forward for American studies. Redding asked his students to read two chapters of Margaret Butcher's *The Negro in American Culture* (1956), which was based on materials gathered by Alain Locke prior to his death. The first chapter Redding selected set aside generalizations about the "Negro" to explore southern Black folk life in particular. Discussing humor, song, theater, and more, Butcher argues that "because of their deeply original and creative character, American culture is most indebted, above all other folk sources, to this lowly but distinctive level of Negro peasant experience."[72] The second chapter Redding assigned provided an overview of the new studies of southern and African American history published in the 1940s and '50s, including W. J. Cash's *The Mind of the South*, Howard Odum's *Southern Regions of the United States*, the Federal Writers' Project's *These Are Our Lives*, Rupert Vance's *Human Factors in Cotton Culture: A Study*

AMERICAN BIOGRAPHICAL LITERATURE: Aspects of American Cultural
and Intellectual History

The rationale:

An examination of the biographies and/or autobiographies of
selected writers, thinkers and participant-observers, with a view
to defining their responses- both anecdotal and philosophic- to
fundamental aspects of American thought, culture, and social behavior in late 19th. and the first half of the 20th. century.
What is the American? Crevecoeur asked the question more than
two centuries ago. Because it is important to know who we are,
who we think we are, and how we conceive ourselves, this seminar
is another attempt to find asnwers.

Order of reading and discussion:(subject to change):

Adams-	THE EDUCATION OF HENRY ADAMS
Kaplan, Justin-	MR. CLEMENS AND MARK TWAIN
Addams, Jane-	TWENTY YEARS AT HULL HOUSE
Dubois, W. E. B.-	DUSK OF DAWN
Lewis, R. W. B.-	EDITH WHARTON
Steffens, Lincoln-	AUTOBIOGRAPHY
Rosengarten, Theo.-	ALL GOD'S DANGERS
Mizener, Arthur-	THE FAR SIDE OF PARADISE
Cowley, Malcolm-	EXILES RETURN
Stegner, Wallace-	THE UNEASY CHAIR; Biography of DeVoto
Wright, Richard-	BLACK BOY
Redding, Saunders-	ON BEING NEGRO IN AMERICA
Baldwin, James-	NOTES OF A NATIVE SON
Haley, Alex-	THE AUTOBIOGRAPHY OF MALCOLM X

FIGURE 4.2. J. Saunders Redding's syllabus for the American Biographical
Literature course he taught at Howard University and the University of Pennsylvania
in 1976. Jay Saunders Redding Papers, John Hay Library, Brown University.

in the Social Geography of the American South, Henderson H. Donald's
The Negro Freedman, and Aptheker's *Documentary History,* many inspired
by Carter G. Woodson's 1926 *The Mind of the Negro as Reflected in Letters
Written during the Crisis, 1800–1860.*[73] A few years later, Redding would
describe how these "biographical and autobiographical works and materials" mostly gathered by Black scholars had "resulted in a reevaluation of
the American past and of that past's relevance to such qualifying abstrac-

tions as 'the American way,' 'the American dream,' and 'the American national character.'"[74]

Other secondary readings for the American Biographical Literature course directly addressed this clash between abstract accounts of the American national character and American realities.[75] Students read two selections from Michael McGiffert's 1964 collection *The Character of Americans*: David Potter's "The Quest for the National Character" and Ethel M. Albert's "Conflict and Change in American Values." Both deal with the question of how to reconcile American studies' quest for national identity and national character with what Albert terms "the persistence of competing, alternative value systems of the different cultures that make up American society."[76] "To detect what qualities Americans share in their diversity may be far more revealing than to superimpose the stereotype of a fictitious uniformity," ventures Potter.[77] Alongside this, students read two chapters, "The Persistent Vision" and "Toward Racism," from Edmund S. Morgan's *American Slavery, American Freedom*. Published the year before Redding taught the course, Morgan's history became known for the assertion that racism enabled the ideal of American equality: "Racism made it possible for white Virginians to develop a devotion to the equality that English republicans had declared to be the soul of liberty."[78] Redding also assigned the introduction to ethnographer Jules Henry's *Culture Against Man* (1963). A latter day Tocqueville, Henry visited schools, nursing homes, and families with institutionalized children, finding there a portrait of "a culture increasingly feeling the effects of almost 150 years of lopsided preoccupation with amassing wealth and raising its standard of living."[79]

In addition to those readings that counterposed idealism with actuality, the final two secondary readings addressed the interplay between the individual life and the broader culture. Redding assigned the "Culture" chapter of Argentinian philosopher Francisco Romero's *Theory of Man*. Romero argues, "Culture is made by [man]. It is made by the average man in his infinitesimal contributions and by the exceptional man with his outstanding conquests. In this way a whole is composed and organized which, in turn, reverts toward each individual, enriching his development and sustaining him at a certain level by a silent compulsion and a complicated interplay of sanctions, external and internal."[80] (Romero's "infinitesimal contributions" finds an echo in Rosengarten's introduction to *All God's Dangers*: "Real history is simply the record of human adjustments to circumstances."[81]) Last, Redding assigned Stephen Butterfield's *Black Autobiography in America*, published in 1974. Butterfield organizes his study into three sections: "The Slave-Narrative Period (ca. 1831–1895),"

"The Period of Search (ca. 1901–1961)," and "The Period of Rebirth (since 1961)." He argued that the "genre of autobiography lives in the two worlds of history and literature, objective fact and subjective awareness."[82] These autobiographies "fill in many of the blanks of America's self-knowledge. They help us to see what has been left out of the picture of our national life by white writers and critics, how our critical judgment has been limited, indeed, crippled, by a blind spot toward Afro-American culture."[83] "To read closely what they have to say," Butterfield adds, is "to allow their message entry into the bloodstream and vital nerve centers, is to look the monster of slavery and racism full in the face, to confront it nakedly, without the shield of interpretation by white historians."[84]

The handouts that survive from Redding's course give some indication of how he encouraged students to mine literary biographies and autobiographies for descriptions and analyses of everyday social life. Redding asked his students, for example, to carefully read the paragraph in which Du Bois describes the class structure and color line of his hometown of Great Barrington, Massachusetts, from the "manufacturers and merchants, whose prosperity was due in no little degree to the new and high tariff," to the "middle class" of "farmers, merchants, and artisans," to the "small proletariat of Irish and German mill workers" who "lived in slums near the woolen mills and across the river clustering about the Catholic Church," to the small number of "colored people" who were "well-known to the old settlers among the whites." Du Bois explains how these "little social knots of people" in a town with "not much that today would be called social life" resulted in a society in which "the color line was manifest and yet not absolutely drawn."[85] Like Du Bois, Nate Shaw is a keen sociologist, and Rosengarten's *All God's Dangers* recounts in great detail his "dealings with landlords, bankers, fertilizer agents, mule traders, gin operators, sheriffs and judges."[86] ("Nate Shaw's record of his life is the history of the Negro—and white—people in the South for almost a hundred years," Redding later wrote, referencing the sharecropping system at the heart of Shaw's memoir.[87]) Lincoln Steffens, for his part, illuminates white middle-class life in Sacramento in the 1870s. Redding directed students to those passages in Steffens's *Autobiography* that describe how school yard trading of "marbles, tops, knives, and all the other tools and properties of boyhood" really offer Sacramento children a training in business and an induction into the town's bourgeois life: "The tendency of the human animal to think what others think, say what the mob says, do what the leaders do or command, and, generally, go with the crowd, is drilled in deep at school, where the playground has its fashions, laws, customs and tyrannies just as Main Street has."[88]

These books not only offer sociological analysis of the real economic relations that gave rise to cultural values and abstract idealizations. They also show the slow and painful and lonely—and sometimes heroic or sustaining—process whereby the author breaks with common custom by taking notice of those real relations that idealizations obscure. In his handouts for American Biographical Literature, Redding focused his students' attention on such moments when an individual, often a child, finds himself at odds with accepted views. In *Dusk of Dawn*, for example, Redding asked students to pay particular attention to a passage in which Du Bois describes how "it was difficult for me at the time to form any critical estimate of any meaning of the world which differed from the conventional unanimity about me."[89] For Du Bois, in another passage Redding reproduced, this tension came from his sense of being "integrally a part of [European civilization] and yet much more significant, one of its rejected parts"; through his experience "in the folds" of this world, Du Bois found himself "imprisoned, conditioned, depressed, exalted and inspired."[90]

In *The Autobiography of Lincoln Steffens*, Redding directed students to chapter 6, "A Painter and a Page." It recounts the months during which the son of a painter comes to live in the Steffens household while serving as a page for the state legislature. He gives Lincoln an insider's view of the ways that House speakers and legislative deals are made ahead of time, and often by the heads of railroad companies. The young page describes this as "good politics," but Lincoln sees the corruption that this euphemism hides:

> I saw that the Legislature wasn't what my father, my teachers, and the grown-ups thought; it wasn't even what my histories and the other books said. There was some mystery about it as there was about art, as there was about everything. Nothing was what it was supposed to be. And Charlie took it as it was; my father took it as it seemed to be; I couldn't take it at all. What troubled me most, however, was that they none of them had any strong feelings about the conflict of the two pictures I had. . . . There was something wrong somewhere, and I could not get it right. And nobody would help me.[91]

Such passages show the particular historical circumstances under which particular individuals arrive at a crisis or crossroads, in which they experience the disconnect between lived reality and American mythmaking. These moments capture on an intimate level what the course as a whole attempted to do within American studies: to juxtapose the individual stories of Americans across nearly a century with the universalizing accounts of American national character and American destiny.

Redding's American Biographical Literature course ended with Alex Haley's *Autobiography of Malcolm X*. Like other courses that Redding taught in the 1960s and '70s, the syllabus emphasized the older roots of the ongoing projects of revolutionary potential and critical self-awareness. Redding frequently encouraged students to draw longer historical connections between contemporary political and aesthetic movements and older cultural formations. "Make a critical comparison of the themes of black writing in the 1920's (Mckay [*sic*], Fisher, Cullen, Hughes, etc.) and black writing today (Baldwin, Jones, Rivers, Reed, etc.)," read question 7 on the Negro in American Literature final exam that Redding used frequently.[92] For Am Civ 175: The Mind of the Negro, which Redding taught at GWU in the summer of 1969, the exam prompts students to "Trace the ideological sources of the current Black Revolution at least as far back as 1900. Be specific. Name names. Cite works."[93] The historical and documentary and biographical and autobiographical sources that served as the foundation and inspiration for Redding's American Biographical Literature course helped to make this case for the long road of revolution. As the front page of the *New York Times Book Review* testified of *All God's Dangers* the year before, "This book demonstrates that The Movement— the freedom movement, the civil rights movement, the black power movement—did not suddenly begin in the 1960's. It was not the primary creation of Northern blacks and Northern white liberals, but was there in the South all along, in men and women like Nate Shaw who were prepared to go along and get along only until they found that moment, that issue and time and circumstance, when it was important to put their lives on the line for something more than survival: freedom. And, if they had to die, they would take some whites with them."[94] For Redding, only by looking closely at the stories of particular people in a specific past—sharecropper Nate Shaw, alcoholic Philadelphia teacher Rosalie Hatton, Boston labor lawyer Richard Henry Dana Jr., border-state enslaved people owned by Manie Morgan in *Old Missouri*, soldiers in the 54th (Negro) Massachusetts Regiment, William Wells Brown and even the fictional Clotel— could we build a basis for solidarity and political organizing that was sounder and more durable than myths of national unity and belonging.

Like the many other literary historical courses that Redding taught over the course of his five-decade career, American Biographical Literature assembled a reading list that didn't accede to the color line. It presented the long history of American literature as one of struggle, revolution, and retrenchment as well as of depression, adjustment, and "infinitesimal contributions."[95] Moving flexibly between documents and literary works, Redding helped students to recognize conventional figures or stock characters where others saw realism, to discern the real social relations that writing transmutes into abstract ideals. He taught them to see a record of true events—a history from below—where others saw mere "biography and social chronicle."[96] Redding's approach to literary study—his classroom materials even more than his published work—valued literature for its proximity to history rather than its distance from it. Redding's courses reconstituted an American tradition by foregrounding conflict rather than burying it under national myth. His vision of writing by Black and white Americans alike as a "literature of necessity" was made in the classrooms of the historically Black colleges in which he taught. It is only by moving from abstractions like "the university" to the real histories of all kinds of institutions, then and now, that we can carry on the literary traditions and national canons that Redding and his students remade in their classrooms.

Cleanth Brooks, Modern Poetry (1963), and Edmund Wilson, Literature of the Civil War (1959)

> To the members of English 300-K
> (Summer Session of 1942, University of Michigan)
> who discussed the problems with me
> and helped me work out some of the analyses
> —dedication to Cleanth Brooks's *The Well Wrought Urn*

> To the Students of English 354
> University of Chicago, Summer, 1939
> —dedication to Edmund Wilson's "Dickens: The Two Scrooges"

Despite the very different genealogy of literary study that we see when we put the methods and career of a scholar like Redding at its center, the New Critical classroom still looms large in both official disciplinary histories and in the casual stories we tell about the past and present of our profession. It is an imaginary, and a powerful one. Simply invoke the history of literary study, and a familiar 35-mm film reel unspools a short featuring the charismatic pedagogue in a mahogany-furnished classroom on a beautiful campus leading rows of GI Bill students through a close reading of a sonnet by John Donne. Cleared of the obfuscating apparatus of scholarly specialization, this vision implies, the New Critic's attention to "the poem itself" conveys the value of literature through a formalist teaching practice at once distinctly literary and deeply democratic. The New Critical classroom becomes the site of a temporary and blissful union of generalist appeal and professional specialization, one that allowed Cleanth Brooks to paste stamps on his classroom close readings and mail them to the *Sewanee Review*.[1] This, as some say with nostalgia as they debate problems of method today, was a time before a split between teaching and research left literary studies without a way to defend ourselves or justify our existence.

The dominance of this powerful imaginary—viewed either as a lost Eden or a primal scene—has discouraged research into New Criticism's history and practices. How did the New Critics actually teach? What was the relationship between formalist close reading and the classroom hour? How did those teachers and students actually use an anthology and textbook like Brooks and Robert Penn Warren's *Understanding Poetry*? What was the relationship between the composite student Brooks describes in the introduction to *The Well Wrought Urn* as able to sense the greatness of Wordsworth's Westminster Bridge sonnet but unable to talk about it, and the actual students in Brooks's 1942 summer session of English 300K at the University of Michigan, whom he thanks in the dedication to that volume for helping him to "work out some of the analyses"? What is the difference between the mythic classroom of New Criticism and the actual classrooms of New Critics?

Our previous chapters restore the missing history of actual teaching practices long concealed by our collective sense of New Criticism as foundational to all teaching in literary study. In our history, historicisms and formalisms are not turned against one another, but are instead difficult to separate. In this history, scholarly tools like indexes or manuscript editions or bibliographies form the foundation of experimental and collaborative projects on discerning literary form like Spurgeon's *Shakespeare's Imagery* or Rickert's *New Methods*. It is a history in which the radical historicisms of World War I–era extension tutorials for working-class adults or Hampton Institute seminars on American literature bring forth new theories and practices of literary value. And it is a history in which teaching and research, often described as alienated from one another in all contexts *except* a midcentury New Critical moment, rely upon one another so fully that, as we have shown, some of the twentieth century's major works of literary scholarship—*Shakespeare's Imagery, The Sacred Wood, Practical Criticism*—were shaped by the teaching of specific classes and particular groups of students. It is a history, in other words, that finds that the methods of formalism and historicism and the spaces of the classroom and the office were always utterly entangled, just as they are now.

This chapter thus pursues this entanglement into two midcentury classrooms. It aims to generate a cross-sectional view of midcentury pedagogy, to view a slice of this moment suspended in time in order to witness the modes of pedagogy that flourish there. We turn for our examples to the midcentury classrooms of Cleanth Brooks and Edmund Wilson, since they are two teachers who seem to embody the divisions of the discipline itself. We know Brooks as a formalist, of course, and Wilson as an historicist; Brooks as a critic with a special relationship to the discipline of English, Wilson as a critic with a special relationship to journalism and common readers. Although the figure of the classroom, as we have shown, often secures such oppositions, the materials of Brooks's and Wilson's own classrooms—their syllabuses, course descriptions, lecture transcripts and notes, handouts, graded papers, and scholarly publications—call into question our habitual distinctions between literary critics and common readers, formalist teaching and historicist research.[2]

Readers might imagine that they already know what Brooks's classroom looked like, since the imaginary New Critical classroom is often specifically imagined as Brooks's classroom. In this classroom are rows of desks filled with postwar students, a mimeographed poem on a single page, and an approachable teacher intent upon clearing away all of the "specialized rubbish . . . standing between the reader of a poem and the poem."[3] Even Brooks himself, in his published writing, figured the classroom as a place at once professional and open to a public, a place that reconciled opposing tensions, a place in which aesthetic experience could be experienced as both rarefied and accessible. Yet in Brooks's actual classroom, this resolution of tensions and balancing of opposing forces comes to seem a more fragile and uncertain thing. Alongside moments in Brooks's teaching when his close readings neatly capture the distinctiveness and value of the literary appear a range of other lower-key, less theorized practices of discernment and evaluation. We examine the uneven methods of Brooks's seminar not to debunk New Critical formalism itself, but to explore how this strong theory of literature was made. At the same time, studying Brooks's classrooms shows us how this strong New Critical theory of literary reading and literary value veils the many other kinds of attention, reading, historical imagination, and textuality that were at work in that same space.

One of Brooks's main contentions in his published work was that formalist pedagogy would provide an account of literary value that historicist scholars had failed to develop. However, when we turn to Edmund Wilson's classroom materials, we see how Wilson's historicist research provides its own aesthetic and mode of value, one that links texts to life experience rather than sanctifying them within a rarefied canon, one that sees literary value accrue to texts as they are read and interpreted over time by varying readerships. Where Brooks operates from a center of literariness and canonicity that he himself builds, Wilson is most interested in the moments in which unliterary texts become literary (or vice versa), and in the moments in which research takes its life from pedagogy as much as from publication. With its understanding of research as an investment of time and energy that conveys value upon its objects of study, Wilson's classroom realizes Brooks's ambitions for pedagogy. In Wilson's classrooms at Smith, Chicago, and Harvard, professional practices connect with public ones, and research methods are capable of generating evaluative judgments.

Cleanth Brooks's English 71: Modern Poetry

In his published writing, Brooks figures the classroom, like literature itself, as compellingly paradoxical. "The Language of Paradox," the first chapter of *The Well Wrought Urn*, is peopled by students who have "the greatest difficulty in accounting for" the "goodness" of poems; scholars for whom poems are significant only in terms of "'facts,' biological, sociological, and economic"; and the Brooks narrator, who performs a close reading of Donne's "The Canonization." Brooks's reading introduces a distinction between richly connotative poetic language and the denotative language of "the scientist . . . purged of every trace of paradox." Brooks suggests that the historicist scholars who research poems rather than really reading them mistake themselves for scientists—blind to the metaphor of Donne's phoenix, they instead "test" its ashes "for their chemical content."[4] These scholars read all poems referentially, failing to understand them as literature. And because they fail to recognize the literariness of poetic language, they cannot help their students develop a good account what the students already sense intuitively on their own: the value or "goodness" of good poems.[5]

Meanwhile, the wider world's growing reverence for facts (of which the quasi-scientific scholars of literature are, to Brooks, a symptom) means that students—and the publics they stand in for—need poetry all the more. Poetry alone, for Brooks, can restore to the world all that rationalism has drained from it. In *The Well Wrought Urn*, poetry's value increases as it becomes more marginal within modern society; in a sense, poetry's confinement to the classroom actually confirms its value. Like the "pretty rooms" that Donne's speaker and his lover build in "The Canonization" to escape the world, only to discover they have "gained the world in each other, now a more intense, more meaningful world," the classroom protects poetry's rarefied value. In doing so, it becomes worldly: "the unworldly . . . become the most 'worldly' of all" (as Brooks says of Donne's lovers).[6] In Brooks's published work, the classroom, like the best poetry, takes the form of paradox.

What pedagogy could hope to match the vision of the classroom found in the pages of *The Well Wrought Urn*?[7] Brooks's archive, housed at the Beinecke Rare Book and Manuscript Library at Yale University, includes reserve lists, syllabuses, and gradebooks from courses Brooks offered at Yale from 1947 to 1975, including English 71: Modern Poetry; English 150, on Wordsworth and Coleridge; and English 160: Twentieth-Century Literature.[8] At the heart of the "Classroom Materials" section of the Brooks collection is a set of transcripts of Brooks's lectures from English 71. Brooks offered Modern Poetry as a yearlong course in the fall of 1963 and spring of 1964; his lectures were recorded and then transcribed in preparation for publication with Bantam Books.[9] The transcripts seem almost verbatim and include student questions and responses, allowing us the rare opportunity to glimpse some of the actual give-and-take of classroom discussion.

English 71 covered poems by Thomas Hardy, A. E. Housman, Gerard Manley Hopkins, William Butler Yeats, Amy Lowell, H.D., John Fletcher, D. H. Lawrence, Edgar Lee Masters, Carl Sandburg, Vachel Lindsay, Edwin Arlington Robinson, Robert Frost, John Masefield, Rupert Brooke, Ezra Pound, T. S. Eliot, and Wallace Stevens in the first term, and poems by E. E. Cummings, Archibald MacLeish, Marianne Moore, Elizabeth Bishop, Hart Crane, Robinson Jeffers, John Crowe Ransom, Louise Bogan, Léonie Adams, and Robert Graves in the second. Both terms featured selections from Robert Stallman's critical anthology *Critiques and Essays in Criticism, 1920–1948*, including essays by T. E. Hulme, Edgell Rickword, Stephen Spender, T. S. Eliot, Robert Penn Warren, René Wellek, and W. K. Wimsatt and Monroe Beardsley. The Yale Course Critique for 1963 (written for students by students) reports that Brooks's English 71 lectures are "centered around individual poems," and that a final exam tests students' understanding of the critical essays and ability to use them "in a close analytical consideration of particular poems."[10] In addition, course reserve lists suggested more than forty volumes of secondary material, including critical studies such as Elizabeth Drew's *T. S. Eliot: The Design of His Poetry*, biographies, and collected letters.

Each class focused on several poems or selections from longer poems written by a single author. Yet the records of the class reveal almost no examples of a close reading in the style of Brooks's reading of "The Canonization" familiar from *The Well Wrought Urn*. Instead, the elements that are so tightly braided in Brooks's exemplary published readings appear in his classroom as individual strands: the parsing of the "plain sense" of a poem; the determination of how its techniques give meaning; the evaluation of the poem; the broader account of poetry's increasingly marginal role in modernity and its inversely proportional value. To read the cism, rather than into the creative effort.

The course, which meets for two hours once a week, opens with a series of discussions on certain aspects of the novel, notably those of Form and Time. Mr. Warren generally reads from his notes, but is always glad to answer questions. Since the class is composed of only 15 students (not counting the frequent auditors) discussion of technical points is possible and encouraged.

After these beginning theory lectures, the class is asked to read several novels as concrete applications of the theories. In 1962–63, the class read Hemingway's Farewell to Arms; Conrad's Lord Jim, Heart of Darkness, and Nostromo; and Faulkner's Sound and Fury. Mr. Warren had originally planned to include Dreiser and Zola, too, but because of a slightly disorganized presentation, was only able to cover his first three authors.

When dealing with specific books, Mr. Warren covers them in strict detail, pointing out themes and techniques on almost every page. One two-hour period last year was, in fact, spent on the first 13 pages of A Farewell to Arms. Digressions are frequent and comparisons to other works are continually made. It is slightly disappointing that Mr. Warren avoids talking about his own work, but he explains this by saying that he does not feel qualified to comment on himself.

The entire grade for the term is based on a long (over 5,000 words) critical paper on a novel or group of novels of the student's choice. Because this paper is not due until the last class before exams, it is often not begun until Christmas vacation. An early start is recommended however, since it gives the student additional excuses to have private conferences with Mr. Warren.

The private conferences are undoubtedly the best part of the course, giving the student an intense exposure to one of America's finest creative and critical minds. The student, when discussing his ideas for the paper, almost immediately gets a feeling of ignorance when confronted with Mr. Warren's knowledge on the subject (no matter what the subject may be).

The paper requires a good deal of research and thought, but grades in the upper 80's are frequently given. Additional work in the course is almost optional, though it is usually done in order that the student might get the full advantage of Robert Penn Warren's genius.

English 71

Contemporary Poetic Theory and Practice.
Mr. Brooks.

The informal approach of Cleanth Brooks is perhaps the most unique feature of English 71. Although Mr. Brooks usually lectures for most of the period, questions from the (small) class are welcome and frequently forthcoming. "Digressions" often ensue which many times form the most interesting and valuable part of the class period. Few students take notes.

The lectures themselves are centered around individual poems. Aesthetic analysis in the manner of the New Critics is stressed while the historical, sociological, and psychological aspects are necessarily deemphasized.

Yeats, Frost, Eliot, and Stevens are studied during the fall term. Six or seven poems are assigned each class period and students are expected to know them thoroughly for class discussion. At the conclusion of the period on each of these poets, a 6-12 page paper on an aspect of the poet's work is required. These papers are generally considered to be the most valuable part of the course since they teach the student to apply independently the analytical methods of Mr. Brooks.

A number of less well-known poets are considered in the spring term including Crane, Ransom, Lowell, and Auden. Six or seven less extensive papers are assigned this term.

Selected critical essays of Hulme, Spender, Eliot, Warren, and Rickword are also read throughout the year to supplement the textual analysis of individual poems dealt with in class. The final exams are usually structured by these essays; students must show that they can apply the theories of these essays in a close analytical consideration of particular poems.

A great deal of personal interest and initiative are necessary for the student to gain from the informal approach since Mr. Brooks emphatically does not "spoon-feed" his students with factual information about the modern poets. Those who can work within the informal rationale, however, will probably find English 71 one of their most valuable courses.

English 77

Daily Themes. Mr. Nangle, Mr. Cain, Mr. Crump, Mr. Gordon.

Puns are inescapable, and such has been the fate of Daily Themes that it has become synonomous with "delirium tremens." Too bad. For while English 77a does keep a student on the go, the work is very much worth the considerable time and trouble it takes --and only the weak will come out of it gibbering.

The very thought of writing a paper a day for a whole term sets many to shuddering. But the facts are that: 1) writing the papers is actually fun for a while; 2) "daily" themes are discontinued for the last five or six weeks, and replaced by short story assignments.

The main purpose of the course is to impose a certain amount of discipline upon the writer which will help him keep writing skills under control. In order to accomplish this, the graders--four in number--make it quite clear that they are interested in a very limited type of fictional expression. Each theme is supposed to deal with a small incident, revealed in dialogue or astute symbolic description which illuminates character, or a change of character. One respondent echoes a common complaint, however: "It can get very tiresome writing little scenes in dormitories or little scenes with dates or little scenes with parents, and the writer can easily become fed up with illuminating character, day in and day out. Finally you're apt to get to the point where you end every illumination with a tag-line like 'He closed the door, finally, decisively.' " The short stories, needless to say, come as a relief.

The student, on the other hand, generally finds that the imposition of such rigid discipline has been helpful, that it has aided him in reining his talent, or lack of it, that in fact the course has fulfilled its purpose admirably.

As for the weekly conferences, they

FIGURE 5.1. Yale Course Critique catalog from 1963, written by students for students, describing Cleanth Brooks's English 71: Contemporary Poetic Theory and Practice. Cleanth Brooks Papers, Yale Collection of American Literature, Beinecke Rare Book and Manuscript Library, Yale University.

archival materials is to understand that pulling all of this together in a single close reading while remaining within "the hour" (as Brooks often mentions) would be quite an achievement. In practice, Brooks spent most classes focusing on smaller parts of poems and appreciating the author's technique, as he does when teaching Hart Crane's *The Bridge*:

> I think maybe the most useful thing that I can do, however, at this moment is to look at some particular passages with you, talk about them, the texture of them, the quality of them, and postpone a bit the matter of the total meaning of the poem and the way in which the parts are held together. As has just been remarked [by a student], the "Proem to Brooklyn Bridge" is really quite magnificent, and many of the figures that are used there come out quite splendidly.[11]

Throughout Brooks's lectures, we found this tension between a formalist reading that would account for the poem's "total meaning" through "the way in which the parts are held together" and a more local and evaluative "talk" about the "texture" and "quality" of particular passages that appreciates their splendor. On the one hand, English 71 occupied itself with deciding, with the aid of essays from the Stallman anthology, whether the poems studied were in fact poetry or whether they were simply prose. This formalist and binary practice of separating the literary from the non-literary was tempered, on the other hand, by a more evaluative approach that placed poems on a spectrum of aesthetic texture and value and even evaluated some parts of poems against other parts of them.

As Brooks's comment about how to approach *The Bridge* suggests, his classes were occupied with the "useful" work of getting a feel for particular poems and parts of poems. Brooks usually began by asking for a summation of the poem's dramatic context. He opens discussion on MacLeish's "Memorial Rain," for example, by asking: "What is the poem Memorial Rain about? What is the dramatic occasion? What is the city? Who's doing the listening? Who's doing the speaking?"[12] Next, Brooks would often read parts of poems line by line, making comments after each reading that either clarified vocabulary or drew attention to different elements of poetic technique, such as metaphor. The "nap" in Marianne Moore's "The Jerboa" refers to "The nap of the fur," he noted;[13] reading Crane's "The Air Plant," he asked, "Why is the airplant called a bird, or almost a bird?"[14] Tracking imagery and mood in MacLeish's "You, Andrew Marvell," Brooks noted that "we get this spacial image of the shadow of night creeping on toward the west. . . . This does much to build in a sense of the solemnity and magnificence but also sombre grandeur, the way in which empires go down under the impact of time." Parsing grammatical structure in "You, Andrew Marvell," he asked the class, "How many 'ands' words occur in [the poem]? Anyone count them?"[15] Investigating the diction of the phrase "frightening gills" from Elizabeth Bishop's "The Fish," "Why frightening?" Brooks asks about the phrase, answering: "I suppose because they seem so vulnerable that one can practically see the blood stream running there at the surface."[16]

As Brooks notes the poems' plain sense and techniques, he also uses appreciative language. Particular techniques or images are "apt" or "brilliant," and individual poems are "admirable" or "magnificent" or "skillful." Brooks's close readings typically end with an evaluative summation. MacLeish's "You, Andrew Marvell" has "a great deal of depth of meaning."[17] In Crane's "The Air Plant," "the imagination is working right straight through. The images are not dead decoration. They demand some kind of leap—answering leap—on the part of the reader."[18] At times, poems are even valued for their statement rather than their technique. MacLeish's "Frescoes for Mr. Rockefeller's City" "is a very brilliant poem. It's a poem which I think actually in its political position is rather sane and fairly balanced."[19] Brooks's evaluative statements seem to hover between an appreciation of the differences between these poems—differences that Brooks's students experience in the close attention afforded to each—and a universal standard of goodness.

At certain points, we can see the moment when close attention to a poem's particular textures and strengths is transformed into a judgment about its status as poetry or prose. Brooks wraps up a close reading of Marianne Moore's "England" with just such a reckoning:

> This is a rather tart defense of one's homeland. The speaker is a little tired of people who throw off on America as being uncultured and incoherent and so on. On the other hand, though she's defending her country, she does it with a sense of humor, and she does it with some sense that she knows the rest of the world and can appreciate the rest of the world. The trouble is is it a poem? Well some of you will say, I suppose, that it is not a poem. It's a piece of prose, rather distinguished prose, but prose.[20]

In such moments of decision, Brooks and his students draw upon Brooks's own theory of aesthetic formalism, supported and developed by the modernist and New Critical essays that Brooks assigned. In response to Brooks's assessment of Moore's "England," a student asks, "Earlier in the year you made remarks about the difference in poetry and a poem.

```
3  Lecture #-1  Mr. Brooks

        as if the night were a kind of black stuff/which had entangled the
    twigs/and the moon rising lifts one strand, one filament after
    another of darkness from them, releasing the twigs, letting them
    show themselves clearer in the moonlight.  It's a very delicate-
    ly built poem, and I think very successful in pointing toward
    one conception of poetry and a conception of poetry very dear to
    Macleish in spite of his committment to the public thing.  Let's
    ask one or two other matters about the poem.

        I notice on page 454 the statement is made - a poem should
    be equal to, not true.  Would anyone like to comment on this doc-
    trine?  Develop it a bit?  The poem should be equal to, not true.
    All right, Mrs.____

    Student:  This is a statement against rhetoric, against saying
    something you might say.

    Brooks:  Yes, it is a statement against rhetoric, at least against
    any kind of embellishment and ornamentation, and that sort of
    thing.  What would you say?

    Student:  I'd say it was kind of against a didactic of type of
    poetry.

    Brooks:  Yes, it's certainly against the didactic.  The poem must-
    n't be preachy, must not sermonize, it must work through implication.  Have
    you run into any parallel statement in our study last time?

    Student:  Well, the                            stated that a poet
    must not simply state his beliefs, he must prove them by a ----.

    Brooks:  Yes, we had Stephen Spender as saying something fairly
    close to this, and we had Mr. Warren in his essay Pure and Impure
    Poetry saying something very close to this - that a poet doesn't
    simply say something or make a statement, he tries to prove his
    statement, tries to prove in his own way; and even more specifically
    I think, didn't we read an essay by T.S. Eliot - no, we have not,
    I beg your pardon- we shall be a little later this semester reading
    a famous essay which some of you know, Hamlet and His Problems which
```

FIGURE 5.2. Transcription of Cleanth Brooks's lecture and student comments and questions on Archibald MacLeish for English 71: Contemporary Poetic Theory and Practice at Yale University (1962). Cleanth Brooks Papers, Yale Collection of American Literature, Beinecke Rare Book and Manuscript Library, Yale University.

Sometime would you come back to that again? I know that a poem goes beyond poetry." Brooks replies:

I would say that poetry as I used it then is the stuff of which poems are made. Precision, accuracy, a world rich in [sic] crisp—a world of the senses that's vivid, a world of exactness, a world of rhythm caught—all the sorts of things which we associate with the gift of the imagination and the arts of language. A poem, however, it seems to me, is more than just this sort of material thrown together in a sack or basket. It's articulated, it has its own form and arrangement.[21]

Several classes before, Brooks elaborated this theory of a poem's "form and arrangement" in relation to MacLeish's "Ars Poetica," which contains the lines "A poem should not mean / but be." As Brooks explains, MacLeish finds his "analogies for poetry not in the usual terms of discourse but in terms of, oh, arts like painting, sculpture." Brooks elaborates: "Poems shouldn't be talky, they shouldn't be wordy. They should have a form which is so tight and condensed that one feels that instead of speaking out, the poem is speaking through the form." Brooks, noting that students should already be "familiar with that [idea] with some of the other poets and critics we've been talking about," mentions an essay by Stephen Spender, Robert Penn Warren's "Pure and Impure Poetry," and Eliot's "Hamlet and His Problems" as well as Alexander Pope's idea that "a poem should do or be in itself what it is talking about."[22]

Poems that fail to transcend the level of "prose" are just as important to the development of English 71's theoretical apparatus. Thus Moore's "Poetry" is of interest despite its failures: "Again, for those of you who say, 'I don't think this is a poem,' still, I think as a document it will be interesting and even exciting."[23] Such interesting failures provide further occasions to delineate the difference between a poem's "form and arrangement" and prose's mundane qualities: Moore's poem is "talky" and "wordy"; it makes statements and uses denotative language. (Indeed, Moore's "Poetry" itself raises the question of this distinction by pulling a quotation from Tolstoy's diary: "nor is it valid / to discriminate against 'business documents and / school-books': all these phenomena are important. One must / make a distinction / however."[24]) Yet Moore's poems fail, for Brooks, because they are excessively referential, containing footnotes citing the sources from which Moore draws quotations. Brooks downplays the importance of such citations: "I suppose it is a kind of amiable pedantry that makes Miss Moore put the quotes around them. Doesn't really matter. You don't have to know the reference."[25] Poems like Moore's seem to invite readers to imagine that their words, phrases, images, and quotations connect to real events—her footnotes evoke the moment when "in her reading in her Brooklyn apartment she picked that up, noted it down, stuck it away in a poem."[26] For Brooks, such references snake outward, endangering the poem's self-enclosed structure; their materiality threatens its universality, much as material source scholarship drains the profession of its account of literature's distinctiveness and its value.

Brooks works to make his classroom as self-contained as good poems should be, and guards against a referentiality that would connect his classroom to the world in non-figural ways. When references to historical events arise in poems in English 71, Brooks resolves them into symbolic situations. For instance, discussing "Memorial Rain," Brooks mentions that the poem is about MacLeish mourning his brother who died in World War I, only to deem this "personal point" irrelevant to the understanding of a poem that could be about any American.[27] Brooks treats the recounting of background or the tracing of allusions as preliminary work that precedes the real work of close reading. Arriving at the Edgar Allan Poe reference in Crane's "The Bridge," Brooks pauses: "Now, obviously, we've got a reference here, and let's see what the reference is, and then maybe we can make some effort to see what the poem is saying. What is the reference? Anybody know it?"[28] A discussion of MacLeish's "Frescoes" begins with a quick explanation of the poem's occasion—but Brooks treats the political import of the context very briefly and misidentifies Diego Rivera before moving on to discuss the way MacLeish handles the "concrete particulars" of the poem.[29]

When the world does enter into the classroom of English 71, it is an already figured world, given shape and meaning by themes and tensions. Brooks's lecture on MacLeish notes that MacLeish exhibits a "whole tendency apparently toward a highly individual and lyrical and private poetry. And yet this is a man whose career has been that of a public man, state department, Fortune magazine, Librarian of Congress, a man terribly interested in politics, very much interested in public affairs." MacLeish's poetry accordingly carries "this anxiety one almost feels inclined to say on the part of Macleish [sic], that poetry not become simply something very private and remote from the concerns of the state." Brooks puts it to his students to decide whether MacLeish "really ever reconciled" these "twin tugs."[30]

While MacLeish's paradoxical position, at once worldly and marginal, recalls the position of modern poetry itself (and the classroom as figured in *The Well Wrought Urn*), other poets seem simply marginal. Brooks introduces Moore, for instance, through her connections to literary coteries and institutions of print. He mentions to his students that she was involved with all of the "little movements and little special magazines," that she taught at the Carlisle Indian School in Pennsylvania, that she now lives in Brooklyn and had been recently awarded the Bollingen Prize, and that she was "a librarian for a while."[31] While Brooks presents MacLeish's life as ahistorical and synchronic, offering at all times an image of poetry's own paradoxical position, Moore's life is a narrative. She changes, develops, and moves. Even the references in her poems, as Brooks's classroom expounds them, link the poems to particular moments along this temporal sequence.

Brooks's story of Moore's life points to a shadowy, alternate version of the classroom that does nevertheless exist for English 71. Less figural and more literal, it is a place where teaching and learning happen in time; this classroom is the setting, "for a while," of a few scenes that are part of an unfolding life. Brooks invokes this more temporal and historically located sense of the classroom at many moments in English 71: when he wishes to "stimulate, provoke" his students into "doing some more reading of MacLeish, thinking about him and finding out for yourself" if he reconciled his "divergent interests," or when Brooks mentions a contemporary culture of letters that holds Elizabeth Bishop's work in "high esteem," even if Brooks himself does not.[32] All of these moments acknowledge literary value as a changing thing. They point to how students' sense of literary value will change over the course of their education and life, and how the culture of letters' consensus about what is valuable changes too, as new members—perhaps even some of Brooks's students—join it.

Brooks's judgment that Moore's failed poem is nevertheless "interesting" captures this more temporal and historical sense of literary value, one that is multiple where Brooks's strong theory is binary. In her analysis of how "interesting" functions as an aesthetic judgment, Sianne Ngai explains exactly this "link between the interesting and ongoingness." As Ngai points out, to declare an object "interesting" is to mark it—like "sticking a Post-It in a book"—in anticipation of returning to it later. In this sense, the aesthetic of the interesting "registers the simple fact (one strangely overlooked by much aesthetic philosophy) that time makes a difference in aesthetic evaluation."[33] Brooks's judgment that Moore's "Poetry" is "interesting" as a "document" seems likewise to point to a more contingent and temporal sense of literary value that exists alongside English 71's strong, theoretical elevation of formal poetry over "talky" prose. Although Brooks's strong theory of literariness cannot account for the way he himself values Moore's poem, his classroom practices nevertheless remain open to the way value accrues to texts by virtue of the attention that we pay to them in the temporality of our experience. This mode of value, like Moore's referential footnotes, extends outward. It links to the ongoing nature of scholarly research, to experiences of aesthetic value that are low-key and long-lasting rather than instantaneous or transcendent, and to a sense of the multiple publics that inhabit the classroom but are not contained by it. Turning to Edmund Wilson's classrooms, we will see how Wilson's historicist method centers around the temporally bound forms of value that we only glimpse in Brooks's classroom.

Edmund Wilson at Smith, Chicago, and Harvard

Brooks's opposition between the self-contained poem and the referential "document" reappears in Wilson's teaching and research as a narrative in medias res. For Wilson, the poem (or, more often, the novel) is always on the verge of taking on the worldly functions of the document, while a document in the correct company holds within it the literary potential of the poem. As Robert Martin Adams noticed in a 1948 review of Wilson's *The Triple Thinkers*:

> *The Triple Thinkers* included observations that the functions of verse were being merged into those of prose,[34] and that literature itself might in time be absorbed into the machinery of social planning.[35] The tendency to think, and in fact to hope, that literature was about to become something else, was common to much of Edmund Wilson's early writing. . . .[36]

Adams, sympathetic to Wilson's search for eddies of literary meaning within "the currents of history," nevertheless means this observation as a criticism. For him, Wilson's utopian fantasy of an order in which literature takes on referential functions is a dodge calculated to "delay or avoid the problem of literary value."[37] Later critics also noticed "something peculiar about Mr. Wilson's taste in fiction. . . . [H]e seems to want it to cease to be art and to turn into document, or at least assume the style of document."[38]

These critics were correct to notice Wilson's attraction to the line between the literary work and the historical document. Yet Wilson's interest in the moment when literature becomes a document, or vice versa, was not a delay tactic or a peculiarity of taste: it was a method. Wilson does not, despite some critics' complaints, avoid the problem of literary value. Rather, he studies and stages the moment when value shifts—the moment when literature becomes referential and touches or transforms the world, the moment when a document becomes literature, and our orientation toward it shifts as a new, provisional canon forms.[39] In a sense, Adams and others are correct that Wilson failed to theorize this method in print, most famously in "The Historical Interpretation of Literature"

(1940). But his historicist interest in how value shifts finds its true home, we argue, in Wilson's temporal, worldly classrooms rather than his printed texts.[40] If we have failed to see and understand the fullest expression of Wilson's method, it is because we have failed to view his classroom as a site of the development and theorizing of method.

Wilson's interest in literature's tendency to "become something else" comes alive in the changing atmosphere of the teaching hour and the summer session. The duration of a single course allows Wilson to track the ways that literary value shifts not only over the course of history, but also through the changes of a reader's serial engagements with a single text. Some of Wilson's courses themselves enact a transformation of the unliterary into the literary, as when he revalues the work of Dickens in a course at the University of Chicago during the summer of 1939, or when he teaches diaries, speeches, memoirs, and journalism in his Literature of the Civil War course at Harvard in 1959–60. Other courses—such as a class on James Joyce at Smith College in 1942 or the Use of Language in Literature at Harvard in 1958—explore the ways that literary texts like *Finnegans Wake* reference the world and thus become, for a moment, documentary.

Wilson pursued the connection between literariness and referentiality through his classrooms in his assignment of theoretical texts and his in-class close-reading exercises. The single theoretical text Wilson assigned to his class on Joyce was Robert Louis Stevenson's "On Style in Literature: Its Technical Elements" (1885). A primer focused on the sounds of consonants and vowels in poetry and prose,[41] Stevenson's essay frames his close-reading protocols by explaining that literature stands apart from the other arts, and much closer to the world, because "the material in which the literary artist works is the dialect of life." The basic elements of literature are "words, the acknowledged currency of our daily affairs," Stevenson notes, and so literature has both "a strange freshness and immediacy of address to the public mind," but is also by this same token limited because, unlike the "plastic and ductile material" available to painters and sculptors, the writer "is condemned to work in mosaic with finite and quite rigid words."[42] Analyzing the sound patterns and structure in the poems of Coleridge and Shakespeare alongside the prose of Milton and Macaulay (in which he triumphs to find in one paragraph "a moment of FV in all this world of K's!"[43]), Stevenson's close reading traverses the literary and the everyday while assiduously avoiding any tight ties between sound and sense. The very nature of language therefore prepares the way for the possibility of the value transfer between poem and document at the core of Wilson's method.

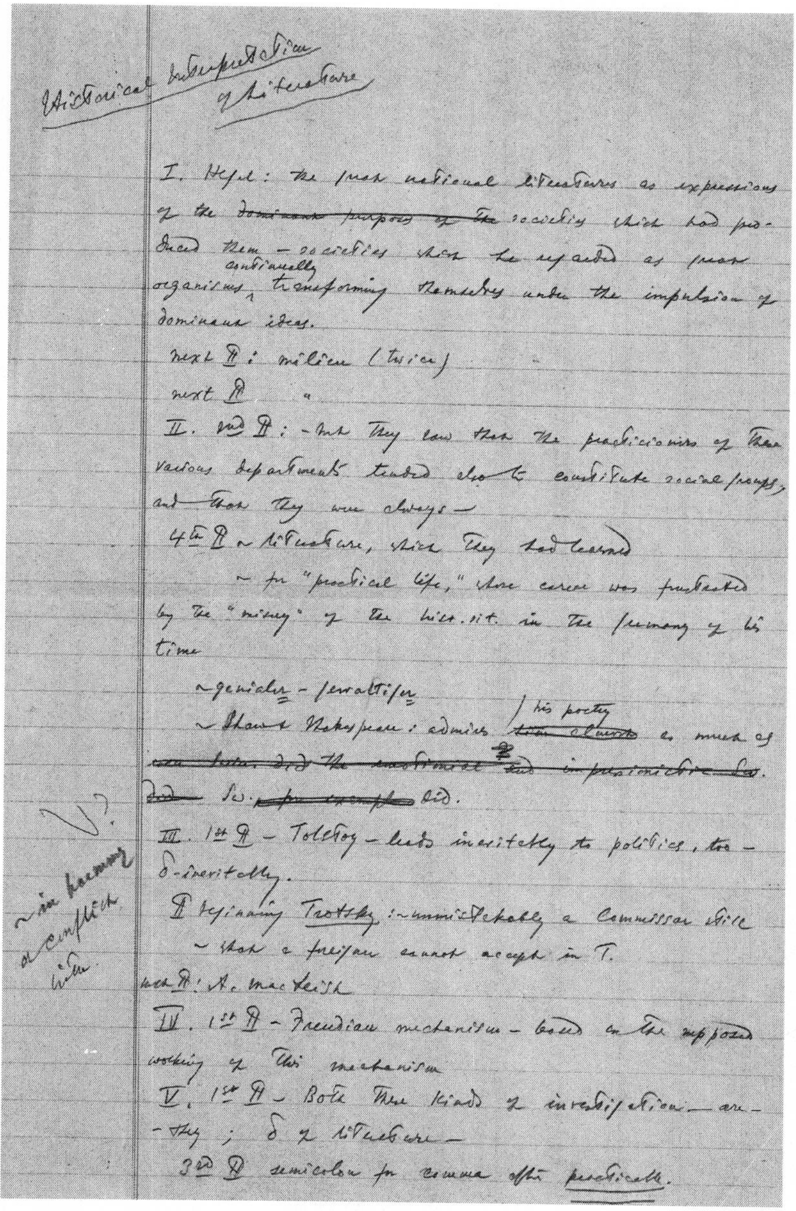

FIGURE 5.3. Notes toward a draft of Edmund Wilson's "Historical Interpretation of Literature" essay made on the back of his class notes for Varieties of Nineteenth Century Criticism at the University of Chicago in 1939. Edmund Wilson Papers, Yale Collection of American Literature, Beinecke Rare Book and Manuscript Library, Yale University.

In another class, Wilson's mimeographed handouts drew students' attention to the worldly, referential origin of a vast catalog of highly canonical literary texts. A handout titled "Sound of Bells" from the Use of Language in Literature course excerpts fourteen different examples of bells represented in literature (including Mother Goose, Edgar Allan Poe, John Milton, John Keats, Henry James, Joyce, and Eliot), while a handout titled "Objects Reflected in Water" excerpts Housman, Percy Bysshe Shelley, W. H. Auden, Yeats, Pope, and James Hogg, and "Bird Song" includes bits of Thomas Nashe, Shelley, Aristophanes in Greek and two translations, Walt Whitman, Matthew Arnold, Bridges, George Gordon, Lord Byron, Eliot, Alfred, Lord Tennyson, Virgil, Milton, and Ivan Turgenev.[44] Rather than the New Critical poem on the page usually associated with the midcentury mimeographed handout, Wilson offered his students long catalogs of parts of poems unified by single referents. He created temporary genres—the birdsong lyric, the reflection rhyme, the bell poem—to compare styles of literary representation. This teaching technique sees a hospitable world organize a temporary but compelling canon—a strong contrast to Brooks, for whom the canon staves off the incursions of a chaotic and hostile world. And rather than imagining the close reading of literary texts as an inherently formalist exercise designed to confirm the literariness, and thus the value, of canonical texts, Wilson modeled a kind of close reading that identifies canonical literature's connection to the world—its everyday referentiality, its commonality with bird-watching guides and unspectacular shoreside sundowns and change-of-class bells—as itself a source of value.

While Wilson's handouts reconnect canonical literature to the world, many of his courses centered on non-canonical texts that had been undervalued precisely because of their enmeshment with the everyday. For example, Wilson's Dickens class opened with a lecture that described how literary culture had undervalued Dickens because of his popularity, a popularity that stems from his connectedness with winter holidays and before-bed reading and memories of school vacations. In Wilson's notes, written in pencil on a yellow legal pad, he wrote:

> Everybody has read Dickens—enormously popular—Pickwick + Xmas Carol in England—symbol of Xmas, cheerful old England—English middle class. Not much criticism: Chesterton + Gissing—perhaps because everybody reads him early ++ the highbrows rather scorn him. Dickens was a great favorite of mine when I was a child—I've kept on reading him off + on all my life. Have come to have ideas about him which I'm going to try to explain in this course. I hope you'll criticize them +

COMPARATIVE LITERATURE 290

Professor Edmund Wilson

OBJECTS REFLECTED IN WATER

1.

And like a skylit water stood
The bluebells in the azured wood.

Housman

2.

He will watch from dawn to gloom
The lake-reflected sun illume
The yellow bees in the ivy-bloom.

Shelley

3.

You who go out alone, on tandem or on pillion,
Down arterial roads riding in April,
Or sad beside lakes where hill-slopes are reflected
Making fires of leaves, your high hopes fallen:

Auden (?)

4.

The trees are in their autumn beauty,
The woodland paths are dry,
Under the October twilight the water
Mirrors a still sky;
Upon the brimming water among the stones
Are nine-and-fifty swans.

Yeats: The Wild Swans at Coole

5.

Oft in her glass¹ the musing shepherd spies
The headlong mountains and the downward skies,
The watery landscape of the pendent woods,
And absent trees that tremble in the floods;
In the clear azure gleam the flocks are seen,
And floating forests paint the waves with green,
Through the fair scene roll slow the ling'ring streams,
Then foaming pour along, and rush into the Thames.

¹Her glass refers to the waters of the river Loddon.

Pope: Windsor Forest

FIGURE 5.4. Handout from Edmund Wilson's Comparative Literature 290: The Use of Language in Literature course at Harvard University in 1958. The handout included literary examples of "Objects Reflected in Water" and (on the following pages) "Bird Song." Edmund Wilson Papers, Yale Collection of American Literature, Beinecke Rare Book and Manuscript Library, Yale University.

don't think that, in writing your papers, you have to accept my ideas—don't hesitate to contradict them.[45]

For the "highbrows," Dickens's enmeshment in everyday life is a mark against him. For Wilson—interested in studying the connections between Dickens's life, his novels, and his historical moment—it is generative. His course goes on to consider "Dickens' style," the ways that his novels related to his own "self-pity" ("I think: literature protected something"), and the ways that Dickens selectively represented the events of his moment (to represent the Chartist agitation of 1840 in *Barnaby Rudge*, Dickens "chose [the] Gordon Riots").[46] Wilson's historicism considers the range of relationships that a novel can have to a life, and that a life can have to an historical moment. He also considers how a reader's relationship to a text changes over time. By marking how he has "come to" his own ideas about Dickens over a lifetime of reading, he acknowledges that his students must arrive at their own conclusions and valuations.

Twenty years later, Wilson turned this historicist model to an apparently even less literary topic. His 1959–60 Literature of the Civil War class at Harvard reanimated the research process of his nearly finished book *Patriotic Gore*. Wilson began his first-day lecture by explaining, "I am going to give you the substance of a book I have been writing on the literature of the American Civil War. By the literature of the Civil War I don't mean simply any literature that deals with the Civil War. I confine myself to the writings of people who actually took part in the war or who had some direct connection with it."[47] Wilson framed his choice of texts as in part an aesthetic one. "The poetry and the fiction and the drama inspired by the war itself are mostly extremely inferior," he notes, while "the diaries, the letters, the memoirs, military, political and social, the speeches and official papers and the journalistic reports are the main literature of the Civil War" because they show that "there has never been an historical crisis in which the actors were more keenly aware of the roles they were playing before the world and in which they were more articulate."[48] Under the pressure of a war carried out within a newly pervasive print culture, he argued, people come to see themselves as historical; therefore the documents of their self-conscious role-playing become literary.[49] Drawing this odd assortment of texts together, Wilson homed in on the moments when such records of everyday experience take on aesthetic form as they are written and read within different historical moments and institutional contexts.

Yet Wilson's historicism resists turning history into the "spirit of the age" or any other strongly unified formation. Indeed, the terrain of his Literature of the Civil War class was both messy and flexible. As he explained to his students, the course "begin[s] with Harriet Beecher Stowe, who did so much to arouse the North by the publication of Uncle Tom's Cabin, and . . . end[s]—next spring—with Justice Holmes, whose whole view of the world and hence professional career were deeply influenced by his experience in the war."[50] Wilson steers clear of reifications, explaining:

> My presentation of these figures will trace a consecutive development but it will not be strictly chronological. . . . My argument . . . will all be presented in a series of literary portraits. I shall be dealing, to be sure, with tendencies, but mainly by implication. Societies and movements and wars are made up of individuals, and my story is all in terms of individuals. Of the career and personality of each I shall try to give a more or less well-rounded picture, so my lectures will be full of details that in a sense will not be relevant to my theses.[51]

Wilson imagined the individual not as a purely psychological subject, but as a bundle of potentially irrelevant but potentially connective details that make up "societies and movements," just as he treated Dickens as both a singular author and an avatar of the Victorian middle class. He rejected the idea of a deep historical truth organizing apparently autonomous individuals and texts. Irrelevancies pose no threat to Wilson's thesis; they are merely details that are not yet relevant. They await a future moment when some other critic might connect them in some new way, just as Wilson himself had gathered together the strange assemblage of Literature of the Civil War.

Wilson's interest in making new connections—between people or texts—informed his teaching as well. Wilson's practice of bringing chance-met friends (like Saul Bellow) along to class, his references to everyday events ("Ford Madox Ford died two days ago"[52]), the scribbled notes, copies of handouts, student papers, lecture plans, and hand-drawn charts of social relations (for teaching Marxist criticism) all offer evidence of his transformation of the classroom into a space that connects different kinds of people and unexpected texts. This principle even applies to the collection of students Wilson accumulated. A single Harvard class found graduate students in philosophy of language, English, and the School of Education alongside undergraduate English, linguistics, history, and philosophy majors, a Radcliffe senior, an otherwise-unidentified student visiting from France, and a Radcliffe linguistics PhD candidate (and research assistant at the Harvard Computation Laboratory on an automatic Russian translation project, "where I've been working on machine inflection"[53]). Whereas Brooks usually set careful boundaries around current events, neatly forming them to fit the literature classroom in which he met his entirely male Yale undergraduate audience, Wilson's classroom sent tendrils outward to connect with the everyday lives of the people—students from France, Russian-translating computers, chance visitors, and Civil War diarists—who crowded his classroom. While Brooks fashioned his classroom as a rarefied space apart from the public sphere, Wilson's classroom cut across multiple publics. When teaching Joyce at Smith, Wilson combined a lecture open to the public with a supplementary two-hour seminar discussion to form a for-credit class in a model familiar from extension school education's combining of lectures and seminars earlier in the century.[54] And while Brooks worked to produce a classroom that felt like a well-wrought urn, Wilson's classroom strove for the effect of a decent railway station bar.

Perhaps most importantly, Wilson's sense of the temporality of interpretation—specifically the sense that texts accrue value as they are read and reread both by individuals and groups—can only truly be modeled in the duration of the class hour and the semester course, stretches of time that forecast a life in which a reader returns to texts again and again, as Wilson has "kept on reading [Dickens] off + on all of my life." In Wilson's 1942 course on Joyce, it became clear that the classroom fosters this temporal model of reading more readily than does the review or the essay. These lectures begin, "I have been reading James Joyce and writing about him ever since a Portrait of the Artist as a Young Man came out in 1916."[55] As he explains in his opening lecture, he "wrote reviews of Ulysses and Finnegans Wake" upon their initial publications, but then he "realized immediately [the] inadequacy of reviews. Such books can hardly be reviewed. As I reread the books, I saw that there was much more in them, both of meaning and of art, than I had understood at first."[56] Joyce can't be reviewed because the mode of the review is a single act of analysis and evaluation; the punctual temporality of the review requires a model of the text as an autonomous object that can be known in a short, if intense, single evaluation and subsequently committed to paper and publication. Rather than offer a representation of life all at once and upfront—as a Dickens novel might—the slow, drawn-out lifelong rereading that Ulysses and Finnegans Wake require produces the sense of "a reality like life's." The reader's slow building up of experience with the text, the accretion of detail and meaning over the successive years of one's life, function to make the experience of reading the novel similar to the experience of living. Instead of imitating reality, the experience of reading Ulysses imitates the structure of the reader's encounter with everyday real life, the composition of a coherent and significant world out of a wealth of incoherent and disconnected detail and experience—an apt description of Wilson's pedagogy and of his classroom itself.

Wilson's role as a public critic and reviewer, the contingency of his various teaching positions, and the everydayness of his classrooms are likely all reasons that his work has rarely been described as having a unified method or viewed as important to the history of literary study at the university. Accounts of Brooks's criticism and his classrooms, by contrast, have been so singular and strong that they have come to stand in for virtually all of midcentury literary study. By looking at the actual teaching of Brooks and Wilson, we have seen the stronger theory undergirding Wilson's varied collection of classrooms and writings. And we have seen that Brooks's teaching was not the string of polished close readings of poems on pages that we have taught ourselves to imagine, but rather often referred to current events, pursued slow-developing readings, and followed student comments down digressive pathways just as many of the other classrooms described in this book do. Despite the centrality of New Criticism to the disciplinary historical imagination of literary studies, therefore, classrooms like Wilson's—referential, historicist, and deeply invested in literary value's origins and contingencies—were equally central to the experience of students of literature.

Brooks's and Wilson's classrooms now join Redding's in our retelling of the real life of midcentury literature classrooms. Together, the three give us a picture of a midcentury that was hardly dominated by New Criticism—a midcentury in which critics taught the forms of literature's referentiality and valued its ties to history. We will complete this midcentury part of the story as we turn in our next chapter to Josephine Miles. For Miles, a poet and a writing workshop teacher and a quantitative researcher of poetry, New Criticism was a distant East Coast fad rather than a sole or primary reference point. In her first-year composition class English 1A at Berkeley, Miles taught students a version of close reading that was connected to both creative writing practice and the interpretation of data. Like Redding, she rejected arguments about the specialness or singularity of literary language, and her quantitative studies of past eras of poetry overturned the idea that major authors were responsible for linguistic change. Miles's five decades' worth of teaching and research gives us a sustained look at a landscape that is perhaps even less familiar to disciplinary history, but arguably even more representative of the history of literary study.

CHAPTER 6

Josephine Miles, English 1A (1940–55)

Josephine Miles began teaching in the English Department at Berkeley as an instructor in 1939. In 1947 she became the first tenured woman in the department's history, and she retired in 1978 as a University Professor. Miles's archive at the Bancroft Library contains not only her tiny scrawled notes for her teaching and her hand-drawn charts for her quantitative literary scholarship, but folder upon folder of letters from former students that Miles taught over the course of her four-decade career. "You undoubtedly don't remember me" or "I have been only one of your many students," these letters begin, for they are not from former graduate students or even from English majors.[1] Instead, they are from students who majored in other fields but took one of Miles's countless sections of English 1A, Berkeley's freshman writing course, or another one of her workshop-style courses on prose or verse composition. A former lumber mill worker and journalism major writes in 1975 to say that he's just found the "Mrs. Dalloway paper" that he wrote for English 1A in the final years of World War II.[2] A social worker writes to tell Miles "how productive your course on the lyric has been on a long range basis."[3] A chemistry teacher writes in 1973 to tell Miles that he can "still remember the stimulating discussions that you were able to generate" in English 1A in 1947; he adds, "now that I am also in the teaching business I frequently wonder if I have aroused the interest of my students."[4]

Nearly all of these former students, writing to Miles decades after having taken a single course with her, allude to the way Miles's teaching roused them—transforming them, through mysterious means, from students into persons pursuing interests through a contemporary world of letters. "The closest parallel I can draw to studying with you is to say it was like adding a new word to your vocabulary; once you've learned it, you cannot recall a time you didn't know it, so completely has it become your possession. So it is, I believe, with all the subtleties you so patiently and effectively led us toward discovering," writes one.[5] "Amidst all the huffing and puffing of the mostly self-concerned English department," writes another, "here was someone talking about what they liked and why, and who was willing to like all kinds of crazy things for all kinds of crazy, but appealing reasons."[6] A lawyer who took Miles's 1A class "in 1946 or 1947" describes how Miles taught her to encourage others to follow their interests to a bookshelf: "I still read poetry and plays," she writes, "although it is usually because one of my children has shown an interest and so I have taken the child who has shown the interest and hauled him or her into the library and taken down a book so we could read some more of whatever interests the child right then."[7] A "chef cooking Creole in Santa Cruz" writes in 1984 to say that picking up a recent volume of Miles's poems "reminds me of all the useful things I learned in your classroom," especially that "knowledge was not a commodity to be obtained in neat little packages, but something messy, nebulous, with holes in it, but which could be relished as such." "As your average guy slogging along under jobs and marriages and National Defense, that continues to mean something to me," he signs off.[8]

Though Miles did teach in the upper division and the graduate program at Berkeley, including the courses History of the Lyric, Graduate Research Methods, and Seventeenth-Century Poetry, and single-author courses on W. B. Yeats and T. S. Eliot, she most consistently taught English 1A and her often wait-listed English 106B: Verse Composition. "I have less often taught informational survey courses and more often taught writing courses or reading courses or courses where I was trying to teach the students how to do something well, and that's different," she explained in an oral interview conducted the year before her retirement.[9] As she declared on the first day of English 1A in Fall 1940, these classes functioned more like a "lab or tool course" resembling a "Machine Shop" in which "Prof doesn't tell & just watches practice."[10] Miles's handwritten notes for years of English 1A courses testify to the workshop style of these classes. Miles made no formal book orders. Instead, she would read off her handwritten shopping list of novels, magazines, journals, a style guide, and a dictionary, with prices marked next to each, for the students to purchase. In place of a formal syllabus, we find sketchy notes planning out the fifteen weeks of class, with major assignments noted and daily theme topics listed: "Class theme for May 12–25 min on something that has struck them funny," read notes from the spring of 1948.[11] In place of lecture notes, we find Miles's jotted responses to individual student essays, which she would read aloud to the entire class so that feedback was public and nearly immediate. In place of class handouts, we find shorthand lists of quick exercises: compose a fifty-word sentence, collaborate on an oral composition, reverse the order of a sentence. And in nearly every semester, Miles records lists of book recommendations fitting a variety of genres and topics. As she explained in the spring of 1941, the course would help students with "getting a wider view of things without being pinched by own groove."[12]

Miles's workshop-style pedagogy was guided by her very clear sense of the role of freshman composition within the university and society. University-level writing, Miles held, should teach students how to take a perspective on material or, in grammatical-theoretical terms, how to "predicate." As Miles explained, freshmen typically arrived at Berkeley knowing how to write with either extreme objectivity or extreme subjectivity. High schools tended to focus on the description or the report, in which students are called upon to convey information in chronological or spatial order. Alternatively, students had written impressionistic pieces, in which "truth + order don't matter." Miles described this divide in high school writing to her summer 1947 students as the "encyl[opedia] vs. sunset" problem.[13] College-level composition, to her mind, needed to move students "toward the center" by teaching them to take a first-person perspective on information rather than simply reporting or emoting.[14] In an essay titled "The Freshman at Composition," Miles suggests that students should learn to write essays with more logics of arrangement— "this, therefore—if, then—either, or," allowing them to arrange and subordinate their material, to ask themselves, "Which in a group of aspects is most important? Important to what? To your point of view."[15] This kind of sorting, subordinating, and arranging happened even at the level of the sentence, Miles emphasizes. "Sentence-making is predication," she explains, "and to predicate is to assert an idea, selecting and treating facts from a point of view." Writing a good sentence, for her, requires students to develop "an individual responsibility of thought."[16]

Teaching students to adopt a perspective on facts, rather than simply report them, Miles thought, had become more necessary than ever in a modern society and a modern research university that regarded individuals as determined by data. "We may be, as the scientists have suggested to us, the victims of sheer uninterpreted data, as meaningless as can be," she wrote in one essay on English 1A. "If so, if we have no attitudes for our facts, we shall have no predicates for our subjects, no themes for our essays, no points for our remarks, no responsibilities for our actions."[17] Miles reminded students that no one could do anything with facts without having ideas about them; a point of view was necessary, at the most basic level, for meaning to exist. Miles regretted divisions and definitions that pitted the so-called "humanities" against the sciences: "Our college of Letters and Science name their divisions Physical Sciences, Social Sciences, and Humanities, as if in only one-third of his study man were humane, beleaguered even there by brute fact and mass pressure. This is a fearful picture, and one perpetuated for some strange reason by 'humanists' themselves."[18] No matter students' eventual areas of interest, majors, or work, Miles aimed for them to understand how to take responsibility for the interpretation they would necessarily do and to encounter knowledge not as a seamless overlay but, in the words of her former student, as "messy, nebulous, with holes in it."[19]

In the same years in which Miles taught freshman writing as a workshop on taking perspectives on data, she was conducting groundbreaking research in quantitative and proto-computational literary study. Well remembered as a beloved teacher of prose and poetry, Miles has only recently been recognized as a foundational figure for quantitative method in literary studies.[20] Miles's earliest quantitative study was her graduate thesis, an analysis of the adjectives favored by Romantic poets, published in 1942 as *Wordsworth and the Vocabulary of Emotion*. Her tabulations, printed in four simple tables in the appendix to the volume, expressed her key findings: that Wordsworth used the language of emotion frequently and consistently across all of his work; that, surprisingly, poets contemporary to Wordsworth used emotion words at roughly the same rate; and that the use of emotion words decreases dramatically in the twentieth-century poetry of T. S. Eliot and Robinson Jeffers. The major discovery of this book, which she would later test across centuries of poetry, was the unexpected degree to which poets' word choices and syntax was shared rather than individually distinctive. A "rogue formalist," as Chris Rovee calls her, Miles used her quantitative work to develop a formalism attentive to poetry rather than poems.[21]

In 1945 Miles began to build a major data set that would help expand her research; it would represent the poetry of the '40s decade of each century, from the 1540s through the 1940s. Each summer, she remembered, "I sat on the patio with my little beat-up traveling typewriter that had only three banks of keys, and typed out these studies of the language of the poets of the 1640s, 1740s, and so on." This work was ideal for Miles: her childhood arthritis had left her unable to drive or walk independently and prevented her from easily traveling to archives to conduct historicist source studies. By contrast, she could "sit outside with and enjoy" counting words in poetry; this was also the kind of work "that students could help with so that they could get support grant money."[22] Miles and her graduate student assistants slowly counted the adjectives, nouns, and verbs used across roughly 1,000-line samples of twenty poets from each decade. From these counts they created summary statistics indicating whether a poet relied more on adjectives or verbs, as well as lists of each decade's "majority vocabulary" and "minority vocabulary."[23] To Miles's mind, almost any kind of counting would shed light on poetic values through time: "When we know so little about what poets have had to say, when we can scarcely tell that cloud has been important to one age and not to another, and in what special way; and how bone and leaf as words now wield a power in poetry they never had before; when we are in this state of curiosity, almost any place in poetry is a good place to begin looking around."[24] Miles added to this data set over the next twenty years; her interpretations of the data set served as the basis of the series of major monographs she published between 1951 and 1974.

In the early 1950s, Miles's quantitative work led her to an historic collaboration with the Electrical Engineering Department at Berkeley. In 1951 Miles's colleague Guy Montgomery died, leaving behind sixty-four shoe boxes of index cards toward a concordance to John Dryden's poetry. Because Miles routinely used concordances for her quantitative scholarship, her department chair George Potter asked Miles to finish Montgomery's project. Working alongside graduate students Helen S. Agoa and Mary Jackman, Miles collaborated with Shirley Rice, Odette Carothers, Penny Gee, and other Electrical Engineering staff members, using their IBM tabulation machine to turn this "departmental obligation and chore" into the first computerized concordance.[25] *Concordance to the Poetical Works of John Dryden* (1957) was thus begun around the time that Fr. Roberto Busa circulated early proof-of-concept drafts of his concordance to the complete works of St. Thomas Aquinas. Digital humanists typically cite Busa's concordance as the origin point for the computational humanities. This is an error, as Miles published her Dryden concordance seventeen years before the first volumes of Busa's 56-volume *Index Thomasticus* began to appear.[26] Through the 1950s and '60s, Miles kept abreast of developments in computerized concordancing even as she continued to expand her own hand counts in attempts to model syntactic forms in poetry and prose that were beyond the reach of early computational linguistics.

The story of Miles's groundbreaking quantitative scholarship and the story of her workshop teaching of English 1A need to be told together in order for us to understand the full meaning and importance of both to the history of literary study. Most crucially, Miles's English 1A courses shaped her scholarly research, particularly her focus on the sentence as the key unit with which to think about poetic form. In 1A, Miles taught her students that the sentence is the basic unit in which the writer takes perspective—qualifying, ordering, linking, opposing, and delimiting her material through corresponding parts of speech and grammar. "The sentence parallels the composition, as being the essence of the whole developed thought. Subject and predicate plus connections and modifications," read her notes for English 1A in the summer of 1945.[27] In fall 1946 she explained, "Statement of idea = sentence. Development of idea = essay. A p[aragraph] is a predication: Inclusion, exclusion, equivalence."[28] She opened class in 1947 by declaring the "Sentence lively + useful. Combines fact + idea by which we live. Subj[ect]—pred[icate]." In 1948 she argued that "our main ways of thought and att[itude]s toward world are flected + given form in single sentences."[29] In 1949, "Sentence is miniature essay. Its sec[tion]s are miniature paragraphs. Axioms, hypotheses, guesses, beliefs, reports of fact + experiences all stateable in 1 sentence + developable in essay."[30]

During these same years, Miles expanded her poetry research beyond the tabulation of "major words" and adjectives to try to model the ghostly sentence structures that informed the poet's orientation to the world in each century. Measuring the proportions of nouns to adjectives to verbs, and eventually to connectives, Miles placed English poets along a spectrum, from "clausal" eras like the Renaissance, which "emphasized causal constructions and highly subordinated clausal forms requiring more verbs," to more "phrasal" eras like Romanticism, which relied upon "highly phrasal and adjectival constructions, qualifying by epithets instead of stating by verbs, suspending time in space."[31] The homely freshman composition grammatical sentence—rather than the poetic line, poetic genres, figures, or images—was at the heart of Miles's entirely new representation of five centuries of literary history.

At the same time, Miles's quantitative work shaped her account of the value of freshman composition, and the humanities more generally, to society. While many other poet-critics of the 1940s and '50s redefined literary and poetic form in opposition to scientific modes of writing and knowing, Miles refused to relinquish literary writing's ability to reference and order the world. For Miles, poems, English 1A papers, and the building of data sets all involved making decisions about representativeness and selection, qualification and connection. Literature, for her, offered not a respite from data, but a master class in working with it in order to speak meaningfully about a world from an individualized perspective. Even as Miles's tabulations of past poetry revealed, against her own initial expectations, the extent to which poets' choices of major vocabulary and syntactic structures were shared with contemporaries and constrained by their moment, her work held a place for the innovations of the individual within a horizon of continuity. In one of her final monographs of quantitative scholarship, *Style and Proportion*, Miles imagined that her careful counting and classifying of past poetry and prose sentence styles era by era would not only give scholars a literary picture of historical change, but would benefit anyone, from first-year college student to seasoned scholar, who wished to know how to write. As she put it, "Students and scholars, no less than artists, enjoy knowing how things work, and perform the better for the knowledge. I have tried looking at literary styles as habitual uses of material and manners that may be discriminated in ways relevant not only to literary textures but also to the needs and feelings of everyday writing. How our language, how our literature has worked, how our writing may work—these are my primary interests."[32] For Miles, the writer served as both the object of and audience for her research. The workshop was everywhere.

Finally, it was in her early years of teaching English 1A that Miles began to collaborate meaningfully with graduate students and teaching assistants, a model of work uncommon in the Berkeley English Department at the time but central to Miles's research as well as her teaching. Miles recalls that when she began teaching 1A in 1940, she asked George Hand, the head of freshman English at the time, "if I could read a batch of his papers to get the drift, [the] idea. He was really shocked and very angry. He said that the way he corrected his papers was none of my business." Miles eventually learned to grade papers alongside her peers; "we younger instructors (really I was the only instructor, but the teaching assistants and I) would get together and correct papers. It was not done in the department. The department was very, very lofty; it didn't bother with us chickens very much."[33] "Us chickens" on the lower rungs of the academic hierarchy had less invested, Miles implies, in obscuring the everyday details and labor conditions of academic work. For them, the ability to see each other's methods and practices in action was worth what they might give up by revealing the mysteries of their craft—or by revealing the work of teaching to involve particular forms of labor at all.

When Miles began, in the mid-1940s, to build her general data sets, she drew on what she had learned about collaborative teaching work and hired some of the same graduate students and teaching assistants who had graded alongside her to help her develop methods for quantifying past eras of poetry. Miles's practice of collaborating with graduate students, staff, and non-tenure-track instructors in her research set her apart from her senior colleagues, who were much more reticent. She remembered, for example, how her colleague Bertrand H. Bronson was doing cutting-edge work in "new methods" but "wouldn't talk about it much," perhaps because he "really felt that any ostensible open discussion of ways and means of anything was obscene. It was just not the gentlemanly way you worked!" This, she noted, was "ironic because Bud Bronson was one of the great pioneers in new methods, in the use of computers in his ballad studies. They never have been followed up. He was a pioneer without a following, and I think this is why."[34] Bronson's refusal to share work or work closely with graduate students meant that his own lines of inquiry did not live on.

For Miles, by contrast, collaboration was essential to the practice of quantitative method, just as quantitative method was useful for reconstructing a collective language from which individual poets made choices that shaped their individual style. Her research looks back to the collaborative experimental classrooms of Richards and Rickert as well as to the quantitative projects of Spurgeon, work that was collaborative both in the creation of its data and in its vision of sharing the data with other scholars. But Miles's research also points forward to a different understanding of quantitative literary study or distant reading. Recent interpretations of what is most essential or valuable about these methods vary. They solve an evidence problem (Andrew Piper), offer more nuanced and precise accounts of change over time in literary history (Ted Underwood), allow us to view a more complex literary field (Katherine Bode), or clarify the process of reduction or modeling literary scholars and critics engage in all of our work (Sarah Allison, Richard Jean So).[35] Miles did quantitative work in part because she had questions that required a different kind of evidence, and also because it allowed her a new view of continuity and change over time. But she began doing quantitative work primarily because it would be collaborative, and continued to do it because what she discovered opened up a new vision of the continuity and collectivity of poetry's past in a place where she expected to find primarily individual style and change between eras.[36] Putting Miles into a new history of distant reading or quantitative literary study thus makes a connection between collaboration and quantification—in Miles's case, between the groups of scholars who create data and the groups of poets whose shared language becomes visible through that data. Miles's own decades' worth of work on the history of poetic forms verified her related insight that the history of poetry is a story of continuity rather than singularity. To return to Miles's teaching of English 1A is to recover the material working conditions among "us chickens" that prepared this continuous vision of poetry's past and future. This connection remains invisible, of course, unless we can see how Miles's teaching of 1A formed her ideas about the role of the sentence in expressing a perspective on data not just for composition students, but also for the history of poetry. Returning to Miles's English 1A classroom thus offers us a composition classroom history of distant reading, a history in which the work of "us chickens" turns out to be at the center, not the margins, of literary study.[37]

English 1A: Taking Perspective

By the time Miles began teaching English 1A in 1940, freshman writing courses had been running in roughly similar format since the late nineteenth century, on several different models. Harvard began offering English A in 1885 as a pure writing course. With no outside readings, first-year students would produce short daily and long fortnightly themes on topics of their choosing. Soon after, as John Brereton describes, other schools devised their own models for the composition course. Yale and Wisconsin offered a literature-based writing course for freshman that required students to write evaluations of or reactions to poems, plays, and novels. At Indiana in the 1890s, Frank Aydelotte developed a nonfiction version of freshman composition, which involved the "close analysis of important essays, a sort of literary nonfiction course with the emphasis upon the structure of the ideas." This model soon spread to Columbia and elsewhere. Colleges like Amherst used expository or creative writing as the basis for the freshman writing course, whereas "less prestigious colleges" focused on "grammar and mechanics drills." As Brereton notes, the freshman composition course that "eventually prevailed was an eclectic mix" of existing approaches, featuring a blend of "personal writing, writing about literature, and writing about ideas."[38]

When Miles herself took English 1B at UCLA in 1928–29, she experienced this mixed-genre approach. Miles and her classmates were required to purchase a dictionary (*Webster's Collegiate*); an anthology of nonfiction essays (Warner Taylor's *Essays of the Past and Present*); a short guide to summarizing and reverse-outlining such essays (Norman Foerster's *Outlines and Summaries: A Handbook for the Analysis of Expository Essays*); a grammar and style guide (Edwin Wooley's *Handbook of Composition*); and a composition textbook offering advice about and specimens of "exposition," "argumentation," "description," and "narrative" (Henry Seidel Canby's *English Composition*). The course reading also included "a novel to be selected by the instructor"; possibilities included *The Ordeal of Richard Feverel*, *The Return of the Native*, *Pride and Prejudice*, and *Framley Parsonage*. Finally, students were required to conduct "outside reading" in "contemporary magazines" such as the *Atlantic Monthly*, *Century*,

Harper's Monthly Magazine, Scribner's Magazine, the *Yale Review*, and the *London Mercury*.[39] The class exemplifies the "eclectic" model: Miles and her classmates practiced literary interpretation, analyzed the structure of important essays, and debated contemporary ideas.

When Miles began teaching English 1A at Berkeley about ten years later, she made a singular revision to this long-standing model of the mixed-mode freshman composition course: she decided to draw her assigned readings exclusively from the contemporary world of letters. Though particular readings varied semester to semester, Miles typically used magazines such as the *New Yorker*, journals like the *Southern Review*, fiction magazines such as *Story*, hobbyist publications, novels (both best-sellers and "modern classics"), and general audience nonfiction like Stuart Chase's *The Proper Study of Mankind* (1948). These wide-ranging readings helped Miles to represent the actually existing world of letters that she wished her students to enter as readers and writers. She often opened the first day of 1A by asking students to "each give one" example of "what sort of things people write now," including "letters, business orders, speeches, applications, articles, stories, poems, plays . . . radio scripts." In place of the essay collections of nineteenth-century prose that provided models for many composition classes, Miles encouraged students to make their own collections drawn from contemporary sources. In one semester, she suggested that the class collectively assemble an anthology of "as much good writing as possible, incl. own," and noted that this anthology should include work that was "as much part of present world as possible."[40]

Miles's course readings aimed to introduce students to actually existing publications and audiences for their writing; accordingly, she left it to students to collect the class readings from local bookshops. She typically ordered only *Webster's Collegiate Dictionary* and Porter G. Perrin's *Writer's Guide and Index to English*, and then distributed a shopping list with projected prices for the remaining readings. In the spring of 1941, for example, Miles opened 1A by giving students the following purchase list of contemporary books and magazines:

1.00	Mrs. Dalloway
1.00	A modern classic {Mann, Proust, Joyce, Shaw or O'Neill}
.25	A current best-seller—see scrap lists
.40	Story magazine Jan–Feb
.25	Poetry Magazine
.40	Harpers
.75	Southern Review
.15	New Yorker

.15   New Republic
.—   A specialty magazine[41]

As the list's contents suggest, Miles called for some texts in common, while leaving other choices to her students. In the spring of 1942, for example, the class all read the January 17 issue of the *New Yorker* as well as the April *Harper's* together. But Miles also wished for her students to make their own selections, and as her mention of "scrap lists" indicates, she introduced students not only to the wide world of contemporary print, but to bibliographic tools—scrap lists, 100 best books lists, recommendation lists from the National Council for Teachers of English, year in review lists, and textbook catalogs—that would help them navigate it.[42]

Knowing that much of her students' present world was the university itself, Miles also taught students to navigate what she called, in the title of her 1968 collection of poetry, the "fields of learning." Miles often had students read the University Bulletin and map the division of disciplines. She encouraged students to browse the course book orders at the university bookshop,[43] and she included writing assignments directed toward the kind of work they would be expected, but perhaps not taught, to do in their future classes. In the fall of 1940, for example, Miles asked students to "fill cards + put courses taken" and also to tell her about their writing "needs."[44] She incorporated readings from other common general education courses such as Philosophy 6B and History 4B, and devoted a week or two to the question of "How to write a bluebook" for their future examinations.[45] Though Miles almost always featured literary readings in 1A, she wished for students to think about what good writing would look like in the field of their chosen major. By the early 1950s, Miles had begun work on a "writing across the disciplines" initiative at Berkeley, known as the Prose Improvement Committee. As she explained later to the *Southern Review*, "We have failed to . . . relate writing to other disciplines. We've taught it too separately. We need to get geographers and astronomers, we need to make the language of their discipline come alive for them in their own writing."[46]

Here, amidst this jostling contemporary world of letters—commentary, stories, memoir, scientific reporting, poetry, blue book exam questions—students would learn to develop what Miles believed they lacked: a level of comfort with opinion and a facility with making claims about information rather than dull reports of it. The contemporary literary world was the context, in other words, in which they would begin to learn "predication" on the level of the essay, the paragraph, the sentence. Rejecting

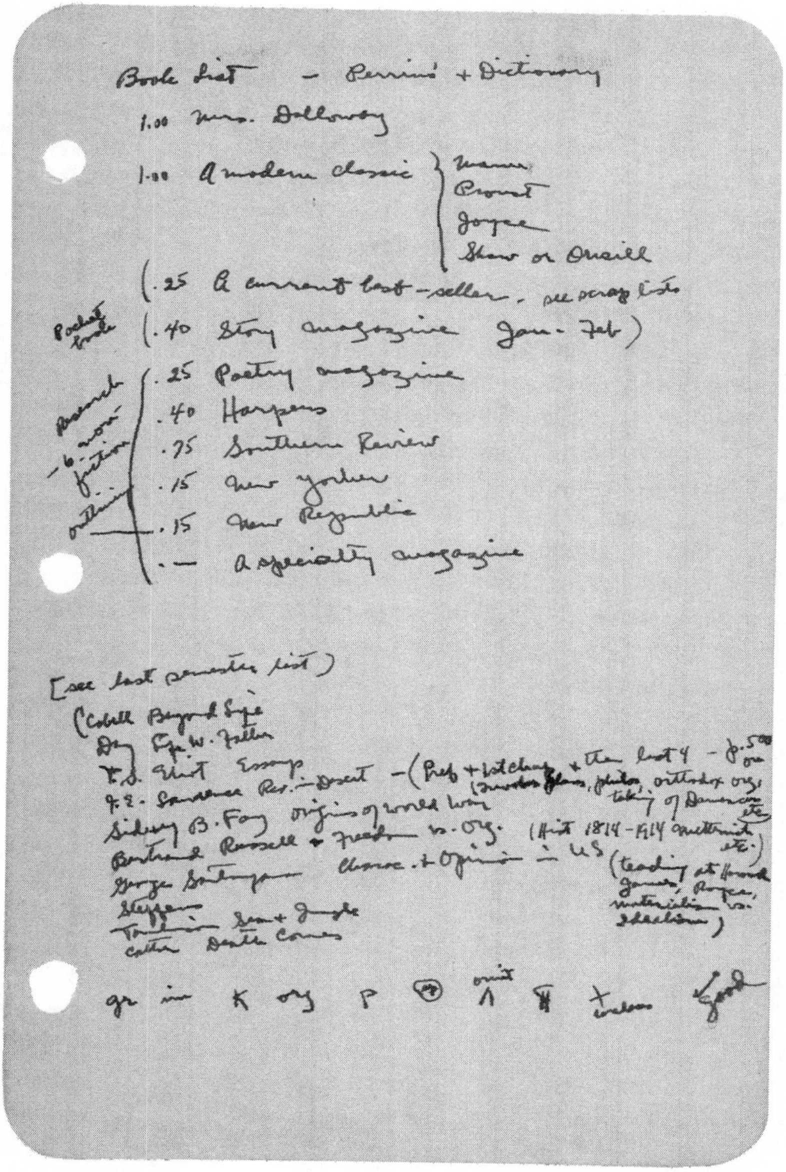

FIGURE 6.1. Josephine Miles's course book list for her English 1A students in 1941. Josephine Miles Papers, Bancroft Library, University of California, Berkeley.

the split between personal writing and factual reportage, Miles and her colleagues at Berkeley often opened 1A by asking students to give shape to a prepared but unordered collection of facts, impressions, or details. For example, Miles's colleague George R. Stewart's *English Composition: A Laboratory Course* (1936) workbook for English 1A opened with a series of exercises on "Organization" in which students were asked to take someone else's raw notes—a random list of celebrities they'd seen; a jotting of impressions in an infirmary; a list of suspects for an unsolved robbery; a series of thoughts about the experience of being a working student—and turn them into an organized outline for an essay.[47] Students began 1A with the sense that facts and details were given, awaiting a governing perspective that would give them order and meaning.

Miles's opening exercise for English 1A likewise asked students to give shape to disordered impressions. Through the early 1940s, Miles used as her opening essay prompt an assignment she herself had written at UCLA: the "corner essay," in which students were directed simply to go stand on a street corner and describe what they saw. Some years she specified the corner of Oxford and University on the campus's western edge; in other iterations of the course, students could choose. Miles would collect these short essays and, in the following class, respond to each one by describing its implicit or explicit point of view: "what facts, chosen on what basis + org[anized] by what function or point or opinion."[48] In her private class notes, she generally sorted them into two categories: "purposeful" or "rambling."[49] Miles's notes jotted next to student names from semester to semester give some indication of how greatly varied her students' observations could be. Students wrote variously about the sight of a "typical prof" walking by; about seeing war "refugees" hop "out of taxi on corner"; they mention a "1943 fire in cafeteria" or describe an "invasion" of "ants"; some simply commented in banal terms about "nature's beauty" or how the "day is lovely." In 1943 Miles notes that many of these essays include the phrase "1st caught my eye," indicating that they've chosen to order their details as a stream of impression, passively registered by the observer. From this reportage style list of details organized by chronology alone—"and . . . and . . . and . . ."—Miles asks her students to consider alternate modes of organization, such as "(1) history, or time tracing (2) type, or space spread (3) explanation—cause and effect (4) personal association + connections (5) balance, compare, contrast."[50] She wishes, ultimately, to make them take greater responsibility for their particular perspective and choice of detail and observation.

From this opening essay designed to demonstrate the importance of writerly perspective, Miles would then have students practice characterizing an author's point of view and developing their own. In the early 1940s, for example, Miles moved on from the corner essay to a study of perspectives in the *New Yorker* paired with a chapter on "Reports" from S. I. Hayakawa's semantics textbook *Language in Action: A Guide to Accurate Thinking, Reading, and Writing* (1939). Hayakawa explains that while we can never entirely avoid "perspective" or "slant," writers can learn to control it. To do this, they must first recognize how slant is encoded into writing at the level of fact, sentence, and word.[51] Hayakawa suggests that students practice by writing both "reports heavily slanted against persons or events he likes" and "reports heavily slanted in favor of persons or events he thoroughly dislikes." This work, he explains, prepares students to try "slanting both ways at once" in an essay modeled on the "Reporter at Large" or "Profiles" departments of the *New Yorker*, which both "offer good examples of the report technique" in which "explicit judgements are few, and a real effort is made to give at least the appearance of 'slanting both ways at once.'"[52]

Miles drew on Hayakawa's model to help her students rewrite their "On the Corner" essays into two different versions. Miles noted that the first set of corner essays were "Almost all = personal impressions, with time or viewpoint the main control." Using Hayakawa's advice to have students practice both impartiality and partiality, Miles prompted her students to rewrite their corner essays twice: first in the style of a "report" and, second, with a "personal slant." Continuing on with Hayakawa as their guide, Miles assigned a whole issue of the *New Yorker*, asking students first to identify "what kind of article is each?" and then to "Write in class on 'slant' of whole mag."[53] To get a handle on the *New Yorker's* particular slant, Miles advises students to "compare" the magazine's "reviews" to the *New York Herald Tribune's* "Books" section. Some semesters, Miles asked students to write specifically an "analysis" of a cartoon from the issue to determine the implicit perspective or worldview it offered or to assess the slant of a particular profile. In the spring 1942 class, for example, they read a profile of Daniel Arnstein, president of the Terminal Taxicab Company in New York City, who had been tasked with helping China open up the Burma Road so that the United States could ship war supplies through to the front. They also wrote analyses of a cartoon of balding men talking bluster about their dinner and the war at a fancy restaurant.[54] After all of these exercises conducted in class on the model of the "daily theme," students finished up their *New Yorker* work with a longer, 1,000-word "char[acter] study" modeled upon the *New Yorker's* "Reporter at Large" feature.[55]

In this series of assignments during the first weeks of English 1A,

Miles's students learned how to identify the perspective of a character sketch, cartoon, or profile and how to control the perspective of their own writing through choice of details, word selection, and the judicious use of facts. Miles was not attempting to teach her students that it was possible or desirable to achieve objectivity; rather, she was helping them to feel comfortable with writing from a perspective. In Miles's teaching, she noted that students tended to "split facts and ideas"; some gravitated toward factual writing because they "fear writing + speaking as too full of idea" and "fear idea as mere opinion" that seemed to have "no connec[tion] with fact." On the other hand, there were the students who "like lang[uage] and toss it around," students whose writing is "glib but not accurate." Both kinds of students "forget," Miles jots in her lecture notes, that "we don't do anything with facts without theories about them."[56] The other major contemporary scene of such problems of perspective—of the apparent crisis of ideas and judgments as mere opinions in the face of an absence of shared values—was modernist fiction and its critical reception. Miles and her students therefore turned, after the corner essay and the *New Yorker* studies, to Virginia Woolf's *Mrs. Dalloway* (1925), read alongside David Daiches's *The Novel and the Modern World* (1939).

Miles would begin discussion about *Mrs. Dalloway* by asking students to consider "how [the] book works": what patterns are established by the book's ordering of material and its movement from character to character?[57] Reading Daiches's chapter on Woolf from *The Novel and the Modern World* gave students a visualization of how "the whole novel is constructed in terms of the two dimensions of space and time."[58] As Daiches explains, the novel proceeds along each of these axes in different sections. In the first set of relations, the novel's perspective remains anchored in time and moves among the perspectives of several characters—Clarissa Dalloway, Septimus, Hugh, Peter, Mr. Dalloway, Lucrezia—while a bell tolling in the background reassures us that we remain in a shared present. In the second set of relations, the novel remains with a single character, but moves through time as Clarissa and others recall past moments and memories. Daiches diagrams each of these movements in tree form. In the first, six characters (A, B, C, D, E, F) are linked by a present moment (T); in the second, a single character is the unifying link between a series of past memories (T1, T2, T3, T4). Daiches then "diagram[m]atically represent[s] the movement of the novel as a whole" as a series of nested trees. These diagrams represent the way the novel travels through Clarissa's present and her past memories before surveying multiple characters in that present, then delving into Lucrezia's thoughts and memories, before

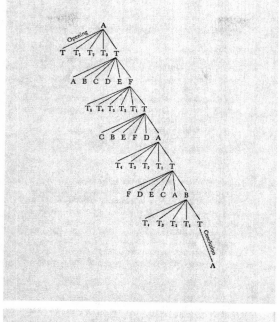

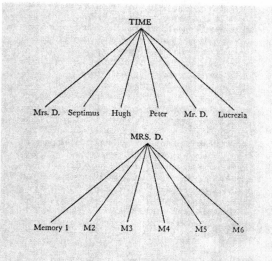

FIGURES 6.2A AND 6.2B. Diagrams of the plot structure of Virginia Woolf's *Mrs. Dalloway* from David Daiches, *The Novel and the Modern World* (1939). Miles assigned Daiches's chapter on Woolf, along with *Mrs. Dalloway*, to her English 1A freshman composition students in the early 1940s. Copyright © 1960 by The University of Chicago. All rights reserved.

conducting yet another survey of multiple characters in the present, and so on.[59]

Daiches developed this schematic account of *Mrs. Dalloway*'s structure as part of his larger inquiry into the modernist novel's new narrative forms. In *The Novel and the Modern World*, Daiches discusses the transition from nineteenth-century realism—in which novelistic plots turned on major events of obvious and shared significance—to twentieth-century realism, in which the postwar loss of shared values sent authors searching for new "patterns of meaning" in response to the breakdown of broad social consensus.[60] The book featured chapters not only on Woolf, but James Joyce, Katherine Mansfield, John Galsworthy, Joseph Conrad, and Aldous Huxley. For Daiches, Woolf and other modern novelists succeed in making their deeply personal value systems seem, however momentarily, objectively held. Joyce, for instance, "solves the problem of selection and significance by finding devices to enable him to show everything as simultaneously both significant and insignificant," while Woolf, "operating by restriction rather than by expansion, solves it by winning the co-operation of the reader's ordinary human tendency to reverie in order to present and to make convincing through a texture largely of reverie her own personal sense of significance."[61] Encountering Daiches's argument in the context of their weeks spent analyzing and practicing the taking of perspective on unordered sensory data, the students would have been able then to place their own practice of perspective-taking in a broader social and historical context, in which all modern writers struggle to objectify their perspectives, to convincingly shape a whole world through their point of view.

As 1A progressed through its series of increasingly complex assignments, moving from the simple corner essay to the analysis of slant in contemporary magazine writing to interpretation of how modern novelists give meaning to subjective experience, the course returned again and again to the idea that the sentence was the core of all of their work. "Frosh don't know sentences. Make some," begin Miles's notes for her first section of 1A in 1940, and the making of sentences and the revising of sentences and the mapping of sentences constituted the daily work of the course for decades.[62] Year after year, students wrote lengthy sentences of fifty words each and revised them; they "co-op[eratively]" wrote one-sentence summaries of their reading; they took topic sentences penned by Miles and wrote group outlines and themes to elaborate upon them; they copied Miles's transcriptions of their faulty sentences and corrected them together; they made "up one memorable sentence on a p[oint] you believe in"; they each chose one sentence from an essay they had read and analyzed its "function + transition."[63] As Miles emphasized nearly

every term, the sentence, followed by the paragraph, were the "fundamental instruments of thought."[64] And sprinkled through all these notes are
Miles's own transcriptions of sentences: her own models, students' error-
ridden sentences, comparative sentences drawn from poems or essays on
similar topics, and beside all these, little reminders to herself to have a
"gentle chat" with the students on "simple and complex" sentences.[65]

In Miles's 1A course, the sentence took pride of place as the most elemental instrument of thought. Paragraphs and essays came to seem like
fuller elaborations of a set of relations and qualifications laid out in single sentences. If the course as a whole prompted students "to anal[yze]
+ organize a mass of material into a meaningful whole," the sentence
represented the primary site where the work of perspective-taking
would begin.[66] Miles's emphasis on the sentence as a machine to think
with helped students to see the sentence—and its predication, in particular—as the primary contact zone between a mind and its material.
The sentence was the place where authors take responsibility for their
opinions, weigh their data, qualify their statements, and so on. The class's
readings and assignments replicated this work on a larger scale: the work
of mapping a field of knowledge, choosing a subject from among a limited if wide-ranging set of options, selecting examples from a sprawling
landscape of potential evidence, and asserting an opinion or argument
that required the subordination of some facts to others, the qualification
of a key idea with the particular conditions that make it true. Through the
1940s and '50s, Miles continued to teach English 1A in a way that invited
first-year writers to imagine themselves as embodied individuals encountering a wide realm of unordered data and evidence. Woolf's modernist fiction was in some semesters replaced by Ruth Benedict's *Patterns of
Culture* or Constance Rourke's *American Humor: A Study of the National
Character*, but the key lesson remained the same: students must survey a
field and consider connections, qualifications, juxtapositions, causalities,
and more in order to shape not just their essays, but also their sentences.

Over the course of the 1940s, the texts and the lessons that Miles
imparted in English 1A migrated into her quantitative scholarship. In
1A, Miles taught students how to predicate; in her research, she began
to think of poetry, too, as an act of predication. Gradually refining her
quantitative methods through her first three monographs, Miles began to
count parts of speech in past poetry, and to think of whole eras of past and
present poetry in terms of their characteristic syntax. Further, because
Miles thought of poetry in terms of sentences, and of sentences as instruments for ordering and subordinating and connecting information, she
saw the work of making these data sets and deciding on representative

samples and modeling past eras in terms of syntax as essentially the same as the work that writers do when they select and structure their sentences and essays. Her refusal to make categorical distinctions between quantitative and qualitative work, between the world of writing and the world of data, sets her very much apart from other famous poet-teacher-critics of her era. To read her groundbreaking quantitative scholarship is also to rediscover a capacious vision for literary study—one that, like English 1A, places the writer rather than the poem at its center.

Counting Sentences

As a poet herself, Miles thought quantitative studies could challenge contemporary critical consensus about how poems should mean and be. She hoped that data—word counts, sentence lengths, adjective taxonomies— could force contemporary critics to reckon with the actual qualities of past poetry rather than treat it as a "mirror" for present tastes and values.[67] Miles took up her dissertation research on Wordsworth's language of feeling against the backdrop of modern poetry's retreat from "named emotion"—a retreat verified by her comparative word counts that showed the steep decline of adjectives in the poetry of Eliot and Jeffers. As she explained in the book's introduction, modern critics including "Richards, Tate, Ransom, Brooks, and the poetry-vs-science theorists" had argued that true poetry *implied* feeling rather than stated it. Faced with a discursive poet like Wordsworth, such critics either banished him "outside and away from 'pure poetry' and 'the tradition'" or reconstructed him in their own image by cherry-picking scattered instances of concrete imagery from *The Prelude* or plucking his "bright blue eggs" from "The Sparrow's Nest."[68] Battling contemporary poetic values with the solidity of word counts, Miles hoped to show what was "essentially poetic" for Wordsworth, if not for her peers: "Wordsworth's persistent and formal naming of emotion, having been so attentively heard as poetry once, and possibly to be heard so again, may be closely observed now to some good end," she wrote in *Wordsworth and the Vocabulary of Emotion*.[69]

For the Wordsworth study, Miles laboriously devised a method for quantifying the language of emotion. She used eighteenth-century philosophical, critical, and reference sources to establish "those words which were considered in Wordsworth's own day to be names of emotions," from "general terms such as *passion* and *affection* [to] the more specific, such as *love, hate, fear*; and signs such as *tears, laughter*, and the word *heart*."[70] She then counted how frequently such words appeared in a given sample of lines of poetry across several corpora: all of Wordsworth's major pub-

TABLE I
NAMED EMOTION IN WORDSWORTH

Poems	Naming per line	Percentages of types of context in amplified third				
		General	Physi-cal	Be-stowal	Personi-fication	Objecti-fication
Early	700/ 4200–1/6	15	47	13	11	14
Lyrical Ballads	760/ 4900–1/7	42	26	20	02	10
Prelude	1270/ 7600–1/6	45	27	10	05	13
Recluse	190/ 850–1 5	25	25	32	05	13
Excursion	1350/ 6550–1/6	43	33	07	05	12
1801–1807	1100/ 6600–1/6	27	27	24	09	13
White Doe	300/ 2000–1/6	27	33	20		20
1808–1820	740/ 7400–1/6	27	24	11	17	21
Memories of Tour	190/ 1000–1 5	24	30	24	12	10
River Duddon	100/ 500–1 5	30	35	10	15	10
Eccles. Sonnets	400/ 2000–1 5	21	14	28	16	21
1823–1837	1500/ 7400–1/5	27	33	10	16	14
1838–1847	350/ 1800–1 5	15	24	38	15	08
Total work	9000/53000–1/6	32	30	15	09	14

To be noted:
a) Except for the first and last items, the earliest and latest work, the proportions are close to those in the total.
b) The earliest and latest items, differing from the rest, lack general statement, emphasize in youth the physical convention of the eighteenth century, in age the bestowal which Wordsworth himself made conventional.
c) The growing literary quality of style is indicated by increase of personification and objectification, not adapted to any changing need.
d) Poems now considered best have largest amount of general statement.

FIGURE 6.3. "Named Emotion in Wordsworth" table from Josephine Miles's dissertation, published in 1942 as *Wordsworth and the Vocabulary of Emotion* (New York: Octagon Books, 1965).

lished works; samples of the work of poets contemporary to Wordsworth, including Alexander Pope, John Armstrong, Samuel Johnson, Oliver Goldsmith, Thomas Gray, William Collins, James Beattie, and William Cowper; and 5,000 lines of Robert Dodsley's miscellany, *A Collection of Poems in Six Volumes by Several Hands*. She also tested representative samples of about 1,000 lines of poetry from other time periods: Shakespeare, Donne, Pope, Eliot, Jeffers. Keeping her counts on handwritten notebook paper charts, Miles compared the total number of emotion words with the total number of lines to calculate a proportion for each. Finally, she classified how these words were used: as expressions of general emotion; as emotions emanating from the physical body; as emotions "bestowed" upon the external world; as emotions personified; or as emotions objectified. Miles's counts did verify that, against the trends of her contemporaries, Wordsworth used the language of emotion consistently in poetry, tending most to use emotions as general statements, as physical sensations, and as bestowed upon the external world or objects in it (what Ruskin would come to call the "pathetic fallacy"). But her counts also revealed something more unexpected. She had begun her quantitative work, she explained, expecting that it would reveal, above all, individual style, allowing her "to be able to recognize a poem of any poet by the singularity of his choices." But Wordsworth, she found to her surprise, shared a common vocabulary with other poets and even prose writers of his time. "Singularity of choice," Miles began to understand, "is part of the commonality of choice that serves a poet in the making of poetry."[71]

The Wordsworth project left Miles curious about the longer arc of poetic languages of emotion. For her next project, Miles narrowed her focus and expanded her scope, tracking just one aspect of emotion language—"the one small device called pathetic fallacy"[72]—over a long century. This second monograph, *Pathetic Fallacy in the Nineteenth Century: A Study of a Changing Relation between Object and Emotion*, examined about 65,000 lines drawn from twenty-four sources: from Collins, Gray, and Cowper through Hopkins, Housman, Amy Lowell's 1915 anthology *Some Imagist Poets*, George Moore's 1924 *Anthology of Pure Poetry*, selections from the March 1940 issue of *Poetry* magazine, and Eliot. Miles's appendix table of frequencies for the volume displayed the "Amount of Pathetic Fallacy in the Work of Twenty-Four Poets" and showed clearly the steep decline of the device over the course of the century. But Miles's close hand counting further revealed how poets began to use the device differently in the nineteenth century. Summarizing her research for *Poetry* magazine, Miles explained that "the eighteenth-century fallacy attributed feelings [to nature] which fitted an outward show of correspondence, the lark gay, the stormy sea angry, the fields smiling, and so on," while "the nineteenth-century fallacy in its decline gave nature many inward causes for feeling." By the mid-nineteenth century, poets attribute emotions to nature that have to do with the sensed qualities of a scene rather than the representative qualities of the object. In Tennyson's "Poor Fancy sadder than a single star," the star is sad not because it is a star but because it sets at twilight and in a land of reeds.[73] For Miles, the changing use of the pathetic fallacy—consistent across poetry and prose—reveals the "changing worldviews and attitudes towards objects" in these eras.[74]

Whereas for her first two projects Miles created data sets of specific figures to answer specific research questions, in her third monograph, *Major Adjectives in English Poetry from Wyatt to Auden*, Miles did something new: she created an open-ended and reusable data set. Wishing to use more efficient and generalizable methods for representing larger corpora of texts, Miles decided to use both concordances and word counts to tally adjectives and high-frequency words. These simpler elements would be easier for a team to identify consistently and also more project-agnostic so that Miles, and potentially others, could use the resulting tabulations to ask and answer multiple questions. As she noted in *Major Adjectives in English Poetry*, "While the earlier studies began with contents of vocabulary and device which seemed significant, and then proceeded to establish some quantitative relationships in context, this study of adjectives begins more formally with a part of speech conventionally isolated, and attempts then to follow some of the main outlines of the pattern of its quantity and quality, stability and variety, in English poetry." The "relatively clear boundaries" of the adjective, verb, noun, or even "special reference or figure" or "device of sound or statement" seemed to Miles "better for counting" than more ambiguous elements like, as she noted, the ambiguously defined "images" that Caroline Spurgeon counted in *Shakespeare's Imagery and What It Tells Us*.[75] Her bibliography for the volume included works like Ruth Benedict's *Patterns of Culture* (which she was also teaching in English 1A by this time), June Downey's *Creative Imagination*, and Erwin Panofsky's *Studies in Iconology*. Miles argued in the introduction that such works provide "an instruction which accepted literary scholarship does not supply, an instruction in the establishing of descriptive norms, for literature as for society." Literary study, Miles implied, had its own encyclopedia vs. sunset problem. In order to develop a true picture of "the whole dense and lively nature of the composition" of English poetry, scholars would need to agree upon the parts in order to describe their function "in frequency and relation."[76]

Miles's attempt to harness word counts to reveal syntax opened a new horizon for studies of poetry. Miles's focus on the ghostly sentence structures of poetry opened new space between the quantifying formalists, who counted meter in order to study poetic form, and the quantifying historicists, who counted and categorized words in poetry in order to get at the "neutral content" of an author's or era's language. While she saw herself as indebted to the work of earlier distant readers such as Rickert and Spurgeon, Miles believed they moved too quickly from poems to the world, and viewed words as containers rather than parts of speech. Miles continually reminded her readers that it was important for critics to make claims about language, not merely about words. To say "that words rather than language are the medium of literature," Miles argued, is a "reduction which seems to me parallel with that which makes HO the medium of the Seven Seas," for "even in its more irrational, magical forms literature makes as much use of syntax as of sound and reference. Language is not the sum of words, for their relationship is part of its character."[77] For

Miles, it was through studying the sentence that poets and critics could perceptively re-inhabit earlier modes of poetic composition: "To many readers such analysis of quantity and connection will seem alien to the modes of poetic creation," she wrote, "but is it not possible that proportions once poetically felt, and then numerically discovered, may be poetically reperceived?"[78]

After the publication of her first three pamphlets as *The Vocabulary of Poetry* in early 1946, Miles began to count not just adjectives but also verbs and nouns across a more evenly selected representation of English poetry over the centuries. This research culminated in a series of pamphlets on the poetry and prose of the '40s decades in each century—*The Primary Language of Poetry in the 1540's and 1640's*, *The Primary Language of Poetry in the 1740's and 1840's*, and *The Primary Language of Poetry in the 1940's*—published together in 1951 as *The Continuity of Poetic Language*. Her aim in focusing on the '40s, as she later noted, was "to discover the degree of continuity in the range of the poetry" by examining the same decade in each century.[79] Adding more graduate students to the team who had helped count for *Major Adjectives*, Miles and her research assistants gathered roughly 1,000-line samples of twenty poets from each decade, selected from Jyotish Chandra Ghosh's *Annals of English Literature, 1475–1925*. Miles presented the 1,000-line samples as "provisionally" "representative" of the poets' work;[80] she typically chose mid-career poems rather than early or late poems. Miles and her students counted, for example, 1,000 lines of Shakespeare's sonnets, all of Pope's *Essay on Man*, the first 123 poems of Robert Herrick's *Hesperides*, and 1,220 lines of eleven poems by Keats. Brad Pasanek, who re-created the hand counts "for a thousand lines of verse," describes the method—"stationed at the boundary between human and machine reading"—as both "monotonous and absorbing."[81]

By expanding their word counts from the adjective alone to the adjectives-verbs-nouns in proportion to one another, Miles and her team were able to order their poets on a scale of syntactic structures, from the verb-heavy "predicative" poets to the more "substantival" poets who used mostly adjectives and nouns. They found, for example, that poets in the 1540s used adjectives-verbs-nouns in roughly a 1-2-2 proportion. Describing the predicative nature of their poetry, which included work by Chaucer as well as medieval ballads, Miles wrote that this was "a verse of fairly laborious thinking process, a language of logic more than names." Poets of the 1740s, meanwhile, showed a proportion of 2-2-1—what Miles described as extremely "qualitative." Miles would later settle on different terms: "clausal" for the more predicative and verbal, phrasal for the more adjectival. She explained that clausal poems "tend to be stanzaic and active . . .

working out an argument or narrative in clearly defined stages and formal external order," while "phrasal poems, and phrasal eras, on the other hand, emphasize line-by-line progression, and cumulative participial modification in description."[82] Miles summarized these proportional counts in the first table of each pamphlet in the '40s series. The table listed the poets and poems counted, their meter, genre, and the proportion of adjectives to verbs to nouns in an average ten lines. These tables offered a snapshot of the poets in relation to one another; the list was ordered from the least to the most adjectival of the poets. When the tables were combined, in *The Continuity of Poetic Language*, they revealed unexpected similarities over time. For example, they showed the reemergence of "the Wyatt and Donne tradition in Cummings and Millay" and the continuation of "the less spare metaphysical tradition in Landor, Emerson, Auden."[83]

The *Continuity* series also took a more qualitative look at the prose of each decade, concluding that poetry and prose share materials: "The language of poetry appears to be a special selection from and formalizing of the language of prose," Miles wrote.[84] In her final *Primary Language* pamphlet on the 1940s, for example, Miles turned from the decade's poetry to its prose, showing that in both, the "characteristic materials" revolve around "questions about number, space, time, mind, matter," and seem to pose one central question: "What is fact and how is it interpreted by mind?"[85] For Miles, the "agreements" of her time were visible in Wallace Stevens's "So and So Reclining on Her Couch," in the "crisp factual beginnings" in *Story* magazine's fiction, in Harvard's *General Education in a Free Society* report, in contemporary medical memoirs, and in the pages of the *Kenyon Review*. Reducing these disparate genres to their major adjectives and core grammatical structures, Miles saw the 1940s as a decade that shuttled back and forth between the discerning mind and the discerned world. The essays, memoirs, and fiction written in this moment obsessed over the "artful creation which wishes to be pure report, the image made by and then scrutinized by mind."[86] Miles moved adeptly, as the 1940s pamphlet shows, from her word counts and proportions to lyrical and compelling reconstructions of the animating questions of an era.

Many of Miles's readers—even her publishers—wanted to retain her fresh and illuminating readings of poets and eras while discarding the data upon which they were based. Reviews of the *Continuity* pamphlets nearly always remarked on a split in Miles's method, between her qualitative close readings and her data tabulations. Vivienne Koch, for example, noted that "a good part of *The Continuity of Poetic Language* is simply the evaluatory judgment of an aware and trained reader in just that type of 'close' criticism Miss Miles seems a little to deplore."[87] These critics suggested that one might discard Miles's careful data tabulations while retaining her charismatic interpretations of them. Even her own publisher, Miles found, shared this attitude. In 1957, when Miles completed work on *Eras and Modes in English Poetry*, the University of California Press refused to publish her tables and data, which by this time included counts from '90s decades alongside her earlier findings from the '40s decades. "It was from '57 on to '64 that a lot of my misery started," Miles recalled, "because I now had all this data but nobody wanted to print it." A "heroic typist at the press" finally did work to allow the Press to publish Miles's data separately. It appeared in 1960 as a large-format supplement to the table-less *Eras and Modes* under the title *Renaissance, Eighteenth-Century, and Modern Language in English Poetry: A Tabular View*. When the Press issued a second edition of *Eras and Modes* in 1964, they included reduced-size versions of the tables.[88]

Despite this lack of interest in her tabulations, Miles continued to expand her data set in the 1960s, now to include tallies and proportions not just for adjectives, nouns, and verbs but also "connectives"—*if, and, but, for*, and so on.[89] By this time, Miles had fully elaborated an account of how her quantitative poetic formalism differed from—and even debunked—the mainstream formalist criticism of her day. By contrast with criticism that tended to focus on the poem as the primary object of interpretation and to overstate its autonomy and originality, Miles's data sets revealed "agreements" and continuities between poets and prose writers, and across centuries. "After a generation of close criticism of individual and autonomous texts," Miles argued, "criticism has still further steps to take, to reach poetry as well as poems, extensions as well as intension, participations as well as isolations."

Read only within the context of her published scholarship and criticism in these years, Miles's work may seem designed to correct the myopia of literary critics who admire a few trees while losing sight of the forest. In this vein, we might see her interventions as akin to some recent computational literary studies work that sees itself as correcting an evidentiary problem in literary studies.[90] But Miles continued to insist—through the 1950s, '60s, and '70s—that a key audience for her quantitative research was the kind of student she taught in English 1A. As she worked to add the connective counts for 1966's *Style and Proportion*, she simultaneously wrote essays such as "What We Compose" to describe how a first-year composition student could benefit from the study of connectives: "One of the simplest ways to observe and follow significant order, then, is to pay close attention to the connectives in a passage . . . additives like *and, then, also*; comparatives like *as, so, how*; disjunctives like *but*; alternatives

like *on the one hand . . . on the other*; causal subordinates like *if, because, for*; descriptive subordinates like *who* and *which*; temporal and spatial locatives like *where* and *there, when* and *then*. Behind these guiding signs lie basic logical patterns of which we profoundly need to be aware." For her it was "important for the young writer to know what these choices are, how they have been made in the past, and how he may make them in the present." For Miles, past poets were once practicing writers. They made choices—of vocabulary, of sentence structures—in the same way that her English 1A students must learn to make them. Both her teaching and her research were devoted to becoming closer to language and its historic possibilities: "It is the grain of the living wood we are after, the character of the language by which we live and compose."[91]

Toward the end of her career in 1976, Miles gave a Faculty Research Lecture at Berkeley that asserted her vision of the individual, even minor writer's importance in the face of the overwhelming evidence for poetic continuity and the commonality of poetic language that her own research provided. Published in *Critical Inquiry* as "Values in Language; or, Where Have *Goodness, Truth,* and *Beauty* Gone?," Miles's lecture begins by considering how poetry changes over time. How, for example, has English poetry moved from "the poetry of social orders" to the "poetry of cosmic scenes" to the poetry of "inner feelings and their correspondences in natural objects of sense and sight"?[92] And what will come next after modernist poetry's refined particularities? Contrary to our expectations, Miles explains, "great poets . . . are not really the innovators," rather "they are the sustainers, the most deeply immersed in tradition, the most fully capable of making use of the current language available to them." It is "minor poets," instead, who introduce "chief new words and structures" in any era. In this sense, both Harold Bloom and "so distinguished a colleague as Fredric Jameson of San Diego" have it wrong—poetic change cannot be traced to major poets' "anxiety of influence," while the fact that it occurs at all disproves Jameson's vision of an individual writer "bound and tied" by the "prison house of language." Instead, Miles writes, "to believe in singularity is not to deny generality; one would not be discernable without the other."[93]

At the end of her talk, Miles turns to address a "you"—an unidentified and potential writer, faced with the daunting task of entering into what may seem like a fully consolidated and complete contemporary world of letters. Miles encourages you to be comforted rather than chastened by the continuities of language before you: the "steadiness of change which can be described so regularly, if one is not imposing one's own interests and limitations, is a fine cultural phenomenon." In her final lines of encouragement, her favored word "agreements"—naming at once the numerical evidence of each era's shared materials and the contract that individual poets make with them—guides the beginner over the bridge from passively, objectively observing to actively, subjectively predicating: "The agreement between talent and talent, and between each talent and each reader, in terms of time and the substances of value as they can be built into art, are at once, as we have tried to trace, good, true, and beautiful to behold. And they can be made by you: your tree, your house, against your sky. Whoever you are. In the agreements of time."[94]

CHAPTER 7

Simon J. Ortiz, Native American Arts (1978)

The opening chapters of this book, on Caroline Spurgeon and T. S. Eliot, showed how their major works of literary criticism—*Shakespeare's Imagery* and *The Sacred Wood*—invented methods and theorized literary value in ways that grew directly out of particular classes that these figures taught at Bedford College for Women and the University of London Extension School. Our final chapter likewise turns to a literature survey class, Ethnic Studies 11: Native American Arts, at the public community College of Marin, in which poet, critic, and activist Simon J. Ortiz experimented with the syllabus format that would prove to be part of the inspiration for his major 1981 essay, "Towards a National Indian Literature: Cultural Authenticity in Nationalism." Ortiz wrote "Towards a National Indian Literature" as he and other writers and scholars of Native American literature raised the question of how Native American literary history would be understood, spoken of, and written in the academy. Offering a decisive answer to the central problem of how a Native literature and culture that had adopted many of the forms of Western literature and culture could be considered authentic, Ortiz's essay has become foundational to the field of Native American literature and Native American studies; it continues to impact how scholars understand the field today. Returning to the College of Marin courses that Ortiz taught and revised in the late 1970s, we can see how his conception of a Native American literary history and his theorization of the connection between the oral tradition and printed literature arose first as solutions to the pedagogical problem of how to teach a literary historical survey that didn't position contemporary writing as belated or inauthentic.

Ortiz—an Acoma Pueblo professor, writer, and activist—turned his attention to the teaching of Native American literature in the American university at a moment when the large body of writing by Native American writers that would come to be called the Native American Renaissance was in progress. The wave of new writing by Native authors starting in the 1960s, along with the Red Power movement and other pan-Indian forms of organizing and cultural consciousness, meant that an American Indian or Native American literature conceived as a kind of national literature with a coherent body of authors and a literary history was coming to seem important and even urgent. N. Scott Momaday had won the Pulitzer Prize for Literature for his 1968 novel *House Made of Dawn*. Pedagogy journals had begun to feature articles on teaching texts like Momaday's *The Way to Rainy Mountain* (1969) to both Indigenous and non-Indigenous students in high schools and colleges. Projects compiling resources on the teaching of Native American literature and culture in primary and secondary schools and in colleges were underway, and Native American studies programs were opening at some institutions and featuring courses on Native American literature as part of formal curricula.[1]

To some, the 1970s moment seemed to present an impasse.[2] The contrast between a lost past oral tradition and a present, possibly less valid, written one seemed unavoidable. Another challenge was posed by the apparent need to subordinate hundreds of distinct languages, cultures, and literary traditions to the single formation "Native American literature" in order to fit the disciplinary and curricular space allocated for it. Some critics questioned whether the very category and idea of the literary misrepresented much past oral and written expression by Native Americans. Others worried about whether a literature and culture that had adopted the rituals and forms of Christianity and Western literature could be considered authentic. Yet if an authentic Native American literature could only exist in a pre-colonized oral past, then of course there seemed to be no possibility for a thriving and vital Native American literature to exist in the present, and no unifying literary history for the new surge of literature by Native American writers Ortiz observed and to which he contributed.

It was in response to these questions and, in particular, to the unavoidable contrast between an "authentic" oral tradition and a less valid written one, that Ortiz wrote "Towards a National Indian Literature," published in *MELUS* in 1981. In it, Ortiz rejected the idea that a contemporary Native American literature was inauthentic or tragically impossible because of genocide, assimilation, and hybridization. Using as an example his own family and pueblo's reappropriation of Christian religious rituals first introduced to them by Spanish colonizers, he argues that these rituals "are now Indian because of the creative development that the native people applied to them" and that "present-day Native American or Indian literature is evidence of this in the very same way." For Ortiz, these creative forms of dissent and adaptation serve as the basis of a long tradition: "And because in every case where European culture was cast upon Indian people of this nation there was similar creative response and development, it can be observed that this was the primary element of a nationalistic impulse to make use of foreign ritual, ideas, and material in their own—Indian—terms. Today's writing by Indian authors is a continuation of that elemental impulse."[3] For Ortiz, the last five hundred post-contact years constituted the national literary tradition—five hundred years in which the continuance of Native American people, cultures, and societies had been built in part out of the adoption and appropriation of colonizers' forms and practices as a response to genocide and the theft of cultural resources. Instead of seeing this new literature by Native American writers as separate from everyday culture, Ortiz insisted on seeing it as continuous with it and obeying similar logics. Acoma songs, dances, and rituals, for example, were "not literary stories," but "it was all literature nevertheless." Despite the importance of "literary" writers like D'Arcy McNickle, N. Scott Momaday, and Leslie Marmon Silko, for Ortiz "it is the voice of countless other non-literary Indian women and men of this nation who live a daily life of struggle to achieve and maintain meaning which gives the most authentic character to a national Indian literature."[4] His essay reimagines authenticity, transforming it from something that might only be discovered in a lost past into something that inheres in the common forms and rituals of everyday life. As Scott Richard Lyons notes, Ortiz's essay would be powerfully influential in bringing "nationalist discourse" not only to the field of Native American literary criticism, but to scholarship in disciplines across Indigenous studies.[5]

Ortiz's experimentation with how to teach Native American literature in the College of Marin classrooms formed the basis of his foundational essay. It was in those classes that Ortiz solved the problem of how to teach the relation between an oral tradition often mistakenly described as past or vanished and a contemporary literature that Ortiz did nevertheless view as a "cultural renaissance of Native American people."[6] In his mid-1970s syllabus drafts and notes and in the new Native American Arts class he taught at Marin for three years, Ortiz worked out his ideas about Native American literature's history. After a more conventional first iteration of his course in spring 1977—in which he followed a survey model that began with older texts, ended with contemporary literature, and assigned weekly readings drawn from the historical period of the week's lecture topic—Ortiz significantly revised his syllabus. Preserving the form of the historical survey that guided his lectures, he changed his text assignments so that each week's readings came from two or three distinct historical moments and genres. By experimenting with the survey's form, Ortiz sought to solve—or at least to be able to allow the class to examine—the tension between the idea of contemporary Native American literature as a form of continuance of the oral tradition and the need to dramatize for his students the literary, cultural, and social effects and historical discontinuities inflicted by white settler society and culture.[7] Even more fundamentally, as Ortiz recorded in his journals, his successive syllabus revisions reckoned with how to teach literature whose meaning resided in its closeness to the everyday lives of people from a wide variety of cultures and geographies under the rubric of the singular, institutionalized curricular formation of "Native American literature" as an academic subject that would be taught to an ethnically diverse range of students in a university classroom.[8] Like many of the other teachers in this book, Ortiz rejected the idea of literature as a thing apart, separate from history and from everyday life.

Simon J. Ortiz and the Universities

By the time he was teaching at College of Marin in the late 1970s, Ortiz had experienced nearly as many educational models as anyone could have in the number of years he had lived. Raised in the Acoma Pueblo, Ortiz learned Acoma culture and the Keres language from his parents and other relatives and members of the community. Ortiz considered this learning both foundational and central to his education. On one curriculum vitae, under a section he titled "Community Background," he explained: "During my developing younger life, I was raised and educated according to the ways of the Acoma People; this has been the basis for all my subsequent education and experience." Ortiz's "formal education," as he called it on the CV, started with elementary school at McCartys Day School in the village of McCartys/Deedzihyana, where his family lived.[9] He later went to a boarding school, St. Catherine Indian School, in Santa Fe, and then Albuquerque Indian School before returning home to attend the local public Grants High School through his graduation in 1960. After graduating high school, Ortiz left for Colorado to enroll at the private, Native student–serving Fort Lewis College for two years before dropping out to join the US Army. Trained as a missile defense technician but ultimately working as a pay clerk, Ortiz remained in the army from 1963 through 1966, during which time he continued to read widely, write poetry, and document his daily life in his journals.

After leaving the army, Ortiz studied English literature at the University of New Mexico for two years, though he left without taking a degree. The comments on his paper for a 1966 Early English Literature class may suggest part of the reason—on one long paper, the instructor made two comments only, one faulting him for not knowing the difference between medieval romance and the Romantic poets, the other a single evaluative line in red ink informing him that "your subject is not clearly defined."[10] (Compare with Ortiz's own comment fifteen years later at UNM, next to an A grade on his student Annie Martinez's final portfolio, "Please remember, all the important things of our people are contained + continued by the language of our stories + songs."[11]) Ortiz's typed journals from his student years record his curricular and extracurricular reading and writing. While reading *Hamlet*, Ortiz noted that he found the class in which the play was assigned uninspiring but that nevertheless the play was good.[12] His journals also record his ironic relation to his English education: his notes for a course on Victorian poetry remark that stanza 39 of *In Memoriam* is "Hilarious"; he transcribes his professor's instruction to "Read [Jerome] Buckley's Books," wryly adding, "I guess Buckley is an author."[13]

After his two years at UNM, Ortiz spent a summer teaching Native American history at Rough Rock Demonstration School while taking an extension school class on Native education that Arizona State University was running there. His extension professor, Robert Roessel, was a central figure at Rough Rock and eventually became president of Navajo Community College (now Diné College). For the course, Ortiz wrote a long paper on why Native students drop out of school, titled "AND WHY NOT?: An Attempt to Explain Why Indian Students, Especially Those Who Show High Potential and Motivation, Drop Out." The essay explains the "intensity of the paradox" felt by Native college and university students.[14] Ortiz begins by describing how his tribe regarded "higher education [as] something that was for the benefit of white people who had money, the educational background, and that peculiar ability for a college education." As Ortiz recalls, when his small cohort of high school graduates asked the tribe to fund their college education, the elders demurred and brought in "BIA personnel who were representatives of the Relocation Program." But the students insisted that it was important that the funds come from their tribe; as Ortiz explains, "The Indian youth . . . can be supported by non-Indian people, they can give him scholarships, grants, stipends, encouragement, but he is not able to feel comfortable without the sanction of his people." This impasse stalled the young graduates: "none of us went to college that fall."[15] Eventually, Ortiz accepted the BIA grant, realizing that this was just the first of the many alienations that his higher education would entail. As an example, Ortiz describes the feeling of realizing that anthropologists such as Adolph Bandelier had spent decades studying traditions such as the *katzina* that Ortiz had been initiated into and warned to "never to divulge the information . . . to young children or white people." Entering the university entails "confrontations, involving the question of whether to be subjective or objective" and whether to accept the university's rewards—"the dissonance of grades, pats on the back, first place ribbons"—or to remain true to the tribe's value of "cooperation, amiability, and being unimposing."[16] Ortiz notes that adopting the objective view of the educational system entailed accepting the premise that "we were . . . second class citizens."[17] He notes that ASU's 1962 cooperative research project, *Higher Education of Southwestern Indians with Reference to Success or Failure,* had found that "those students who succeeded most were those who were not as American Oriented as the others."[18]

After his summer at Rough Rock, Ortiz attended the University of Iowa's International Writing Program for a year in 1968–69 on a fellowship before returning to UNM to advise Native American students as a counselor-instructor in a College Enrichment–Upward Bound program. He also taught, in the following years, at Pembroke State University (a Native student–serving school, now the University of North Carolina at Pembroke), at Navajo Community College (NCC), and at the Institute of American Indian Arts (IAIA). As he designed and taught workshops and lit survey classes at this range of institutions—most of them Native student serving, but in very different contexts—he began to consider what the Native American literary canon might be, how it might take shape in the form of a syllabus, and how that syllabus might relate to his students' lives and their sense of identity. Much of this he recorded in his journals from these years.

"You could have an introduction to Native American literature": *Experiments in Teaching, 1974–76*

Ortiz's journals from the 1970s show him experimenting with a number of possible course plans for teaching Native American literature. At this time, Ortiz was writing daily. In page upon typewritten page, he reflected on the day's events, wrote poems, composed letters to friends and family, recorded his thoughts about his reading, drafted speculative reading lists, and planned the structure and rationales of courses real and imagined.

The stacks of loose-leaf typed pages of his journals gather together poetry and prose, course descriptions and messages to his unborn child, notes about the weather and records of his extensive travels.

In these journals Ortiz returns again and again to the question of what exactly "Native American literature" might be. If it was clear that colleges and universities were going to need a full set of Native American literature courses that would fit within the existing modes of teaching literature and hierarchies of organizing literary study—surveys and courses dedicated to a genre, period, or author—it was not as obvious how one might go about defining the literature, let alone constructing the courses.[19] In a May 5, 1974, journal entry (dated "Cinco de Mayo"), Ortiz ventriloquized the mix of optimism and uncertainty people in the academy seemed to feel about it: "Introduction to Native American literature. I don't know what they mean by that." "You could have an introduction to Native American literature."[20] Energized by the moment's openness to possibilities, Ortiz mapped out multiple courses that could belong to a university curriculum in Native American literature.

One of the fundamental difficulties at the outset for Ortiz was the way the syllabus, class hour, and available texts all seemed to predetermine courses that presented literature as separate from daily life. This easier path was thus "basically an academic approach." In this vein, Ortiz imagined an "Intro to Native Am. Lit" course that was "purely a survey." It would begin with pre-contact literature and present a continuous history that would end with contemporary responses. An introductory week would ask "what is Indian lit, what are some definitions?"; then would come a multipart survey, including "the forms: legend, folktale, myths, etc."; "prayer, chant, wordless lit"; "visual lit, i.e., hieroglyphs, pictographs, sacred paraphernalia"; and "rituals and the accompanying lit." Next would be "recorded lit. which has been translated & reworked" by white anthropologists and linguists; and two final sections, one on "very recent, contemporary lit written by non-Indians" and one on "lit. written in Indian and non-Indian by Indian writers, again very new." Ortiz imagined two further classes building on these final two weeks. The first, Written Indian Literature (Written by Non-Indians) could stretch "from European contact to the present," including written reflections in Spanish and English, "attitudes, reflections, portraits" of Indians including "'romanticized' Indians by Hawthorne, Longfellow, Melville," "translations and reworkings (anthologies, ethnographs by BAE)," as well as "contemporary work being done." Written Indian Literature (Written by Indians), by contrast, could be "necessarily very contemporary, from 1930s to present," examining "reflections/interpretations of American life by Indians" as well as "Indian life by Indians."[21]

He also planned a more literal study of the oral tradition. "Traditional Indian Literature" could focus on "the literature transmitted by the vocal method," looking at many genres: legend, prayer, chant, folktale, "explanations and instructions," orations, and translations.[22] It would teach students "'the word as sacred' concept, continuance/survival regard for Indian lit," and end with "contemporary traditional material" by powwow singers, everyday singers, "the very new American Indian Theater idea," which Ortiz would have encountered during his time at Pembroke, and music and spoken word by musicians like Paul Ortega. In this framework, course readings would necessarily be published materials, but such materials would act as a "resource" for reconstructing the oral tradition rather than as true primary texts.[23]

These imagined courses, all examples of the "academic approach," had limitations. As he wrote, "One of the problem (seemingly?) areas seems to be a feeling that Indian literature cannot be taught (or allowed to be) as a purely academic discipline, i.e., in a college oriented or 'education' oriented course." This was the case, Ortiz thought, "because the way literature is taught at home, in the community, in [t]he prayers, songs, is not taught as 'literature,' but as a function, an extension of the 'word as sacred' idea." What might it look like to teach an actual experience of oral literature that nonetheless could carry a course number and be a part of a formal academic program at a US university? One might, Ortiz thought, pursue this goal through anthropological methods, attempting at the outset to understand the idea of oral literature's place within specific cultural contexts and activities in an analytical way. Alternatively, he thought, one might create an artificial version of the conditions necessary to actually re-create the *experience* of the oral tradition. If you were not a member of a particular tribe with the specific individual and collective experience necessary to understanding their literature, perhaps "there would have to be set up almost another thing, a cult (?), a far parallel being studying to be a Zen buddhist monk." Even then, however, something would be missing; the real way would be what Ortiz describes abstractly but extensively as a kind of living out of the "word as sacred idea": "The ultimate working out of the 'word' being living the life—you don't even have to say anything— although it is manifested and is continued by some method, mostly by the word, physical and spiritual word, life being measured by nonendings, always the continual process."[24]

While teaching in the 1970s at IAIA, NCC, and other Native student–

serving schools, Ortiz explored ways to offer students this more immersive course on Native American literature. He experimented with teaching students to write poetry and fiction, and to translate into and out of Indigenous languages. These were techniques for teaching students about how the literary forms of oral traditions were inextricable from everyday life and everyday experience. In the pages of his May 1974 journals, Ortiz drafted the course description and book list of the five-week Native American lit class he would teach at NCC June 10 through July 12 that same summer. It was another iteration of how one might teach the oral tradition in relation to written literature, this time including some work in creative writing as well as critical reading. "Designed as a survey with particular emphasis on the American Indian's particular method of literary expression, that it has been and is vocal as compared to that which is written," the course combined the three different types of texts Ortiz would identify going forward as core elements of his literature surveys—creation legends, traditional stories, and "the poetry found in the chant, song prayer, and drama"; autobiography and historical and migration narratives; and contemporary literature by Native American writers. While the class would necessarily read written materials and published texts, Ortiz noted, the emphasis would be on using them as "resource and reference material" to illuminate core "techniques of 'telling'" in the literary tradition. Texts written by non–Native Americans would be included, Ortiz noted, because in some cases it was the only available access to a story or genre—and "because some of it is accurate" even though "a lot of it is very bad."[25]

In this class, Ortiz tried to split the difference between the academic and the experiential approaches. The class would not only teach Native American literature as literature in the "common academic definition," but would also convey Ortiz's belief at the time that to the Native American writer "the language, the word, is indeed sacred because it is an extension of himself complimenting that which is around him." To put it as Momaday did in *The Way to Rainy Mountain*, Ortiz said, "his literature is the idea that he, the man, has of himself." Along with the literature survey, Ortiz introduced two creative workshop elements in order to move the class's response to the literature survey from "appreciation" to "inspiration"—some writing of creative literature, and some work on "the translation of Indian literature from the native language to another language and of course from another language into an [I]ndian language."[26]

The creative writing elements that Ortiz included in his course at NCC (and in his more fully hybrid reading and creative writing summer class at the IAIA) did not reappear in the Native American literature survey class he would go on to teach at Marin. This is likely because most of his Marin students were not Native American, and thus could not participate in the creation of Native literature as his NCC students could. But in his self-evaluation for one of his three Marin classes, Ortiz did note that his students "seemed especially enthused by the context of the oral tradition" and that the "song, story, poem, and other forms of literature found in Native American societies as well as some newer developments in that tradition" seemed to offer "insight into the student's own sense of self in the contemporary American setting."[27] As he moved from teaching students at NCC and IAIA to teaching students at the College of Marin, Ortiz taught non-Native students to conceive of a literature that was an integrated part of social life and a mode of continuance—all without fetishizing Native American experience as mystically unalienated and without idealizing Native American literature as magically healing the rifts caused by colonization and capitalism.

Ethnic Studies 11: Native American Arts at the College of Marin, Spring 1978

At Marin, Ortiz taught in the Ethnic Studies program for three years, from fall 1976 through spring 1979. Located in Kentfield, California, just north of San Francisco, Marin was a community college with a two-year program. The Ethnic Studies program had grown out of course offerings from various departments and had become a department with instructors and courses of its own just a few years earlier, in 1973.[28] By 1978 the department had seven instructors, all of them men: four in La Raza Studies (Joaquin Gallardo, Antonio Medrano, Don Ortez, and Juan Rios), one in Asian Studies (Bill Tsuji, the new department's first chair), and one in Black Studies (Walter Turner, the chair in 1978). The department acted as a center for the academic study of "the special contributions and problems of ethnic minorities in the cultural and historical development of the United States," and directed itself toward "education and the alleviation of racism and prejudice which has so long been a part of life in the U.S.A."[29] Their roster of classes rotated, but an Introduction to Ethnic Studies class and Ethnic Studies 3: Principles of Racism and Prejudice were offered most semesters.

Marin served a diverse body of students, many of whom would eventually transfer into the University of California system to finish a four-year degree. Each Ethnic Studies course catalog included a full page of detailed information about how Marin credits would transfer for admission and for departmental credit into the UC system; the back of some of the catalogs emphasized, in large decorative letters, that "ALL ETHNIC STUDIES COURSES QUALIFY FOR TRANSFER CREDIT" in the UC system schools.[30] The Marin curriculum also suggests that many of the students would eventually work in the public school system or in community support services. Ortiz's courses, for example, incorporated weeks on the teaching of Native American literature in the US public school system and prompted students to consider "the importance of applying the American Indian oral tradition of literature to the American education system."[31] The department described their curriculum as directed toward students with both personal and preprofessional interests in ethnic studies, singling out students aiming for careers in law, social work, health care, and primary, secondary, and university education as particularly in need of ethnic studies coursework. They also worked to support "the relationship between the College and the community" by offering programs in the local Sausalito School District, in San Quentin Prison, and by offering services to a variety of community organizations including the American Indian Survival School, the Ex-Offenders Program, and La Familia.[32] In addition, they supported a number of student organizations, providing faculty advisers to groups including the Native American Student Union, the La Raza Student Organization, and the Black Students Association.

At Marin, Ortiz was hired to teach creative writing, the Ethnic Studies program's intro class, and Native American literature and history classes in the Ethnic Studies program. He spent three years in the department before leaving to join the University of New Mexico's Native American Studies program. Ortiz's pathway to college and university teaching, through his publication record rather than formal credentials, was not available in many disciplines. This relative flexibility meant that literature departments in the later 1960s and '70s were, as Robert Warrior points out, early locations of the teaching of Native American studies by Native American faculty.[33] Ortiz's own May 1974 journal entry registered the difficulty of finding faculty with the relevant expertise. Describing classes on "Specific Tribal Literature" in well-documented languages "such as Navajo or Sioux," Ortiz notes that they "should be taught by a person who knows the tribal lit as a native and is academic oriented as well with linguistic and literary background (ANYBODY?)."[34] On a copy of his own CV filed at Marin in the late 1970s, Ortiz explained how he had experience and publications in place of a formal degree: "Although I do not have any college degrees my experience and publications have allowed me to be qualified for college level teacher employment. I hold a California Community College Teaching Credential."[35]

For colleges and universities working to bring more Native American professors into higher education, the revaluing of nontraditional career paths like Ortiz's offered one solution to the absence of a significant pool of formally trained candidates. Writing one of the sheaf of official "confirmation of employment and moral character" letters that the Marin administration required that Ortiz have previous employers submit, Bill J. Wahpepah, the director of the American Indian Adult Education program, wrote warmly about Ortiz's generous mentoring of the students in his programs, noting that he also was an important model for young Native American writers. Wahpepah added in a closing, separately set-off line: "It is not often you see an Acoma poet at College of Marin."[36] The line seems to congratulate the College of Marin on its good fortune in managing to hire a rare teacher of Native American literature who is himself a well-known poet from a small, traditional Indigenous community. But the full, sly meaning of the line is legible only to an initiated audience who had already had the chance to read Ortiz's new collection of journey poems *Going for the Rain*. Newly published when Wahpepah was writing his letter, the collection contains a poem titled "Many Farms Notes," in which a sheep remarks to the poet, "You don't see many Acoma poets passing through here."[37] Wahpepah's reference is friendly but pointed: there were not many Acoma poets, or Native American people of any kind, teaching in institutions like Marin, and to get a job at a place like Marin—especially given the higher-education credentialing process that would stand as an almost insurmountable barrier in the way of anyone from Acoma at that historical moment—required accomplishments like publishing a major poetry collection with a publisher like Harper and Row. While he might be marginally qualified from the perspective of the institution, Wahpepah's coded reference said that he was overqualified from the perspective of many other measures of accomplishment.

Though his Ethnic Studies 11 class bore the general title "Native American Arts" in the course catalog, Ortiz explained in his course description that his focus would be on the "Native American art of oral literature" as "conveyed through the song, story, poem, prayer, autobiographical narrative, etc. which is a complement to the representative or visual art of painting, sculpture, pottery, weaving, etc. that is more popularly known by the general public."[38] Ortiz taught an iteration each spring semester—1977, 1978, and 1979—during his three years at Marin.[39] Though the three versions differed radically from one another, in all three versions of the class, as in his own poetry and other writing, Ortiz aimed to capture the "continuance" of the oral tradition while accounting for, as he saw it, the fact that "it has been only since the 1960's that Native American writers have been published to any extent; before then it was as if we were truly invisible, truly the 'vanishing Indian' of the U.S.A.'s vainglorious wish."[40] Framing literature by Native Americans as central to Indigenous cultural and social life, Ortiz added that "this artform of the Native American is through which he perceives and expresses his religion, history, culture, value system, experiences, the relationship he shares with the universe, the continuance of his traditions, and his survival."[41] The class, the syllabus noted in the first week, would cover the forms of traditional oral expression and language necessary to understand not just Native American literary and cultural history, but also contemporary Native American literature.

The class's carefully designed literature survey structure followed the oral tradition from its earliest available traces (knowledge of which was changing rapidly as the scholarly field grew) to the present day. Like many Native American literature surveys of the time, Ortiz's syllabus traveled the familiar sweep of the historical literature survey. As Ted Underwood explains, from the beginning of its early nineteenth-century use, the general English literary historical survey "stressed the causal connections between broad stages of development" rather than the "distinct character of narrowly defined periods" characteristic of the period course that became popular in the 1840s.[42] The survey form was therefore suitable for representing an Indigenous oral literature as a form of cultural continuance, an incremental and still ongoing tradition that connected very different cultures and times, from the longest-ago written records to the present resurgence of writing by Native American authors from different tribes, nations, and geographical locations.[43]

In the first part of the semester, the class focused on pre-contact literature, including weeks on creation stories, migration traveling and journey stories, story cycles like Coyote and others, and tribal memory and traditional autobiography. The course began with creation stories as the "beginning development of language and literature." The first week offered a general introduction to the "sources, elements, context, history, techniques, forms: stories, prayers, religious instructions, songs, dances, which are the source of contemporary literature." Weeks two and three turned to creation stories as "the beginning, development of language and literature" ("often mislabeled as 'mythology' or 'legend' or 'folklore,'" Ortiz added in the 1978 and 1979 iterations of the syllabus). In weeks four, five, and six, the class moved through early accounts of travel and migration stories, the "further development of religious and social institutions, crises overcome, continuance," as well as story cycles like the Coyote stories, human and animal relationships, and "the earth as ordinary yet vital knowledge."[44]

The syllabus then moved on to examine literature, culture, and society during contact and colonization, following the development of the oral tradition as resistance to colonialism and mode of generational continuance. Week seven treated tribal memory and historical narrative and traditional autobiography, mentioning as examples (but not assigned reading) Momaday's *The Way to Rainy Mountain* and Mountain Wolf Woman's autobiography. Weeks eight and nine treated "ritual literature in the religious ceremony and other artforms embodied in the Native American dance" and the transmission of culture and knowledge through "anecdotes, narratives which teach customs, practice, insight related from one generation to another, one geographical area to another."[45] And weeks ten and eleven continued to study oral forms in order to show students how stories collected by white ethnographers and anthropologists as part of the colonial project nevertheless could furnish a record of Indigenous people's resistance to colonization.[46]

Ortiz's survey ended with four final weeks devoted to contemporary literature and culminated with the idea of the current cultural renaissance.[47] Ortiz asked the class to consider how to read contemporary Native American literature now in the light of their new knowledge of Native American literary history. As Ortiz put it on the syllabus, in these weeks the class would study the "traditional forms of the contemporary Native American literature embodied in the prayer, song, ritual literature; traditional forms of the contemporary novel and dramatic literature in the oral narrative and ritual drama."[48] Pausing to imagine the complex interchanges between past and present literatures, Ortiz drew on previous weeks' lectures and discussions to show students how many of the functions of contemporary Native American literary forms were performed in the past by other genres and forms. He spent a week on short stories, essays, and criticism; a week on new novels; and a week on poetry.[49]

In both this survey-like structure and choice of texts, Ortiz's class was not exceptional; it followed a common approach to the teaching of Native American oral literature at the time. Patricia Russo's American Indian Literature class, taught in the spring 1978 semester at San Diego State University, offers a useful comparison. Her course states similar aims, includes somewhat similar texts, and also moves, survey-like, from earlier oral literature to the contemporary present, beginning with ethnolinguistic translations or reconstructions of myths, moving through anthropologist-mediated autobiographies, and ending with contemporary literature written in English. On her syllabus, Russo describes a course that would "survey American Indian Literature from the oral traditions (creation and origin stories, trickster-hero and legendary stories, poetry and song) to

Eth. St. 11 NATIVE AMERICAN ARTS   MWF 10 AM   FA 134

Instructor: Simon J. Ortiz
             Ethnic Studies Department

This course will focus upon the Native American art of
oral literature conveyed through the song, story, poem, prayer,
autobiographical narrative, etc. which is a complement to
the representative or visual art of painting, sculpture,
pottery, weaving, etc. that is more popularly known by the
general public. This particular artform is not just 'art'
in the sense that it comes from the spiritual as well, nor
is it just verbal ororal in that it utilizes dramatic ritual
as well though not in the same sense as 'theater art.' This
artform of the Native American is through which he perceives
and expresses his religion, history, culture, value system,
experiences, the relationship he shares with the universe,
the continuance of his traditions, and his survival.

Required textbooks: Sun Chief, Simmons
                     Indian Tales, de Angulo
                     The Man To Send Rain Clouds, Rosen
                     The First Skin Around Me, White

Course Outline

Jan. 17 - 21

Introduction to Native American literary expression and language - sources, elements, context, history, techniques, forms:
stories, prayers, religious instructions, songs, dances, which
are the source of contemporary written literature

Jan. 23 - 28

Creation, the beginning, development of language and literature -
often called 'mythology' or 'legend' or 'folklore'
Reading: Sun Chief

Jan. 31 - Feb. 4

Creation stories of the Hopi, the Kiowa, other Hano
Reading: Sun Chief
          Indian Tales

FIGURES 7.1A AND 7.1B. The first two pages of Simon J. Ortiz's 1977 syllabus for
Ethnic Studies 11: Native American Arts at the College of Marin. Simon J. Ortiz Papers,
MSS-372. Arizona State University Library: Labriola Center.

the literature of contemporary American Indian authors."[50] The standard
chronological models of the literature survey required that the class move
from a past cast as oral to a present cast as written, from a past in which
Indigenous languages are mediated by white ethnologists and Indigenous
life stories by white anthropologists to a present in which Native American writers express themselves (primarily) in English. For Russo, as for
Ortiz in his 1977 version of the class, lectures and accompanying texts

α

Feb. 7 - 11   (No class Feb. 11)

Emergence into the upper world through various levels of
development, struggle, and experience
Reading: Sun Chief
          Indian Tales

Feb. 14 - 18

Migration, travelling, journey stories, the further development of religious and cultural and social institutions,
crises overcome, continuance
Reading: Sun Chief
          Indian Tales

Feb. 21 - 25

The cycles, Coyote stories, invention and discovery, awareness of relationship among human beings, animals, the earth
as ordinary yet vital knowledge
Reading: Indian Tales

Feb. 28 - Mar. 4

The tribal memory, historical narrative such as in The Way
To Rainy Mountain, and traditional autobiography as in Mountain
Wolf Woman
Reading: Sun Chief

Mar. 7 - 11   (Midterm essay exam Mar. 7)

Anecdotes, brief narratives which teach rules of custom,
practice, insight related from one generation to another, one
geographical area to another
Reading: Sun Chief
          Indian Tales

Mar. 14 - 18

Ritual literature in the religious ceremony and other artforms
embodied in the Native American dance
Reading: Sun Chief
          Indian Tales

Mar. 21 - 25

Literature which has been gathered into written form by anthro-
pologists into publications like the Bulletins of the Bureau of
American Ethnology, Technicians of the Sacred, Castenanda's Don
Juan and Journey to Ixtlan

progress through history, and progress seemed to culminate in Native
American authors writing in English.

After teaching Native American Arts as a traditional survey, Ortiz
decided to experiment with an entirely new model. He reconfigured his
reading assignments, assigning three texts each week: one traditional
story, an autobiography, and contemporary literary work. The new three-
genre structure created a weekly contrast between three separate moments
in Native American literary history. Rather than trekking through representative texts from a long and continuous literary history, Ortiz's weekly

Eth. St. 11 NATIVE AMERICAN ARTS   MWF 10 AM   DH-103
Spring 1978
Instructor: Simon J. Ortiz, Ethnic Studies Department

This course focuses upon the Native American art of oral literature conveyed through the song, story, poem, prayer, autobiographical
narrative, etc., which is a complement to the representative or visual
art of painting, sculpture, pottery, weaving, etc. that is more popularly known by the general public. This literature is not just "art"
in the sense that it comes from the spiritual as well, nor is it just
verbal or oral in that it utilizes dramatic ritual as well though not
in the same sense as "theater art." This artform of the Native American
is through which he perceives and expresses his religion, history,
culture, value system, experiences, the relationship he shares with
the universe, the continuance of his traditions, and his survival, in
particular his resistance against colonialism.

Required textbooks: The Man To Send Rainclouds, Rosen
                       Indian Tales, de Angulo
                       Lame Deer: Seeker of Visions, Lame Deer & Erdoes
                       A Good Journey, Ortiz

Course Outline
Jan. 16 - 20
Introduction to Native American oral literary expression and lan-
guage - sources, elements, context, history, techniques, forms:
stories, prayers, religious instructions, songs, dances, which
are the source of contemporary written literature
Reading: pp 247 - 266 Lame Deer
             1 - 27 Indian Tales
            65 - 66 A Good Journey
Jan. 23 - 27
Creation, the beginning development of language and literature -
often mislabeled as 'mythology' or 'legend' or 'folklore'
Reading: pp 29 - 52 Indian Tales
           11 - 16, 119 - 138 Lame Deer
Jan. 30 -
Feb. 3
Creation stories of the Hopi, the Kiowa, other Hano
Reading: pp 174 - 181 Lame Deer
           53 - 86 Indian Tales
Feb. 6 - 10
Emergence into upper world through various levels of development,
struggle, knowledge derived from experience
Reading: pp 87 - 120 Indian Tales
           183 - 197 Lame Deer
           155 - 160 Man to Send Rain Clouds

FIGURES 7.2A AND 7.2B. The first two pages of Simon J. Ortiz's 1978 syllabus for
Ethnic Studies 11: Native American Arts at the College of Marin. This year, Ortiz moved
from a historical survey format to a format that featured constellations of texts from
different eras and genres each week. Simon J. Ortiz Papers, MSS-372. Arizona State
University Library: Labriola Center.

reading clusters drew students' attention to historical discontinuities and
identifications across time. He saw the change as an experiment in how to
posit a new relation between the resurgence of Native American cultural
production underway at the moment of his teaching and the millennia-
long oral tradition with which the new work enjoyed an important and

2.

Feb. 13 – 17
Migration, travelling, journey stories, further development of
religious and cultural and social institutions, crises overcome,
continuance
Reading: pp 164 – 168, 82 – 92 Man To Send Rain Clouds
         198 – 224 Lame Deer

Feb. 20 – 24
The cycles, Coyote stories, invention and discovery, awareness of
relationship among human beings, animals, the earth as ordinary yet
vital knowledge
Reading: pp 108 – 118 Lame Deer
         121 – 136 Indian Tales
         15 – 16, 29 – 34, 39 – 42 A Good Journey

Feb. 27 – Mar. 3
The Tribal memory, historical narrative such as in The Way to Rainy
Mountain and traditional autobiography as in Mountain Wolf Woman
Reading: pp 17 – 40 Lame Deer
         128 – 138 A Good Journey

Mar. 6 – 10   Mid-term exam
Anecdotes, narratives which teach customs, practice, insight related
from one generation to another, one geographical area to another.

Mar. 6 – 10   Mid-term exam
Ritual literature in the religious ceremony and other artforms
embodied in the Native American dance
Reading: pp 137 – 163 Indian Tales
         198 – 224 Lame Deer, 236 – 246
         54 – 61 A Good Journey

Mar. 20 – 24 No classes

Mar. 27 – 31
Anecdotes, narratives which teach customs, practice, insight related
from one generation to another, one geographical area to another
Reading: pp 164 – 197 Indian Tales
         139 – 173 Lame Deer

Apr. 3 – 7
Development of oral literature which has come from struggle against
colonialism
Reading: pp 42 – 70 Lame Deer, 225 – 235

         72 – 81, 132 – 138 A Good Journey
         128 – 144 Man To Send Rain Clouds

Its remembering but it's also something else—the memory.

necessarily complex relationship. (He also introduced some substitute
texts that better fit the new model; in 1978, for example, Ortiz exchanged
the more contemporary "transcribed" autobiography *Lame Deer: Seeker of
Visions* for *Sun Chief* and replaced the *First Skin* poetry anthology with his
own newly published poetry collection *A Good Journey* [1977].[51])

At least one important model for Ortiz's weekly constellation of readings was N. Scott Momaday's *The Way to Rainy Mountain* (1969). Momaday's book had topped the list of texts Ortiz brainstormed in 1974 as
he prepared to teach at NCC and IAIA; by the mid-1970s, it had already
made its way into curricula in high school and college classes. Moma-

day's famous history of the Kiowa people's migration and survival is told through the triangulation of three kinds of text: the traditional oral story, historical document, and Momaday's family's personal stories recounted through an authorial narrator's first-person voice. Momaday himself refers to the three different modes of the twenty-four sections of *The Way to Rainy Mountain* as "the mythical, the historical, and the immediate"; critic Christopher Teuton categorizes them similarly as "part oral tradition, part history, part personal reminiscence."[52] *The Way to Rainy Mountain* famously represents all three modes of writing about the past on each double-paged spread. Critics have tended to read *The Way to Rainy Mountain* as a work of modernist fragmentation,[53] but the book's more proximate formal history lies in Momaday's education in English literature at the University of New Mexico (BA, 1958) and Stanford University (PhD, 1963).[54] The book's form embodies the model of historical contrast familiar from the period course as a way of writing history not as a continuous story, but as a series of moments of identification across wide gaps of space and time. Momaday's history is itself a kind of syllabus, an outline for the study of Kiowa history that accommodates the presence of gaps and breaks. Joining mediated past, document, and present first-person subjective account, Momaday creates the "vivid evocation of vanished worlds" and fleeting but repeated moments of identification across time that Underwood describes as the characteristic of the literary period course so especially well-suited to national imagining in the England of the 1840s.[55] This model, which supported early nineteenth-century projects of national imagining in England, is one that Momaday adopts to his own purpose of putting into print a form of Kiowa national imagining that might support his tribe's recovery of political and cultural sovereignty.

Inspired in part, therefore, by Momaday's adoption of classroom forms to the writing of Kiowa history, with its own complex relation to the forms of university literary study and its definitions of literariness, Ortiz revised his single-semester survey syllabus. In the very first week of his 1978 class, Ortiz gave an overview of the "Native American oral literary expression and language," "which are the source of contemporary written literature." He organized the week's reading to use the idea of prayer as a line connecting mediated versions of animal stories, autobiography, and contemporary poetry. He started off with the final chapter of John Fire Lame Deer's autobiography ("as told to," and as Julian Rice points out, as partly fabricated by Richard Erdoes[56]), a text that follows the figure of a "hippy Indian" as medicine man through a life narrative that connects gonzo journalism as well as visionary activist writing to tell a series of stories about seven-day benders and American Indian Movement (AIM) sit-ins. In that chapter, "Blood Turned to Stone," Lame Deer ends with the words of a prayer:

> When an Indian prays he doesn't read a lot of words out of a book. He just says a very short prayer. If you say a long one you won't understand yourself what you are saying. And so the last thing I can teach you, if you want to be taught by an old man living in a dilapidated shack, a man who went to the third grade for eight years, is this prayer, which I use when I am crying for a vision: "Wakan Tanka, Tunkashila, *onshimala* ... Grandfather Spirit, pity me, so that my people may live."[57]

For the same first week, students in Ortiz's class read the introduction to linguist Angulo's *Indian Tales* (1953). The first chapter introducing the Father Bear–Mother Antelope–Baby Fox family ends with the mother sitting up after her husband and baby have gone to bed, the night before setting out on the journey that forms the book: "She looked into the shadows and sang softly a song to the night. It said: 'Dream for my child so that he will have power.'"[58] And as his third text, Ortiz assigns a contemporary prayer, "A Morning Prayer and Advice for a Rainbowdaughter" from *A Good Journey*, his own newly published collection of poems. Part of section 2 of *A Good Journey*, "Notes for My Child," centers around the figure of Ortiz's daughter Rainy Dawn, born on July 5, 1973. The first half of the poem is the prayer, beginning *"For this morning"*—a particular prayer for particular day. The second half of the poem is *"Advice"*: "learn how to make good bread," "enjoy yourself as a child," "pray, in whatever fashion," "learn how to recognize sadness," "respect your parents, brothers and sisters, all your kin, friends, and most of all yourself, learn this well." It ends "this is not all, certainly not all, because there is so much / more, and you will learn that."[59] Emphasizing ongoingness at the end of the poem, Ortiz teaches his own poem as an example of how traditional prayer forms continue within the new form of the poem, and shows how prayer might coexist alongside quotidian advice about baking and playing.

In other weeks, Ortiz constellated other texts in the same pattern of traditional story, modern autobiography, and contemporary literature. During the week of February 27, he lectured on "the Tribal memory, historical narrative such as in The Way to Rainy Mountain and traditional autobiography such as in Mountain Wolf Woman."[60] Students did not read *Rainy Mountain* or *Mountain Wolf Woman*, but rather the chapter "That Gun in the New York Museum Belongs to Me" of Lame Deer's autobiography, in which Lame Deer complains jokingly, "In the Museum of the American Indian in New York are two glass cases. A sign over them reads: 'Famous Guns of Famous Indian Chiefs.' They have five or six guns there, Sitting Bull's among them. A note text to one of those old breech-loaders says that it belonged to the famous Chief Lame Deer, killed in a battle with General Miles, who generously donated the gun to the New York museum. I don't know what right old Bear Coat Miles had to be that free with other people's property. That gun didn't belong to him. It belongs to me. I am the only Lame Deer left."[61]

Ortiz pairs this ironic chapter on colonizers' theft and fetishization of a worthless example of a weapon that is itself a symbol of the depredations of settler colonialism with his own ironic poem about the incursion of modern travel and communications infrastructures onto Acoma land. The poem describes how "RAILROADS, ELECTRIC LINES, GAS LINES, PHONE COMPANIES," and (in the present of the poem) "CABLE TV" use right-of-way laws to survey, record, divide, and steal Indian lands. Thinking about how tribal memory and historical narrative always come into focus around attempts at destroying them, Ortiz figures the traditional modes of dwelling on the land of his home through his childhood view of their invasion by a succession of expanding utility companies. Because of the railways "the village, Deedzihyana, / I come from is called McCartys / on the official state maps"; the "electric lines connect up Acu / with America," the "El Paso Natural Gas pipeline / blew up in the spring of 1966" and "ran / through our best garden and left stones."[62] Highway construction has similar effects; "When the Interstate was coming through" the excavations uncover "four kivas" that had been lost and forgotten. The phone is confusing: "When I was a boy, I didn't know / whether or not you could talk in Acoma / into the telephone and even after I found / that you could I wasn't convinced / that the translation was coming out correctly / on the other end of the line."[63] And cable TV probably also has its own designs on Ortiz's home: "I don't know much about CATV / and I would like to think / that it's better that way / but then I get this unwanted feeling / I better learn something about it."[64] Ortiz details how an Indigenous past is now perhaps always going to be accessed through text mediated through colonizers, through a mediated communications infrastructure (an infrastructure that includes the press on which Ortiz's own poems were printed) that literally appropriated Acoma land while connecting Acu closer and closer to a settler United States. Yet, like Lame Deer, Ortiz offers his map of settler theft and cultural destruction as the ironically enabling conditions of his own history writing.[65]

Toward the end of the semester, Ortiz explicitly took up the question of how traditional forms relate to contemporary literature. During the

week of April 17–21, Ortiz lectured on the "traditional forms of the contemporary Native American literature embodied in the prayer, song, ritual
literature; traditional forms of the contemporary novel and dramatic literature in the oral narrative and ritual drama."[66] The readings for this week
included texts that thematize historical difference. In addition to a selection from Angulo's *Indian Tales* and poems from *A Good Journey*, Ortiz
taught three selections from the new anthology *The Man to Send Rain
Clouds*: Anna Lee Walters's poem "Come, My Sons" and two of Leslie
Marmon Silko's short stories, "The Man to Send Rain Clouds" and "Yellow Woman." "Yellow Woman"—now widely anthologized—meditates
reflexively on its status as story, posing the question of whether it is continuous with traditional tales or a representation and rewriting of them
from the other side of the social and cultural gulf opened by European
invasion. Silko's story rewrites one of the traditional Laguna Pueblo stories about the Yellow Woman figure. These tales exist in multiple versions,
but all of them include a ka'tsina spirit who abducts Yellow Woman, and
all describe Yellow Woman's eventual return home, usually pregnant.[67]
Silko's story opens when the narrator and her lover, Silva, wake up on
the bank of a river where they have met, had sex, and slept. The unnamed
narrator returns with Silva, whom she had just met the day before, to his
home; she eats some apricots, makes some food, and they have sex again;
she thinks about her husband and children, but remains with Silva; she
accompanies Silva to town to sell the beef from some stolen cows. On the
way to town, they encounter a rancher who threatens Silva with arrest;
Silva kills him. Yellow Woman returns home to her family, planning to tell
them that she had been abducted by a Navajo man.

The central question of the story is also a central question for its main
character. Yellow Woman, through whose first-person perspective the
story is told and whose thoughts we follow as the story unfolds, spends
the story wondering whether she and Silva are the Yellow Woman and
ka'tsina spirit of Laguna myth, or whether she is a modern Laguna woman
and Silva is "some Navajo." When Silva refers to her as "Yellow Woman,"
the only name she has in Silko's story, she replies that she had been joking
when she said, the night before, that she and her lover were figures from
Laguna myth: "But I only said that you were him and that I was Yellow
Woman—I'm not really her—I have my own name and I come from the
pueblo on the other side of the mesa. Your name is Silva, and you are a
stranger I met by the river yesterday afternoon." She insists that "the old
stories about the ka'tsina spirit and Yellow Woman can't mean us."[68] But
in response, Silva answers, "What happened yesterday has nothing to do
with what you will do today, Yellow Woman." In some moments, the nar-

rator tries to restabilize the distance between the mythic past and the living present: "'I don't believe it. Those stories couldn't happen now,' I said." Silva, however, insists that a belief in modernity as a rupture without a continuous connection to the past is an illusory one: "He shook his head and said softly, 'But someday they will talk about us, and they will say, "Those two lived long ago when things like that happened."'" In response, the narrator wonders if the original "Yellow Woman had known who she was—if she knew that she would become part of the stories."[69] In this way, Silko reflects on the question of whether traditional retold and repeated stories have only a figural relation to a modern present, or whether the present is so continuous with the oral tradition that any modern short story's narrator might be transformed, through the passage of time, into the figure at the center of a traditional story with many tellings. Is Silko a contemporary fiction writer or a Laguna storyteller? Like the form of Ortiz's syllabus, Silko's story does not offer us an answer, but presents the question.

At the end of the second page of the copy of the Spring 1978 Native American Arts syllabus in his archive at the Labriola National American Indian Data Center at Arizona State University, Ortiz has written: "It's remembering / But it's also something else than memory."[70] With his revision of his Native American Arts syllabus, Ortiz sought to offer his students more than one model of literary history so that they might be able to grapple with what he viewed as the radical break in the literary tradition caused by European colonization. He even imagined that they might turn literary history into a new tool for understanding and rebuilding Native American life and culture, imagining a version of history that could acknowledge the almost unimaginable social and cultural destruction of Indigenous life by white settlers while also supporting a vision of Native American life in North American that was ongoing, culturally and socially continuous. For Ortiz, part of the promise of teaching literary history in this way was the possibility that it might raise the individual experiences expressed in the literary texts he assigned into something more than individual, something else than personal memory.

That something else than memory, Ortiz suggests, is a form of continuance that literature in its everyday, unliterary forms carries out through expressing the "voice of countless other non-literary Indian women and men of this nation who live a daily life of struggle to achieve and maintain meaning." As he writes in "Towards a National Indian Literature," the oral tradition "as transmitted from ages past" is not alone "the inspiration and source for contemporary Indian literature." That is, an imagined unified past that dictates and justifies the canon in the present is not the only model possible. Rather, for Ortiz, Native American literature receives its national character in part by looking toward a desired future: "It is also because of the acknowledgement by Indian writers of a responsibility to advocate for their people's self-government, sovereignty, and control of land and natural resources; and to look also at racism, political and economic oppression, sexism, supremacism, and the needless and wasteful exploitation of land and people, especially in the U.S., that Indian literature is developing a character of nationalism which indeed it should have."[71] In his national literature–building essay, as on his syllabus, Ortiz represents this different orientation to literary history by triangulating forms of literature rather than telling a continuous history. Alongside contemporary novels like D'Arcy McNickle's *Wind from an Enemy Sky*, Momaday's *House Made of Dawn*, and Silko's *Ceremony*, the essay places the oral ceremony through which his uncle Steve turns the reenactment entrance of conquistador Santiago and missionary Chapiyuh to an anticolonial purpose, as well as the stories and music made by southern textile workers (recorded by Bob Hall in *Southern Exposure*).

These forms of literature transmit messages across time to construct solidarity rather than securing a mythic past that acts as an alibi for an imperfect future. The voice of these forms of literature, Ortiz emphasizes, is thus "not a mere dramatic expression of a sociohistorical experience" but rather "a persistent call by a people determined to be free; it is an authentic voice for liberation."[72] And within the essay, we see the traces of Ortiz's classroom creation of a Native American literary history that has a past and yet leaves open the possibility of imagining a future that is not determined by it. By using his syllabus to unify a wide collection of unlike texts from unlike sources with questionable transmission histories into a usable past, Ortiz confronts a problem in the history of literary study of which his teaching is an important part. As we have shown in this book, a narrow vision of our profession's past does not fit with the many professors, students, methods, and texts that have actually been in it. Ortiz models the difficulty and promise of writing a history that does not separate the practice of critique from the making of culture.

Conclusion

THE PAST WE NEED NOW

This book ends in the 1970s, on the cusp of major changes to higher education that shaped the classroom teaching of English today: the financialization of student debt starting in the late 1970s; the withdrawal of state funding for public universities that began with Proposition 13 in California in the early 1980s; the massive expansion of university administration and the attendant growth, among other things, of "student life" management; the financial crises that decimated the endowments of private universities; and the casualization of academic labor, through which all kinds of colleges and universities have attempted to solve the resulting budgetary crises by cutting instructional costs. These changes have paved the way for new systems of assessment and ranking designed to force a market logic of competition on a pool of resources whose shrinking has been engineered by the architects of austerity measures. They have led administrators to deeply cut funding for humanities research, and indeed at many institutions to cut funding for open-ended and basic research of all kinds. They have created a professorial underclass of adjuncts, assessed but not supported, teaching high loads without contracts or health benefits, performing the same kind of research necessary to college-level teaching without being paid for it, and responsible, at many institutions, for an increasingly large percentage of the undergraduate curriculum, especially the crucial early years containing introductory courses and required classes. In the broadest view, these changes have resulted in the transformation of education into a private risk and a private good.[2] In particular, these changes threaten to make liberal arts education the province of wealthy private universities alone while everyone else narrows their focus to "job training."

Within the discipline of English, there has been a tendency to experi-

ence these changes to the economic basis of higher education as tied—
perhaps even in causal ways—to the method changes the discipline supposedly underwent in these same decades. In the 1970s, most disciplinary
histories tell us, English professors stopped teaching "Great Books" and
began to analyze any old thing: Tide boxes, safety-pin earrings, new short
story collections by ethnic authors, the Enclosure Acts, SlimFast commercials, and newly inclusive poetry anthologies. The last wave of major
disciplinary histories spoke in terms of a dawning or already arrived crisis
in the discipline, but framed it as a crisis of disciplinary purpose or reading method or canons or curriculum.[3] Today, critics continue to view the
1970s as a moment of misguided method.[4] And implicitly or explicitly,
many of the critics who pinpoint the 1970s as a moment when literary
study went wrong or went too far suggest that part of the problem is that
methods claimed forms of political efficacy or agency for themselves, and
yet failed to protect us from the large-scale changes to university funding
structures whose effects on English departments have become increasingly apparent in recent years.[5] Some critics go further, suggesting that
mistaken—usually historicist and critical—methods are the cause of
current de-professionalization.[6] These stories of dissipation and decline
evince longing for a midcentury moment of power and authority and, in
some cases, advocate for a return to the methods that critics supposedly
practiced then and the literary judgments they freely expressed.

We hope that this book will put to rest, once and for all, the feeling
that our discipline's midcentury flourishing was a uniform "Big English"
moment of formalist purpose or canonical focus or exceptionally democratic teaching methods to which we should longingly look back, or to
which we should aspire to return to find a solution to the problems of our
present moment. We hope, also, that this book helps dispel the sense that
our discipline has happened in a monolithic and uniform place called "the
university"—an abstraction modeled upon elite research universities that
"diversified" in the 1970s.[7] We've shown instead the longer histories of
methods and texts that most disciplinary histories associate exclusively
with the post-'68 research university. We have described how working-
class adult students in London read Du Bois's *Souls of Black Folk* in 1915;
we have shown how scholars have remade national literature courses to
talk about race in America and decolonized literature surveys since at least
the 1930s. We have shown how methods of cultural studies—including
the close analysis of apparently ephemeral documents or materials of a
culture and the incorporation of first-person experiences into "objective" accounts—originated with African American literary historians

like J. Saunders Redding. We have shown that a critical attention to what Edward Said called "the category of literature as something created, made to serve various worldly aims," featured as a familiar part of literary study, perhaps particularly in access-oriented and minority student–serving institutions.[8] We have shown how "identity politics" has flourished in all eras: Josephine Miles, for example, taught a high proportion of women writers, including the published work of her own female students, in the early 1940s at Berkeley; T. S. Eliot ditched Edward Fitzgerald and George Meredith to spend extra time on Ruskin with his working-class students. Far from being a post-'68 phenomenon, ideology critique—Marxist and otherwise—threads through literature classrooms across the entire twentieth century. We see it as a staple especially of early Negro in American Literature courses or classes on Irish types and stereotypes in drama. The New Critics, we have shown, had no particular monopoly on democratizing and student-centered classroom pedagogy. And almost every classroom we have discussed here offers evidence that literary historicism is not borrowed from history departments, but has a long and continuous classroom life in English.

The fact that we find in classrooms a longer history for the supposedly revolutionary methodological shifts of the 1970s does not mean, of course, that significant change didn't happen in that decade and after, both the result of progressive social movements and individual struggles, as well as of the backlash against them. In the United States, university enrollments tripled between 1960 and 1980—a larger increase than the famed GI Bill years, which saw a huge influx of mostly white veterans and federal tuition dollars. These decades saw the slow dissolution of the color line and an enormous increase in women undergraduate students; yet these same students found it was harder than before to secure faculty positions.[9] These decades saw Ford Foundation investments in area studies and Black studies and Native American studies; at the same time, the 1970s marked the beginning of anti-tax movements and state-level disinvestment from higher education that continues today. These decades saw the creation of public policies designed to bring groups of students who had been excluded from state-funded education into universities, as well as the beginnings of decades of legal challenges to these same policies. The Higher Education Act of 1965 inaugurated federal student assistance programs, which expanded dramatically through the end of the century; at the same time, the rise of for-profit universities funneled this federal money into private hands.[10] Looking back now, we might tell a post-1968 story that is not about the democratic and anti-racist expansion of the university, but about the two-steps-forward/one-step-back shuffle of that incomplete project.[11] In literary study, the year 1968 and the decades that followed stand as shorthand for the twinned opening of the university and the literary canon; for an anti-elitism that both opened admissions and denounced New Critical formalism as conservative and exclusionary. Yet these years in fact saw neither the decisive democratization of the university nor the arrival of the methods we associate with them. As we have shown, there is a much longer twentieth-century history of both threading through institutions of all kinds.[12]

If we really wish to think about how large-scale institutional changes in the second half of the twentieth century profoundly and radically altered how English professors work, we need to look at how major changes in funding structures left both humanities faculty and the general public with a sense that humanities teaching and humanities research were vastly different, even incompatible, activities.[13] The second half of the twentieth century saw a major increase in federal funding for research, mostly from the Department of Defense and for the sciences. These changes in federal funding were accompanied by state-level funding cuts so deep that most US flagship public universities became private in all but name. Universities sought to fill the gap by monetizing scientific research, increasing university-industry partnerships, and pursuing patents and licensing fees as a major source of revenue. In this new financial landscape, with state money largely gone and federal money earmarked for the sciences, the humanities were increasingly funded by internal discretionary money, a backchannel reward for the tuition dollars their general education teaching generated.[14] But while administrators funded English departments with the revenue generated by their own teaching, prestige followed research within the university more generally; therefore universities also directed some of the funds that humanities teaching generated into the creation of institutes, residential fellowships, and faculty leave that would stimulate research. The usual story we tell to explain the creation of this research infrastructure is that humanities research was not widespread before the post-WWII rise in science research, and that universities invented it to make humanities faculty easy to assess and manage in the university's new science-research-centric model. But once we see how—perhaps unlike in the sciences—humanities research and teaching were woven together in the first decades of the twentieth century, we can assess what these changes actually did: pull research and teaching apart. In extreme cases, an adjunct faculty came to do most of the revenue-generating general education teaching, while tenure-line faculty had reduced teaching loads that enabled them to pursue the research imagined as their primary work. In nearly all cases, this split meant that the assessment and valuation of teaching remained on campus, while journals, publishers, and disciplinary organizations measured the merit of research.

Despite a history and present of interdigitated, inter-reliant, even inseparable practices of teaching and research, English professors' everyday experience and understanding of our work has come to be granularly shaped by these institutional separations—from the subsections of the reports we submit for annual reviews to the way we make our summer plans to the productivity programs and applications we rely upon to do "our own work" (where "work" is writing for publication). And while professors may admire their friends who publish often and teach rarely at elite research universities and think with pity (or self-pity) of those stuck with high teaching loads at small colleges and comprehensive universities, the practical working world, as it styles itself, has very different values. It indicts the universities for arbitrarily tethering economically valuable teaching to valueless literary scholarship. Beleaguered students, complain *Economist* columnists, involuntarily fund our worthless humanities research when they overpay for their badly taught courses. Different as these two valuations of research may be, one firmly within and one clearly outside the academy, they both assume that teaching and research are fundamentally opposed, fundamentally different activities with fundamentally different kinds of value. And crucially, they read out of these apparent differences the idea that teaching and research are fundamentally separate activities that have been arbitrarily yoked together through accidents of history.

Though English professors intuitively know that research and knowledge production happen in the classroom as much as in the library or the study, the absence of a shared and official history and collective memory of their inseparability has left us vulnerable to interests inside and outside the university that profit from declaring humanities research valueless and teaching a failing endeavor to be radically reinvented. English professors' collective amnesia about their discipline's past has left us without a unified and detailed response to higher ed disruptors' persistent characterization of teaching within the discipline as ineffective and untheorized. The separation of teaching and research enables the cleansing of pedagogy from the expensive stain of disciplinary knowledge. An entirely new industry of education technologists, assessment providers, and teaching and learning professionals has sprung up. Nourished by the foundational fiction that disciplines have never possessed serious pedagogies, many of these experts regard no pedagogical tip as too basic to be taught at "brown bag" lunchtime professional development seminars or in a for-profit "webinar." A major strategy has been the repackaging of long-standing disciplinary teaching practices as dehistoricized "innovations" to be taught as though for the first time to resistant or ignorant faculty. Experienced teachers of literature have the uncanny experience of meeting the "flipped classroom" (i.e., doing the reading before class), the strategy of the "think pair share" (i.e., facilitating class discussion, now with a memorable rhyming name), or the "active learning environment" (i.e., the seminar) in their guise as innovative interventions designed to help a casualized faculty do ever more with ever less. The disciplines have been allowed to keep the dehistoricized "lecture," which has become a general description of just how bad teaching was in the past (unless it is recorded and put online, which is innovative). Meanwhile, baroque assessment regimes have grown like Spanish moss on the existing canopy of teaching infrastructure so thickly that assessment—requiring a de-disciplined language of critical thinking and transferable skills so generalized as to never convince—seems increasingly to insist that it is the rationale for teaching itself. In the assessment regime, the only good teaching is the perfect teaching that has not happened yet, but which will take place in a near but fully transformed and fully de-disciplined future.

This future already exists on many campuses, though its utopian promise has not quite been realized. At an entire category of schools, primarily for-profit universities, faculty are imagined as content producers and no more; they sign nondisclosure agreements, have no role in governance, and no tenure protections or intellectual property rights.[15] These schools treat teaching as job training alone, and a whole range of institutions from regional state universities and small private colleges have begun to follow suit. As a result of these changers, a two-tier model of American higher education has emerged. A small handful of elite institutions remain committed to liberal arts education for a cadre of future "leaders" with flexible, management-oriented abilities, while everyone else gets an increasingly vocationalized curriculum imagined as a first round of job training that looks ahead to a lifelong series of returns for reskilling.

This book has begun the work of stitching back together the long history of how our teaching has made our scholarship and how scholarship has happened in classrooms. Rather than take part in method wars that inadvertently express or even exacerbate the divide between teaching and research by restaging scholars/critics battles and pitting historicists' teaching style against formalists', we imagine a larger ecosystem of knowledge production that takes place in classrooms, libraries, and studies, an ecosystem of knowledge in which many methods have comfortably coexisted.[16] Knowledge production in the classroom has been difficult to talk about in part because we have come to accept that knowledge production involving students must imitate the forms of professional research the university can count: work like co-writing an article with a student, directing a senior thesis, perhaps working on a collective project in a humanities lab, generally individualized and often requiring additional, uncompensated work. But the evidence of research in the literature classroom is everywhere once we look for it, from the collective close reading that unfolds in the classroom hour to the course lecture whose question-and-answer period restructures a book chapter (and sometimes becomes visible in the book or article's dedication), from class trips to the library to the creation of new reference tools. More formal research in the literature classroom thus looks like a small island—but is actually a glimpse of a submerged continent where scholarship and teaching live together. Professors read as much scholarship when constructing a new syllabus as when writing an article, and they are likely to read more widely and across more fields and even disciplines when they read for teaching. Students therefore are a key audience for scholarship, even if they never publish themselves or even if they never read a single page of a scholarly journal. The citation metrics that universities increasingly use (which are based on models for assessing scientific research) mistake citation for engagement and counts for values; they fail to trace how teachers and students use scholarship, and therefore actively devalue these long-standing practices.[17] Making this history of lived but uncounted use visible is urgent in an era in which universities and colleges conclude, via citation counts, that published humanities scholarship is like a metaphorical marketplace of all supply and no demand.

In this book we have shown how English classrooms—not only at research universities but at extension schools, liberal arts colleges, southern "trade" schools during segregation, public land-grant universities, and community colleges—have fostered the practices of these kinds of literary and historical research in students, not as apprenticeship training for embryo professors, but as core practices of reading and thinking. We've shown T. S. Eliot lecturing on G. P. Baker's *The Development of Shakespeare as a Dramatist* to grocers and schoolteachers; we've shown J. Saunders Redding vocalizing the debate in Dickens studies over the autobiographical content of *David Copperfield* to a classroom of teachers-to-be at Hampton; we've shown Josephine Miles assigning David Daiches's 1939 study of the modern novel to first-year students at Berkeley; we've shown how during World War I Caroline Spurgeon brought her working-class students to do original research on medieval manuscripts in the British Museum. We've given examples of how classics of literary scholarship—

The Sacred Wood, The Well Wrought Urn, Shakespeare's Imagery, To Make a Poet Black, The Triple Thinkers, "Towards a National Indian Literature"— were fundamentally shaped by classrooms in which professors tuned their teaching to the particular interests, lives, and needs of particular groups of students.

We need now more than ever a fuller and more detailed history of how English has actually been practiced in all kinds of classrooms.[18] We need now more than ever to experience that past as part of our collective intellectual history and to describe its importance as central to the mission of higher education. Ours is a moment in which administrators at regional public universities justify the shuttering of humanities departments and programs by framing their place in access-oriented institutions as a misguided midcentury blip of largesse while positing their removal as a return to healthy vocational form.[19] As our book has shown, this is a false history. Literary study was not a long-ago elite formation that somehow opportunistically adapted to the more pragmatic needs of mass education; it was often cultivated alongside or even as part of vocational education. The disciplinary shape of English bears the marks of this history, but it will be visible to us and to others only once we see classrooms at vocational programs, night schools, community colleges, and technical institutes as part of our intellectual genealogies.

This book also redefines what the "outcomes" of the English classroom have been and are, to give us back a more capacious history of who has made our discipline and of what literary study has contained. And we've started to show how this history includes what Fred Moten and Stephano Harney call "the undercommons," the imagined collective of the contingently employed teachers, teaching assistants, instructors, university staff, and indebted students who have also helped make those major works.[20] Defenses of literary study today either advocate for the potential or actual economic value of teaching literature (critical thinking, soft skills), or locate its value in its refusal to live in a world in which economic value is the only kind of value, and in which capitalist modes of thought are the only modes of thought. In this book, we have shown the very many more ways—both abstract and localized—that actual students and teachers have valued literature and all that's gone under that name. Our moment, in which both the risk and the rewards of education have become private and individual, and in which higher education is becoming ever more polarized, requires the biggest possible version of our past that we can build together. We need to leave aside histories of literary study that accept a narrow vision fabricated for the convenience of others, and replace them with a history that remembers the institutions and people who have actually made literary study in the university. We will do it using careful historical research, reanimations of long past conversations, and wild imaginings of the world as otherwise—all practices that we have developed and used for over a century in our English classrooms.

Acknowledgments

Many of the teachers we write about in this book brought their students closer to literature by making the material conditions of writing visible. A full accounting of all the people and institutions who made this book would require more reading than we are willing to assign you. But here is the general outline.

The most difficult part of this project was finding teaching materials in archives and special collections; this book would not exist without the expertise of a number of special collections librarians and university archivists who helped us immensely, both over email and in person. We especially need to thank Shannon Supple (now at Smith College Libraries) and Kathi Neal for their help at the Bancroft Library at the University of California, Berkeley; Adrienne Sharpe at the Beinecke Rare Book and Manuscript Library at Yale University; Donzella Maupin, Andreese A. Scott, and their colleagues at Hampton University Museum Archives; Jean B. Bischoff at G. R. Little Library, Elizabeth City State University; Holly Snyder, Tim Engels, and Jennifer Betts at the Hay Library at Brown University; Liz Harper and Jason Brady at Hunter Library, Western Carolina University; Timothy Provenzano, Joyce Martin, and Jeston Morris at the Labriola National American Indian Data Center at Arizona State University; librarians at the Louisiana State University Libraries Special Collections; Marc Carlson at the Special Collections and University Archives at McFarlin Library, University of Tulsa; Joellen El Bashir at the Moorland-Spingarn Research Center at Howard University; Annabel Valentine at Royal Holloway Special Collections, University of London; Tansy Barton and her colleagues at the Senate House Library, University of London; Nanci Young at the Smith College Archives; Kassandra A. Ware at Spelman College Archives Department; Julia Gardner (now at Cornell University Library) and the staff at the University of Chicago

Library's Special Collections Research Center; Carlene Cummings and Anne Coleman in special collections at the University of North Carolina at Pembroke; and Tony Kurtz at Western Washington University Archives. Richard Vela corresponded with us about Pembroke courses; Kim Christian and Mary Anne Hansen helped us connect with tribal college librarians.

We could not have written this book without financial support and research leave. A postdoctoral fellowship from the Pembroke Center for Research and Teaching on Women at Brown University supported Laura during the earliest stages of this project. An American Council of Learned Societies Collaborative Research Grant, along with the support of the College of Arts and Sciences at the University of North Florida and Swarthmore College, gave us an invaluable year of simultaneous research leave and enough financial support to visit some key overseas archives. A James Michener Faculty Fellowship supported Rachel during the middle stage of the project. We'd like to thank the Office of Research and Sponsored Programs, graduate dean John Kantner and English Department chair Keith Cartwright at UNF, as well as the Swarthmore English Department chairs Nora Johnson and Betsy Bolton, Swarthmore's Office of Sponsored Programs (especially Tania Johnson), and Swarthmore's Business Office (especially Denise Risoli). The Office of the Provost at Swarthmore College (especially Marcia Brown and Joanne Kimpel) has supported us in multiple ways.

We are so very grateful to everyone who invited us to present this work on their campuses: Jordan Stein, Matthew Hart, Adam McKeown, Sean Latham, Benjy Kahan, Lauren Coates, Mary Mullen, Joe Drury, Paul Fleming, Aaron Jaffe, Andrew Epstein, and Jon Eburne. Thanks as well to Jim Hansen, Vicki Mahaffey, Lauren Goodlad, and members of the British Modernities Group at the University of Illinois at Urbana-Champaign; to John Pollack, Zack Lesser, and members of the Penn History of Material Texts; Hoyt Long, Stacie Williams, and members of the University of Chicago Digital Humanities Forum; Seth Koven, Lynn Hollen Lees, and members of the Delaware Valley British Studies Seminar; and Eric Hayot and members of the Penn State Center for Information and Humanities.

This book was made stronger by the Press's two reviewers: our deepest thanks to Deidre Shauna Lynch, who helped us see the project's full stakes, and to the other, anonymous reader. Alan Thomas at the University of Chicago Press saw the value in a book about teaching's role in the discipline's history and, along with Randy Petilos, guided us through publication. Erin DeWitt has been a thoughtful as well as thorough copy editor. Before the book even came to formal review, it was made better by the readers who generously responded to individual chapters: Bill Cohen, Rita Felski, Anthony Foy, Matt Hooley, Evan Kindley, Seth Koven, Jenni Lieberman, and Kathy Lou Schultz. Jed Esty and Tim Yu read early off-shoots of this project for us. The Junior Faculty Works in Progress group at Swarthmore—including Laura Holzman, Cheryl Jones-Walker, Ayse Kaya, Min Kyung Lee, and Eric Song—gave us helpful feedback on ear-lier drafts of this project, as did the Faculty Writing group at UNF: Chris Gabbard, Stephen Gosden, Tru Leverette, Jenni Lieberman, Betsy Nies, Sarah Provost, and Nicholas de Villiers.

Many others have helped us with research and manuscript prepara-tion. James Beasley put his knowledge of rhetoric and composition his-tory at our disposal. Carolyn Smith generously gave us total access to the Josephine Miles papers that she had gathered for years in preparation to write a biography of Miles. Jess Holler's incredibly detailed and creative research assistance during the project's early stages inspired us. Hali Han has helped us immensely in the final stages of manuscript preparation. Michael Boyles of UNF's Center for Instruction and Research Technol-ogy generously offered to prepare our images.

Lara Cohen read countless drafts of our book proposal and introduc-tion; our respect for Lara is immense and so her enthusiasm has been both authorizing and sustaining. Heather Love has supported us and this project from the beginning; she treated us as peers when we were junior scholars and that meant so much. Jeremy Braddock was one of our ear-liest and best readers; he showed us that the book was making a bigger claim than we yet knew ourselves. Eric Song has been our most dedicated and careful reader through every stage of this process, despite his deep skepticism about the value of our methods and the validity of our claims. Ben Knights recognized us, early on, as fellow scholars of pedagogy; we've valued his friendship immensely. Brian Glavey recognized, perhaps even more than we did, the value of describing classroom practice, and he reminds us of it every so often. Sarah Hayford has been our resident sociologist (even though she's a demographer); she's answered myriad queries, copyedited paragraphs in a pinch, and—most importantly—listened patiently on the telephone to updates on the project's progress for over a decade. Tim Burke has continually helped us see that our work was relevant to the present and the future of the university, not just its past. In countless conversations, Yumi Shiroma has helped us see how our project fit into a landscape of contemporary criticism and a threatened profession. Over the years, Jordan Stein has thought with us about how disciplinary history might be different. Chris Foley read every word of the "Dead Teacher's Social" manuscript with a sharp editorial eye and sharper sense of humor. From the beginning, Margreta de Grazia believed that we could do it. John Shaw, Paul Saint-Amour, Sam Kimball, Jim English, Peter Logan, and Talia Schaffer have offered us extraordinary support at the moments that mattered most.

This book has been shaped by many intellectual communities, beginning with the Penn Modernist Studies group and the Penn Material Texts Seminar, and later the P19 group. The Swarthmore English Department has cared for and thought with both of us through the years. We have been lucky to have the intellectual community and companionship of Nat Anderson, Farid Azfar, Sarah Allison, Nancy Bentley, Hester Blum, Sara Bryant, Keith Cartwright, Linda Chen, Eileen Clancy, Rebecca Colesworthy, Debra Rae Cohen, Jon Eburne, Sierra Eckert, Merve Emre, Lynne Farrington, Talissa Ford, Anthony Foy, Mitch Fraas, Alex Gillespie, Jonathan Goodwin, Elizabeth and Charles Hayford, Andy Hines, Claire Jarvis, Nora Johnson, Bonnie Jones, Cheryl Jones-Walker, Priya Joshi, Nabil Kashyap, Ayse Kaya, Damien Keane, Aislinn Kelly, Lauren Klein, Anna Kornbluh, John Pat Leary, Zack Lesser, Anna Levine, Clark Lunberry, Jane Malcolm, Baki Mani, Bill Maxwell, Matthew Merlino, Mary Mullen, Aaron Parrett, Gina Patniak, Mearah Quinn-Brauner, Jill Rappoport, Martha Schoolman, Peter Schmidt, Kathy Lou Schultz, Peggy Seiden, Jon Shaw, Juliet Shields, Peter Stallybrass, Kate Stanley, Emily Steinlight, K. Elizabeth Stevens, Dennis Yi Tenen, Kate Thomas, Dan Traister, Whitney Trettien, Robin Wagner-Pacifici, Megan Ward, Ted Underwood, Nicholas de Villiers, Alisha Walters, Patty White, Beth Womack, Connie Xhu, and Matt Zucker.

Our families and friends have both materially and spiritually supported this project. Our mothers, Mary Glackin and Deborah Sagner, accompanied us on early research trips and cared for our then-small children. Lillian and George Albro, and Kevin and Karen Heffernan, and Bill Dineen provided love and childcare that made it possible for us to travel for research and stay late at work. We are grateful for the love and support of our friends and family: Sarah Hayford; Kathleen Glackin and Carole Rykaczewski; Mary Heffernan; Leslie, Matt, Aiden, Alex, and Hailey Potter; BethAnn, Jami, Adrienne, and Julia Albro-Fisher; Matthew, Jackie, and Ben Buurma; Jacob, Jennifer, Bevin, Bellamie, and Bowie Buurma; Becka, Larry, Maddie, and Abby Buurma and Jack McMaster; Tom Foley and Carolyn Bradley; Julie, Jodie, Cosmo, and Madeleine Foley, and Roxanna Hibdon; Holly Barton, Anne Kapoor, Sun Ha Lee, and Kelly Winship. Talissa and Zev Ford, Hunter McCorkel, Basha Smolen, and Ruth Smolen provided encouragement and friendship in Philadelphia; Martha Schoolman and Caitlin Wood, Nicholas de Villiers and Sam Trask, Anne

Pfister and John Arnold, Andrea Phillips, and Ashley McKay provided encouragement and friendship in Florida. Aaron, Nann, and Maizy Parrett along with Akilah, Imara, and Zahari Lane provided encouragement and friendship in Helena.

We remember Margaret Glackin, and Ruth and Alan Sagner here; they believed in the value of literary study and the university.

The friendship of our families has been the soil in which this book took root and grew, and Frances Ruth and Lowell have grown up alongside the book. Prudence Foley has aged considerably. Chris and Tim have given their love and good humor to us; we are all lucky to have each other.

We dedicate this book to our teacher Elaine Freedgood and to the inventive students of English 261 at the University of Pennsylvania and English 009Z and 083 at Swarthmore College, who helped launch this project in the spring of 2009.

Earlier versions of two chapters of this book were previously published: Chapter 2 originally appeared in *PMLA* 33, no. 2 (March 2018), published by the Modern Language Association of America; and chapter 5 first appeared in *New Literary History* 43, no. 1 (Winter 2012): 113–35, copyright © 2012 *New Literary History*, The University of Virginia. We thank the editors of these journals for the opportunity to work through some of the ideas in this book first in their pages.

Appendix

ARCHIVES AND COLLECTIONS CONSULTED

Cleanth Brooks Papers, Yale Collection of American Literature, Beinecke Rare Book and Manuscript Library, Yale University

Course Catalog Collection, Hampton University Archives

Josephine Miles Papers, Bancroft Library, University of California, Berkeley

Simon J. Ortiz Papers, Labriola Center, Arizona State University

Oxford Extension Delegacy Papers, University of Oxford Archives

J. Saunders Redding Papers, Hampton University Archives

Jay Saunders Redding Papers, John Hay Library, Brown University

I. A. Richards Collection, Magdalene College, University of Cambridge

Senate House Library, University of London Archive

D. Nichol Smith Papers, Bodleian Library, University of Oxford

Papers of Professor Caroline Spurgeon, Royal Holloway Archives and Special Collections, University of London

University of Chicago Press Records, 1892–1965, Special Collections Research Center, University of Chicago Library

Edmund Wilson Papers, Yale Collection of American Literature, Beinecke Rare Books and Manuscript Library, Yale University

Notes

Introduction

1. "Although teaching and learning are allegedly at the heart of higher education, scholars have made relatively few attempts (and with limited results) to penetrate the changing classroom and curricula of the American campus," writes John R. Thelin in his overview of American higher education research. See Thelin, "Essay on Sources," 447.

2. This is what Christopher Hilliard, in *English as a Vocation: The 'Scrutiny' Movement,* refers to as "the habit of thinking about literary criticism, like literature itself, in terms of major authors" (9). And even institutional histories tend to focus on elite schools. Gerald Graff, for example, explains that his *Professing Literature: An Institutional History* was based on evidence gathered from a very particular set of higher educational institutions: "Though I refer generically to 'academic literary studies' and 'the literature department,' most of my evidence is drawn from research-oriented departments of English at major universities" (2). Classic histories of higher education in general have disproportionately focused on elite colleges and universities. See, for example, Rudolph, *The American College and University;* and Veysey, *The Emergence of the American University.* Thelin notes that "historical writing about higher education" lags in covering "community colleges," as well as "correspondence schools, extension courses, 'diploma mills,' and now Internet 'virtual universities.'" Thelin, "Essay on Sources," 449.

3. It is common for scholars to invoke the classroom as a place where otherwise good methods go to die. For example, Richard Poirier, in 1970, writes that "my attack is less on the so-called new criticism or on the 'anatomy of criticism' . . . than on classroom versions of these." Poirier, "What Is English Studies?," 5. Or Derek Attridge describing deconstruction as "dead," living on zombie-like only in "in some guides to literary theory and first-year university classrooms." Attridge, *Reading and Responsibility,* 34.

4. Wilson, *The Wound and the Bow,* 1; Brooks, *The Well Wrought Urn,* v; Richards, *Practical Criticism,* 1; Rickert, *New Methods for the Study of Literature,* vi.

5. As Ben Knights argues in *Pedagogic Criticism,* "the study and interpretation of texts" in English are inextricable from the "social forms and rituals of pedagogy" (1).

6. *Hampton Bulletin,* May 1941, 64–65.

7. On this topic, see also Burnett, "On Lamentations for a Lost Canon." Burnett writes, "The myth of the canon as some set of texts that was once widely taught on

American university campuses until it was finally abandoned in the 1980s is, in fact, a product of 1980s' and 1990s' debates about higher education."

8. Nor should we understand literary historicism as an accident of higher education's institutional history and the post-WWII imperative for humanities departments to follow models of scientific research. For this, see Geiger, *To Advance Knowledge*; and Wellmon, *Organizing Enlightenment*.

9. Rhetoric and composition studies, by contrast, has a much longer tradition of seeing classroom method and practice as part of the main line of their disciplinary history, reflecting the greater value they accord to teaching and their more collective approach to teaching practice. As John Brereton noted in 1994, "We now know a good deal more about composition instruction than, say, instruction in English literature." Brereton, *The Origins of Composition Studies in the American College, 1875–1925*, xiv. For additional rhetoric and composition histories that research teaching as part of intellectual genealogies, see Berlin, *Rhetoric and Reality*; Connors, *Composition-Rhetoric*; Crowley, *Composition in the University*; Harris, *A Teaching Subject*; Miller, *The Formation of College English*; and Stock, *Composition's Roots in English Education*.

10. Of course, practices of literary scholarship and lecturing on modern literature are much older, but most disciplinary historians focus on the late nineteenth century because it is a moment of professionalization. As William Riley Parker puts it, "Our research and criticism are old; our jobs are new." Parker, "Where Do English Departments Come From?," 342.

11. Warner, "Professionalization and the Rewards of Literature," 2; Douglas, "Some Questions about the Teaching of Works of Literary Art," 37; Parker, "Where Do English Departments Come From?," 343; Court, *Institutionalizing English Literature*; Graff, *Professing Literature*, 3.

12. Guillory, "Literary Study and the Modern System of the Disciplines," 37.

13. Such often-cited polemics include John Churton Collins's *The Study of English Literature: A Plea for Its Recognition and Reorganization at Universities* (1891); Hiram Corson's *The Aims of Literary Study* (1894); and Bliss Perry's "The Life of a College Professor" (1897).

14. Atherton, *Defining Literary Criticism*, xx. Graff notes that Arnoldian humanists—those "bitter critics of the profession"—have been generally overcited and warns against "thinking of institutions as if they were unmediated projections of the values, methods, and ideologies of major individuals and movements." Graff, *Professing Literature*, 5.

15. Martin, "Criticism and the Academy," 270.

16. Assuming that all "teacher-critics" practiced evaluative judgment and that calls for "objectivity" in literary study came from philologists has produced erroneous accounts of this era. For example, Michael Warner points to R. G. Moulton, who put forward a model of "inductive criticism" set against "judicial criticism" as a paragon of the new professional practices in English. For Warner, Moulton should be shelved with the scholar-philologists; yet, as Alexandra Lawrie has shown by researching syllabuses, Moulton developed his "inductive" methods through teaching contemporary novels to extension school students. We suggest that many such "professional" practices of literary study—the teaching of literary history, a focus on the forms and themes of individual texts—have long nineteenth-century classroom histories and were often taught to nontraditional and non-apprenticing students and publics; they only later come to seem the result of philology's supremacy in the professionalization

era. See Warner, "Professionalization and the Rewards of Literature," 13–16; and Lawrie, *The Beginnings of University English*, 93–94.

17. Guillory, "Literary Study and the Modern System of the Disciplines," 33; Graff, *Professing Literature*, 14.

18. Veysey, *The Emergence of the American University*, 221.

19. Graff, *Professing Literature*, 14, 10.

20. For an overview of the new formalism, see Levenson, "What Is New Formalism?" For strategic formalism, see Levine, *Forms*. For post-critical reading, see Felski, *The Limits of Critique*. For surface reading, see Best and Marcus, "Surface Reading: An Introduction," in "The Way We Read Now," ed. Best and Marcus, special issue, *Representations* 108, no. 1 (2009): 1–21, along with the other essays in that issue. For recent defenses of aesthetic experience, see Aubry, *Guilty Aesthetic Pleasures*; Clune, "Judgment and Equality"; and North, *Literary Criticism*.

21. For example, Joseph North in *Literary Criticism* sees the history of the discipline as revolving around "a central axis of dispute . . . between literary 'scholars' and literary 'critics,' the key distinction being between those who treated the study of literature as a means by which to analyze culture and those who treated the study of literature as an opportunity to intervene in culture" (1–2). Caroline Levine likewise uses the figure of division when she opens *Forms* by imagining a "literary critic today" who can "do a formalist reading of Charlotte Brontë's *Jane Eyre*" and can "take stock of the social and political conditions that surrounded the novel's production," but experiences "her formalism and her historicism" as "belong[ing] to separate realms"—one involving "close reading methods" and the other "historical research methods" (1).

22. Jane Gallop, for example, argues that "when New Criticism took over English studies, it injected methodological rigor into what had been a gentlemanly practice of amateur history" and that "the most valuable thing English ever had to offer was the very thing that made us a discipline, that transformed us from cultured gentlemen into a profession: close reading." Gallop, "The Historicization of Literary Studies and the Fate of Close Reading," 182–83.

23. Some scholars have challenged the idea that the professionalization of English happens through or depends upon the arrival of German-style philological research. See Lynch, *Loving Literature*; and Glazener, *Literature in the Making*. For a more expansive account of philology and its pedagogies, see Turner, *Philology*.

24. Williams, *The Long Revolution*.

25. For a parallel account of how early American formalisms emerged from mechanistic approaches to literary composition, see Tenen, "The Emergence of American Formalism."

26. For longer genealogies of the digital humanities that connect early twentieth-century scholarly tool-making with later computational approaches, see Bode, *A World of Fiction*; and Klein, "Feminist Data Visualization." See also Klein, "Dimensions of Scale: Invisible Labor, Editorial Work, and the Future of Quantitative Literary Studies."

27. Guillory's genealogy for literary studies is, like those of many of his contemporaries, very formalist—it tracks from Adam Smith to T. S. Eliot to Cleanth Brooks. For histories of English that account for traditions of historicism in the discipline, see Wellek, *The Rise of English Literary History*. For an extended description of this problem, see Kucich, "The Unfinished Historicist Project."

28. Viswanathan, *Masks of Conquest*; Crawford, *Devolving English Literature*; Gere,

"Kitchen Tables and Rented Rooms"; Rose, *The Intellectual Life of the British Working Classes.*

29. Atherton, *Defining Literary Criticism*; Lawrie, *The Beginnings of University English*; Dale and McDonell, "Lessons from the Past?"; Dale, *The Enchantment of English*; Renker, *The Origins of American Literature Studies*; Robson, *Heart Beats*; Fisher, *Reading for Reform*; Baer, *Indigenous Vanguards*; Savonick, "Insurgent Knowledge"; Glazener, *Literature in the Making*; Lynch, *Loving Literature*; Emre, *Paraliterary.*

30. Dana A. Williams describes the persistence of these integrated approaches to literary history in curricula at several historically Black colleges and universities; she also notes that HBCUs are responsible for the undergraduate education of a majority of African American doctorate earners. See Williams, "'The Field and Function' of the Historically Black College and University Today."

31. Graff, *Professing Literature*, 258.

32. Guillory, *Cultural Capital*, 339.

33. For retrospective accounts from teachers, see Graff and Warner, "Part III: Memoirs and Personal Accounts." For a student memoir, see Altick's *A Little Bit of Luck.* The Centre for Contemporary Cultural Studies Archive at Cadbury Research Library, University of Birmingham, houses a collection of student notes, but this kind of collecting is rare in general. Of course, many university lectures were published by university presses, from the eighteenth century onward, some of them based on students' notes. On earlier eighteenth-century practices of student note taking, see Eddy, "The Interactive Notebook."

34. Wilson, lecture notes for English 356A: Varieties of Nineteenth Century Criticism, University of Chicago, summer 1939, Edmund Wilson Papers, YCAL MSS 187, box 163, folder 4045, Beinecke Rare Book and Manuscript Library, Yale University (hereafter EWP).

35. Blair, *Too Much to Know*; Clark, *Academic Charisma and the Origins of the Research University*, 6.

36. Collini, "A Lot to Be Said," 35. See also Collini, *Common Reading*; Thaventhiran, *Radical Empiricists*; and Kramnick and Nersessian, "Form and Explanation."

37. Eliot, "Lecturer's Report for Modern English Literature (First Year) [1916]," quoted in Schuchard, *Eliot's Dark Angel*, 38.

38. Richards, *Interpretation in Teaching*, 24.

39. Gates, "'. . . and Bid Him Sing,'" vii.

40. Redding, English 365: The Negro in American Literature syllabus (1975), box 24, folder 10, Jay Saunders Redding Papers, John Hay Library, Brown University.

41. Said, "Opponents, Audiences, Constituencies and Community," 159.

42. Adams, "Masks and Delays," 277.

43. Published as Miles, *Wordsworth and the Vocabulary of Emotion.*

44. Miles, *Poetry, Teaching, and Scholarship*, 86.

45. Memo from John E. Jordan, May 28, 1971, box 8, folder 19, Josephine Miles Papers, Bancroft Library, University of California, Berkeley.

46. Walker, "American Studies at the George Washington University."

47. Redding, Proposed Syllabus for American Civilization, 1971–1972, George Washington University, MS 98.1, box 25, folder 19, Jay Saunders Redding Papers, John Hay Library, Brown University.

48. Graff, *Professing Literature*, 7.

Chapter One

1. Matching Spurgeon's own careful organization, Spurgeon's collection of teaching notes has been beautifully and extensively cataloged by the staff at the Royal Holloway Archives and Special Collections, University of London.

2. Many scholars describe the institutions where modern literature had been taught for much of the nineteenth century, long before Oxford and Cambridge established their modern English literature degrees. See Court, *Institutionalizing English Literature*; Eagleton, "The Rise of English Studies"; Lawrie, *The Beginnings of University English*; Palmer, *An Account of the Study of the English Language and Literature from Its Origins to the Making of the Oxford English School*; Viswanathan, *Masks of Conquest*.

3. Haas, "Caroline F. E. Spurgeon (1869–1942)," 99.

4. See Court, "The Social and Historical Significance of the First English Literature Professorship in England."

5. In addition to her notes for Ker's lectures, Spurgeon preserved notes from Faithfull's lectures on Shelley, Byron, and Keats as well as Sélincourt's lecture on Elizabethan literature. For Ker's role in shaping the English degree at Oxford and elsewhere, see Chambers and Edwards, "Ker, William Paton (1855–1923), Literary Scholar."

6. Haas, "Caroline F. E. Spurgeon," 101.

7. George Eliot herself attended lectures at Bedford College (then Ladies' College). See Ashton, *Victorian Bloomsbury*, 15.

8. For a description of the "intellectual *entente cordiale*" established between the Sorbonne and the less recognized University of London, whereby University of London students of English could travel to the Continent for formal legitimation, see Haas, "Caroline F. E. Spurgeon," 101.

9. Haas, 101. As Haas describes, Spurgeon's friend Edith Morley obtained the title of professor through internal promotion at Reading in 1908; she was made a professor of English language rather than English literature. The British Federation of University Women, founded in 1907, indicates how many women were already part of academia at this time; many of them, like Morley and Spurgeon, were central to the formation of English literature departments.

10. Juliette Dor argues that Spurgeon "contributed very significantly to the restructuring of English studies. Not only did she write on the topic, not only did she put it into practice at Bedford, but she also took a major part in national reassessment committees of British education." Dor, "Caroline Spurgeon (1869–1942) and the Institutionalization of English Studies as a Scholarly Discipline," 55.

11. Palmer, *Account of the Study*, 34.

12. Guillory, "Literary Study and the Modern System of the Disciplines," 33.

13. Shairp, "Lecturer's Report for Seminar on Shakespeare and England."

14. Haas suggests that, for women academics, the war "brought unprecedented opportunities. Like others Spurgeon was able to extend her sphere of work, consolidate her position, and move into the public eye." Haas, "Caroline F. E. Spurgeon," 104.

15. Spurgeon, "Lecturer's Report for Seminar on the Age of Johnson."

16. Spurgeon was not the only teacher to take her University of London extension school students to use collections in the British Museum. Elizabeth Macrae's 1919 University College extension course—the Literature and Historical Sources from Which Our Knowledge of the Classical and Mediaeval Periods of History Are

Derived—was another from among the several courses and seminars that made trips to the British Museum "and other places where original documents and MSS. can be seen." Macrae, *Syllabus of a Tutorial Class in Historical Literature by Miss Elizabeth Macrae. First Year. The Literature and Historical Sources from Which Our Knowledge of the Classical and Mediaeval Periods of History Are Derived*, 3.

17. During WWI, most collections from the British Museum were transferred to other locations for safety; see Kavanagh, *Museums and the First World War*, 30–31.

18. Spurgeon, "Lecturer's Report for Seminar on the Age of Johnson."

19. For the early modern methods that scholars used to make reference works, see Blair, *Too Much to Know*.

20. Spurgeon's sense of the role that information management plays in the creation of critical sensibilities of undergraduates was not singular. Maurice S. Lee sees the nineteenth century's strategies of information management—"from bibliographic ordering and bureaucratic regulation to the quantification of literature and literary practices"—as a shaping influence on "the content and uses of literature" in that era. See Lee, *Overwhelmed*, 4.

21. Spurgeon, "Notebook: 'Art of Reading,'" 5, Papers of Professor Caroline Spurgeon, PP 7/3/1/20, Royal Holloway Archives and Special Collections, University of London (hereafter PPCS).

22. Spurgeon, 5.

23. See John Henry Newman's "Preface" to *Discourses on the Scope and Nature of University Education, Addressed to the Catholics of Dublin* (1852), v.

24. Spurgeon, *Keats's Shakespeare*, 55, 549.

25. Spurgeon's approach to studying literary history via the material traces of critical opinion, both lay and scholarly, and citation and reworking by other authors represented a more widespread approach to the teaching of early modern literature in particular. David Nichol Smith, for example, used this method to teach his disciplinary history course, Lectures on the History of English Studies, at Oxford in the same year that Spurgeon taught Art of Reading at Bedford. A denizen of archives and bookshops, Nichol Smith was a dedicated historian of the lesser literary genres, particularly periodical journalism and correspondence. He opened his Lectures on the History of English Studies by setting aside the very short history of literary study as a taught subject in the university to instead find the discipline's origins in the work of men "whom in contempt—often unmerited—we are tempted to call antiquaries, grubbers, researchers." In a series of eight lectures, he tells the story of the evolution of the apparatuses of modern scholarly knowledge as a story of editorial accuracy and editorial error, books borrowed and cited, library access, scholarly rivalries, bibliographic disagreements, and archival acquisitions. Though today Nichol Smith is remembered, if at all, as one of the dry bibliographers that the New Critics so often caricatured, his approach to literary history, like Spurgeon's, sought to invite students to participate in an imperfect but capacious world of literary production: "I ask you to come with me into the work-shop," Nichol Smith invited students at the end of his course's first lecture, "to see the workers at work." Nichol Smith, "Lectures on the History of English Studies, 1913," Lectures, Essays, and Notes of D. Nichol Smith, MS Eng. Misc. D47, folder 4388, Bodleian Library, Oxford University. For a book-length treatment of this literary culture that encompasses the figures central to Smith's disciplinary history course, see Lynch, *Loving Literature*.

26. Spurgeon thanks "my two successive secretaries, Miss M. A. Cullis and Miss

Agnes Latham," as well as "Miss Lois Latham for her expert copying and drafting of some of my charts" in the acknowledgments to *Shakespeare's Imagery and What It Tells Us*, viii. Latham went on to become a professor of English at Bedford.

27. Tuke, *A History of Bedford College for Women*, Chart V: "Students at Bedford College 1849–1937."

28. Tuke, 233.

29. Tuke, 295.

30. Tuke, 296.

31. Tuke, 247. See also Dor, "Caroline Spurgeon," 55.

32. Spurgeon, "Notebook: 'The Teaching of English,'" PPCS, PP 7/3/1/27. Course description from London County Council: Summer Courses for Instructors in Evening Institutions, Session 1914–15.

33. Spurgeon's English literature seminar model also set the pattern for Honors instruction in other departments at Bedford, notably French and German. Tuke, *A History of Bedford College*, 248.

34. Spurgeon, "Notebook: 'Art of Reading,'" 1, PPCS, PP 7/3/1/20.

35. Spurgeon, 2v.

36. Spurgeon, 4.

37. Spurgeon, 2.

38. Spurgeon, 2v.

39. Spurgeon, 2v.

40. Spurgeon, 4.

41. Spurgeon, 3v.

42. Spurgeon, 10.

43. Spurgeon, 10, 11.

44. Spurgeon, 11.

45. Spurgeon had been offering a course of eight lectures called Some Aspects of John Ruskin and His Influence in Modern Thought Since 1907. She planned a book based on the lectures but gave up the project when she could not secure permission from George Allen to quote from Ruskin's *Works*. See Spurgeon, "Ruskin," PPCS, PP 7/4/3.

46. Spurgeon, "Notebook: 'Art of Reading,'" 12, PPCS, PP 7/3/1/20.

47. Spurgeon, 12–13.

48. Spurgeon, 13.

49. Spurgeon, 2.

50. Spurgeon, 14.

51. Spurgeon, 12v.

52. Spurgeon, 23.

53. Though Spurgeon taught index making as part of liberal education, it is also the case that professional indexing was a new career open to women at this time. See Duncan, "'The Gladdest Surprise': Nancy Bailey's Indexing Office."

54. Spurgeon, "Notebook: 'Art of Reading,'" 15, PPCS, PP 7/3/1/20.

55. Spurgeon did give examples beyond Ruskin, walking her students step-by-step through the use of reference books and the construction of indexes and back again in each case. She taught them how to set out to write a general research paper on Defoe, consulting first the bibliographies of the *Cambridge History of Literature*, the Subject Index of the London Library, and the articles in the *Dictionary of National Biography* (especially the chronological list of the subject's works). Reading through these

indexes, articles, and bibliographies, she writes, "You will soon see what works you need specially to read. You will find that his famous Review has been reprinted, and that there is a copy of it in the British Museum, which you will try to see. You see that he is a very prolific writer, but that his work falls under 4 heads chiefly—Journalism, politics, social + industrial matters, fiction. You will keep various slips dealing with various sections of these headings." She also included a description of how to do a narrower paper on Defoe's place in the history of fiction, proceeding differently. Spurgeon, "Notebook: 'Art of Reading,'" 19–22, PPCS, PP 7/3/1/20.

56. While *Shakespeare's Imagery and What It Tells Us* is probably the best known of Spurgeon's works, her massive *500 Years of Chaucer Criticism and Allusion, 1357–1900* may be the most cited.

57. Spurgeon, *Shakespeare's Imagery*, ix.

58. Spurgeon, x. Spurgeon did not publish further monographs nor her results because of poor health and her eventual death in 1942, but the notecards are archived in the Folger Shakespeare Library.

59. Spurgeon, 11.

60. Spurgeon, 11. In her 1936 review of the book, Kathleen Tillotson objected to this aspect of Spurgeon's method, noting that "her emphasis is always on the 'stuff or content' of the image, rather than on the relation perceived or the underlying mental process; the 'stuff' is perhaps the only aspect of an image which can be counted or classified, but it is not the image itself." Tillotson, review of *Shakespeare's Imagery and What It Tells Us*, 460.

61. Spurgeon, *Shakespeare's Imagery*, Chart I.

62. Spurgeon notes in "Appendix I: Difficulties Connecting with the Counting and Classifying of Images" that "the difficulties connected with the counting and classifying of images could hardly be believed by one who has not experienced them" before explaining her system of primary references and secondary cross-references. Spurgeon, 359.

63. Marjorie Garber views Spurgeon as a pioneer of distant reading methods that now seem new. See Garber, as well, for a detailed account of how Shakespeare was taught in nineteenth-century classrooms, in the United States especially: "Character study, philology, social and cultural history, textual studies, the history of style, were all part of the early flowering of Shakespeare teaching, and are with us in various degrees today." Garber, *The Muses on Their Lunch Hour*, 124, 135.

64. Spurgeon, *Shakespeare's Imagery*, 10.

65. Spurgeon, x.

66. Spurgeon, 124. *Shakespeare's Imagery* includes marginal citations giving the relevant act, scene, and line of each figure she mentions.

67. Spurgeon, 117–18.

68. Barthes, *The Preparation of the Novel*, 909. Here Spurgeon, like Barthes, implicitly claims to locate herself before the canon's formation, prior to value judgment, if only temporarily and imaginatively; note that for Spurgeon this acknowledges Shakespeare as a stylistically uneven writer even as she also claims that her method might be used for purposes of author attribution of contested texts.

69. Edward Maisel, in his 1938 *An Anatomy of Literature*, argues that this sort of "neutral content" analysis whereby critics like Spurgeon "isolate the image involved from any specific text and examine it for what it tells us about the author, the state of knowledge at the time of writing, and the like, and on a larger scale to note recurrent

content concerns, has always been one of the most fruitful techniques of enlightened scholarship." Along with Spurgeon, Maisel cites Hoxie Neale Fairchild, John Livingston Lowes, and Frederick Prescott as neutral content critics. Maisel, *An Anatomy of Literature*, 61.

70. Spurgeon, *Shakespeare's Imagery*, 202.

71. Dick, "Dusty Answer," 51.

72. Spurgeon, *Shakespeare's Imagery*, 42.

73. "A writer refers to a thing in quite a different mood and with quite a different poetic impulse from that which produces a simile or metaphor. . . . If a poet, then, continually draws upon certain classes of things, certain qualities in things and certain aspects of life, for his illustrations, we are justified, I suggest, in arguing that those qualities and those aspects specially interested him and appealed to him." Spurgeon, 42.

74. Spurgeon, 80. Although she approvingly references a range of works on metaphor from the last decades—Middleton Murry on "Metaphor" in *Countries of the Mind* (1922), *Poetic Imagery* (1924) by H. W. Wells, *The World of Imagery* (1927) by Stephen J Brown, and *Intensifying Similes in English* (1918) by T. H. Svaratengren—she starkly contrasts her work to theirs.

75. Describing the importance of metaphor in her introduction, she writes, "I incline to believe that analogy—likeness between dissimilar things—which is the fact underlying the possibility of metaphor, holds within itself the very secret of the universe," before abandoning further consideration of such questions to "an abler pen than mine." Spurgeon, 6.

76. Such criticisms try to locate Spurgeon within the long tradition associating literary women with the quotidian domestic detritus of the process of producing great literature; for another example, see Cleanth Brooks's discussion of Marianne Moore's referential and quotidian poems in chapter 5.

77. Hyman complains that "when she points out that the running metaphor in the early historical plays is 'the rash and untimely cutting or lopping of fine trees,' 'deep' psychology would note its association with the figures of kings and interpret it as the destruction of authority in a father-symbol, if not specifically castration; Miss Spurgeon interprets it as an interest in orchards." Though his tone conveys that Hyman thought his was the obvious literary reading and Spurgeon's the comically naive one, today Hyman's castration anxieties probably sound more comical than Spurgeon's orchards. Hyman, "The Critical Achievement of Caroline Spurgeon,"102.

78. Hyman, 104.

79. Hyman, 108. Hyman enumerates major critics and strands of criticism influenced by Spurgeon: less obvious examples include work by Marxists like Kenneth Muir, Cleanth Brooks's *The Well Wrought Urn*, William Troy's writing on Henry James in the *New Republic*. Obvious examples include G. Wilson Knight's work on Shakespearean imagery and E. M. W. Tillyard's evocation of the everyday worldview of educated early modern people in *The Elizabethan World Picture*. Hyman could have mentioned many more critics and works, including Milton Rugoff's *Donne's Imagery* (1939). Hyman does acknowledge that in *The Philosophy of Literary Form* (1941), Kenneth Burke names *Shakespeare's Imagery* as one of "the three most fertile works on literature since *The Sacred Wood*." Burke quoted in Hyman, 107. By 1955, however, Spurgeon's accomplishments had come to seem more enduring and more impressive to Hyman. Revising the 1948 "Critical Achievement" piece for the "Caroline Spur-

geon and Scholarship in Criticism" chapter in the revised edition of *The Armed Vision*, he notes that Spurgeon should survive "as an example of scholarship at its best, creative enough to discover a mine of wealth for criticism, not quite creative enough to mine it herself." He also praises her moderation and declares that she should serve as an example "in contrast to Lane Cooper at one extreme and Knight and Murry at the other, as a warning to scholars and critics. They would do well to keep one foot on the ground; not both [as in the case of Cooper's concordances], not neither [as in the case of Knight's 'two travesties on criticism' and Murry's 'literary metabiology']." Hyman, *The Armed Vision*, 196, 195.

80. Hannon, "Imagery and the Adding-Machine," 12–13.

81. See for examples of these debates the "Literature and the Professors" special double issue: "Literature and the Professors: A Symposium," *Southern Review* 6, no. 2 (1940): 225–69; and "Literature and the Professors: A Symposium," *Kenyon Review* 2, no. 3 (1940): 403–42.

82. Spurgeon, "Notebook: 'The Teaching of English,'" 5, PPCS, PP 7/3/1/20.

83. John Henry Newman, *Discourses on the Scope and Nature of University Education*, 2nd ed. (1959), vi, 208, 209.

Chapter Two

1. Tillyard, *The Muse Unchained*, 98; Collini, "'Non-Fiction Prose' to 'Cultural Criticism,'" 16; McDowell, "Early Modern Stereotypes and the Rise of English," 32–33. Steven Matthews notes that Eliot himself dismissed such accounts of his outsized influence on literary study: "Eliot was assiduous, near the end of his life, in pointing out . . . that he did not 'invent' the Early Modern period for the modern age, nor establish the accepted canon of its texts. But this has been the continuing belief of academic criticism." Matthews, *T. S. Eliot and Early Modern Literature*, 6.

2. Ransom, *The New Criticism*, 138.

3. See Gilbert and Gubar, *No Man's Land*; Brooker, *Mastery and Escape*; and Lamos, *Deviant Modernism*.

4. Guillory, *Cultural Capital*, 188.

5. Guillory, "The Ideology of Canon-Formation," 179, 185. Also see Collini, "'Non-Fiction Prose,'" 16.

6. Schuchard, *Eliot's Dark Angel*, 25–51. See also Styler, "T. S. Eliot as Adult Tutor," 53–54. For a consideration of Eliot's teaching at Harvard in the early 1930s, see Bush, "'As if you were hearing it from Mr. Fletcher or Mr. Tourneur in 1633': T. S. Eliot's 1933 Lecture Notes for English 26 ('Introduction to Contemporary Literature')" and "'Intensity by Association,'" and Nash, "T. S. Eliot's Views on James Joyce." For the lecture notes themselves, see Eliot, *The Complete Prose of T. S. Eliot*, vol. 4, *English Lion, 1930–1933*, ed. Harding and Schuchard. And for Schuchard's first publication of the syllabuses and discussion of their implications, see "T. S. Eliot as Extension Lecturer, 1916–1919," published in two issues of the *Review of English Studies* 25, nos. 98 and 99. The Modern English Literature tutorial syllabuses also appear in Eliot, *The Complete Prose of T. S. Eliot*, vol. 1, *Apprentice Years, 1905–1918*, ed. Brooker and Schuchard.

7. The University of London Joint Committee for the Promotion of the Higher Education of Working People was formed in 1909 to coordinate joint efforts between

the Workers' Educational Association (founded in 1903) and the University of London's Board to Promote the Extension of University Teaching (founded in 1900).

8. Eliot, *The Letters of T. S. Eliot*, vol. 1, *1898–1922*, 168.

9. Mansbridge, *University Tutorial Classes*, 1.

10. Eliot, "Lecturer's Report for Modern English Literature (First Year) [1916]," quoted in Schuchard, *Eliot's Dark Angel*, 38.

11. Eliot, *Letters*, 1:177.

12. Terry Eagleton depicts extension school teaching as "distracting the masses from their immediate commitments." See Eagleton, "The Rise of English," 23. Chris Baldick portrays extension lectures as bourgeois and dilettantish. See Baldick, *The Social Mission of English Criticism, 1848–1932*, 76. See also Fieldhouse, "Conformity and Contradiction in English Responsible Body Adult Education, 1925–1950."

13. Alexandra Lawrie discusses the failure of disciplinary historians to look at material evidence of teaching practices. See *The Beginnings of University English*, 5–6. See Rose, "The Whole Contention Concerning the Workers' Educational Association."

14. Lawrie, *The Beginnings of University English*, 112.

15. Rose describes how students in 1914 challenged the Historical Association to write more about working people: "The influence of the WEA on British historiography is another topic, but worth exploring: Tawney insisted that his classic *The Agrarian Problem in the Sixteenth Century* owed much to his Tutorial Class students." Rose, *Intellectual Life of the British Working Classes*, 276.

16. University-based "extension" education, as opposed to adult education more broadly, might be said to have started in 1876 when the London Society for the Extension of University Teaching began offering courses for workers. Oxford University offered extension lectures around the country beginning in 1878.

17. Goldman, *Dons and Workers*, 5.

18. Quoted in Burrows, *University Adult Education in London*, 38. For a transcript of the parliamentary hearing that Burrows quotes, see Great Britain, Parliament, House of Commons, *Sessional Papers*, vol. 40, 150.

19. Mansbridge, *University Tutorial Classes*, 83–84, 26.

20. Mansbridge, 9.

21. The first extension tutorials—R. E. S. Hart's The Dissolution of the Monasteries, H. Frank Heath's Tennyson, and W. R. L. Blackiston's Combustion and Oxidation—were piloted at Toynbee Hall in 1900–1901 and their popularity grew in the following years.

22. Goldman, "The First Students in the Workers' Educational Association," 51–52. See also Rose, *Intellectual Life of the British Working Classes*, 264.

23. Quoted in Burrows, *University Adult Education in London*, 39. The WEA's magazine, first published in 1910, was titled *The Highway*.

24. In 1916 Eliot, for example, told the Oxford Extension Delegacy that he could teach short lecture courses on a range of French literature topics including "Tendencies of Contemporary French Thought," "The Novel in France," and "French Literary Criticism." Oxford University Extension Report 1915–16, Syllabuses and Examination Papers 1916–17, Oxford Extension Delegacy Papers, CE 3/22/33, University of Oxford Archives. At the same time, he offered the University of London's Extension School a dozen topics for tutorial courses, including "sociology of primitive peoples" and "social psychology." See Burrows, *University Adult Education in London*, 43.

25. University of London syllabuses were enclosed in wrappers with standard information about the "Method of Conducting Tutorial Classes" or the "Method of Conducting Classes and Lectures," describing the length of classes, the protocols for turning in assigned essays (as well as rules regarding tutors' ability to excuse "some portion of the written work" at their discretion), and in some cases information about library and book access. Publishing extension school syllabuses was common in the United States as well.

26. Davies, *Syllabus of a Course of Tutorial Classes Some Writers of the XIXth Century and After*, 3; Henderson, *Syllabus for a Tutorial Class in Aspects of Victorian Literature (First Year)*, 3; Atkinson, *Syllabus of a Course of Tutorial Classes on the Social History of England*, 3.

27. Parry, "Introduction," *Cambridge Essays on Adult Education*, 8.

28. Mansbridge notes that students generally asked for "historical or economic study," only later desiring "the study of Philosophy or Literature" once the tutorial experience had "broaden[ed] out" their interests. Mansbridge, *University Tutorial Classes*, 59.

29. Slater, *Syllabus of a Course of Tutorial Classes on The Worker and the State*; Tayler, *The Condition of the People (An Introduction to the Social History of the People)*.

30. Epstein, *Syllabus for a Course of Tutorial Classes on Descriptive Economics (Modern Society in Its Economic Aspect)*, 3. See also Epstein, *Syllabus for a Course of Tutorial Classes on Descriptive Economics (Modern Society in Its Economic Aspect)*; and Epstein, *Syllabus for a Course of Twenty Lectures (Modern Society in Its Economic Aspect)*."

31. Bloor, *Syllabus of a Course of Lectures on Ideals and Issues of the Present Struggle*; Palmer, *Syllabus for Problems of Social Economics Arising from the War*; Shairp, *Syllabus of a Course of Ten Lectures on the Literary Inspiration of the Great War*; Freeman, *Syllabus of a Tutorial Class on the Economic Problems of Demobilisation*.

32. Alexandra Lawrie finds that even pre-WEA-era University of London extension syllabuses from the late nineteenth century encouraged scholarly work: "These English Extension syllabuses were structured along scholarly lines that prioritized systematic and analytical treatment of each work." See Lawrie, *The Beginnings of University English*, 77.

33. For statistics on paper completion, see Lawrie, 61–62. Jonathan Rose notes that "the history of education, like literary history, has been written mainly from the perspective of the suppliers rather than the consumers"; and that "the WEA and Ruskin College were the most influential continuing education movements in twentieth-century Britain, and their institutional histories have been thoroughly chronicled," but mainly from the position of the institution rather than the student. Rose, *Intellectual Life of the British Working Classes*, 256.

34. Brierley, *Syllabus for a Tutorial Class in Psychology*.

35. Tayler, *Syllabus for Course of Tutorial Classes on The Condition of the People*, 2; Farley, *Syllabus of a Course of Tutorial Classes on Poverty: Suggested Causes and Remedies (First Year's Work in Sociology)*, 1; Pringle, *Syllabus for Modern Economic Problems*.

36. Jack, "Lecturers' Report for the Life of the Nineteenth Century as Represented in Literature."

37. Eliot, "Lecturer's Report for Modern English Literature (First Year) [1916]," quoted in Schuchard, *Eliot's Dark Angel*, 37, 38.

38. Mansbridge, *University Tutorial Classes*, 43.

39. See Rose, *Intellectual Life of the British Working Classes*, 276.

40. McDonald, *Learning to Be Modern*, 3.

41. Eliot, *Syllabus for a Course of Tutorial Classes on Modern English Literature*, 3.

42. Eliot, 5.

43. Eliot wrote in his lecturer's report: "We devoted at the end four evenings to Ruskin and one to George Borrow." Quoted in Schuchard, *Eliot's Dark Angel*, 38.

44. Eliot, *Letters*, 1:216.

45. Eliot, *Syllabus for a Course of Tutorial Classes on Modern English Literature (Second Year's Work)*, 6.

46. Eliot, "Lecturer's Report for Modern English Literature (First Year) [1916]," quoted in Schuchard, *Eliot's Dark Angel*, 38.

47. Eliot, *Syllabus for a Course of Tutorial Classes on Modern English Literature (Second Year's Work)*, 8.

48. Eliot, "Lecturer's Report for Modern English Literature (First Year) [1916]," quoted in Schuchard, *Eliot's Dark Angel*, 38.

49. Eliot, *Letters*, 1:263.

50. Eliot, *The Sacred Wood*, 10.

51. Eliot, "The Function of Criticism," 32.

52. Eliot, *The Sacred Wood*, 68.

53. Eliot, *Letters*, 1:249.

54. Eliot, *Syllabus for a Course of Tutorial Classes on Modern English Literature (Third Year's Work)*, 1.

55. Eliot, 3.

56. Eliot, 7.

57. Mansbridge, *University Tutorial Classes*, 9.

58. Eliot, *Letters*, 1:353.

59. Murry, review of *The Sacred Wood*, by T. S. Eliot, 194.

60. *New Statesman*, review of *The Sacred Wood*, by T. S. Eliot, 733.

61. Lynd, "Buried Alive," 359.

62. Goldring, "Modern Critical Prose," 7.

63. *New Statesman*, review of *The Sacred Wood*, by T. S. Eliot, 733. See also Moore, review of *The Sacred Wood*, by T. S. Eliot, 336–39.

64. Guillory, *Cultural Capital*, 167–69.

65. Eliot, *The Sacred Wood*, xiv.

66. Eliot, 70. Jan Gorak argues that *The Sacred Wood* aimed to "dismantle" Edwardian and Georgian notions of literary genius; he notes, "As an adult education lecturer, when Eliot considered how to present this important period to a non-academic audience, all he found were books by Edward Dowden, Walter Raleigh, and A. C. Swinburne that relayed the myth of genius to the untrained reader." Gorak contends that Eliot's engagement with minor poets and appreciation of non-expressive elements of the writing process deepened in the years after *The Sacred Wood*, when Eliot became the prime reviewer of early modern scholarship for the *Times Literary Supplement*. Gorak, "From Prodigality to Economy," 1070.

67. Eliot, *The Sacred Wood*, 123, 96.

68. Eliot, 78.

69. Eliot, "The Function of Criticism," 32.

70. Eliot, *The Sacred Wood*, 9, 10.

71. Eliot, 69.

72. Eliot, 112, 29, 68.

73. Eliot, 83.

74. Eliot, 71.

75. Eliot, 79.

76. Eliot, 138.

77. Eliot, ix.

Chapter Three

1. Richards, *Practical Criticism*, 13.

2. Richards, 3.

3. Williams, *Writing in Society*, 182.

4. Brooks, "I. A. Richards and 'Practical Criticism,'" 587.

5. Wood, "William Empson," 220.

6. Not everyone credits Richards with the overnight transformation of English studies. Wallace Martin writes that "it is doubtful whether this belief in 'the close study of actual texts' was something that did not exist before Richards's lectures and won universal assent immediately thereafter." Martin, "The Critic and the Institutions of Culture," 296. Likewise, John Constable dispels the fiction that Richards was responsible for putting practical criticism on the Tripos: "the English Tripos at Cambridge had long been setting unattributed pieces for comment, though within the context of a specific time period." Constable, "Editorial Introduction," xvi.

7. North, *Literary Criticism*, 35. See also Collini, "On Highest Authority." Collini argues that "Richards claimed for literary criticism two of the most powerful forms of justification available in British culture: the moral and the scientific."

8. In *Experimental*, Natalia Cecire describes the general context for this groundswell of experimentalism in the early twentieth century, noting that "one does not have to look far to find examples in this period of attempts to generalize 'scientific' and 'experimental' thought in ways that could meaningfully extend its purview into areas hitherto typically dominated by arts and letters" (18).

9. For discussions of *Practical Criticism* in the context of contemporary experimental psychology, see Goodblatt and Glicksohn, "Conversations with I. A. Richards"; see Helen Thaventhiran on Practical Criticism's similarities to "experimental investigations in subjective accentuation" in Cambridge psychology laboratories. Thaventhiran, *Radical Empiricists*, 63–64. For discussion of Practical Criticism as indebted to Ivan Pavlov and behaviorism, see West, *I. A. Richards and the Rise of Cognitive Stylistics*. Joshua Gang also sees Richards as indebted to behaviorism; see Gang, "Behaviorism and the Beginnings of Close Reading." Murray Krieger describes Richards as "a would be neurologist" in *The New Apologists for Poetry*, 57. Alongside those who read Richards as borrowing from the sciences is the school that sees him as prefiguring cybernetics, computer programming, and communication theory. Jessica Pressman, along with Mark Garrett Cooper and John Marx, trace the genealogy that links I. A. Richards to Marshall McLuhan. See Pressman, *Digital Modernism*; and Cooper and Marx, "Television, or New Media," in *Media U*. Meanwhile, scholars of rhetoric and composition stand alone in their embrace of Richards as a figure who worked within their discipline, instead of borrowing from outside it. See, for example, Brown, "I. A. Richards' New Rhetoric."

10. Tate, "Poetry in the Laboratory," 113.

11. Werner, "Teaching Books Instead of Authors."

12. Aydelotte, *English as Training in Thought*, 355.

13. Campbell, "Introductory Course in Literature," 745, 747.

14. Rickert, *New Methods for the Study of Literature*.

15. Rickert, v. Brian Lennon writes that "Rickert's articulation of a practice of close reading modeled on cryptanalysis is entertaining to regard amid the excitement of latter-day digital humanists who would have us believe that their cryptanalytic derivation of a 'distant reading' is unprecedented in literary studies." See Lennon, *Passwords*, 100.

16. Rickert, *New Methods*, x.

17. Chapin and Thomas, *A New Approach to Poetry*, viii, x, ix.

18. Chapin and Thomas, 152.

19. I. A. Richards to Dorothy Richards, November 20, 1923, in *Selected Letters of I. A. Richards*, 28.

20. Baldick, *The Social Mission of English Criticism, 1848–1932*, 151. See Tillyard: "If properly set [the test] cannot be faked." *The Muse Unchained*, 82. See also Hugh Bredin: "[Richards] clearly considered that the test which he had devised, however unnatural, brought to light deficiencies in reading which normally were concealed or disguised." Bredin, "I. A. Richards and the Philosophy of Practical Criticism," 28.

21. Rickert, *New Methods*, xi; Richards, *Interpretation in Teaching*, 24.

22. John Fekete argues that Richards inaugurated "the major North American pedagogical tradition." Fekete, *The Critical Twilight*, xviii. For a standard account of how Richards influenced the New Critics, see Fry, "I. A. Richards." See Alan Brown for an account of the "persistence of the practical criticism exercise in English pedagogy" and indeed in the "structure of the teaching relation *per se*." Brown, "On the Subject of Practical Criticism," 326.

23. An exception to this rule: John Constable, in his editorial introduction to volume 4 of Richards's *Selected Works*, has painstakingly reconstructed the early Practical Criticism courses. Constable, "Editorial Introduction."

24. Richards, *Speculative Instruments*, 104. Though Richards did propose to his students a model of poetic meaning, he was not, as others have noted, much of a close reader himself. See, for example, Thaventhiran, *Radical Empiricists*, 85.

25. Richards, Lecture I, 1, Notebook 21: Practical Criticism 1925, I. A. Richards Collection, Magdalene College, Cambridge University (hereafter IARC).

26. Richards, Lecture 1, [o]v, Notebook 21, IARC.

27. Richards, *Practical Criticism*, 3.

28. Richards, Lecture I, 1–2, Notebook 21, IARC.

29. Richards, *Interpretation in Teaching*, 29. Richards continues, "We have to remember, unless we are to forget all that we have to teach, that what the writer meant is not to be simply equated with what he wrote." Some have argued that Richards developed his (supposedly literary) theories of ambiguity in meaning from the experience of interpreting the protocols. See Berthoff, "I. A. Richards and the Philosophy of Rhetoric." See also Childs, *The Birth of the New Criticism*, 12.

30. Richards, Lecture 1, 4, Notebook 7: Practical Criticisms, IARC.

31. Richards, 15.

32. Richards, Lecture I, 4, Notebook 7, IARC.

33. Richards, Lecture I, 10, Notebook 21, IARC.

34. Richards, 9.

35. Richards, 12.

36. Richards, 12.

37. Richards, 2.

38. Richards, Lecture IV, 1, Notebook 21, IARC.

39. Richards, Lecture V, 1, Notebook 21, IARC.

40. Richards, 1.

41. Richards, 13.

42. Russo, *I. A. Richards*, 93.

43. See Russo, *I. A. Richards*, 93. See also Hilliard, *English as a Vocation*, 35.

44. Russo, *I. A. Richards*, 93.

45. Richards, *Practical Criticism*, 338.

46. Richards, 334.

47. Richards, 335.

48. Richards, 337.

49. Richards, 335.

50. Richards, 336.

51. Richards, Lecture I, 2, Notebook 7, IARC.

52. Richards, 2.

53. Richards, 3.

54. Richards, 5.

55. Richards, Lecture IX, 2, Notebook 7, IARC.

56. Richards, Lecture I, 4, Notebook 7, IARC.

57. Constable describes how Richards considered writing a book on paraphrase with Ogden in 1928. Constable, "Editorial Introduction," xxvii.

58. Richards, Lecture VIII, 1, Notebook 7, IARC.

59. Richards's notes include a caret pointing up to the added-in word "interpreting," which may indicate his own uncertainty about the distinction.

60. Richards, Lecture I, 2, Notebook 7, IARC.

61. Richards, Lecture VI, 1, Notebook 7, IARC.

62. Richards, 3.

63. Richards, Lecture IX, 4, Notebook 7, IARC.

64. Richards, 1.

65. Richards, 1.

66. Richards, 2.

67. Richards, 2.

68. Richards, 3.

69. On Richards's planned book with Ogden, see Constable, "Editorial Introduction."

70. See Scala, "'Miss Rickert of Vassar' and Edith Rickert at the University of Chicago (1871–1938)."

71. See Scala, "Scandalous Assumptions: Edith Rickert and the Chicago Chaucer Project."

72. See Furnivall, *Frederick James Furnivall*, 165–69.

73. Rickert and Furnivall, *The Babees' Book*, xi.

74. Rickert, "'What Has the College Done for Girls,'" 11.

75. Rickert, "As 100 College Girls Write Letters," 13.

76. See Snell, "A Woman Medievalist Much Maligned," 45. See also Kahn, *The Codebreakers*; and Veggian, "From Philology to Formalism." For disciplinary histories

of cryptography in general and Rickert and Manly's work specifically, see Lennon, *Passwords*.

77. Kahn, *The Codebreakers*, 171.

78. Manly, "The President's Address," xlviii.

79. Manly, liv.

80. Greenlaw, "Recent Movements for Co-operative Research in the Humanities," 93–96.

81. John C. Gerber notes that "until 1930 or so, heads of departments of English *did* hire women, and sometimes a good many of them." "Women in English Departments before 1930," 9.

82. See Robinson, "Electronic Textual Editing."

83. Manly and Rickert, *The Text of the Canterbury Tales*, xiii.

84. Rickert, *Chaucer's World*, v.

85. Rickert, *New Methods*, 2.

86. Manly and Rickert, *The Writing of English*, v.

87. Manly and Rickert, v.

88. Manly and Rickert, 415.

89. Manly and Rickert, *Contemporary British Literature*, iii.

90. Manly and Rickert, v.

91. Manly and Rickert, 17, 143.

92. Edith Rickert to G. J. Laing, October 23, 1924, University of Chicago Press Records, 1892–1965, box 396, folder 2, Special Collections Research Center, University of Chicago Library (hereafter UCPR).

93. Rickert, *New Methods*, v.

94. Manly, "Introductory Note," x.

95. Rickert, *New Methods*, 213, 59, 86.

96. "By the statistical method it is possible to set down and summarize the facts about the numerous stylistic devices upon which literary effects depend: the numbers and proportions of different types of images; the numbers and proportions of different types of words; the numbers and proportions of different types of thought formations in the sentence; the numbers and proportions of different types of rhythm and of sound; and so on," writes Rickert. "By the graphic methods we can go a step further and show, not merely dominant features, but relationships, such as successive variations and ranges of variation of a particular phenomenon." *New Methods*, 18, 19.

97. Rickert, 55–56.

98. Rickert, 56, 57n1.

99. Rickert, 203–4. Rickert used *The Teacher's Word Book* as a sort of everyday language baseline for comparison; the book compiled an alphabetical list of the 10,000 words found to occur most widely in printed books for children. Thorndike, *The Teacher's Word Book*.

100. Rickert, *New Methods*, 223.

101. Rickert, 219.

102. Rickert, 61.

103. Rickert, 137.

104. Rickert, 86–87, 88.

105. Jones, "A Detective School of Criticism."

106. Rickert, *New Methods*, 54.

107. Rickert, 255.

108. For example, in trying to determine which image words "awaken sense impressions of more than one kind," Rickert notes that "this classification represents the responses of twelve people who agreed as to the primary appeal; in regard to the first subsidiary appeal, 11 of them agreed in 5 cases, 10 in 8 cases, 9 in 11 cases, and 7 in all." Rickert, 32.

109. Rickert, 6–7.

110. Rickert, 7.

111. Typescript Press Release, New Methods for the Study of Literature, June 1, 1929, UCPR, box 396, folder 2.

112. Woodbridge, "Literary Suicide."

113. William Wilbur Hatfield to Donald Bean, October 13, 1926, UCPR, box 396, folder 2.

114. Review of *New Methods for the Study of Literature*, by Edith Rickert, *English Journal* (April 1927), UCPR, box 396, folder 2.

115. Squire, review of *New Methods for the Study of Literature*, by Edith Rickert, 101–2.

116. Tate, review of *New Methods for the Study of Literature*, by Edith Rickert, 281.

117. "The Study of Literature," *London Times*.

118. Jones, "A Detective School of Criticism."

119. Rinaker, review of *New Methods for the Study of Literature*, by Edith Rickert.

120. Christ, "Letter to the Editor."

121. Donnelly, "Words and Their Use."

122. Christ, "Letter to the Editor."

123. Press questionnaire, UCPR, box 102, folder 1.

124. "English Teachers Are Testing Poems," *Y News*, 1. For Rowe's courses, see *Brigham Young University Annual Catalogue, 1928–29*, 18; and *Brigham Young University Division of Continuing Education Class Schedule, 1929–30*, 4.

125. Contract issued by Donald Bean, February 24, 1928, UCPR, box 396, folder 2. Quotation is from letter from Bean to Mr. Crippen, May 8, 1929, UCPR, box 102, folder 1.

126. Edith Rickert to Donald Bean, August 12, 1928, UCPR, box 396, folder 2.

127. Press questionnaire, UCPR, box 102, folder 1.

128. Chapin and Thomas, *A New Approach to Poetry*, vii.

129. Chapin and Thomas, 23.

130. Chapin and Thomas, 9.

131. Chapin and Thomas, 52.

132. Chapin and Thomas, 14.

133. Chapin and Thomas, 53n1.

134. Chapin and Thomas, 77.

135. Chapin and Thomas, 151–52.

136. Chapin and Thomas, 152.

137. Chapin and Thomas, 153, 155.

138. *Bookman*, unsigned review of *The Real Rhythm in English Poetry*, by Katharine M. Wilson and *A New Approach to Poetry*, by Elsa Chapin and Russell Thomas.

139. Chapin and Thomas, 157.

140. Chapin and Thomas, 158.

141. Chapin and Thomas, 163.

142. Chapin and Thomas, 164.

143. Chapin and Thomas, vii.

144. Chapin and Thomas, 165.

145. Richards, Lecture IX, 3, Notebook 7, IARC.

146. For more recent replications of the Practical Criticism experiment, see Hilliard, "Leavis, Richards, and the Duplicators" as well as chapter 4, "Will Teachers Bear Scrutiny?" from *English as a Vocation*; and Arthur, "Plus Ça Change . . . : *Practical Criticism* Revisited." See also Goodblatt and Glicksohn, "From Practical Criticism to the Practice of Literary Criticism"; and Mathieson, *Teaching Practical Criticism*. Ann Berthoff's composition textbook was also inspired by Richards's experiments. See Berthoff, *Forming Thinking Writing*. Elsewhere Berthoff writes, "Every teacher of English in the country from the grades through graduate school can be a researcher in the ways and means of teaching literacy." Berthoff, "I. A. Richards and the Philosophy of Rhetoric," 209n18.

Chapter Four

1. Redding, "The Black Youth Movement," 587.

2. Lawrence P. Jackson takes Redding as the prime representative of this generation and its critical values. Jackson, *The Indignant Generation*, 9.

3. Lisa Giaffo compiled Redding's papers for the John Hay Library at Brown University. Faith Berry gives an excellent bibliography for Redding in *A Scholar's Conscience*.

4. For a memoir of being an African American student of English at Columbia in these years, see Davis, "Columbia College and Renaissance Harlem."

5. Gates, "'. . . and Bid Him Sing,'"xiv.

6. See *Annual Report of the Librarian of Congress for the Fiscal Year Ended June 30, 1938*, xii.

7. *Annual Report, National Endowment for the Humanities, 1965–66*, 22.

8. See "Job Offers," MS 98.1, box 6, folders 18–24, Jay Saunders Redding Papers, John Hay Library, Brown University (hereafter JSRP-B).

9. Gates, "'. . . and Bid Him Sing,'" vii.

10. Redding, *To Make a Poet Black*, xxix.

11. Redding, English 332 exam, box 24, folder 10 JSRP-B.

12. Redding, English 365: Negro in American Literature syllabus, box 24, folder 22, JSRP-B. The editors of *The Negro Caravan* likewise reject the idea of "Negro literature": "Negro writers [are] American writers, and literature by American Negroes [is] a segment of American literature." Brown, Davis, and Lee, *Negro Caravan*, 7. Laura Helton traces similar ideas in libraries around the same time, showing how librarian Dorothy Porter reclassified books by Black authors, removing them from 325.26, a catch-all Dewey classification "where librarians shelved anything black," to categories appropriate to their contents and topics: "Porter moved Booker T. Washington's *Selected Speeches*, which some libraries placed at 325.26, to the Dewey class for American oratory. She moved Du Bois's books to history and literature (Catalogue 149). . . . These acts built on a tradition of countercataloging at black institutions, from Du Bois's turn-of-the-century bibliographies at Atlanta University to the filing systems developed at the Tuskegee and Hampton Institutes to organize black newspaper data." Helton, "On Decimals, Catalogs, and Racial Imaginaries of Reading," 105.

13. Warren, *What Was African-American Literature?*, 6. See also Joyce A. Joyce's

periodization of author positions for African American literary critics in "The Black Canon."

14. Redding, *No Day of Triumph*, 119. See also Porter, *The Blackademic Life*.

15. Hugh Gloster memo, Correspondence 1955–65, box 1, J. Saunders Redding Papers, Hampton University Archives (hereafter JSRP-H).

16. Maxwell, *F.B. Eyes Digital Archive*.

17. Memo from Clarence Mondale to Redding, May 7, 1969, box 7, folder 50, JSRP-B. In response to an invitation from Bowdoin College professor John Walker in 1977 to participate in the Black Emeritus Professor Program, Redding wrote, "Since I have quite severe reservations about what is called 'the black experience' and the on-going effort to define and segregate that experience in terms of race, I'm afraid that the ideological ground I stand on and the assumptions I make render me unsuited to participate in the projected Black Emeritus Professor Program." See box 6, folder 2, JSRP-B. In print, Redding denounced Black Arts writers like Nikki Giovanni and Amiri Baraka as "cultural and national separatists" writing "in a language that Whitey is scornfully challenged to understand." See Redding, "James Weldon Johnson and the Pastoral Tradition."

18. Michael Bibby invokes Redding as a poetry critic whose "nonrecognition of race" at midcentury was ultimately consistent with "the New Critical color-blind poetics that reified the implicit whiteness of modernism." Bibby, "The Disinterested and Fine," 495. Melissa Girard argues that Redding's critical values imported New Criticism's misogyny into African American literary studies. Girard, "J. Saunders Redding and the 'Surrender' of African American Women's Poetry." Andy Hines, by contrast, argues that midcentury African American writers including Melvin Tolson and, perhaps, Redding attempted "to register literariness and personhood at the same time" against New Criticism's attempt to divide the field between "pure poetry" and "propaganda." See Hines, "Vehicles of Periodization."

19. Lackey, "Redeeming the Post-Metaphysical Promise of J. Saunders Redding's 'America.'"

20. Brown, *The Postwar African-American Novel*, 132.

21. In 1967, for example, English 245: Studies in American Literature included readings by "Whitman, Poe, Melville, James, Twain, Hemingway, Faulkner, Baldwin, and Ellison," with the added explanation that "in 1967–68, the focus will be upon crises in self-discovery as revealed in works dealing with the relationship of Americans and Europeans and with that of Negroes and whites." *Cornell University Announcements, College of Arts and Sciences* 58 (1967–68), 110. In 1968 a graduate seminar on "problems of freedom in American culture" included a reading list of novels by "Twain, James, Dos Passos, Bellow, and Ellison." *Cornell University Announcements, College of Arts and Sciences* 59 (1968–69), 270.

22. Addison Gayle made a similar argument in 1967: he suggested that the academy's penchant for metaphysical poetry and literary criticism in the style of Sainte-Beuve and Taine had defined work by Black writers as unliterary: "Few white students to whom I have talked have knowledge of any Negro Writer outside of the 'Big Three,' Wright, Baldwin, and Ellison." Gayle describes how a white English professor and "former chairman of the department of a university renowned for its English department, on reading a paper of mine with Saunders Redding as the subject, implored me to find out if the works of Saunders Redding could be found in the University

Library. . . . This was in 1965 and Saunders Redding's first book appeared in 1939."
Gayle, "The Critic, the University, and the Negro Writer," 176–77.

23. Scott Zaluda, for example, finds Alain Locke and his colleagues at Howard
University practicing very similar approaches in the classroom. Among other things,
students at Hampton used Otelia Cromwell, Lorenzo Dow Turner, and Eva B. Dykes's
1931 collection of *Readings from Negro Authors, for Schools and Colleges,* in which students "were encouraged, for example, to seek out what were called 'collateral' readings
for a short story by Turner's former student, Zora Neale Hurston. The text suggested
that alongside Hurston's 'Drenched in Light,' students could read Louisa May Alcott,
Dickens, and Tolstoy; similarly, after reading another short story by an African American author, students could go to the library to read stories by O. Henry and the Jew-
ish author Israel Zangwill." Zaluda writes that "it is important to recognize that well
before formal courses in African American history, society, and culture were being
sanctioned for announcement in college catalogues, student writers had been working
hard to produce a literature of African American contemporary life and history." See
Zaluda, "Lost Voices of the Harlem Renaissance," 247–48, 246.

24. *Hampton Bulletin,* May 1941, 64–65; *Hampton Bulletin,* May 1942, 71. In 1943 the
course was renamed Literature of the United States, transformed from a 400-level to
a 300-level class, and the description updated to emphasize learning goals rather than
structure and the importance of rhetoric: "This is a 'springboard' course designed to
awaken in young people a thorough and appreciative recognition of 1) what American
writers have had to say 2) how they have said it and 3) how they are saying it." This
course description revision coincided with the creation of the new Communications
Center at Hampton; integrated into the English Department, its emphasis on oral
presentation invoked, in the Hampton context, a twinned nineteenth-century history of rhetorical education and abolitionist oration. *Hampton Bulletin,* May 1943, 94,
Hampton University Archives.

25. *Hampton Bulletin,* May 1943 (Course Catalog for 1943–44), 94; *Hampton Bulletin,* April 1947 (Course Catalog for 1946–47 and 1947–48), 88–89: English 313, for-
merly Negro Literature, becomes The Negro in American Literature: "Study of American Literature by and about Negros, with emphasis upon racial life and character as
reflected in this body of writing. Attention to historical and critical studies in field."
Hampton Bulletin, May 1943 and May 1947, Hampton University Archives.

26. Redding, English 364: The Negro in American Literature, box 24, folder 10,
JSRP-B.

27. *Cornell University Announcements, College of Arts and Sciences* 62 (1970–71):
89, and 63 (1971–72): 70.

28. *Cornell University Announcements, College of Arts and Sciences* 62 (1970–71): 89.

29. Guillory, *Cultural Capital,* 6. Guillory is not alone in worrying that the addition
of minority authors to existing courses obscures politics, yet others worry for different reasons. David Palumbo-Liu argues that "the institutionalization of multiculturalism that parallels the modes of inserting ethnicity into the general curriculum—
certain 'texts' deemed worthy of representing the 'ethnic experience' are set forth,
yet the critical and pedagogical discourses that convey these texts into the classroom
and present them to students and readers in general may very well mimic and reproduce the ideological underpinnings of the dominant canon, adding 'material' to it
after a necessary hermeneutic operation elides contradiction and smooths over the
rough grain of history and politics, that is, those very things that have constructed the

'ethnic' in the United States." See Palumbo-Liu, *The Ethnic Canon*, 2. Hazel V. Carby argues that the diversification of course reading lists substituted for actual institutional change. See Carby, "The Multicultural Wars."

30. Jackson argues that these logics of romantic authorship and voice were ascendant at midcentury, when the assumption "that the writer's prime obligation to improve society was fulfilled by creating literature that shaped the moral, ethical, and psychological structure of the individual" led to the canonization of novels by Ellison and Baldwin. Redding, by contrast, favored the critical writings of Ellison and Baldwin over their psychological fictions and taught them regularly as part of English 332, which presented his "literature of necessity" tradition of African American writing. One could, of course, read the novels of Ellison and Baldwin within Redding's tradition; this is part of the point. Redding did not ascribe to midcentury logics that sharply divided "literary" from "unliterary" genres. Jackson, *The Indignant Generation*, 4.

31. These glimpses of a pluralistic history, Redding hoped, would overturn commonly held stereotypes: "In black American literature (including pamphlets, speeches and sermons as well as poetry and fiction) from the 1850's to 1910, the evidence against the Sambo (or Plantation) image of the Negro created by certain white writers is overwhelming," reads a prompt that Redding asked his English 365: The Negro in American Literature students to write in support of their final exam at Cornell. English 365, box 24, folder 10, JSRP-B.

32. Redding, review of *The Confessions of Nat Turner*, by William Styron.

33. Redding, *To Make a Poet Black*, 25. Lauri Ramey describes how Redding's views on the "three foundational figures" of Jupiter Hammon, Lucy Terry, and Phillis Wheatley were "at best, grudgingly respectful and, at worst, outright dismissive." For Ramey, this "ambivalence" toward the originators of the African American literary tradition "haunts this genre to the present." Ramey, *A History of African American Poetry*, 57.

34. Redding, *To Make a Poet Black*, 24. Much of what Redding registered as William Wells Brown's impressionability might be due to his extensive incorporation or plagiarism of a wide variety of sources. For a book-length study of how Brown's plagiarism related to his vision of a racially integrated nation, see Sanborn, *Plagiarama!*.

35. Redding, *To Make a Poet Black*, 25.

36. Redding, *No Day of Triumph*, 45.

37. Redding, 43. Much later, Redding's *No Day of Triumph* would come to serve as inspiration for the editors of the *Heath Anthology of American Literature*. Paul Lautner recalls how they gathered for their first meeting in 1983, "at the Seamen's Church Institute, a sailors' haven in New York near the Battery, built on the site of a place in which Melville had lived." They decided to begin by reading "a few potential selections," and Eleanor Tignor read from the opening of Redding's *No Day of Triumph*, "which gave us the impetus to undertake that necessary reexamination of what most understood to be the American Literary terrain." See Lautner, "The Making of the Heath Anthology," 35.

38. Lovell, "The Things So Strange and Marvellous," 218.

39. *Phylon*, unsigned review of *No Day of Triumph*, by J. Saunders Redding, 87.

40. Lovell, "The Things So Strange and Marvellous," 220.

41. *Phylon*, unsigned review of *No Day of Triumph*, 88.

42. Wright continues, "Redding's main task is to expose, exhibit, declare, and he

does this job in a dramatic and unforgettable manner, offering his own life as evidence." Wright, "Introduction," n.p.

43. Redding, Course notes: The Novel, 2nd semester, Sept '54, box 24, folder 9, JSRP-B.

44. Redding.

45. Redding.

46. Redding. Redding's citation of scholars in his lectures challenges broad characterizations of Hampton as a trade school, in distinction to graduate degree–granting institutions like Howard University or Morehouse. As James D. Anderson has pointed out, Hampton, like Tuskegee, has been mischaracterized as a trade or agricultural school, when in fact its primary mission was teacher training. See Anderson, The Education of Blacks in the South, 1860–1915. And while Michael Winston describes the obstacles that segregation in the South posed to the scholarship of African American faculty, Redding seems to have had no trouble keeping up with recent scholarship not only in his core fields of seventeenth-century literature and American culture, but in fields such as Victorian literature as well. See Winston, "Through the Back Door."

47. Redding, Course notes: The Novel, 2nd semester, Sept '54, box 24, folder 9, JSRP-B.

48. Redding.

49. Forster, The Life of Charles Dickens, 1:34.

50. Redding, "The Negro Author."

51. Lofton, review of They Came in Chains, by Milton Meltzer.

52. Redding, The Lonesome Road, cover.

53. For the planned sequel to Stranger and Alone, see Jackson, The Indignant Generation, 2.

54. George Marion describes the New York Times' refusal to review Aptheker's anthology in Stop the Press!, 47.

55. Redding, review of The New Stars: Life and Labor in Old Missouri, by Manie Morgan, November 15, 1952, box 20, folder 17, JSRP-B.

56. Redding, review of The Sin of the Prophet, by Truman Nelson, Herald Tribune, February 5, 1952, box 20, folder 20, JSRP-B.

57. Redding, review of The Sin of the Prophet.

58. Redding, review of In the Castle of My Skin, by George Lamming, October 20, 1953, box 20, folder 28, JSRP-B.

59. American Studies had been founded at GWU in 1936 by Robert Bolwell as a program in American civilization offered through the English Department. In 1968 it became an independent and interdisciplinary program. See Walker, "American Studies at the George Washington University." See also American Studies Department Records (1953–1998), Special Collections Research Center, RG0082, George Washington University.

60. Mondale and Redding's co-taught Am Civ 71–72 course explored, week by week, a series of national oppositions: Europe/America, East/West, North/South, City/Country, Immigrant/Native, Elitism/Equality, and Black/White. The course mixed historical materials with fiction. Each week centered on a novel: Henry James's The American for Europe/America; Mark Twain's Huckleberry Finn for North/South; William Faulkner's Absalom, Absalom! for City/Country; Saul Bellow's The Adventures of Augie March for Immigrant/Native, F. Scott Fitzgerald's The Great Gatsby for Elitism/Equality; and Redding's Stranger and Alone for Black/White. Lectures

were accompanied by images such as slides of southern plantation architecture (for North/South), Alfred Stieglitz's photographs (for Immigrant/Native), "changes in city layout and planning" (for City/Country), and WPA art and photography (for Elitism/Equality). Other primary readings were drawn from Willard Thorp, Merle Curti, and Carlos Baker's anthology *American Issues*, vol. 1: *The Social Record* and vol. 2: *The Literary Record*, with the exception of the final week on Black/White. As supplementary reading for Black/White, Redding improvised to fill the gaps in *American Issues*. He assigned excerpts from Williams Wells Brown's *Clotel* (anthologized in selections in Sterling Brown, Arthur P. Davis, and Ulysses Lee's 1941 *The Negro Caravan* and republished in a new edition that same year). Redding also suggested Herbert Aptheker's *Documentary History*, W. E. B. Du Bois's *Dusk of Dawn: An Essay toward an Autobiography of a Race Concept*, E. Franklin Frazier's *The Negro Family in the United States*, Langston Hughes's *Poems*, Richard Wright's *Native Son*, Gunnar Myrdal's *An American Dilemma*, *The Autobiography of Malcolm X*, and Eldridge Cleaver's *Soul on Ice*.

61. Professor Jennifer James and her students have researched GWU's segregated past. See Wilson, "Student Research Spotlight's GW's Segregated Past."

62. Mondale, "Spring Disturbance." For an archival and interview-based history of Black studies across college campuses, see Fenderson, Stewart, and Baumbartner's special issue of *Journal of African American Studies*, "Expanding the History of the Black Studies Movement."

63. Memo from Clarence Mondale to Redding, May 7, 1969, box 7, folder 50, JSRP-B.

64. Redding, "Afro-American Studies." In draft form, the op-ed was titled "On the Scholarly Validity of Afro-American Studies." See box 20, folder 12, JSRP-B.

65. Adler, Van Doren, and Ducas, *Negro in American History*, vol. 1, xi.

66. Davis and Redding, *Cavalcade*. *Cavalcade* was updated under the direction of Joyce A. Joyce in 1991. See Joyce, Redding, and Davis, *The New Cavalcade*. For *Cavalcade*'s place in the long history of African American literary anthologies, see Kinnamon, "Anthologies of African-American Literature from 1845–1994."

67. In 1975 Redding wrote to Mary Schimke, an English instructor at Stanford University, to request a copy of her syllabus for her course Tellers and Tales: An Autobiographical Approach to American Literature. Redding assigned many of the same authors that Schimke had, including Henry Adams, Lincoln Steffens, Richard Wright, and Alex Haley/Malcolm X. Yet where Schimke's syllabus emphasized ethnic diversity and authorial voice (she included *Black Elk Speaks*, Alfred Kazin's *A Walker in the City*, Abigail McCarthy's *Private Faces/Public Places*, and John Steinbeck's *Travels with Charley*), Redding's syllabus focused on American social history. Letter from Mary McEwen Schimke to Redding, June 18, 1975, box 2, folder 152, JSRP-B.

68. Redding, American Biographical Literature syllabus, box 24, folders 17 and 20, JSRP-B.

69. For example, Daniel Mannix and Malcolm Cowley's anthology of slave ship captain's narratives, *Black Cargoes*, appeared in 1962; Charles Nichols's anthology of slave narratives, *Many Thousand Gone*, in 1963. Arna Bontemps's *Great Slave Narratives* appeared in 1969, as did Gilbert Osofsky's *Puttin' on Ole Massa*. The *New York Times* and Arno Press published, under the general editorship of William Loren Katz, a 44-volume series, *The American Negro: His History and Literature* (1968–71), a reprinting of historical and literary sources. William Katz's *Eyewitness: The Negro*

in American History: A Living Documentary of the Afro-American Contribution to U.S. History was published in 1974.

70. Redding, American Biographical Literature syllabus, box 24, folders 17 and 20, JSRP-B.

71. Kaplan, *Mr. Clemens and Mark Twain*, 19.

72. Butcher and Locke, *The Negro in American Culture*, 19.

73. Butcher and Locke, 261.

74. Redding, "The Negro in American History," 292.

75. John S. Gilkeson argues that the "myth and symbol" school was discredited in the late 1960s by the realization that American culture was neither integrated nor shared. See his *Anthropologists and the Rediscovery of America, 1886–1965*, 156–58. See also Buell, "Commentary," 13–16.

76. Albert, "Conflict and Change in American Values."

77. Potter, "The Quest for National Character."

78. Morgan, *American Slavery, American Freedom*, 386.

79. Henry, *Culture Against Man*, 4–5.

80. Romero, *Theory of Man*, 121.

81. Redding quoted this line of Rosengarten's a few years later in "The Negro in American History," 292.

82. Butterfield, *Black Autobiography in America*, 1.

83. Butterfield, 3.

84. Butterfield, 3–4.

85. Du Bois, *Dusk of Dawn*, 9–10.

86. Rosengarten, "Preface," 3.

87. Redding, "The Negro in American History," 303.

88. Steffens, *Autobiography*, 25. Butterfield's *Black Autobiography in America* commends Redding's *No Day of Triumph* for this kind of sociological acuity: "The beauty of *No Day of Triumph*," Butterfield writes, "is in the way its author enters into the voices of his characters and lets their experience draw the picture of class structure and race relations in the South. Throughout *No Day* we are given a clear understanding of the way human beings in a particular area produce and distribute wealth, buy and sell commodities, work together, exploit labor and cope with exploitation, what they think of themselves and each other, how they associate, and how their values and ideas are related to the way they earn their living. Redding's autobiography is full of wages, factories, bosses, workers, shacks, cotton fields, sharecroppers, and important economic detail of every sort. These facts have aesthetic, as well as sociological, importance for they contrast with and complement the verbal tradition of abolitionist oratory in his family background, and thus help to structure the work. They are also the basis of his larger, human 'validities,' their content and mode of existence." Butterfield, *Black Autobiography in America*, 153.

89. Du Bois, *Dusk of Dawn*, 25.

90. Du Bois, *Dusk of Dawn*, 3.

91. Steffens, *Autobiography*, 46–47.

92. Redding, The Negro in American Literature final examination, box 24, folder 22, JSRP-B.

93. Redding, Am Civ 175 final examination, box 25, folder 19, JSRP-B.

94. Geiger, review of *All God's Dangers*, by Theodore Rosengarten.

95. Romero, *Theory of Man*, 121.

96. For Redding's critique of "objective" history, see "The Negro in American History."

Chapter Five

1. Despite the disciplinary historical treatment of New Criticism as a unified movement that powerfully conjoined publication and pedagogy, as Frank Lentricchia notes, "*The* New Criticism was in fact no monolith but an inconsistent and sometimes confused movement." Lentricchia, *After the New Criticism*, xii–xiii. And, accordingly, despite a tendency to treat the methods of New Criticism as settled, many critics have contributed to a long debate over how to interpret what Mark Jancovich calls the "cultural politics" of the New Criticism. Jancovich opposes what he describes as a tendency for critics to assume that New Criticism was apolitical, or implicitly conservative, by providing context and politics for some of the New Critics. Jancovich, *The Cultural Politics of the New Criticism*. And counter to those who interpret New Criticism as seeking to bring scientific method to literary study, Gerald Graff places New Criticism "squarely in the romantic tradition of the defense of the humanities" as an "antidote to science and positivism." Graff, *Literature Against Itself*, 133–34.

2. Our pairing of Brooks and Wilson can also be read in terms of the dynamic between professional and amateur reader specific to the midcentury American moment but newly important in the present moment. See in this regard the essays in *The Critic as Amateur*, edited by Vadde and Majumdar, which explore the shifting interdigitation of professional and amateur criticism during the late nineteenth and twentieth centuries. As Vadde and Majumdar note in their introduction, their aim in the collection is in part to "recover a story of literary study and institutional crossover that might combat" recent "backlash against experts" (127).

3. Said, "Opponents, Audiences, Constituencies and Community," 159.

4. Brooks, *The Well Wrought Urn*, 5, 18, 21.

5. Richard Strier describes the marriage of interpretive and evaluative practices that lies at the heart of New Criticism in "How Formalism Became a Dirty Word and Why We Can't Do Without It."

6. Brooks, *The Well Wrought Urn*, 15.

7. Accounts of Brooks's actual classrooms are few and far between. In *Cleanth Brooks and the Rise of Modern Criticism*, Mark Winchell mentions that Brooks was a "remarkably popular teacher among both graduate and undergraduate students" and discusses a few of those students briefly (292–94).

8. English 71 was officially titled Contemporary Poetic Theory and Practice, but Brooks and others referred to it colloquially as Modern Poetry.

9. The lectures were never actually published.

10. Brooks, Yale Course Critique 1963, Cleanth Brooks Papers, YCAL MSS 30, box 81, folder 1657, Beinecke Rare Book and Manuscript Library, Yale University (hereafter CBP).

11. Brooks, Modern Poetry Lecture #5 transcript [corrected and retyped], February 13, 1963, YCAL MSS 30, 1–2, box 81, folder 1662, CBP.

12. Brooks, Modern Poetry Lecture #1 transcript [corrected and retyped], February 4, 1963, YCAL MSS 30, 9, box 81, folder 1658, CBP.

13. Brooks, Modern Poetry Lecture #3 transcript [corrected and retyped], February 8, 1963, YCAL MSS 30, 14, box 81, folder 1660, CBP.

14. Brooks, Modern Poetry Lecture #4 transcript [corrected and retyped], February 11, 1963, YCAL MSS 30, 2, box 81, folder 1661, CBP.

15. Brooks, Lecture #1, 6–8, CBP.

16. Brooks, Lecture #3, 19, CBP.

17. Brooks, Lecture #1, 9, CBP.

18. Brooks, Lecture #4, 7, CBP.

19. Brooks, Modern Poetry Lecture #2 transcript, February 6, 1963, YCAL MSS 30, 4, box 81, folder 1659, CBP.

20. Brooks, Lecture #3, 7, CBP.

21. Brooks, 7–8.

22. Brooks, Lecture #1, 3–6, CBP.

23. Brooks, Lecture #3, 11–12, CBP.

24. Moore, "Poetry," 26.

25. Brooks, Lecture #3, 4, CBP.

26. Even Moore's footnote-free poems are treated, by Brooks, as documents that contain obscure, excessively particular references: "I don't know what that means." "I think this is probably an old-fashioned or whimsical touch." "Since I don't know the Hebrew language, this is suggestive, and I am willing to take it on faith. It sounds right, but I don't know." "Is this Thoreau? Could be. Don't remember. Someone of the sort." "Don't ask me what that means. I can think of a dozen things it might mean." Brooks, Lecture #3, 1–17, CBP.

27. Brooks, Lecture #1, 10, CBP.

28. Brooks, Lecture #5, 14–15, CBP.

29. Brooks, Lecture #1, 25, CBP. Brooks says that Rockefeller commissioned José Clemente Orozco to paint the frescoes, though they were actually painted by Diego Rivera. When a student explains that the "Mexican artist," intending to satirize Rockefeller, included an image of Lenin, Brooks interrupts: "Yes, Yes, but what happened was that Mr. Rockefeller paid the artist for his work but didn't use the murals in Rockefeller center. And Macleish [sic] decides then that he will provide some frescoes for Mr. Rockefeller's city." Brooks, 23–24.

30. Brooks, 1–3.

31. Brooks, Lecture #3, 1–2, CBP.

32. Brooks, Lecture #2, 14, CBP.

33. Ngai, "Merely Interesting," 786–87.

34. See Wilson, "Is Verse a Dying Technique?" in *The Triple Thinkers*, 15–30.

35. See Wilson, "Marxism and Literature," in *The Triple Thinkers*, 197–212.

36. Adams, "Masks and Delays," 277.

37. Adams, 277.

38. Foster, review of *Patriotic Gore*, by Edmund Wilson, 526.

39. If some academic critics saw Wilson as an historicist who had no account of literary value, others saw—and continue to see—Wilson as a common reader critic for whom questions of value were simple and settled. Both reception histories obscure his very productive career-long struggle with the problem of how to properly interpret and properly value literature within the framework of his historical interests and investment in historicist—often Marxist—methodologies.

40. Wilson was widely criticized for failing to provide a strong theory of how historical approaches account for the value of literature in "The Historical Interpretation of Literature" (1940), in which he describes the historicist methodologies of Vico,

Taine, and Marx and Engels but attributes their success to their intuitive appreciation of "literature of 'Grade A.'" See Wilson, "The Historical Interpretation of Literature," in *The Triple Thinkers*, 272.

41. Teaching students to suspend sense in order to "follow the adventures of a letter through any passage that has particularly pleased you," Stevenson's essay must have struck Wilson as especially useful for approaching *Finnegans Wake*.

42. Stevenson, "On Style in Literature," 549.

43. Stevenson, 560.

44. Wilson, handouts for Comparative Literature 290: The Use of Language in Literature, Harvard University, fall 1959, YCAL MSS 187, box 163, folders 4055–56, EWP.

45. Wilson, lecture notes for English 354: Charles Dickens, University of Chicago, summer 1939, YCAL MSS 187, box 163, folder 4044, EWP.

46. Wilson, lecture notes for English 354: Charles Dickens.

47. Wilson, lecture notes for English 175: The Literature of the American Civil War, Harvard University, 1959–60, YCAL MSS 187, box 163, folder 4053, EWP.

48. Wilson, lecture notes for English 175: The Literature of the American Civil War, EWP.

49. This general revaluing also extended to the fiction and poetry Wilson did include. Puzzled reviewers wanted to know why Wilson apparently "consciously avoid[ed] close engagement" with canonical literature and included "such irrelevant figures as Poe, Stephen Foster, Frederick Goddard Tuckerman, Thomas Holly Chivers, Ezra Pound, and, of all people Adelaide Crapsey" instead of "Melville, Whitman, and Timrod." See H. Foster Charles's review of *Patriotic Gore*, by Edmund Wilson, 525.

50. Wilson, lecture notes for English 175: The Literature of the American Civil War, EWP.

51. Wilson, lecture notes for English 175.

52. Wilson, lecture notes for English 356a: Varieties of Nineteenth-Century Criticism, University of Chicago, 1939, YCAL MSS 187, box 163, folder 4045, EWP.

53. Wilson, lecture notes for Comparative Literature 290: The Use of Language in Literature, Harvard University, fall 1959, YCAL MSS 187, box 163, folder 4057, EWP.

54. On this model of the extension class that combined the public lecture open to a wide audience with the small accompanying seminar for enrolled students, see Lawrie, *The Beginnings of University English*, 59.

55. Wilson, lecture notes for English 30: An Introduction to James Joyce, Smith College, 1942, YCAL MSS, box 163, folder 4048, EWP.

56. Wilson, lecture notes for English 30.

Chapter Six

1. Glen Koskela to Josephine Miles, March 20, 1975, box 10, folder 5, and Annie Roth to Josephine Miles, September 12, 1978, box 10, folder 7, Josephine Miles Papers, Bancroft Library, University of California, Berkeley (hereafter cited as JMP).

2. Koskela to Miles, March 20, 1975, JMP.

3. Barbara Kirschenblatt-Gimblett to Josephine Miles, January 21, 1972, box 10, folder 5, JMP.

4. Arthur Cho to Josephine Miles, June 9, 1973, box 10, folder 5, JMP.

5. William Ruchte to Josephine Miles, January 30, 1973, box 10, folder 7, JMP.

6. Dan Aldeson to Josephine Miles, August 3, 1984, box 10, folder 4, JMP.

7. Kirschenblatt-Gimblett to Miles, January 21, 1972, JMP.

8. Aldeson to Miles, August 3, 1984, JMP.

9. Miles, *Poetry, Teaching, and Scholarship*, 81.

10. Miles, Fall 1940 English 1A lecture notes, carton 8, folder 47, JMP.

11. Miles, Spring 1948 English 1A lecture notes, carton 8, folder 48, JMP.

12. Miles, Spring 1941 English 1A lecture notes, carton 8, folder 47, JMP.

13. Miles, Summer 1947 English 1A lecture notes, carton 8, folder 48, JMP.

14. Miles, "The Use of Reason," in *Working Out Ideas*, 23.

15. Miles, "The Freshman at Composition," in *Working Out Ideas*, 6.

16. Miles, 5, 6.

17. Miles, 8–9.

18. Miles, "The Use of Reason," 18.

19. Koskela to Miles, March 20, 1975, JMP.

20. See Rovee, "Counting Wordsworth by the Bay"; and Pasanek, "Extreme Reading."

21. Rovee, "Counting Wordsworth by the Bay," 406. Even as Miles sought to correct the tendency of formalists to view past poets as "mirrors" for present values, her dissertation credited Richards and Ogden's *The Meaning of Meaning*, Stuart Chase's *The Tyranny of Words*, and other "work of the type of Barfield's *Poetic Diction*, Bateson's historical study, Lowes', Empson's, Spurgeon's on Shakespeare's images, and R. P. Blackmur's 'close criticism,'" for pioneering in general terms her own more specific analyses. Miles, *Wordsworth and the Vocabulary of Emotion*, 7.

22. Miles, *Poetry, Teaching, and Scholarship*, 128.

23. Majority vocabulary is considered to be words used more than 10 times in 1,000 lines by 10 poets or more, and minority vocabulary is considered to be words used 10 times in 1,000 lines by 4 poets or more.

24. Miles, *Wordsworth and the Vocabulary of Emotion*, 8.

25. Miles to Lester A. Hubbard, October 12, 1957, box 8, folder 13, JMP.

26. See Buurma and Heffernan, "Search and Replace." As Brad Pasanek says, "Enough with Father Busa, let us praise Mother Miles." Pasanek, "Extreme Reading," 2. See also Melissa Terras and Julianne Nyhan's research on the women who operated the punch card machines that made the *Index Thomasticus*: "Father Busa's Female Punch Card Operatives." As we also note in "Search and Replace": "There are good reasons, of course, that scholars and journalists like to begin with Busa: he was the first concordance-maker to automate all five stages of the process, in 1951. Busa also sought out high-profile partnerships with Thomas Watson of IBM and others; he foregrounded the innovative nature of his work, and his index incorporated new programming approaches as they developed through the later 1950s and '60s."

27. Miles, Summer 1945 English 1A lecture notes, carton 8, folder 47, JMP.

28. Miles, Fall 1946 English 1A lecture notes, carton 8, folder 48, JMP.

29. Miles, Spring 1947 English 1A lecture notes, carton 8, folder 48, JMP.

30. Miles, Fall 1949 English 1A lecture notes, carton 8, folder 48, JMP.

31. Miles, "Values in Language," 11.

32. Miles, *Style and Proportion*, vi.

33. Miles, *Poetry, Teaching, and Scholarship*, 76, 77.

34. Miles, 77.

35. Piper, "There Will Be Numbers"; Underwood, *Distant Horizons*; Bode, *A World of Fiction*; Allison, *Reductive Reading*; So, "All Models Are Wrong."

36. Despite some recent scholarly discussion, collaboration in quantitative literary study and digital humanities has not been discussed in proportion to its importance to the field; as Gabriele Griffin and Matt Steven Hayler note, "Collaboration in DH research has not been ignored, but it is still under-discussed in the field." Griffin and Hayler, "Collaboration in Digital Humanities Research—Persisting Silences."

37. Miles herself aimed to credit the work of the graduate students and IBM machine operators who might otherwise have been viewed as unimportant; she credited two of her graduate students, Mary Jackman and Helen S. Agoa, on the cover of the Dryden index rather than herself, and spoke in the preface to the concordance and in later interviews about the centrality of her collaboration with Penny Gee of Berkeley's Cory Hall computing lab. See Buurma and Heffernan, "Search and Replace."

38. Brereton, *The Origins of Composition Studies*, 17, 16, 15.

39. Miles, "Themes for English 1B, 1928–29," carton 9, folder 26, JMP.

40. Miles, Fall 1940 English 1A lecture notes, carton 8, folder 47, JMP.

41. Miles, Spring 1941 English 1A lecture notes, carton 8, folder 47, JMP.

42. See, for example, Miles, citation of "Adler 100 best," in Spring 1942 English 1A lecture notes, carton 8, folder 47, JMP.

43. See Miles, assignment of "ASUC book list," in Fall 1953 English 1A lecture notes, carton 8, folder 48, JMP.

44. Miles, Fall 1940 English 1A lecture notes, carton 8, folder 47, JMP.

45. See, for example, Miles, note on "blue bookwork" in the Fall 1945 English 1A lecture notes, carton 8, folder 47, JMP.

46. Hammond, "An Interview with Josephine Miles," 622.

47. Stewart, *English Composition*.

48. Miles, Fall 1943 English 1A lecture notes, carton 8, folder 47, JMP.

49. Miles, Spring 1952 English 1A lecture notes, carton 8, folder 48, JMP.

50. Miles, Spring 1943 English 1A lecture notes, carton 8, folder 47, JMP.

51. For example, Hayakawa prompts students to attempt to write a report that can be "verified" and "agreed upon" excluding "all evidence of the writer's approval or disapproval." This is a difficult task; students must use facts that can be verified, avoid "loaded words" ("homeless unemployed" not "tramp"; "Chinese" not "Chinaman"), and avoid inferences or guesses about other people's states of mind and future behavior (don't say "he is a thief"; say "he was convicted of theft"). He reminds his readers that even apparently neutral descriptions are shaped by inclusions and exclusions of details. The goal of a report, Hayakawa explains, is not pristine objectivity—"we cannot attain complete impartiality while we use the language of everyday life"—but "to attain enough impartiality for practical purposes." Hayakawa, *Language in Action*, 33–36.

52. Hayakawa, 41.

53. Miles, Fall 1941 English 1A lecture notes, carton 8, folder 47, JMP.

54. Bainbridge, "Hu Shih's Musketeer, II," *New Yorker*, January 17, 1942; cartoon on p. 25 of same issue.

55. Miles, Fall 1941 English 1A lecture notes and Spring 1942 English 1A lecture notes, carton 8, folder 47, JMP.

56. Miles, Summer 1947 English 1A lecture notes, carton 8, folder 48, JMP.

57. Spring 1942 English 1A lecture notes, carton 8, folder 47, JMP.

58. Daiches, *The Novel and the Modern World*, 172.

59. Daiches, 176.

60. Daiches, 188.

61. Daiches, 190.

62. Miles, Fall 1940 English 1A lecture notes, carton 8, folder 47, JMP.

63. Miles, Spring 1942 English 1A lecture notes, carton 8, folder 47; and Spring 1952 English 1A lecture notes, carton 8, folder 48, JMP.

64. Miles, Summer 1943 English 1A lecture notes, carton 8, folder 47, JMP.

65. Miles, Spring 1952 English 1A lecture notes, carton 8, folder 48, JMP.

66. Miles, Spring 1948 English 1A notes, carton 8, folder 48, JMP.

67. Miles, *Eras and Modes in English Poetry*, 128.

68. Miles, *Wordsworth and the Vocabulary of Emotion*, 1; Miles, *Eras and Modes*, 128.

69. Miles, *Wordsworth and the Vocabulary of Emotion*, 1.

70. Miles, 16.

71. Miles, *Style and Proportion*, 19.

72. Miles, *Pathetic Fallacy in the Nineteenth Century*, 186.

73. Miles, "The Pathetic Fallacy and the Thing in Itself," 212.

74. Miles, *Pathetic Fallacy in the Nineteenth Century*, 191.

75. Miles, *Major Adjectives in English Poetry*, 305, 309.

76. Miles, 307.

77. Miles, *The Continuity of Poetic Language*, 45n7.

78. Miles, 3–4.

79. Miles, "Preface to the Octagon Edition," i.

80. Miles went back and forth on the question of whether data sets were representative or descriptive: "I therefore mean to make no statement about any more than the lines under consideration," she wrote. Miles, *The Continuity of Poetic Language*, 41.

81. Pasanek, "Extreme Reading," 356–57.

82. Miles, *Eras and Modes*, 11.

83. Miles, *The Continuity of Poetic Language*, 551–52.

84. Miles, 161.

85. Miles, 459.

86. Miles, 471.

87. Koch, "Continuity of Poetic Language," 367. See also John Arthos's review of *The Primary Language of Poetry in the 1640's; The Primary Language of Poetry in the 1740's and 1840's*, by Josephine Miles, 80–81.

88. Miles remembered, "That was at the behest of the editorial committee of the University Press" and its chairman, who was "a real hero to me because he told the press that that data was important enough." Miles noted, "Though the University has published a good deal of my work, I don't think that the manager of [the] University Press and chief editor ever was happy about having to do it. So this was a case where the editorial committee stepped in and defended me and really rescued me after years of trouble." Miles, *Poetry, Teaching, and Scholarship*, 129.

89. Miles's turn to connectives in the 1960s was quite ambitious, as these words are numerically dominant and therefore daunting to count by hand. Inspired by innovations in computer concordancing, Miles imagined a future in which connectives could be machine counted. Noting that new work by Stephen Parrish of the Cornell concordance group had made it easier to add frequency and context to concordance words, Miles dreamed of the possibilities. In a review of the Cornell Arnold and Yeats concordances, she wrote: "While concordances first were useful as directions for the locating of passages and allusions, and more recently have become resources for the

study of variations of meaning . . . they may also serve more fully than we yet realize to illuminate the structures of poetry as well as its references." They could give us a sense of what it means, for example, that Yeats is the poet of "of." "The particle terms, like the referential, are clues to style, to tone, to structure. Pronouns stand in place for nouns, and connective phrases and clauses are replacive for adjective and adverb modifiers; and each possible replacement suggests a choice of value. The poetry of *in* and *of* may be quite different from the poetry of *to* and *from* or *by* and *because*. . . . It is possible then that even without full listings, machine counts can make us aware of structural clues to relations between terms." Miles, review of *Concordance to the Poems of Matthew Arnold*, by Stephen M. Parrish; *Concordance to the Poems of W. B. Yeats*, by Stephen M. Parrish; *Concordance to the Poems of Wallace Stevens*, by Thomas F. Walsh, 290–92.

90. For example, in *Enumerations*, Andrew Piper argues that literary critics move too hastily from particular examples to generalizations: "In traditional critical practices, we only ever hear about the passages and works that fit our thesis. . . . We almost *never* hear about the ones that did not, how many were considered, and how prevalent the phenomenon is that we are observing more generally" (11).

91. Miles, "What We Compose," in *Working Out Ideas*, 26.

92. Miles, "Values in Language," 12–13.

93. Miles, 11.

94. Miles, 13.

Chapter Seven

1. The teaching of Native American literature in English departments, ethnic studies departments, and in newly formed and forming Native American studies programs was new, though some colleges and universities, including the University of Arizona, had been teaching classes on Native American society and culture since the 1930s. Joseph Bruchac remembers: "It was in 1970 that the first Native American literature course was taught at Skidmore, during their one-month winter term. I wasn't allowed to teach it, though by then I was being allowed to teach a single course in Black Literature. 'Topics in American Indian Literature' was taught by a senior faculty member who used a lot of work from anthropologists and a little contemporary Indian writing. He used Kroeber's *The Inland Whale*, some creation stories, threw in a few poems by poets who were Indian." Bruchac, "Four Directions," 2.

2. In 1970 Ortiz attended the conference "Indian Voices: The First Convocation of American Indian Scholars" at Princeton University, where he likely heard the discussions between several of the directors of and teachers in newly formed Native American Studies programs that took place during the panel on "Native American Studies Programs: Review and Evaluation" led by W. Roger Buffalohead. As Buffalohead noted about the development of history curricula, "When you first get into it, it is pretty easy to say you are going to develop an American Indian History course, but unless you want it to be something different from what has passed for American Indian History, in college textbooks or in a lot of other writings, then you have to get down to the serious work of how you are going to incorporate all history, for example, into the program. How are you going to emphasize oral histories sufficiently? You are actually supposedly telling the Indian student like it is, for him, from the Indian point

of view of history, rather than saying or concentrating solely on written materials, etc." *Indian Voices*, 168. This debate has persisted; on the question of authenticity and the definition of "Native American literature," see Treuer, *Native American Fiction*; and Parker, *The Invention of Native American Literature*.

3. Ortiz, "Towards a National Indian Literature," 8.

4. Ortiz, 12.

5. Lyons, "The Fine Art of Fencing," 89, 90.

6. Ortiz, "Journal Entries, 1970–71, 1973–74," Simon J. Ortiz Papers, MSS-372, box 19, folder 1, Labriola Center, Arizona State University (hereafter cited as SJOP). In his introduction to *Woven Stone* (1992), Ortiz notes that despite the long oral tradition, "it has been only since the 1960s that Native American writers have been published to any extent" (30). Other critics and literary historians see the history of written and published Native American literature differently; in the introduction to anthology *The Remembered Earth: An Anthology of Contemporary Native American Literature* (1979), editor Geary Hobson argues that "even in its written form, in the English language, Native American literature is quite old within the framework of American literature" (4), going on to survey literature by Native American authors published in the nineteenth and twentieth centuries.

7. David Treuer argues that Native American writers' combination of these forms seeks to work out the fact that the Western literary forms of the poetry, novels, and short stories written by Native American writers are often fundamentally at odds with traditional stories. Treuer, *Native American Fiction*.

8. Questions about how Native American studies courses and programs might compromise with or change any institutions in which they could live and thrive began long before such programs and courses were widely established, and still continue today. See Cook-Lynn, "Who Stole Native American Studies?"

9. Ortiz, "College of Marin Personnel Folder, 1976–79," MSS-372, box 46, folder 9, SJOP.

10. Ortiz, "Notes and Papers from English Literature Coursework, 1966," MSS-372, box 1, folder 2, SJOP.

11. Annie Martinez portfolio for English 488-001, Summer 1980, "Student Work from Native American Literature," MSS-372, box 48, folder 4, SJOP.

12. Ortiz, "Journals, 1964–1966," MSS-372, box 17, folder 14, SJOP.

13. Ortiz, "Coursework on Victorian Novel and Early English Novel, 1968 Spring," MSS-372, box 1, folder 7, SJOP.

14. Ortiz, "AND WHY NOT?: An Attempt to Explain Why Indian Students, Especially Those Who Show High Potential and Motivation, Drop Out," writing for Dr. Robert A. Roessel Extension Course ASU, 1968 Summer Indian Education, MSS-372, box 1, folder 8, SJOP.

15. Ortiz, 12, 11.

16. Ortiz, 14, 17.

17. "There was . . . a distinct disadvantage in being Indian in certain situations, mainly social. And of course this awareness overlapped into our intellectual and academic activity." Ortiz, 17.

18. Ortiz, 13.

19. Many of the new anthologies of Native American literature past and present created in the 1970s were also engaged in the project of attempting to create a "Native

American literature" out of the diverse range of texts belonging to very different cultures and languages that might be part of such a formation; see n. 25 for some of the anthologies Ortiz considered teaching in his own class.

20. Ortiz, "Journal Entries, 1970–71, 1973–74," SJOP.

21. Ortiz, "Journal Entries, 1970–71, 1973–74," SJOP.

22. Ortiz, "Journal Entries, 1970–71, 1973–74," SJOP. The "explanations and instructions" genre helps explain Ortiz's useful poem "How to Make a Good Chili Stew," which has seemed frivolous to some critics.

23. Ortiz, "Journal Entries, 1970–71, 1973–74," SJOP. ·

24. Ortiz, "Journal Entries, 1970–71, 1973–74," SJOP.

25. Ortiz, "Journal Entries, 1970–71, 1973–74," SJOP. Ortiz's seventeen-book list of possible readings included individual works by Native American writers like N. Scott Momaday's *The Way to Rainy Mountain* (1969), Leslie Marmon Silko's *Laguna Woman: Poems* (1974) (referred to in Ortiz's list as "Leslie's book," possibly not published at the time Ortiz made the list), and James Welch's *Riding the Earthboy 40* (1971), along with recent anthologies of new poetry and fiction including *The Man to Send Rain Clouds* (1974), *The American Indian Speaks* (1969), and *From the Belly of the Shark* (1973). It also included collections of translations, adaptations, and rewritings (primarily by white translators and poets) of prayers, myths, and stories: *Shaking the Pumpkin: Traditional Poetry of the Indian North Americas* (1972), edited by Jerome Rothenberg, Theodora Kroeber's *The Inland Whale* (1959), and Jaime de Angulo's *Indian Tales* (1953). Ortiz also listed some "recorded" or "as told to" autobiographies like *Sun Chief* (1942), *Black Elk Speaks* (1932), and *Lame Deer: Seeker of Visions* (1959). And he included Vine Deloria Jr.'s work of political and cultural criticism *We Talk, You Listen* (1970) and the *Chronicles of American Indian Protest* (1971), a collection of historical documents chronicling the struggle against European invasion from 1622 until the present.

26. Ortiz, "Journal Entries, 1970–71, 1973–74," SJOP.

27. Ortiz, Native American Arts self-evaluation, 1978, "College of Marin Personnel Folder, 1976–79," SJOP.

28. For context on the creation of ethnic studies programs in the United States in the 1960s and '70s, see Yamane, *Student Movements for Multiculturalism*, 12–18.

29. Spring 1978 Ethnic Studies Catalog, 2, College of Marin, MSS-372, box 46, folder 7, SJOP.

30. Spring 1978 Ethnic Studies Catalog, College of Marin, SJOP.

31. Ortiz, American Indian Art Final Exam, Fall 1976, "College of Marin Exams, 1976–79," MSS-372, box 46, folder 8, SJOP.

32. Spring 1978 Ethnic Studies Catalog, College of Marin, SJOP.

33. Warrior, "Literature and Students in Native American Studies."

34. Ortiz, "Journal Entries, 1970–71, 1973–74," SJOP.

35. Ortiz, "College of Marin Personnel Folder, 1976–79," SJOP. Despite his lack of a formal degree, Ortiz had taken far more credits than would have made up the balance of courses for a BA at a single institution: 45 credit hours at Fort Lewis College, 80 at the University of New Mexico, and 30 at the University of Iowa, as well as coursework in education at Arizona State University and in linguistics at UNM during the early 1970s.

36. Recommendation letter from Bill Wahpepah, "College of Marin Personnel Folder, 1976–79," SJOP. Bill Wahpepah was also a Bay Area activist who had this to

say about the public school system: "It's still a war with our people . . . except now they have . . . political weapons such as [an] education system, that are designed to make our children become something other than what they are. We want them to be proud American Indians." Williams, "Bill Wahpepah and Dennis Banks at Oakland Indian School."

37. Ortiz, "Many Farms Notes," 29.

38. Ortiz, Spring 1977 Native American Arts syllabus, College of Marin, MSS-372, box 48, folder 6, SJOP.

39. Ortiz may also have taught one earlier version of the class at Marin in fall 1976, for which we have seen only a three-question "American Indian Literature" exam with Ortiz listed as the instructor and without a course number; it is labeled "1976" in pencil on top.

40. Ortiz, *Woven Stone*, 30. This interpretation of Native American literary and cultural history has not been, of course, universally shared, at the time or since. In his introduction to *The Remembered Earth* anthology (which Ortiz himself used in his 1979 iteration of the class) and elsewhere, Geary Hobson discusses how many writers and critics, including Ortiz, imagined a huge gap between the individual oral traditions of hundreds of tribes and the contemporary moment of literary production. As Hobson notes in the introduction to his 1979 anthology of new creative writing, "even in its written form, in the English language, Native American literature is quite old within the framework of American literature" (4). As Christopher Teuton notes, the strong emphasis on the oral tradition in the 1970s and '80s meant that the preponderance of nineteenth-century Native American literature, which was often not strongly related to the oral tradition, was sometimes ignored. See Teuton, *Deep Waters*.

41. Ortiz, Spring 1977 Native American Arts syllabus, SJOP.

42. Underwood, *Why Literary Periods Mattered*, 84–85.

43. A few years later, at the University of New Mexico, Ortiz would teach two separate courses, one on the oral tradition and one on modern and contemporary Native American literature. See Ortiz, "Outlines, Syllabi, Readings, 1979–1980," MSS-372, box 47, folder 4, SJOP.

44. Spring 1977 Native American Arts syllabus, box 48, folder 6.

45. Ortiz, Spring 1977 Native American Arts syllabus, SJOP.

46. In weeks ten and eleven, the 1978 and 1979 syllabuses departed from the 1977 first iteration to make the resistance to colonization a much stronger focus. In the 1977 version, Ortiz taught about the collections of oral literature collected by white anthropologists and ethnographers "into publications like the *Bulletins of the Bureau of American Ethnology*, *Technicians of the Sacred*, Castenada's *Don Juan* and *Journey to Ixtlan*." Ortiz, Spring 1977 Native American Arts syllabus, SJOP. The later iterations of the course replace week ten's study with the study of the "development of oral literature which has come from struggle against colonialism." Ortiz, Spring 1978 Native American Arts syllabus, College of Marin, MSS-372, box 48, folder 6, SJOP. And again, week eleven in 1977 introduces "other Tribal literary artforms from around the world which are similar to Native American forms of oral literature," while week eleven in 1978 and 1979 continue with the topic of "oral tradition and resistance." Ortiz, Spring 1977 Native American Arts syllabus and Spring 1978 Native American Arts syllabus, SJOP.

47. Ortiz, Spring 1977 Native American Arts syllabus, SJOP.

48. Ortiz, Spring 1977 Native American Arts syllabus, SJOP.

49. Ortiz selected texts for the class from the basic three categories he tended to use: sources that would represent traditional story cycles, autobiographies translated and edited by anthropologists, and contemporary fiction and poetry by Native American writers. In the 1977 syllabus, Ortiz listed *Sun Chief: The Autobiography of a Hopi Indian* (1942) by Don C. Talayesva, edited by Leo W. Simmons; Angulo's *Indian Tales* (1953), a very loose adaptation and synthesis of anthropological recordings of animal stories drawn from different California tribes; *The Man to Send Rain Clouds* (1974), an anthology of prose (with a few poems and some visual artwork) by Native American writers, edited by white Dickinson College English professor Kenneth Rosen; and *The First Skin Around Me: Contemporary American Tribal Poetry* (1976), edited by white poet and critic James L. White. (Note that on his required textbooks, Ortiz lists only Leo W. Simmons as the author of *Sun Chief*, in accordance with the first editions of the book; new editions by the early 1970s listed Don C. Talayesva as author and Simmons as editor.)

50. Patricia Russo, Native American Literature Syllabus, San Diego State University, 1978, MSS-372, box 48, folder 7, SJOP.

51. Ortiz, Spring 1978 Native American Arts syllabus, SJOP.

52. See Teuton, *Deep Waters*, 58, 54.

53. Teuton comments, "Critics have described how the work's self-conscious, modernist structure signals its ambition to place multiple traditions into conversation, as the narrative embraces competing epistemologies that influence the narrator's understanding of his experience" (57).

54. Momaday's Stanford dissertation was an edition of the poems of Frederick Goddard Tuckerman. Edmund Wilson's *Patriotic Gore: Studies in the Literature of the American Civil War* (discussed in chapter 5) had sparked a revival of interest in Tuckerman. See *The Complete Poems of Frederick Goddard Tuckerman*.

55. Underwood, *Why Literary Periods Mattered*, 101.

56. Rice, "A Ventriloquy of Anthros."

57. Lame Deer and Erdoes, *Lame Deer, Seeker of Visions*, 281–82.

58. Angulo, *Indian Tales*, 13.

59. Ortiz, *A Good Journey*, 66.

60. Ortiz, Spring 1978 Native American Arts syllabus, SJOP.

61. Lame Deer and Erdoes, *Lame Deer*, 8.

62. Ortiz, *A Good Journey*, 133, 134.

63. Ortiz, 135, 136.

64. Ortiz, 136–37.

65. Matching Ortiz's poetic critique of colonizers' use of communication infrastructure was his concurrent interest in the organization and dissemination of information in forms that met the needs of Native American communities. During the fall of 1978, Ortiz coauthored, along with Roxanne Dunbar-Ortiz, a report titled "Traditional and Hard-to-Find Information Required by Members of American Indian Communities: What to Collect; How to Collect It; and Appropriate Format and Use" for the White House Pre-Conference on Indian Library and Information Services On or Near Reservations. The report opens with an epigraph from Momaday's *The Way to Rainy Mountain*. Roxanne Dunbar-Ortiz with Simon Ortiz, "Traditional and Hard-To-Find Information Required by Members of American Indian Communities: What to Collect; How to Collect It; and Appropriate Format and Use," Ephemera folder 7, SJOP.

66. Ortiz, Spring 1978 Native American Arts syllabus, SJOP. We have silently corrected minor typographical errors in the syllabus.

67. On versions of the Yellow Woman story, see Beidler et al., "Silko's Originality in 'Yellow Woman.'"

68. Silko, "Yellow Woman," 34, 35. In a later essay, "Yellow Woman and a Beauty of the Spirit," Silko describes Yellow Woman as representing "all women in the old stories" (70). Silko's Yellow Woman appeals to her because "she dares to cross traditional boundaries of ordinary behavior during times of crisis in order to save the Pueblo"; Yellow Woman's "power lies in her courage and her uninhibited sexuality" (70). Of all the stories Silko might have drawn on or adapted in her short story, the one about her abduction by the ka'tsina seems, at first glance, to be the least representative of what Silko admires about Yellow Woman.

69. Silko, "Yellow Woman," 37.

70. Ortiz, Spring 1978 Native American Arts syllabus, SJOP.

71. Ortiz, "Towards a National Indian Literature," 12.

72. Ortiz, 12.

Conclusion

1. Childress, *The Adjunct Underclass*, 31–38. On casual labor as part of the ecosystem of higher education, see Bousquet, *How the University Works*.

2. See Labaree, "Public Goods, Private Goods." See also Readings, *The University in Ruins*. In *The Blackademic Life*, Lavelle Porter notes the increasingly pervasive assumption that education is now a private rather than a public good, and the accompanying assumption that higher education institutions are both monolithic and elite; his work shows how these assumptions can be resisted in part through strategies for offering a better view of the actual, varied conditions of higher education, including through fiction.

3. These disciplinary historians variously framed the conflict as a civil war between cultural studies and English studies; a revolutionary replacement of the discipline-specific concept of literature with the seemingly boundless concept of cultural "texts"; an abandonment of the "traditional" canon for a "multicultural" one. See Bergonzi, *Exploding English*; and Abrams, "The Transformation of English Studies, 1930–1995."

4. Many commentators within and outside the discipline of literary study, of course, study the connection between actual demographic change and changes to method and curriculum. See, for example, Alan Kernan's "Introduction: Change in the Humanities and Higher Education"; Hunt, "Democratization and Decline?"; and Oakley, "Ignorant Armies and Nighttime Clashes." And still other commentators from humanities disciplines are doing work that connects the history of institutions to the present and future of the study of the humanities; see, for example, the essays in Hutner and Mohamed, *A New Deal for the Humanities*.

5. Joseph North, for example, sees the years after 1968 as a definitive turning point for the discipline, in which the scholars edged out the critics once and for all by making "any attack on the historicist/contextuality paradigm" seem rooted in "cultural conservatism, particularly if the offending party makes use of such terms as 'criticism,' 'aesthetic,' 'sensibility,' and similar." North, *Literary Criticism*, 4. Simon During sees 1968 as the end of a fifty-year period in which the English department became the "most exciting and popular institution in the academic humanities" and in which

critics produced, in the wake of Eliot's *The Sacred Wood*, countless "path-breaking and exciting works," while the years after 1968 saw the "dissipation" of these energies in multiple directions: toward identity politics, anti-elitism, deconstruction, and literary sociology. During, "Studying Literature Today." Others see this 1970s moment as the rise of ideology critique, which seems to them to be the powerfully dominant form that eclipses other methods. For Stephen Best and Sharon Marcus, the 1970s are the watershed moment when ideology critique first took hold and a Jamesonian (or Althusserian) "symptomatic reading" began to edge out everything else. Best and Marcus, "Surface Reading." For Rita Felski, "critique" as the "critical mood" of a variety of otherwise very varied theory-driven methods ("hermeneutics of suspicion" à la Pierre Macherey and Fredric Jameson; New Historicism, postcolonial theory, queer theory, cultural materials) became dominant around this same time, its brightness outshining the lesser stars of humanities method with less purchase on understanding structures of power. Felski notes, by citing Helen Small's *The Value of the Humanities*, the fact that "the work of the humanities is frequently descriptive, or appreciative, or imaginative, or provocative, or speculative, more than it is critical." Small, *The Value of the Humanities*. However, Felski also notes that "critique" is far from the only method in the humanities, but argues that the "critical mood" is often "feted as the most serious and scrupulous form of thought" at the expense of the other modes. Felski, *The Limits of Critique*, 19–20.

6. For Joseph North, the return to formalism promises to counter historicism's conservatism by "using works of literature for the cultivation of aesthetic sensibility, with the goal of more general cultural and political change." North, *Literary Criticism*, 3. For Michael Clune, the return to aesthetic judgment promises a means of "contesting the neoliberal hegemony of the market." Clune, "Judgment and Equality," 910. See also Clune, "The Humanities' Fear of Judgment." Like Walter Benn Michaels before them, Clune and North argue that 1970s-era new methods, for all their progressivism, failed to counteract the neoliberal ascendency of these years, and perhaps even unknowingly participated in it by denouncing too loudly and for too long the elitism of literary tastes and canons. Michaels, *The Shape of the Signifier*.

7. The imagining of higher education as a monolithic research university goes alongside the tendency to overrepresent the perspectives of elite private universities; Gordon Hutner and Feisal Mohamed point out, for example, how few expert faculty from public universities were on the committee that authored the American Academy of Arts and Sciences' congressionally mandated report *The Heart of the Matter: The Humanities and Social Sciences for a Vibrant, Competitive, and Secure Nation*. Hutner and Mohamed, "Introduction," in *A New Deal for the Humanities*, 1.

8. Said, "Figures, Configurations, Transfigurations," 67.

9. See Judith Glazer-Raymo, "Academia's Equality Myth," drawn from her book, *Shattering the Myths: Women in Academe*, excerpted in Bender and Smith, *American Higher Education Transformed, 1940–2005*.

10. On for-profit education in relation to the privatization of American higher education, see Cottom, *Lower Ed*.

11. In *We Demand: The University and Student Protests*, Roderick Ferguson describes "the heterogeneous publics whose due has never been received, whose dreams have never been fully activated, and whose histories and identities are rarely acknowledged as part of our 'public'" (5). And Mary Mullen has described how the immense "political and social pressure to defend" the university, and the role of the

humanities within it, "encourage[s] scholars to forget the daily struggles within their own institutions and not only accept, but actively seek to maintain, existing institutional arrangements as an ideal present and desired future." Mullen, "Coda," in *Novel Institutions*, 212.

12. Important scholarship also exists on the different but related point that the forms of new access the university took were largely ones that did not threaten the increasingly privatized order of higher education; see, for example, Walcott, "The End of Diversity."

13. Mark Garrett Cooper and John Marx argue that "the culture wars mobilized key factions by avoiding discussion of structural changes in favor of wedge issues." Cooper and Marx, "By the Numbers," in *Media U*, 206.

14. See Bender and Smith, "Introduction," in *American Higher Education Transformed, 1940–2005*, 6. Christopher Newfield offers a slightly different narrative about the funding of humanities departments in *The Great Mistake*.

15. See Cottom, *Lower Ed*.

16. We therefore disagree with claims like Caroline Levine's that a representative contemporary literary critic writing about a novel "would most likely keep her formalism and her historicism analytically separate, drawing from close reading methods to understand the literary forms, while using historical research methods to analyze sociopolitical experience." We agree that the effects of method debates in recent years have meant that formalism and historicism have come to *seem* to "belong to separate realms and call for different methods," but as we have argued in this book, in practice such methods are more often closely connected. See Levine, *Forms*, 1.

17. For some initial work on the possibilities, difficulties, and limitations of incorporating citations on syllabuses in citation metrics see Konkiel, "What Do Syllabi-Based Altmetrics Actually Mean?"; Rhody, "The Syllabus as HuMetrics Case Study"; and the International Studies Association, "How to Count What Counts: TIS the Season for Syllabi Metrics?" See also the Open Syllabus Project, https://opensyllabus.org/.

18. We give only a part of the story here. Another important area of research is the history of the interrelations between primary, secondary, and tertiary education, a topic we touch on only briefly here in our account of Edith Rickert's teaching of high school teachers. For an account of why we need to understand the history of K–12 education in the United States and of the costs of viewing K–12 teaching as ahistorical, see Goldstein, *The Teacher Wars*.

19. Buurma and Heffernan, "Elite Colleges Have No Monopoly on the Liberal Arts."

20. Harney and Moten, *The Undercommons*.

Bibliography

Abrams, M. H. "The Transformation of English Studies, 1930–1995." *Daedalus* 126, no. 1 (Winter 1997): 105–31.

Adams, Robert Martin. "Masks and Delays: Edmund Wilson as Critic." *Sewanee Review* 56, no. 2 (April 1948): 272–86.

Adler, Mortimer J., Charles Van Doren, and George Ducas, eds. *The Negro in American History*. Vol. 1. Chicago: Encyclopedia Britannica Educational Corporation, 1969.

Albert, Ethel M. "Conflict and Change in American Values." In *The Character of Americans: A Book of Readings*, edited by Michael McGiffert. Homewood, IL: Dorsey Press, 1964.

Allison, Sarah. *Reductive Reading: A Syntax of Victorian Moralizing*. Baltimore: Johns Hopkins University Press, 2018.

Altick, Richard. *A Little Bit of Luck: The Making of an Adventurous Scholar*. Philadelphia: Exlibris, 2002.

Anderson, Amanda. "Theory and the Changing Forms of Institutional Prestige." *Symploke* 27, no. 1 (October 3, 2019): 427–32.

Anderson, James D. *The Education of Blacks in the South, 1860–1915*. Chapel Hill: University of North Carolina Press, 1988.

Angulo, Jaime de. *Indian Tales*. New York: North Point Press, 1997.

Annual Report, National Endowment for the Humanities, 1965–66. Washington, DC: National Endowment for the Humanities, 1966.

Annual Report of the Librarian of Congress for the Fiscal Year Ended June 30, 1938. Washington, DC: United States Government Printing Office, 1939.

Arthos, John. Review of *The Primary Language of Poetry in the 1640's*; and *The Primary Language of Poetry in the 1740's and 1840's*, by Josephine Miles. *Journal of Aesthetics and Art Criticism* 10, no. 1 (September 1951): 80–81.

Arthur, Anthony. "Plus Ça Change . . . : *Practical Criticism* Revisited." *College English* 38, no. 6 (February 1977): 583–88.

Ashton, Rosemary. *Victorian Bloomsbury*. New Haven, CT: Yale University Press, 2012.

Atherton, Carol. *Defining Literary Criticism: Scholarship, Authority, and the Possession of Literary Knowledge, 1880–2002*. New York: Palgrave Macmillan, 2006.

Atkinson, Mabel. *Syllabus of a Course of Tutorial Classes on the Social History of*

England. London: University of London Press, 1911. EM 6/6/1, Senate House Library, University of London.

Attridge, Derek. *Reading and Responsibility: Deconstruction's Traces*. Edinburgh: Edinburgh University Press, 2010.

Aubry, Timothy. *Guilty Aesthetic Pleasures*. Cambridge, MA: Harvard University Press, 2018.

Aydelotte, Frank. *English as Training in Thought*. New York: Educational Review Publishing, 1912.

Baer, Ben Connisbee. *Indigenous Vanguards: Education, National Liberation, and the Limits of Modernism*. New York: Columbia University Press, 2019.

Bainbridge, John. "Hu Shih's Musketeer, II." *New Yorker*, January 17, 1942.

Baldick, Chris. *The Social Mission of English Criticism, 1848–1932*. Oxford: Clarendon Press, 1983.

Barfield, Owen. *Poetic Diction: A Study in Meaning*. Middletown, CT: Wesleyan University Press, 1973.

Barthes, Roland. *The Preparation of the Novel: Lecture Courses and Seminars at the Collège de France, 1978–1979 and 1979–1980*. Edited by Nathalie Léger. Translated by Kate Briggs. New York: Columbia University Press, 2011.

Beidler, Peter, Heather Holland, Ann Cavanaugh Sipos, Jian Shi, Nora El-Aasser, Melissa Fiesta Blossom, Carolyn Leslie Grossman, Jennifer A. Thornton, and Vanessa Holford Diana. "Silko's Originality in 'Yellow Woman.'" *Studies in American Indian Literatures* 8, no. 2 (1996): 61–84.

Bender, Thomas, and Wilson Smith, eds. *American Higher Education Transformed, 1940–2005: Documenting the National Discourse*. Baltimore: Johns Hopkins University Press, 2008.

Bergonzi, Bernard. *Exploding English: Criticism, Theory, Culture*. Oxford: Oxford University Press, 1990.

Berlin, James A. *Rhetoric and Reality: Writing Instruction in the American Colleges, 1900–1985*. Carbondale: Southern Illinois University Press, 1987.

Berry, Faith. *A Scholar's Conscience: Selected Writings of J. Saunders Redding, 1942–1977*. Lexington: University of Kentucky Press, 1992.

Berthoff, Ann. *Forming Thinking Writing: The Composing Imagination*. Portsmouth, NH: Boynton/Cook Publishers, 1982.

Berthoff, Ann. "I. A. Richards and the Philosophy of Rhetoric." *Rhetorical Society Quarterly* 10, no. 4 (Autumn 1980): 195–210.

Best, Stephen, and Sharon Marcus. "Surface Reading: An Introduction." In "The Way We Read Now," edited by Best and Marcus, special issue. *Representations* 108, no. 1 (Fall 2009): 1–21.

Bibby, Michael. "The Disinterested and Fine: New Negro Renaissance Poetry and the Racial Formation of Modernist Studies." *Modernism/Modernity* 20, no. 3 (September 2013): 485–501.

Blair, Ann. *Too Much to Know: Managing Scholarly Information before the Modern Age*. New Haven, CT: Yale University Press, 2011.

Bloor, R. H. U. *Syllabus of a Course of Lectures on the Ideals and Issues of the Present Struggle*. London: University of London Press, 1917. EM 2/21/14, Senate House Library, University of London.

Bode, Katherine. *A World of Fiction: Digital Collections and the Future of Literary History*. Ann Arbor: University of Michigan Press, 2018.

Bontemps, Arna. *Great Slave Narratives*. Boston: Beacon Press, 1969.

Bookman. Unsigned review of *The Real Rhythm in English Poetry*, by Katharine M. Wilson, and *A New Approach to Poetry*, by Elsa Chapin and Russell Thomas." 1930. Box 102, folder 1, University of Chicago Press Records, 1892–1965, Special Collections Research Center, University of Chicago Library.

Bousquet, Marc. *How the University Works: Higher Education and the Low-Wage Nation*. New York: NYU Press, 2008.

Bredin, Hugh. "I. A. Richards and the Philosophy of Practical Criticism." *Philosophy and Literature* 10, no. 1 (April 4, 1986): 26–37.

Brereton, John. *The Origins of Composition Studies in the American College, 1875–1925: A Documentary History*. Pittsburgh: University of Pittsburgh Press, 1996.

Brierley, S. S. *Syllabus for a Tutorial Class in Psychology*. London: University of London Press, 1917. EM 6/6/5C, Senate House Library, University of London.

Brigham Young University Annual Catalogue, 1928–29. Provo, UT: Brigham Young University Press, 1928.

Brigham Young University Division of Continuing Education Class Schedule, 1929–30. Provo, UT: Brigham Young University Press, 1929.

Brooker, Jewel Spears. *Mastery and Escape: T. S. Eliot and the Dialectic of Modernism*. Amherst: University of Massachusetts Press, 1994.

Brooks, Cleanth. "Current Critical Theory and the Period Course (NECEA Conference)." *CEA Critic* 12, no. 7 (1950): 1–6.

Brooks, Cleanth. "I. A. Richards and 'Practical Criticism.'" *Sewanee Review* 89, no. 4 (October 1, 1981): 586–95.

Brooks, Cleanth. *The Well Wrought Urn: Studies in the Structure of Poetry*. New York: Harcourt, Brace and World, 1947.

Brown, Alan. "On the Subject of Practical Criticism." *Cambridge Quarterly* 8, no. 4 (1999): 293–327.

Brown, Stephanie. *The Postwar African-American Novel: Protest and Discontent, 1945–50*. Oxford: University of Mississippi Press, 2013.

Brown, Stephen J. *The World of Imagery: Metaphor and Kindred Imagery*. London: Kegan Paul, Trench, Trubner, 1927.

Brown, Sterling A., Arthur P. Davis, and Ulysses Lee, eds. *Negro Caravan: Writings by American Negroes*. New York: Citadel Press, 1941.

Brown, Stuart C. "I. A. Richards' New Rhetoric: Multiplicity, Instrument, and Metaphor." *Rhetoric Review* 10, no. 2 (Spring 1992): 218–31.

Bruchac, Joseph W. "Four Directions: Some Thoughts on Teaching Native American Literature." *Studies in American Indian Literatures* 3, no. 2 (Summer 1991): 2–7.

Buell, Lawrence. "Commentary." In *Locating American Studies: Evolution of a Discipline*, edited by Lucy Maddox, 13–16. Baltimore: Johns Hopkins University Press, 1999.

Burnett, L. D. "On Lamentations for a Lost Canon." *Chronicle of Higher Education*, May 10, 2016.

Burrows, John. *University Adult Education in London: A Century of Achievement*. London: University of London/National Institute of Adult Education, 1976.

Bush, Ronald. "'Intensity by Association': T. S. Eliot's Passionate Allusions." *Modernism/Modernity* 20, no. 4 (November 2013): 709–27.

Butcher, Margaret Just, and Alaine Leroy Locke. *The Negro in American Culture*. 1956. Reprint, Champaign: University of Illinois Press, 1972.

Butterfield, Stephen. *Black Autobiography in America.* Amherst: University of Massachusetts Press, 1974.

Buurma, Rachel, and Laura Heffernan. "Elite Colleges Have No Monopoly on the Liberal Arts." *Chronicle of Higher Education,* July 15, 2018.

Buurma, Rachel Sagner, and Laura Heffernan. "Search and Replace: Josephine Miles and the Origins of Distant Reading." *Modernism/Modernity,* Print Plus, 3, no. 1 (2018).

Campbell, O. J. "Introductory Course in Literature." *English Journal* 17, no. 9 (1928): 740–48.

Carby, Hazel V. "The Multicultural Wars." *Radical History Review* 54 (1992): 7–18.

Cecire, Natalia. *Experimental: American Literature and the Aesthetics of Knowledge.* Baltimore: Johns Hopkins University Press, 2019.

Chambers, R. W., and A. S. G. Edwards. "Ker, William Paton (1855–1923), Literary Scholar." In *Oxford Dictionary of National Biography.* Oxford: Oxford University Press, 2004.

Chapin, Elsa, and Russell Thomas. *A New Approach to Poetry.* Chicago: University of Chicago Press, 1929.

Chase, Stuart. *The Tyranny of Words.* New York: Harcourt, Brace, 1938.

Childress, Herb. *The Adjunct Underclass: How America's Colleges Betrayed Their Faculty, Their Students, and Their Mission.* Chicago: University of Chicago Press, 2019.

Childs, Donald J. *The Birth of the New Criticism: Conflict and Conciliation in the Early Works of William Empson, I. A. Richards, Robert Graves, and Laura Riding.* Montreal: McGill-Queens Press, 2013.

Christ, Martha F. "Letter to the Editor." *Saturday Review of Literature,* July 30, 1927.

Clark, William. *Academic Charisma and the Origins of the Research University.* Chicago: University of Chicago Press, 2008.

Clune, Michael W. "The Humanities' Fear of Judgment." *Chronicle of Higher Education,* August 26, 2019.

Clune, Michael W. "Judgment and Equality." *Critical Inquiry* 45, no. 4 (Summer 2019): 910–34.

Collini, Stefan. "A Lot to Be Said." Review of *Literary Criticism: A Concise Political History,* by Joseph North. *London Review of Books,* November 2, 2017.

Collini, Stefan. *Common Reading: Critics, Historians, Publics.* Oxford: Oxford University Press, 2009.

Collini, Stefan. "'Non-Fiction Prose' to 'Cultural Criticism': Genre and Disciplinarity in Victorian Studies." In *Rethinking Victorian Culture,* edited by Juliet John and Alice Jenkins. Houndmills, UK: Palgrave Macmillan, 1999.

Collini, Stefan. "On Highest Authority: The Literary Critic and Other Aviators in Early Twentieth-Century Britain." In *Modernist Impulses in the Human Sciences, 1870–1930,* edited by Dorothy Ross, 152–70. Baltimore: Johns Hopkins University Press, 1994.

Collins, John Churton. *The Study of English Literature: A Plea for Its Recognition and Reorganization at Universities.* London: Macmillan, 1891.

Connors, Robert. *Composition-Rhetoric: Backgrounds, Theory, and Pedagogy.* Pittsburgh: University of Pittsburgh Press, 1997.

Constable, John. "Editorial Introduction." In *I. A. Richards, Selected Works, 1919–1938.* Vol. 4, *Practical Criticism.* London: Routledge, 2011.

Cook-Lynn, Elizabeth. "Who Stole Native American Studies?" *Wičazo Ša Review* 12, no. 1 (1997): 9–28.

Cooper, Mark Garrett, and John Marx. *Media U: How the Need to Win Audiences Has Shaped Higher Education*. New York: Columbia University Press, 2018.

Cornell University Announcements, College of Arts and Sciences 58 (1967).

Cornell University Announcements, College of Arts and Sciences 59 (1968).

Cornell University Announcements, College of Arts and Sciences 62 (1970).

Cornell University Announcements, College of Arts and Sciences 63 (1971).

Corson, Hiram. *The Aims of Literary Study*. New York: Macmillan, 1894.

Cottom, Tressie McMillan. *Lower Ed: The Troubling Rise of For-Profit Colleges in the New Economy*. New York: New Press, 2017.

Council on Interracial Books for Children, ed. *Chronicles of American Indian Protest*. New York: Fawcett, 1971.

Court, Franklin E. *Institutionalizing English Literature: The Culture and Politics of Literary Study, 1759–1900*. Stanford, CA: Stanford University Press, 1992.

Court, Franklin E. "The Social and Historical Significance of the First English Literature Professorship in England." *Proceedings of the Modern Language Association* 103, no. 5 (October 1988): 796–807.

Crawford, Robert. *Devolving English Literature*. Edinburgh: Edinburgh University Press, 1992.

Crowley, Sharon. *Composition and the University: Historical and Polemical Essays*. Pittsburgh: University of Pittsburgh Press, 1998.

Daiches, David. *The Novel and the Modern World*. Chicago: University of Chicago Press, 1939.

Dale, Leigh. *The Enchantment of English: Professing English Literatures in Australian Universities*. Sydney: Sydney University Press, 2012.

Dale, Leigh, and Jennifer McDonell. "Lessons from the Past?" *Modern Language Quarterly* Special Issue 75, no. 2 (June 1, 2014): 119–27.

d'Arms, John H., Alvin B. Kernan, William G. Bowen, and Harold T. Shapiro. "Funding Trends in the Academic Humanities, 1970–1995: Reflections on the Stability of the System." In *What's Happened to the Humanities?*, edited by Alvin Kernan, 32–60. Princeton, NJ: Princeton University Press, 1997.

Davies, Alice. *Syllabus of a Course of Tutorial Classes Some Writers of the XIXth Century and After*. London: University of London Press, 1913. EM 6/6/3, Senate House Library, University of London.

Davis, Arthur P. "Columbia College and Renaissance Harlem: An Autobiographical Essay." *Obsidian* 4, no. 3 (1978): 90–113.

Davis, Arthur P., and J. Saunders Redding, eds. *Cavalcade: African American Writing from 1790 to the Present*. Boston: Houghton Mifflin, 1971.

Deloria, Vine, Jr. *We Talk, You Listen*. New York: Macmillan, 1970.

Dick, Anne Bayard. "Dusty Answer." *Sewanee Review* 44, no. 2 (1936): 249–52.

Dinshaw, Carolyn. *How Soon Is Now?: Medieval Texts, Amateur Readers, and the Queerness of Time*. Durham, NC: Duke University Press, 2012.

Donnelly, Francis. "Words and Their Use." Review of *New Methods for the Study of Literature*, by Edith Rickert. *Saturday Review of Literature*, March 12, 1927.

Dor, Juliette. "Caroline Spurgeon (1869–1942) and the Institutionalization of English Studies as a Scholarly Discipline." *PhiN-Beiheft* 4 (2009): 55–66.

Douglas, Wallace W. "Some Questions about the Teaching of Works of Literary Art." *ADE Bulletin* 25 (May 1970): 31–44.

Du Bois, W. E. B. *Dusk of Dawn: An Essay toward an Autobiography of a Race Concept*. New Brunswick, NJ: Transaction Publishers, 1984.

Duncan, Dennis. "'The Gladdest Surprise': Nancy Bailey's Indexing Office." In *Index, A History of The*. London: Oxford University Press, forthcoming.

During, Simon. "Studying Literature Today." *Golias Research* (blog), October 2017. https://www.academia.edu/30274913/Studying_literature_today_2016_.

Eagleton, Terry. "The Rise of English Studies." In *Literary Theory: An Introduction*. Minneapolis: University of Minnesota Press, 1983.

Eddy, Matthew Daniel. "The Interactive Notebook: How Students Learned to Keep Notes during the Scottish Enlightenment." *Book History* 19, no. 1 (2016): 86–131.

Eagleton, Terry. "The Rise of English." In *Literary Theory: An Introduction*, 2 ed. Minneapolis: University of Minnesota Press, 1996.

Eliot, T. S. *The Complete Prose of T. S. Eliot*. Vol. 1, *Apprentice Years, 1905–1918*, edited by Jewel Spears Brooker and Ronald Schuchard. Baltimore: Johns Hopkins University Press, 2014.

Eliot, T. S. *The Complete Prose of T. S. Eliot*. Vol. 4, *English Lion, 1930–1933*, edited by Jason Harding and Ronald Schuchard. Baltimore: Johns Hopkins University Press, 2015.

Eliot, T. S. "The Function of Criticism." In *Selected Essays, 1917–1932*, 12–24. London: Faber and Faber, 1932.

Eliot, T. S. *The Letters of T. S. Eliot*. Vol. 1, *1898–1922*, edited by Valerie Eliot and Hugh Haughton. New Haven, CT: Yale University Press, 2011.

Eliot, T. S. *The Sacred Wood: Essays on Poetry and Criticism*. New York: Alfred A. Knopf, 1921.

Eliot, T. S. *Syllabus for a Course of Tutorial Classes on Modern English Literature*. London: University of London Press, 1916. EM 6/6/5, Senate House Library, University of London.

Eliot, T. S. *Syllabus for a Course of Tutorial Classes on Modern English Literature (Second Year's Work)*. London: University of London Press, 1917. EM 6/6/5, Senate House Library, University of London.

Eliot, T. S. *Syllabus for a Course of Tutorial Classes on Modern English Literature (Third Year's Work)*. London: University of London Press, 1918. EM 6/6/5, Senate House Library, University of London.

Emre, Merve. *Paraliterary: The Making of Bad Readers in Postwar America*. Chicago: University of Chicago Press, 2017.

"English Teachers Are Testing Poems." *Y News* 7, no. 38. February 17, 1928.

Epstein, M. *Syllabus for a Course of Tutorial Classes on Descriptive Economics (Modern Society in Its Economic Aspect)*. London: University of London Press, 1912. EM 6/6/2, Senate House Library, University of London.

Epstein, M. *Syllabus for a Course of Tutorial Classes on Descriptive Economics (Modern Society in Its Economic Aspect)*. London: University of London Press, 1915. EM 6/6/5A, Senate House Library, University of London.

Epstein, M. *Syllabus for a Course of Twenty Lectures (Modern Society in Its Economic Aspect)*. London: University of London Press, 1914. EM 6/6/4, Senate House Library, University of London.

Farley, R. P. *Syllabus of a Course of Tutorial Classes on Poverty: Suggested Causes and Remedies (First Year's Work in Sociology)*. London: University of London Press, 1917. EM 6/6/1, Senate House Library, University of London.

Fekete, John. *The Critical Twilight: Explorations in the Ideology of Anglo-American Literary Theory from Eliot to McLuhan*. London: Routledge and Kegan Paul, 1977.

Felski, Rita. *The Limits of Critique*. Chicago: University of Chicago Press, 2015.

Felski, Rita. *Uses of Literature*. Malden, MA: Wiley-Blackwell, 2011.

Fenderson, Jonathan, James Stewart, and Kabria Baumbartner. "Expanding the History of the Black Studies Movement." *Journal of African American Studies* 16, no. 1 (March 2012): 1–20.

Ferguson, Roderick. *We Demand: The University and Student Protests*. Berkeley: University of California Press, 2017.

Fieldhouse, Roger. "Conformity and Contradiction in English Responsible Body Adult Education, 1925–1950." *Studies in Education of Adults* 17 (October 1985): 121–34.

Fisher, Laura R. *Reading for Reform: The Social Work of Literature in the Progressive Era*. Minneapolis: University of Minnesota Press, 2019.

Forster, John. *The Life of Charles Dickens*. Vol. 1. London: Chapman and Hall, 1872.

Foster, Charles H. Review of *Patriotic Gore: Studies in the Literature of the American Civil War*, by Edmund Wilson. *New England Quarterly* 35, no. 4 (December 1962): 524–27.

Freeman, Arnold. *Syllabus of a Tutorial Class on the Economic Problems of Demobilisation*. London: University of London Press, 1916. EM 6/6/5B, Senate House Library, University of London.

Fry, Paul H. "I. A. Richards." In *The Cambridge History of Literary Criticism*. Vol. 7, *Modernism and the New Criticism*, edited by A. Walton Litz, Louis Menand, and Lawrence Rainey, 179–99. Cambridge: Cambridge University Press, 2000.

Furnivall, Frederick James. *Frederick James Furnivall: A Volume of Personal Record*. London: Oxford University Press, 1911.

Gallop, Jane. "The Historicization of Literary Studies and the Fate of Close Reading." *Profession*, 2007, 181–86.

Gang, Joshua. "Behaviorism and the Beginnings of Close Reading." *ELH* 78, no. 1 (2011): 1–25.

Garber, Marjorie. *The Muses on Their Lunch Hour*. New York: Fordham University Press, 2016.

Gates, Henry Louis, Jr. "'. . . and Bid Him Sing': J. Saunders Redding and the Criticism of American Negro Literature." In *To Make a Poet Black*. Ithaca, NY: Cornell University Press, 1988.

Gayle, Addison. "The Critic, the University, and the Negro Writer." In *The Addison Gayle Jr. Reader*. Edited by Nathaniel Norment Jr. Urbana: University of Illinois Press, 2009.

Geiger, H. Jack. Review of *All God's Dangers*, by Theodore Rosengarten. *New York Times Book Review*, October 20, 1974.

Geiger, Roger L. *To Advance Knowledge: The Growth of the American Research Universities, 1900–1940*. New York: Oxford University Press, 1986.

Gerber, John C. "Women in English Departments before 1930—and after: A Note." *Women's Studies Newsletter* 4, no. 2 (1976): 9.

Gere, Anne Ruggles. "Kitchen Tables and Rented Rooms: The Extracurriculum of Composition." *College Composition and Communication* 45, no. 1 (1994): 75–92.

Gilbert, Sandra, and Susan Gubar. *No Man's Land: The Place of the Woman Writer in the Twentieth Century*. Vol. 1, *The War of the Words*. New Haven, CT: Yale University Press, 1998.

Gilkeson, John S. *Anthropologists and the Rediscovery of America, 1886–1965*. Cambridge: Cambridge University Press, 2010.

Girard, Melissa. "J. Saunders Redding and the 'Surrender' of African American Women's Poetry." *PMLA* 132, no. 2 (March 2017): 281–97.

Glazener, Nancy. *Literature in the Making: A History of U.S. Literary Culture in the Long Nineteenth Century*. Oxford: Oxford University Press, 2015.

Glazer-Raymo, Judith. "Academia's Equality Myth." In *Shattering the Myths: Women in Academe*. Baltimore: Johns Hopkins University Press, 1999.

Goldman, Lawrence. *Dons and Workers: Oxford and Adult Education since 1850*. Oxford: Clarendon Press, 1995.

Goldman, Lawrence. "The First Students in the Workers' Educational Association: Individual Enlightenment and Collective Advance." In *A Ministry of Enthusiasm: Centenary Essays on the Workers' Educational Association*, edited by Stephen K. Roberts. London: Pluto Press, 2003.

Goldring, Douglas. "Modern Critical Prose." *Chapbook* 2, no. 8 (February 1920): 7–14.

Goldstein, Dana. *The Teacher Wars: A History of America's Most Embattled Profession*. New York: Doubleday, 2014.

Goodblatt, Chanita, and Joseph Glicksohn. "Conversations with I. A. Richards: The Renaissance in Cognitive Literary Studies." *Poetics Today* 31, no. 3 (2010): 387–432.

Goodblatt, Chanita, and Joseph Glicksohn. "From Practical Criticism to the Practice of Literary Criticism." *Poetics Today* 24, no. 3 (2003): 207–36.

Gorak, Jan. "From Prodigality to Economy: T. S. Eliot on the 'Minor Elizabethans.'" *Modern Language Review* 108, no. 4 (2013): 1064–85.

Graff, Gerald. *Literature Against Itself: Literary Ideas in Modern Society*. Chicago: University of Chicago Press, 1979.

Graff, Gerald. *Professing Literature: An Institutional History*. Chicago: University of Chicago Press, 1987.

Graff, Gerald, and Michael Warner, eds. "Part III: Memoirs and Personal Accounts." In *The Origins of Literary Studies in America: A Documentary Anthology*. New York: Routledge, 1989.

Great Britain. Parliament. House of Commons. *Sessional Papers*. Vol. 40. London: H. M. Stationery Office, 1915.

Greenlaw, Edwin. "Recent Movements for Co-Operative Research in the Humanities." *Journal of the Proceedings and Addresses of the Association of American Universities, Twenty-Sixth Annual Conference*. November 31, 1924, 93–96.

Griffin, Gabriele, and Matt Steven Hayler. "Collaboration in Digital Humanities Research—Persisting Silences." *Digital Humanities Quarterly*, Social Foundations of Aesthetic Forms Series, 12, no. 1 (2018). http://www.digitalhumanities.org/dhq/vol/12/1/000351/000351.html.

Guillory, John. *Cultural Capital: The Problem of Literary Canon Formation*. Chicago: University of Chicago Press, 1993.

Guillory, John. "The Ideology of Canon Formation: T. S. Eliot and Cleanth Brooks." *Critical Inquiry* 10, no. 1 (September 1983): 173–98.

Guillory, John. "Literary Study and the Modern System of the Disciplines." In *Disciplinarity at the Fin de Siècle*, edited by Amanda Anderson and Joseph Valente. Princeton, NJ: Princeton University Press, 2002.

Haas, Renate. "Caroline F. E. Spurgeon (1869–1942): First Woman Professor of English in England." In *Women Medievalists and the Academy*, edited by Jane Chance, 99–109. Madison: University of Wisconsin Press, 2005.

Hammond, Karla M. "An Interview with Josephine Miles." *Southern Review* 19, no. 3 (July 1983): 606–31.

Hampton Bulletin. Hampton, VA: Hampton Institute, 1941.

Hannon, Rachel M. "Imagery and the Adding-Machine." *College English* 6, no. 1 (October 1, 1944): 6–13.

Harney, Stefano, and Fred Moten. *The Undercommons: Fugitive Planning and Black Study*. New York: Autonomedia, 2013.

Harris, Joseph. *A Teaching Subject: Composition since 1966*. Upper Saddle River, NJ: Prentice Hall, 1996.

Hayakawa, S. I. *Language in Action: A Guide to Accurate Thinking, Reading, and Writing*. New York: Harcourt, Brace and World, 1939.

Helton, Laura E. "On Decimals, Catalogs, and Racial Imaginaries of Reading." *PMLA* 134, no. 1 (January 1, 2019): 99–120.

Henderson, B. L. K. *Syllabus for a Tutorial Class in Aspects of Victorian Literature (First Year)* [1919–21]. London: University of London Press, n.d. EM 6/6/6, Senate House Library, University of London.

Henry, Jules. *Culture Against Man*. New York: Random House, 1963.

Hilliard, Christopher. *English as a Vocation: The 'Scrutiny' Movement*. Oxford: Oxford University Press, 2012.

Hilliard, Christopher. "Leavis, Richards, and the Duplicators." In *The Critic as Amateur*, edited by Aarthi Vadde and Saikat Majumdar. New York: Bloomsbury Academic, 2019.

Hines, Andy. "Vehicles of Periodization: Melvin B. Tolson, Allen Tate, and the New Critical Police." *Criticism* 59, no. 3 (Summer 2017): 417–39.

Hobson, Geary, ed. "Remembering the Earth." In *The Remembered Earth: An Anthology of Contemporary Native American Literature*. Albuquerque: University of New Mexico Press, 1981.

Hunt, Lynn, Alvin B. Kernan, William G. Bowen, and Harold T. Shapiro. "Democratization and Decline?: The Consequences of Demographic Change in the Humanities." In *What's Happened to the Humanities?*, edited by Alvin Kernan, 17–31. Princeton, NJ: Princeton University Press, 1997.

Hutner, Gordon, and Feisal G. Mohamed, eds. *A New Deal for the Humanities: Liberal Arts and the Future of Public Higher Education*. New Brunswick, NJ: Rutgers University Press, 2016.

Hyman, Stanley Edgar. *The Armed Vision: A Study in the Method of Modern Literary Criticism*. Rev. ed. New York: Vintage Books, 1955.

Hyman, Stanley Edgar. "The Critical Achievement of Caroline Spurgeon." *Kenyon Review* 10, no. 1 (January 1, 1948): 92–108.

Indian Voices: The First Convocation of American Indian Scholars. San Francisco: Indian Historian Press, 1970.

International Studies Association. "How to Count What Counts: TIS the Season for Syllabi Metrics?" https://www.isanet.org/Publications/ISQ/Posts/ID/5108/How-to-Count-What-Counts-TIS-the-Season-for-Syllabi-Metrics.

Jack, A. A. "Lecturers' Report for the Life of the Nineteenth Century as Represented in Literature." University of London Joint Committee for the Promotion of the Higher Education of Working People Lecturers' and Examiners' Reports, Session 1914–15, Summer 1914. EM 2/23/74, Senate House Library, University of London.

Jackson, Lawrence P. *The Indignant Generation: A Narrative History of African-American Writers and Critics.* Princeton, NJ: Princeton University Press, 2010.

Jancovich, Mark. *The Cultural Politics of New Criticism.* Cambridge: Cambridge University Press, 1994.

Jones, Llewellyn. "A Detective School of Criticism." *Chicago Illinois Post,* February 25, 1927.

Joyce, Joyce A. "The Black Canon: Reconstructing Black American Literary Criticism." *New Literary History* 18, no. 2 (1987): 335–44.

Joyce, Joyce Ann, J. Saunders Redding, and Arthur P. Davis, eds. *The New Cavalcade: African American Writing from 1790 to the Present.* Washington, DC: Howard University Press, 1991.

Kahn, David. *The Codebreakers: The Comprehensive History of Secret Communication from Ancient Times to the Internet.* New York: Macmillan, 1967.

Kaiser, Jo Ellen Green. "Disciplining the Waste Land, or How to Lead Critics into Temptation." *Twentieth Century Literature* 44, no. 1 (Spring 1998): 82–99.

Kaplan, Justin. *Mr. Clemens and Mark Twain: A Biography.* New York: Simon and Schuster, 1991.

Katz, William Loren, ed. *The American Negro: His History and Literature (1968–71).* New York: Arno Press and the New York Times, 1968.

Kavanagh, Gaynor. *Museums and the First World War: A Social History.* London: Leicester University Press, 1994.

Kernan, Alvin. "Introduction: Change in the Humanities in Higher Education." In *What's Happened to the Humanities?,* edited by Alvin Kernan, 3–14. Princeton, NJ: Princeton University Press, 1997.

Kinnamon, Keneth. "Anthologies of African-American Literature from 1845–1994." *Callaloo* 20, no. 2 (Spring 1997): 461–81.

Klein, Lauren F. "Feminist Data Visualization; Or, the Shape of History." *Lauren F. Klein Digital Humanities, Data Studies, and Early American Literature* (blog), January 24, 2017. http://lklein.com/conference-papers/feminist-data-visualization-or-the-shape-of-history/.

Klein, Lauren. "Dimensions of Scale: Invisible Labor, Editorial Work, and the Future of Quantitative Literary Studies." *PMLA* 135, no. 1 (January 2020): 23–29.

Knights, Ben. *Pedagogic Criticism: Reconfiguring University English Studies.* Basingstoke, UK: Palgrave Macmillan, 2017.

Koch, Vivienne. "Continuity of Poetic Language." *Poetry* 79, no. 6 (March 1952): 360–67.

Konkiel, Stacey. "What Do Syllabi-Based Altmetrics Actually Mean?" *Altmetric Blog,* September 27, 2016. https://www.altmetric.com/blog/syllabi-altmetrics-meaning/.

Kramnick, Jonathan, and Anahid Nersessian. "Form and Explanation." *Critical Inquiry* 43, no. 3 (Spring 2017): 650–69.

Krieger, Murray. *The New Apologists for Poetry.* Minneapolis: University of Minnesota Press, 1956.

Kroeber, Theodora. *The Inland Whale: Nine Stories Retold from California Indian Legends.* Berkeley: University of California Press, 1963.

Kucich, John. "The Unfinished Historicist Project." *Victoriographes* 1, no. 1 (September 2011): 58–78.

Labaree, David F. "Public Goods, Private Goods: The American Struggle Over Educational Goals." *American Educational Research Journal* 34, no. 1 (January 1, 1997): 39–81.

Lackey, Michael. "Redeeming the Post-Metaphysical Promise of J. Saunders Redding's 'America.'" *New Centennial Review* 12, no. 3 (2012): 217–43.

Lame Deer, John (Fire), and Richard Erdoes. *Lame Deer: Seeker of Visions: The Life of a Sioux Medicine Man.* New York: Simon and Schuster, 1972.

Lamos, Colleen. *Deviant Modernism: Sexual and Textual Errancy in T. S. Eliot, James Joyce, and Marcel Proust.* Cambridge: Cambridge University Press, 1998.

Lautner, Paul. "The Making of the Heath Anthology." *Editors' Notes: Bulletin of the Conference of Editors of Learned Journals* 11, no. 1 (Spring 1992): 34–39.

Lawrie, Alexandra. *The Beginnings of University English: Extramural Study, 1885–1910.* Houndmills, UK: Palgrave Macmillan, 2014.

Lee, Maurice S. *Overwhelmed: Literature, Aesthetics, and the Nineteenth-Century Information Revolution.* Princeton, NJ: Princeton University Press, 2019.

Lennon, Brian. *Passwords: Philology, Security, Authentication.* Cambridge, MA: Harvard University Press, 2018.

Lentricchia, Frank. *After the New Criticism.* Chicago: University of Chicago Press, 1980.

Levenson, Marjorie. "What Is New Formalism." *PMLA* 122, no. 2 (2007): 558–69.

Levine, Caroline. *Forms: Whole, Rhythm, Hierarchy, Network.* Princeton, NJ: Princeton University Press, 2017.

"Literature and Professors: A Symposium." *Southern Review* 6, no. 2 (1940): 225–69.

"Literature and Professors: A Symposium." *Kenyon Review* 2, no. 3 (1940): 403–42.

Lofton, William H. Review of *They Came in Chains,* by Milton Meltzer. *Journal of Negro History* 35, no. 4 (1950): 459–61.

Lovell, John. "The Things So Strange and Marvellous." *Journal of Negro Education* 12, no. 2 (1943): 217–20.

Lowenfels, Walter, ed. *From the Belly of the Shark: A New Anthology of Native Americans.* New York: Vintage Books, 1973.

Lynch, Deidre Shauna. *Loving Literature: A Cultural History.* Chicago: University of Chicago Press, 2015.

Lynd, Robert. "Buried Alive." *Nation* 4 (December 4, 1920): 359–60.

Lyons, Scott Richard. "The Fine Art of Fencing: Nationalism, Hybridity, and the Search for a Native American Writing Pedagogy." *JAC* 29, nos. 1/2 (2009): 77–105.

Macrae, Elizabeth. *Syllabus of a Tutorial Class in Historical Literature by Miss Elizabeth Macrae. First Year. The Literature and Historical Sources from Which Our Knowledge of the Classical and Medieval Periods of History Are Derived.* London:

University of London Press, 1919. EM 6/6/5c, Senate House Library, University of London.

Maisel, Edward. *An Anatomy of Literature*. New York: Standard and Hall, 1938.

Manly, John. "Introductory Note." In *New Methods for the Study of Literature*, by Edith Rickert. Chicago: University of Chicago Press, 1928.

Manly, John. "The President's Address: New Bottles." *PMLA* 35 (1920): xlvi–lx.

Manly, John, and Edith Rickert. *Contemporary British Literature: Outlines for Study, Indexes, Bibliographies*. New York: Harcourt, Brace, 1921.

Manly, John, and Edith Rickert. *The Text of the Canterbury Tales: Studied on the Basis of All Known Manuscripts*. Chicago: University of Chicago Press, 1940.

Manly, John, and Edith Rickert. *The Writing of English*. New York: Henry Holt and Company, 1919.

Mannix, Daniel, and Malcolm Cowley. *Black Cargoes: A History of the Atlantic Slave Trade, 1518–1865*. New York: Viking Press, 1962.

Mansbridge, Albert. *University Tutorial Classes: A Study in the Development of Higher Education among Working Men and Women*. London: Longmans, Green, 1913.

Marion, George. *Stop the Press!* New York: Fairplay Publishers, 1953.

Martin, Wallace. "The Critic and the Institutions of Culture." In *The Cambridge History of Literary Criticism*. Vol. 7, *Modernism and the New Criticism*, edited by A. Walton Litz, Louis Menand, and Lawrence Rainey. Cambridge: Cambridge University Press, 2000.

Martin, Wallace. "Criticism and the Academy." In *The Cambridge History of Literary Criticism*. Vol. 7, *Modernism and the New Criticism*, edited by A. Walton Litz, Louis Menand, and Lawrence Rainey. Cambridge: Cambridge University Press, 2000.

Mathieson, Margaret. *Teaching Practical Criticism: An Introduction*. London: Routledge, Kegan, and Paul, 1985.

Matthews, Steven. *T. S. Eliot and Early Modern Literature*. Oxford: Oxford University Press, 2013.

Maxwell, William J. *Eyewitness: The Negro in American History: A Living Documentary of the Afro-American Contribution to U.S. History*. New York: Pitman Publishing, 1974.

Maxwell, William J. *F.B. Eyes Digital Archive: FBI Files on African American Authors and Literary Institutions Obtained through the US. Freedom of Information Act (FOIA)*. Digital Archive. http://digital.wustl.edu/fbeyes/.

McDonald, Gail. *Learning to Be Modern: Pound, Eliot, and the American University*. Oxford: Clarendon Press, 1993.

McDowell, Nicholas. "Early Modern Stereotypes and the Rise of English: Jonson, Dryden, Arnold, Eliot." *Critical Quarterly* 48, no. 3 (Autumn 2006): 25–34.

Michaels, Walter Benn. *The Shape of the Signifier: 1967 to the End of History*. Princeton, NJ: Princeton University Press, 2006.

Micir, Melanie, and Aarthi Vadde. "Obliterature: Toward an Amateur Criticism." *Modernism/Modernity* 25, no. 3 (September 2018): 517–49.

Miles, Josephine. *The Continuity of Poetic Language: Studies in English Poetry from the 1540s to the 1940s*. Berkeley: University of California Press, 1951.

Miles, Josephine. *Eras and Modes in English Poetry*. Berkeley: University of California Press, 1957.

Miles, Josephine. *Major Adjectives in English Poetry: From Wyatt to Auden*. Berkeley: University of California Press, 1946.

Miles, Josephine. "The Pathetic Fallacy and the Thing in Itself." *Poetry* 63, no. 4 (January 1944): 210–18.

Miles, Josephine. *Pathetic Fallacy in the Nineteenth Century: A Study of a Changing Relation Between Object and Emotion*. Berkeley: University of California Press, 1942.

Miles, Josephine. *Poetry, Teaching, and Scholarship: Oral History Transcript and Related Material, 1977–1980*. Berkeley: University of California Press, 1980.

Miles, Josephine. "Preface to the Octagon Edition." In *The Continuity of Poetic Language: Studies in English Poetry from the 1540s to the 1940s*. New York: Octagon Books, 1965.

Miles, Josephine. *The Primary Language of Poetry in the 1540's and 1640's*. Berkeley: University of California Press, 1948.

Miles, Josephine. Review of *Concordance to the Poems of Matthew Arnold*, by Stephen M. Parrish. *Victorian Studies* 8, no. 3 (March 1965): 290–92.

Miles, Josephine. *Style and Proportion: The Language of Prose and Poetry*. Boston: Little Brown, 1967.

Miles, Josephine. "Values in Language: Or, Where Have *Goodness, Truth*, and *Beauty* Gone?" *Critical Inquiry* 3, no. 1 (Autumn 1976): 1–13.

Miles, Josephine. "What We Compose." *College Composition and Communication* 14, no. 3 (1963): 146–54.

Miles, Josephine. *Wordsworth and the Vocabulary of Emotion*. Berkeley: University of California Press, 1942.

Miles, Josephine. *Working Out Ideas: Predication and Other Uses of Language, Curriculum Publications*. Berkeley: Bay Area Writers Project, 1979.

Miller, Thomas P. *The Formation of College English: Rhetoric and Belles Lettres in the British Cultural Provinces*. Pittsburgh: University of Pittsburgh Press, 1997.

Milton, John R., ed. *The American Indian Speaks: Poetry, Fiction, Art, Music, Religion*. San Leandro, CA: Dakota Press, 1969.

Momaday, N. Scott. *The Way to Rainy Mountain*. Albuquerque: University of New Mexico Press, 1969.

Mondale, Clarence. "Spring Disturbance." *George Washington University News* 13, no. 2 (Summer 1969).

Moore, Marianne. "Poetry." In *Observations*, edited by Linda Leavell. New York: Farrar, Straus and Giroux, 2016.

Moore, Marianne. Review of *The Sacred Wood*, by T. S. Eliot. *The Dial*, March 1921.

Morgan, Edmund S. *American Slavery, American Freedom*. New York: Norton, 1975.

Moten, Fred, and Stefano Harney. "The University and the Undercommons: Seven Theses." *Social Text* 22, no. 79 (Summer 2004): 101–15.

Mullen, Mary. *Novel Institutions: Anachronism, Irish Novels, and Nineteenth-Century Realism*. Edinburgh: Edinburgh University Press, 2019.

Murry, John Middleton. *Countries of the Mind: Essays in Literary Criticism*. London: W. Collins Sons, 1924.

Murry, John Middleton. Review of *The Sacred Wood*, by T. S. Eliot. *New Republic*, April 13, 1921.

Nash, John. "T. S. Eliot's Views on James Joyce: The Harvard Teaching Notes." *James Joyce Quarterly* 56, no. 1 (2019): 115–31.

Neihardt, John G. *Black Elk Speaks: Being the Life Story of a Holy Man of the Oglala Sioux*. Lincoln: University of Nebraska Press, 2000.

Newfield, Christopher. *The Great Mistake: How We Wrecked Public Universities and How We Can Fix Them*. Baltimore: Johns Hopkins University Press, 2016.

Newman, John Henry. *Discourses on the Scope and Nature of University Education, Addressed to the Catholics of Dublin*. Dublin: James Duffy, 1852.

Newman, John Henry. *Discourses on the Scope and Nature of University Education*. 2nd ed. London: Longman, Green, Longman, and Roberts, 1959.

New Statesman. Review of *The Sacred Wood*, by T. S. Eliot. March 26, 1921.

Ngai, Sianne. "Merely Interesting." *Critical Inquiry* 34, no. 4 (Summer 2008): 786–87.

Nichols, Charles. *Many Thousand Gone: The Ex-Slaves' Account of Their Bondage and Freedom*. Leiden: E. J. Brill, 1963.

North, Joseph. *Literary Criticism: A Concise Political History*. Cambridge, MA: Harvard University Press, 2017.

Oakley, Francis. "Ignorant Armies and Nighttime Clashes: Changes in the Humanities Classroom, 1970–1995." In *What's Happened to the Humanities?*, edited by Alvin Kernan. Princeton, NJ: Princeton University Press, 1997.

Ogden, C. K., and I. A. Richards. *The Meaning of Meaning: A Study of the Influence of Language upon Thought and of the Science of Symbolism*. New York: Harcourt Brace, 1923.

Ortiz, Simon J. *A Good Journey*. Berkeley: Turtle Island Foundation, Netzahaulcoyotl Historical Society, 1977.

Ortiz, Simon J. "Many Farms Notes." In *Going for the Rain*. New York: Harper and Row, 1976.

Ortiz, Simon J. "Towards a National Indian Literature: Cultural Authenticity in Nationalism." *MELUS* 8, no. 2 (1981): 7–12.

Ortiz, Simon J. *Woven Stone*. Tucson: University of Arizona Press, 1992.

Osofsky, Gilbert. *Puttin' on Ole Massa*. New York: Harper and Row, 1969.

Palmer, D. J. *An Account of the Study of the English Language and Literature from Its Origins to the Making of the Oxford English School*. London: Oxford University Press, 1965.

Palmer, Mabel. *Syllabus for Problems of Social Economics Arising from the War*. London: University of London Press, 1916. EM 6/6/5B, Senate House Library, University of London.

Palumbo-Liu, David. *The Ethnic Canon: Histories, Institutions, and Interventions*. Minneapolis: University of Minnesota Press, 1995.

Parker, Robert Dale. *The Invention of Native American Literature*. Ithaca, NY: Cornell University Press, 2002.

Parker, William Riley. "Where Do English Departments Come From?" *College English* 28, no. 5 (February 1962): 339–51.

Parry, R. St. John, ed. "Introduction." In *Cambridge Essays on Adult Education*. Cambridge: Cambridge University Press, 2014.

Pasanek, Brad. "Extreme Reading: Josephine Miles and the Scale of the Pre-Digital Digital Humanities." *ELH* 86 (2019): 355–86.

Perry, Bliss. "The Life of a College Professor." *Scribner's Magazine* 22 (1897).

Phylon. Unsigned review of *No Day of Triumph*, by J. Saunders Redding. Vol. 4, no. 1 (1943): 87–89.

Piper, Andrew. *Enumerations: Data and Literary Study.* Chicago: University of Chicago Press, 2018.

Poirier, Richard. "What Is English Studies, and If You Know What That Is, What Is English Literature?" *ADE Bulletin* 25 (May 1970): 3–11.

Porter, Lavelle. *The Blackademic Life: Academic Fiction, Higher Education, and the Black Intellectual.* Evanston, IL: Northwestern University Press, 2019.

Potter, David. "The Quest for National Character." In *The Character of Americans,* edited by Michael McGiffert. Homewood, IL: Dorsey Press, 1964.

Pressman, Jessica. *Digital Modernism: Making It New in New Media.* Oxford: Oxford University Press, 2014.

Pringle, E. H. *Syllabus for Modern Economic Problems.* London: University of London Press, 1911. EM 6/6/2, Senate House Library, University of London.

Ramey, Lauri. *A History of African American Poetry.* Cambridge: Cambridge University Press, 2019.

Ransom, John Crowe. *The New Criticism.* Norfolk, VA: New Directions, 1941.

Readings, Bill. *The University in Ruins.* Cambridge, MA: Harvard University Press, 1997.

Redding, J. Saunders. "Afro-American Studies." *New York Times,* September 20, 1970.

Redding, J. Saunders. "The Black Youth Movement." *American Scholar* 38, no. 4 (1969): 584–87.

Redding, J. Saunders. *The Lonesome Road.* New York: Doubleday, 1958.

Redding, J. Saunders. "James Weldon Johnson and the Pastoral Tradition." *Mississippi Quarterly* 28, no. 4 (Fall 1975): 417–21.

Redding, J. Saunders. "The Negro Author: His Publisher, His Public and His Purse." *Publishers Weekly,* March 24, 1945.

Redding, J. Saunders. "The Negro in American History: As Scholar, as Subject." In *The Past Before Us: Contemporary Historical Writing in the United States,* edited by Michael G. Kammen. Ithaca, NY: Cornell University Press, 1980.

Redding, J. Saunders. *No Day of Triumph.* New York: Harper and Bros., 1942.

Redding, J. Saunders. *On Being Negro in America.* Indianapolis: Bobbs-Merrill, 1951.

Redding, J. Saunders. Review of *The Confessions of Nat Turner,* by William Styron. *Providence Journal,* October 20, 1967.

Redding, J. Saunders. *To Make a Poet Black.* Ithaca, NY: Cornell University Press, 1988.

Renker, Elizabeth. *The Origins of American Literature Studies: An Institutional History.* Cambridge: Cambridge University Press, 2010.

Rhody, Jason. "The Syllabus as a HuMetrics Case Study." *Medium,* October 18, 2016. https://medium.com/@jasonrhody/the-syllabus-as-humetrics-case-study -616e60fe35ad.

Rice, Julian. "A Ventriloquy of Anthros: Densmore, Dorsey, Lame Dear, and Erdoes." *American Indian Quarterly* 18, no. 2 (1994): 169–96.

Richards, I. A. *Interpretation in Teaching.* New York: Harcourt, Brace, 1938.

Richards, I. A. *Practical Criticism: A Study of Literary Judgment.* London: Kegan, Paul, Trench, and Trubner, 1929.

Richards, I. A. *Selected Letters of I. A. Richards.* Edited by John Constable and Richard Luckett. Oxford: Oxford University Press, 1990.

Richards, I. A. *Speculative Instruments.* Chicago: University of Chicago Press, 1955.

Rickert, Edith. "As 100 College Girls Write Letters." *Ladies' Home Journal* 30 (February 1913).

Rickert, Edith. *Chaucer's World.* Edited by Clair C. Olson and Marin M. Crow. New York: Columbia University Press, 1948.

Rickert, Edith. *New Methods for the Study of Literature.* Chicago: University of Chicago Press, 1928.

Rickert, Edith. "'What Has the College Done for Girls': A Personal Canvass of Hundreds of Graduates of Sixty Colleges, I: Has the College Injured the Health of Girls?" *Ladies' Home Journal* 29 (January 1912).

Rickert, Edith, and Frederick James Furnivall. *The Babees' Book: Medieval Manners for the Young.* London: Chatto and Windus, 1908.

Rinaker, Clariss. Review of *New Methods for the Study of Literature,* by Edith Rickert." *Journal of English and Germanic Philology* 27, no. 1 (January 1928): 133–35.

Robinson, Peter M. W. "Electronic Textual Editing: *The Canterbury Tales* and Other Medieval Texts." In *Electronic Textual Editing,* edited by Lou Burnard, Katherine O'Brien O'Keeffe, and John Unsworth, 128–54. New York: MLA, 2001.

Robson, Catherine. *Heart Beats: Everyday Life and the Memorized Poem.* Princeton, NJ: Princeton University Press, 2012.

Romero, Francisco. *Theory of Man.* Berkeley: University of California Press, 1964.

Rose, Jonathan. *The Intellectual Life of the British Working Classes.* New Haven, CT: Yale University Press, 2001.

Rose, Jonathan. "The Whole Contention Concerning the Workers' Educational Association." In *The Intellectual Life of the British Working Classes,* 256–97. New Haven, CT: Yale University Press, 2002.

Rosengarten, Theodore. "Preface." In *All God's Dangers: The Life of Nate Shaw.* New York: Alfred A. Knopf, 1974.

Rothenberg, Jerome, ed. *Shaking the Pumpkin: Traditional Poetry of the Indian North Americas.* New York: Doubleday, 1972.

Rovee, Chris. "Counting Wordsworth by the Bay: The Distance of Josephine Miles." *European Romantic Review* 28, no. 3 (2017): 405–12.

Rudolph, Frederick. *The American College and University: A History.* New York: Alfred A. Knopf, 1961.

Russo, John Paul. *I. A. Richards: His Life and Work.* Baltimore: Johns Hopkins University Press, 1989.

Russo, Patricia. "Native American Literature Syllabus, San Diego State University, 1978." Box 48, folder 7, Simon J. Ortiz Papers, MSS-372, Simon J. Ortiz Papers, Labriola Center, Arizona State University, n.d.

Said, Edward. "Figures, Configurations, Transfigurations." In *Subject to Change: Teaching Literature in the Nineties,* edited by Susie Tharu. Hyderabad: Orient Longman, 1998.

Said, Edward. "Opponents, Audiences, Constituencies and Community." In *The Anti-Aesthetic: Essays on Postmodern Culture,* edited by Hal Foster. New York: New Press, 1998.

Sanborn, Geoffrey. *Plagiarama!: William Wells Brown and the Aesthetic of Attractions.* New York: Columbia University Press, 2016.

Savonick, Danica B. "Insurgent Knowledge: The Poetics and Pedagogy of Toni Cade Bambara, June Jordan, Audre Lorde, and Adrienne Rich in the Era of Open Admissions" (2018). CUNY Academic Works.

Scala, Elizabeth. "'Miss Rickert of Vassar' and Edith Rickert at the University of Chicago (1871–1938)." In *Woman Medievalists and the Academy*, edited by Jane Chance. Madison: University of Wisconsin Press, 2005.

Scala, Elizabeth. "Scandalous Assumptions: Edith Rickert and the Chicago Chaucer Project." *Medieval Feminist Forum: A Journal of Gender and Sexuality* 30, no. 1 (Fall 2000): 27–37.

Schuchard, Ronald. *Eliot's Dark Angel: Intersections of Life and Art.* New York: Oxford University Press, 1999.

Schuchard, Ronald. "T. S. Eliot as Extension Lecturer, 1916–1919." *Review of English Studies* 25, no. 99 (August 1974): 292–304.

Shairp, Mordaunt. "Lecturer's Report." University of London Board to Promote the Extension of University Teaching, Walworth Road, Shakespeare and England lecture course, Michaelmas Term 1915., n.d.

Shairp, Mordaunt. "Lecturer's Report for Seminar on Shakespeare and England." Joint Committee for the Promotion of the Higher Education of Working People Lecturers' and Examiners' Reports, Session 1915–16. EM 2/23/79, Senate House Library, University of London.

Shairp, Mordaunt. *Syllabus of a Course of Ten Lectures on the Literary Inspiration of the Great War.* London: University of London Press, 1919. EM 2/21/14, Senate House Library, University of London.

Silko, Leslie Marmon. *Laguna Woman: Poems.* New York: Greenfield Review Press, 1974.

Silko, Leslie Marmon. "The Man to Send Rain Clouds." In *The Man to Send Rain Clouds: Contemporary Stories by American Indians*, edited by Kenneth Rosen. New York: Viking Press, 1974.

Silko, Leslie Marmon. "Yellow Woman." In *The Man to Send Rain Clouds: Contemporary Stories by American Indians*, edited by Kenneth Rosen. New York: Viking Press, 1974.

Silko, Leslie Marmon. "Yellow Woman and a Beauty of the Spirit." In *Yellow Woman and a Beauty of the Spirit.* New York: Simon & Schuster, 1996.

Slater, Gilbert. *Syllabus of a Course of Tutorial Classes on the Worker and the State.* London: University of London Press, 1911. EM 6/6/1, Senate House Library, University of London.

Small, Helen. *The Value of the Humanities.* Oxford: Oxford University Press, 2013.

Smith, Wilson, and Thomas Bender. *American Higher Education Transformed, 1940–2005: Documenting the National Discourse.* Baltimore: Johns Hopkins University Press, 2008.

Snell, William. "A Woman Medievalist Much Maligned: A Note in Defense of Edith Rickert (1871–1938)." *PhiN-Beiheft* 4 (2009): 41–54.

So, Richard Jean. "All Models Are Wrong." *PMLA* 132, no. 3 (May 1, 2017): 668–73.

Spurgeon, Caroline F. E. *500 Years of Chaucer Criticism and Allusion (1357–1900).* Cambridge: Cambridge University Press, 1920.

Spurgeon, Caroline F. E. *Keats's Shakespeare: A Descriptive Study Based on New Material.* London: Oxford University Press, 1928.

Spurgeon, Caroline. "Lecturer's Report for Seminar on the Age of Johnson." Joint Committee for the Promotion of the Higher Education of Working People Lecturers' and Examiners' Reports, Session 1915–16. EM 2/23/79, Senate House Library, University of London.

Spurgeon, Caroline F. E. *Shakespeare's Imagery and What It Tells Us*. Cambridge: Cambridge University Press, 1935.

Squire, J. C. Review of *New Methods for the Study of Literature*, by Edith Rickert. *London Mercury*, May 1927.

Steffens, Lincoln. *The Autobiography of Lincoln Steffens*. Vol. 1, *A Boy on Horseback/Seeing New York First*. New York: Harcourt, Brace and World, 1931.

Stevenson, Robert Louis. "On Style in Literature: Its Technical Elements." *Contemporary Review* 47 (April 1885).

Stewart, George. *English Composition: A Laboratory Course*. Vol. 2. Henry Holt, 1936.

Stock, Patricia Lambert, ed. *Composition's Roots in English Education*. Portsmouth, NH: Boynton/Cook Publishers, 2012.

Strier, Richard. "How Formalism Became a Dirty Word and Why We Can't Do Without It." In *Renaissance Literature and Its Formal Engagements*, edited by Mark David Rasmussen, 208–15. New York: Palgrave, 2002.

Styler, W. E. "T. S. Eliot as Adult Tutor." *Notes and Queries* 19, no. 2 (February 1972): 53–54.

Svaratengren, T. H. *Intensifying Similes in English*. Lund, Sweden: Gleerupska universitetsbokhandeln, 1918.

Talayesva, Don C. *Sun Chief: The Autobiography of a Hopi Indian*. Edited by Leo W. Simmons. New Haven, CT: Yale University Press, 1963.

Tate, Allen. "Poetry in the Laboratory." *New Republic*, December 18, 1929.

Tate, Allen. Review of *New Methods for the Study of Literature*, by Edith Rickert. *New Republic*, April 27, 1927.

Tayler, J. Lionel. *Syllabus for the Course of Tutorial Classes on the Condition of the People*. London: University of London Press, 1912. EM 6/6/1, Senate House Library, University of London.

Tenen, Dennis Yi. "The Emergence of American Formalism." *Modern Philology* 117, no. 2 (November 2019): 257–83.

Terras, Melissa, and Julianne Nyhan. "Father Busa's Female Punch Card Operatives." In *Debates in Digital Humanities, 2016*, edited by Matthew K. Gold and Lauren F. Klein. Minneapolis: Minnesota University Press, 2016.

Teuton, Christopher B. *Deep Waters: The Textual Continuum in American Indian Literature*. Lincoln: University of Nebraska Press, 2018.

Thaventhiran, Helen. *Radical Empiricists: Five Modernist Close Readers*. Oxford: Oxford University Press, 2015.

Thelin, John R. "Essay on Sources." In *A History of American Higher Education*. 2nd ed. Baltimore: Johns Hopkins University Press, 2011.

"The Study of Literature." *London Times*. May 26, 1927. University of Chicago Press Records, 1892–1965, box 396, folder 2, Special Collections Research Center, University of Chicago Library.

Thorndike, Edward L. *The Teacher's Word Book*. New York: Columbia University Press, 1921.

Tillotson, Kathleen. Review of *Shakespeare's Imagery and What It Tells Us*, by Caroline F. E. Spurgeon. *Review of English Studies* 12, no. 48 (October 1936): 458–61.

Tillyard, E. M. W. *The Muse Unchained: An Intimate Account of the Revolution in English Studies at Cambridge*. London: Bowes and Bowes, 1958.

Treuer, David. *Native American Literature: A User's Manual.* Saint Paul, MN: Graywolf Press, 2006.

Tuckerman, Frederick Goddard. *The Complete Poems of Frederick Goddard Tuckerman.* Edited by N. Scott Momaday. New York: Oxford University Press, 1965.

Tuke, Margaret. *A History of Bedford College for Women.* London: Oxford University Press, 1939.

Turner, James. *Philology: The Forgotten Origins of the Modern Humanities.* Princeton, NJ: Princeton University Press, 2014.

Underwood, Ted. *Distant Horizons: Digital Evidence and Literary Change.* Chicago: University of Chicago Press, 2019.

Underwood, Ted. *Why Literary Periods Mattered: Historical Contrast and the Prestige of English Studies.* Stanford, CA: Stanford University Press, 2015.

Vadde, Aarthi, and Saikat Majumdar. "Introduction: Criticism for the Whole Person." In *The Critic as Amateur.* New York: Bloomsbury Academic, 2019.

Veggian, Henry. "From Philology to Formalism: Edith Rickert, John Matthews Manly, and the Literary/Reformist Beginnings of U.S. Cryptology." *Reader: An Interdisciplinary Journal* 54 (Spring 2006): 67–89.

Veysey, Laurence. *The Emergence of the American University.* Chicago: University of Chicago Press, 1965.

Viswanathan, Gauri. *Masks of Conquest: Literary Study and British Rule in India.* New York: Columbia University Press, 1989.

Walcott, Rinaldo. "The End of Diversity." *Public Culture* 31, no. 2 (May 1, 2019): 393–408.

Walker, Robert H. "American Studies at George Washington University." *American Quarterly* 22, no. 2 (1970): 528–38.

Warner, Michael. "Professionalization and the Rewards of Literature." *Criticism* 27, no. 1 (Winter 1985): 1–28.

Warren, Kenneth. *What Was African-American Literature?* Cambridge, MA: Harvard University Press, 2012.

Warrior, Robert Allen. "Literature and Students in Native American Studies." In *Studying Native America: Problems and Prospects*, edited by Russell Thornton, 111–29. Madison: University of Wisconsin Press, 1998.

Welch, James. *Riding the Earthboy 40.* Cleveland: World Publishing, 1971.

Wellek, René. *The Rise of English Literary History.* Chapel Hill: University of North Carolina Press, 1941.

Wellmon, Chad. *Organizing Enlightenment: Information Overload and the Invention of the Modern Research University.* Baltimore: Johns Hopkins University Press, 2015.

Wells, Henry W. *Poetic Imagery, Illustrated from Elizabethan Literature.* New York: Russell and Russell, 1924.

Werner, W. L. "Teaching Books Instead of Authors." *English Journal* 18, no. 10 (1929): 836–41.

West, David W. *I. A. Richards and the Rise of Cognitive Stylistics.* London: Bloomsbury, 2012.

West, David W. "Practical Criticism: I. A. Richards' Experiment in Interpretation." *Changing English* 9, no. 2 (October 1, 2002): 2017–213.

Williams, Ben. "Bill Wahpepah & Denis Banks at Oakland Indian School, KPIX

Eyewitness News Report." Bay Area Television Archive, January 11, 1977. https://
diva.sfsu.edu/collections/sfbatv/bundles/190877.

Williams, Dana A. "'The Field and Function' of the Historically Black College and
University Today: Preparing African American Undergraduate Students for
Doctoral Study in the Humanities." *Profession*, November 2013.

Williams, Raymond. *The Long Revolution*. London: Chatto and Windus, 1961.

Williams, Raymond. *Writing in Society*. London: Verso Modern Classics, 1983.

Wilson, B. L. "Student Research Spotlights GW's Segregated Past." *GW Today*,
April 30, 2018. https://gwtoday.gwu.edu/student-research-spotlights-gw
%E2%80%99s-segregated-past.

Wilson, Edmund. "A Guide to *Finnegans Wake*." In *Classics and Commercials: A
Literary Chronicle of the Forties*. New York: Farrar, Straus and Giroux, 1950.

Wilson, Edmund. *The Triple Thinkers: Twelve Essays on Literary Subjects*. New York:
Farrar, Straus and Giroux, 1976.

Wilson, Edmund. *The Wound and the Bow: Seven Studies in Literature*. Oxford:
Oxford University Press, 1941.

Winchell, Mark Royden. *Cleanth Brooks and the Rise of Modern Criticism*. Charlot-
tesville: University of Virginia Press, 1996.

Winston, Michael. "Through the Back Door: Academic Racism and the Negro
Scholar in Historical Perspective." *Daedalus*, The Future of Black Colleges, 100,
no. 3 (Summer 1971): 678–719.

Womack, Craig S. "A Single Decade: Book-Length Native Literary Criticism
between 1986 and 1997." In *Reasoning Together: The Native Critics Collective*,
edited by Daniel Heath Justice, Christopher B. Teuton, and Craig S. Womack.
Norman: University of Oklahoma Press, 2008.

Wood, Michael. "William Empson." In *The Cambridge History of Literary Criticism*. Vol. 7, *Modernism and the New Criticism*, edited by A. Walton Litz, Louis
Menand, and Lawrence Rainey. Cambridge: Cambridge University Press, 2000.

Woodbridge, Homer E. "Literary Suicide." Review of *New Methods for the Study of
Literature*, by Edith Rickert. *New York Herald Tribune Books*, July 26, 1927. Box
396, folder 2, University of Chicago Press Records, 1892–1965, Special Collections Research Center, University of Chicago Library, n.d.

Wright, Richard. "Introduction." In *No Day of Triumph*, by J. Saunders Redding.
New York: Harper, 1942.

Yamane, David. *Student Movements for Multiculturalism: Challenging the Curricular
Color Line in Higher Education*. Baltimore: Johns Hopkins University Press,
2002.

Zaluda, Scott. "Lost Voices of the Harlem Renaissance: Writing Assigned at
Howard University, 1919–31." *College Composition and Communication* 50, no. 2
(December 1998): 232–57.

Index

Pages in italics refer to illustrations.